Effective Strategies for Combatting Social Engineering in Cybersecurity

Rajeev Kumar
Moradabad Institute of Technology, India

Saurabh Srivastava
Moradabad Institute of Technology, India

Ahmed A. Elngar
Beni-Suef University, Egypt

IGI Global
Scientific Publishing
Publishing Tomorrow's Research Today

Vice President of Editorial	Melissa Wagner
Managing Editor of Acquisitions	Mikaela Felty
Managing Editor of Book Development	Jocelynn Hessler
Production Manager	Mike Brehm
Cover Design	Phillip Shickler

Published in the United States of America by
IGI Global Scientific Publishing
701 East Chocolate Avenue
Hershey, PA, 17033, USA
Tel: 717-533-8845
Fax: 717-533-8661
E-mail: cust@igi-global.com
Website: https://www.igi-global.com

Library of Congress Cataloging-in-Publication Data

ISBN13: 9798369366653
EISBN13: 9798369366677

British Cataloguing in Publication Data
A Cataloguing in Publication record for this book is available from the British Library.

Table of Contents

Detailed Table of Contents

This Chapter discusses the application of Natural Language Processing (NLP) in the legal domain for entity identification and the generation of hierarchy-based applications. NLP techniques, such as Named Entity Recognition (NER) and information extraction, are utilized to analyse legal documents, extract key information, and understand contextual relationships. The integration of NLP facilitates tasks such as legal document summarization, contract analysis, automated document generation, and legal research, thereby enhancing the efficiency and accuracy of legal processes. The creation of hierarchical structures within documents, language translation, sentiment analysis, and compliance monitoring further contribute to the comprehensive utilization of NLP in the legal field. The abstract highlights the transformative impact of NLP in streamlining legal workflows, improving information retrieval, and ensuring compliance with evolving legal standards. Most judicial systems in the world, centered around the Supreme Court as the highest-level court, grapples with a substantial caseload, receiving over 7,500 cases annually but hearing fewer than 150. The Supreme Court's unique role in interpreting the constitutionality of laws and establishing precedents underscores its significant influence. Challenges arise from the overwhelming caseload, leading to increased use of plea bargains and potential concerns about justice. To address these issues, a proposed research initiative suggests employing machine learning and natural language processing to accelerate Supreme Court decisions, aiming to uncover pivotal aspects that greatly influence the outcomes, and enhance our comprehension on India legal system's functioning and constraints. This chapter presents a methodology for sentiment-based summarization of legal documents using Natural Language Processing (NLP) techniques. The process involves pre-processing the text, conducting sentiment analysis to label sentences as positive, negative, or neutral, and then summarizing the document while incorporating the identified sentiments. Special attention is paid to legal-specific considerations such as terminology and context.

The social engineering attack is one of the most common forms of cyber-attacks. Attackers are using psychological tricks and more covert tactics to coerce victims into disclosing private information that belongs to them or that has been approved by authorities. Social skills are commonly employed to manipulate people by tricking, revealing, and acting upon them. This chapter discuss many types of social engineering assaults, the methodology for analyzing these attacks and data gathering methods utilized as case studies. This chapter also encompass the consequences, implications, legal and regulatory concerns, as well as strategies to mitigate them, such as awareness initiatives, security protocols, and technology remedies with contingency measures that are regularly utilized. The chapter finishes by providing insights and recommendations for organizations to enhance their security measures against social engineering assaults. It highlights the importance of maintaining constant awareness and adjusting cyber security defenses as necessary.

Social engineering is one of the biggest dangers in the digital world today. Attacks using social engineering are extremely dangerous to individuals and organizations by exploiting human psychology to compromise security controls to steal sensitive information. This study explores the different forms of social engineering attacks, analyzes real-world cases, and investigates the strategies attackers employ. It aims to assess the potential consequences for individuals and organizations targeted by these attacks. The study also assesses the effectiveness of current prevention methods, proposing enhanced strategies and best practices to implement measures to reduce the vulnerability with social engineering. By understanding the intricate tactics of attackers and the vulnerabilities they exploit, this research aims to provide a robust framework for improving security awareness and defense mechanisms against social engineering threats.

In the digital era, the proliferation of social engineering attacks poses a significant threat to cybersecurity. Unlike traditional cyber threats that exploit technical vulnerabilities, social engineering attacks manipulate human psychology to gain unauthorized access to sensitive information and systems. This paper explores the evolving landscape of social engineering, examining its various forms such as phishing, pretexting, baiting, and tailgating. The core of this study focuses on developing comprehensive defense strategies to mitigate the risks associated with social engineering. We advocate for a multi-layered approach that integrates technological solutions, such as advanced email filters and anomaly detection systems, with human-centric measures, including rigorous training programs and awareness campaigns. We highlight the importance of fostering a security-conscious culture within organizations and analysed the critical role of both technology and human behavior in safeguarding information assets in the age of social engineering.

Social engineering entails obtaining important information. Attackers may request varied victim details. After targeting someone, attackers aim to steal their bank account information or passwords or breach into their machine to install malicious software to take control. Social engineering is simpler than software infiltration because attackers exploit victim confidence. Tricking someone into giving their password is simpler than hacking it. Trusting people and things is crucial to security. Finding out if someone is who they say they are is crucial. Trusting a website and giving your personal information: when? Thus, every respected security expert agrees that the weakest link in the security system is the believer. Even with locks and deadbolts on our doors and windows, guard dogs, alarm systems, floodlights, barbed wire fences, and armed guards, the pizza delivery man at the gate can get in. This chapter expands on social engineering and safety.

Social engineering remains an enduring and emerging threat in cybersecurity. This chapter delves into the fluid landscape of social engineering threats, examining the strategies employed by cyber criminals and providing valuable perspectives on the current defence mechanisms that organizations and individuals can utilize for the efficient reduction of these vulnerabilities. The development of social engineering threats is propelled by a profound grasp of human psychology, coupled with the growing dependence on digital communication and information-sharing channels. This paper underscores the importance of collaboration among individuals, organizations, and security experts in the continuous effort to combat social engineering. It highlights the significance of staying informed about emerging threats and continuously improving defensive strategies to confront the constantly evolving landscape of social engineering attacks. This article introduces a comprehensive framework designed to address these challenges and shape the future of cybersecurity.

In today's world, where digital interactions and online transactions are crucial for both personal and professional activities, social engineering attacks have become more common and sophisticated, threatening data security and organizational integrity. These attacks exploit a lack of awareness to gain illegal access to systems. While research includes various studies and methods for preventing these attacks, a thorough analysis of effective strategies is lacking. Current methods involve health campaigns, frameworks with human security sensors, user-focused approaches, and vulnerability models. This chapter thoroughly examines different types of social engineering attacks, such as phishing, vishing, and pretexting, highlighting the human element as the weakest link in cybersecurity. It then delves into prevention methods, stressing the need for awareness training and behavioral changes among users as a key defense. This chapter seeks to equip readers with practical insights and tools to protect against social engineering attacks by integrating current research and best practices.

Social engineering attacks exploit human behavior to bypass security measures, posing a growing threat in cybersecurity. This paper examines future defenses against these attacks by analyzing recent incidents and common attack vectors like phishing, pretexting, baiting, and tailgating, which leverage psychological manipulation. Key trends include AI and machine learning for real-time detection, and zero-trust architecture for stringent access controls and continuous identity verification. The development of regulatory frameworks and industry standards is also crucial for shaping effective defenses. As technology evolves, so do attack methods, necessitating comprehensive solutions that integrate technological, individual, organizational, and governmental strategies to safeguard society.

This book chapter will provide an in-depth exploration of blockchain technology, covering its history, fundamental principles and practical applications. The chapter begins with an introduction to the decentralized nature of blockchain, explaining how it works to provide security, immutability and transparency in a trustless environment. It also examines various types of blockchain including public, private and permissioned and explores the advantages and limitations of each. This chapter looks at the future of blockchain technology discussing emerging trends and potential developments in the field. It highlights ongoing research and development efforts aimed at improving the functionality and security of blockchain, as well as exploring new use cases and business models. Overall, this book chapter will provide a comprehensive introduction to blockchain technology, offering insights into its workings, practical applications and potential impact on various industries.

Social engineering in social media and online interactions has emerged as a critical concern in the digital age, driven by the increasing interconnectivity and sharing of personal information online. This study is motivated by the growing prevalence of cyberattacks that exploit human psychology rather than technical vulnerabilities, targeting individuals through platforms where they share personal details. By examining various social engineering techniques such as phishing, pretexting, and baiting. This research highlights the methods attackers use to manipulate individuals and the specific vulnerabilities they exploit in social media environments. The study leverages data from recent cases and surveys to analyze the effectiveness of these techniques and the impact on both individuals and organizations. The findings underscore the significant risks posed by social engineering attacks, revealing the psychological underpinnings that make such tactics so effective.

Deepfakes, a recent and compelling technique that is used in social engineering attacks, allows cybercriminals to falsify audio, videos, and video to deceive individuals. These deepfakes can be used in phishing attacks, where fake hyperlinks lure victims into providing sensitive information. Deepfakes in social engineering attacks pose a significant cybersecurity threat. This spread of falsehood and misrepresentation on social media platforms has been shown to have a significant impact, with falsehood spreading farther, faster, deeper, and more broadly than the truth. The use of deepfakes in social engineering attacks raises ethical concerns, as these technologies can be used to manipulate individuals and spread disinformation on social media networks. The present chapter highlights the types of social engineering attacks, the meaning of deepfake technology, the positive side (benefits) of deepfake technologies, and the possible threats of deepfakes, with some real-time cases of the Indian political and entertainment industry followed by possible solutions.

Advancements in digital technologies have made it difficult to distinguish between real and fake media, leading to privacy and security threats. Deepfake, a combination of deep learning and fake, is a technique used to replace or mask someone else's face in images or videos. Social engineering (SE) attacks exploit human attributes and psychology to bypass technical security measures for malicious acts. Deepfake videos, created using artificial intelligence (AI), pose a significant threat to society, politics, and businesses. Deepfakes pose a significant threat, they can be combated through legislation, regulation, corporate policies, voluntary action, education, training, and the development of technology for deepfake detection, content authentication, and prevention. Common deepfakes include pornographic videos, political deepfakes, financial crimes, and synthetic audio. The paper explores deepfake technology, its benefits, challenges, and detection techniques.

Phishing attacks pose significant threats by tricking individuals and organizations into divulging sensitive information through deceptive websites and emails. This research paper presents a Phishing Detection System (PDS) designed to mitigate such threats using advanced machine learning techniques. The system's architecture includes data collection, feature extraction, a detection engine, and a response module. It employs machine learning algorithms such as Naive Bayes, K-Nearest Neighbors, Decision Tree, and Random Forest to optimize detection accuracy. The PDS provides real-time alerts, blocks malicious sites, and quarantines suspicious emails, achieving high detection accuracy with minimal false positives and negatives. Future enhancements focus on scalability, advanced machine learning integration, and user education. This system represents a significant advancement in cybersecurity by offering robust protection and actionable insights against phishing threats.

Preface

In the digital age, the convergence of advanced technologies and human behavior presents a complex cybersecurity challenge, particularly through the lens of social engineering. Social engineering attacks exploit psychological manipulation rather than relying solely on technical vulnerabilities. By leveraging human trust and deception, these attacks become particularly difficult to defend against, evolving alongside advancements in artificial intelligence, machine learning, and other technologies. This dynamic environment heightens the risk of cyber threats, underscoring the need for comprehensive and innovative strategies to address these emerging vulnerabilities.

Effective Strategies for Combatting Social Engineering in Cybersecurity offers a thorough exploration of these challenges, providing a well-rounded approach to understanding and countering social engineering threats. This book delves into the theoretical aspects of social engineering, including the psychological principles that drive these attacks, while also offering practical solutions through real-world case studies and applications. By bridging the gap between theory and practice, the book equips readers with actionable strategies to enhance their defenses.

Key to our solution is a multi-faceted approach that begins with a deep understanding of social engineering tactics and their psychological underpinnings. The book provides detailed case studies and practical applications of technologies such as deep learning and machine learning, demonstrating how these can be utilized to detect and prevent social engineering attacks. Additionally, we address the ethical considerations associated with cybersecurity, including data privacy, consent, and accountability, to ensure that strategies are not only effective but also responsible.

Education and training play a crucial role in building resilience against social engineering. Our book emphasizes the importance of awareness programs to prepare individuals and organizations to recognize and respond to these threats. Furthermore, we explore the latest technological tools and collaborative approaches involving industry and government perspectives, examining emerging trends and future directions in social engineering defense.

Designed for a broad audience—including researchers, academics, students, tech professionals, and policymakers—this book aims to advance the discourse on social engineering and contribute to the development of more effective cybersecurity practices. By integrating insights from various fields and focusing on practical applications, we hope to provide valuable guidance for mitigating social engineering threats and shaping future research and policy.

We invite readers to engage with this book to gain a deeper understanding of social engineering and explore effective strategies for combatting it. Together, we can navigate the complexities of the digital world and build a more secure and resilient future.

Chapter 1: Types of Social Engineering Attacks and Case Studies

Social engineering attacks exploit human psychology to trick individuals into divulging confidential information, bypassing technical defenses. This chapter delves into various social engineering techniques, including phishing, pretexting, baiting, and tailgating. It outlines the stages of these attacks and presents detailed case studies from various organizations, highlighting the repercussions these breaches have had on them. By examining these real-world examples, the chapter underscores the importance of vigilance, employee training, and security awareness programs. It advocates for continuous education and robust security protocols to mitigate risks and challenges, ultimately fostering a more informed and secure community.

Chapter 2: Exploring Social Engineering Attacks involving Insights from Case Studies

Social engineering remains one of the most prevalent forms of cyberattacks, relying on psychological manipulation rather than technical vulnerabilities. This chapter provides an in-depth analysis of different types of social engineering attacks and the methodologies used to study and understand them. Through various case studies, it explores the consequences and implications of these attacks, including legal and regulatory concerns. The chapter also discusses strategies for mitigation, such as awareness initiatives, improved security protocols, and technological solutions. The goal is to enhance organizational security measures and promote constant vigilance against evolving social engineering tactics.

Chapter 3: Social Engineering in the Digital Age: A Critical Examination of Attack Techniques, Consequences, and Preventative Measures

In the digital era, social engineering poses significant threats by exploiting human psychology to undermine security controls and steal sensitive information. This chapter explores various forms of social engineering attacks and real-world cases, assessing the strategies employed by attackers and the effectiveness of current prevention methods. By analyzing these tactics, the chapter aims to provide a robust framework for improving security awareness and defense mechanisms. It proposes enhanced strategies and best practices for reducing vulnerability to social engineering, focusing on both technological and human-centric measures.

Chapter 4: Cybersecurity in the Age of Social Engineering: Implementing Effective Defense Strategies

As social engineering attacks become more sophisticated, traditional cybersecurity measures are often insufficient. This chapter examines the evolving landscape of social engineering, including tactics like phishing, pretexting, and baiting. It advocates for a comprehensive defense strategy that integrates advanced technological solutions, such as email filters and anomaly detection systems, with human-centric measures, including rigorous training and awareness campaigns. Emphasizing the importance of a security-conscious culture, the chapter explores how organizations can blend technology and human behavior to enhance their defenses against social engineering threats.

Chapter 5: Exploration of Social Engineering in the Digital Era of Stealth

Social engineering exploits the inherent trust individuals place in technology and each other, making it easier for attackers to obtain sensitive information. This chapter highlights how social engineering tactics can be less complex than technical breaches, relying instead on manipulating trust. It discusses various methods attackers use to deceive their victims and underscores the need for vigilance in verifying identities and safeguarding personal information. By expanding on the nature of social engineering and its impact, the chapter aims to reinforce the importance of maintaining strong security practices and awareness.

Chapter 6: Empowering Cyber Resilience: Effective Strategies for Combating Social Engineering Threats

Social engineering is a persistent and evolving threat in the cybersecurity landscape. This chapter explores the strategies employed by cybercriminals and evaluates current defense mechanisms available to organizations and individuals. Emphasizing the role of understanding human psychology and the impact of digital communication, it highlights the need for collaboration among stakeholders to effectively combat social engineering. The chapter introduces a comprehensive framework designed to address these challenges and promote ongoing improvements in defensive strategies to adapt to emerging threats.

Chapter 7: Securing the Weakest Link: Comprehensive Approaches to Social Engineering Attacks Prevention

The human element often represents the weakest link in security systems, particularly in the context of social engineering. This chapter reviews various user-centric approaches and prevention methods, such as health campaigns and frameworks where humans act as security sensors. It identifies gaps in current strategies and emphasizes the need for a more integrated human-centric framework. As social engineering tactics evolve, the chapter advocates for ongoing research and the implementation of advanced tools to stay ahead of fraudsters, providing best practices for avoiding common attacks.

Chapter 8: Protecting Against Social Engineering Using Wireshark: Effective Strategies with Real-World Examples

Defending against social engineering attacks requires innovative approaches, including the use of network analysis tools like Wireshark. This chapter explores how Wireshark can be utilized to detect and mitigate social engineering threats. It covers configuring Wireshark for optimal security monitoring, setting up filters and profiles, and analyzing network traffic for signs of phishing and malware communications. By providing real-world examples and effective strategies, the chapter demonstrates how Wireshark can be a valuable asset in safeguarding against social engineering attacks.

Chapter 9: Emerging Trends and Future Directions in Social Engineering Defense

As social engineering attacks become more sophisticated, organizations face significant challenges in mitigating these threats. This chapter explores current social engineering threats and the strategies for countering them. It provides a historical perspective on the evolution of social engineering, examines modern tactics used by cybercriminals, and forecasts future trends. The chapter also discusses advancements in technology and tools for detection and prevention, while addressing ethical and legal considerations. It emphasizes the need for proactive defense strategies to address emerging threats effectively.

Chapter 10: Exploring the Future Landscape: Emerging Trends in Social Engineering Defense

The shift to online platforms, accelerated by the COVID-19 pandemic, has introduced new challenges in cybersecurity, particularly in education. This chapter examines how artificial intelligence (AI) and data mining techniques can be applied to enhance student performance prediction and address the challenges faced in diverse learning environments. It evaluates various machine learning models and their effectiveness in predicting student outcomes, using a comprehensive dataset. The chapter highlights the potential of AI and data mining to personalize learning experiences and improve educational support.

Chapter 11: A Comprehensive Guide to Blockchain Technology and Its Role in Enhancing Cybersecurity and Combating Social Engineering

Blockchain technology offers promising solutions for enhancing cybersecurity and combating social engineering. This chapter provides an in-depth exploration of blockchain's fundamental principles, including its decentralized nature, security features, and practical applications. It examines different types of blockchain, such as public, private, and permissioned, and discusses their advantages and limitations. The chapter also looks at emerging trends and future developments in blockchain technology, offering insights into its potential impact on various industries and its role in improving cybersecurity.

Chapter 12: Social Engineering in Social Media and Online Interactions

Social media and online interactions have become prime targets for social engineering attacks, exploiting the vast amounts of personal information shared on these platforms. This chapter investigates how social engineering tactics are employed in online environments, including social media platforms. It explores various techniques used by attackers to manipulate individuals and gain unauthorized access to sensitive information. The chapter also discusses strategies for protecting against these threats and enhancing security in digital interactions.

Chapter 13: The Use of Deep Fakes in Social Engineering Attacks: A Case Study on Social Media Engagements

Deepfake technology, which creates realistic but fabricated audio and video content, poses a significant threat in social engineering attacks. This chapter examines how deepfakes are used in phishing and other deceptive practices, with a focus on social media engagements. It highlights the ethical concerns and potential impact of deepfakes on various sectors, including politics and entertainment. By analyzing real-time cases, the chapter explores both the benefits and risks of deepfake technology and proposes solutions for mitigating its negative effects.

Chapter 14: The Rising Threat of Deepfake Technology and Frightening Advancements in Social Engineering

The rise of deepfake technology, which leverages artificial intelligence to create convincing fake media, presents new challenges for cybersecurity. This chapter explores the implications of deepfakes for privacy and security, discussing their use in social engineering attacks and the broader societal impact. It covers various types of deepfakes, including pornographic, political, and financial content, and examines detection techniques and preventive measures. The chapter emphasizes the need for legislation, corporate policies, and technological advancements to combat the threats posed by deepfakes.

Chapter 15: Phishing Detection System Using Machine Learning

Phishing attacks, which deceive individuals into revealing sensitive information, remain a significant cybersecurity threat. This chapter presents a Phishing Detection System (PDS) that utilizes advanced machine learning techniques to identify and mitigate phishing threats. It details the system's architecture, including data collection, feature extraction, and detection algorithms such as Naive Bayes, K-Nearest Neighbors, and Random Forest. The chapter highlights the system's effectiveness in providing real-time alerts, blocking malicious sites, and reducing false positives. It also discusses future enhancements and the importance of user education in strengthening phishing defenses.

Chapter 16: Assortment of Social Engineering Attacks in the New Digital Era

Social engineering involves stealing secrets. Assaults seek different information each person. Deception is used to gain passwords, financial data, and viruses. This spyware may steal passwords, financial data, and computer control. Attackers utilize social engineering because victim confidence is easier to influence than program weaknesses. Phishing for a password is easier than cracking it. Fast technical change has increased social engineering assaults, which target psychology rather than technology. Hackers utilize many methods to deceive people into disclosing sensitive information or taking digital security risks. We discuss numerous digital social engineering attacks in this chapter. Discussing phishing, pretexting, baiting, quid pro quo, and whaling. We also explore attackers' psychological manipulation and their massive damage to people and organizations. We emphasize awareness, education, and training to prevent social engineering assaults and protect crucial data in the digital era.

Chapter 1

Sentiment-Based Summarization of Legal Documents Using Natural Language Processing (NLP) Techniques

Shyamala Devi N.
https://orcid.org/0000-0003-4413-4775
VISTAS Chennai, India

Grace Hannah J.
https://orcid.org/0000-0002-9997-3157
Vels Institute of Science,Technology, and Advanced Studies, India

ABSTRACT

This Chapter discusses the application of Natural Language Processing (NLP) in the legal domain for entity identification and the generation of hierarchy-based applications. NLP techniques, such as Named Entity Recognition (NER) and information extraction, are utilized to analyse legal documents, extract key information, and understand contextual relationships. The integration of NLP facilitates tasks such as legal document summarization, contract analysis, automated document generation, and legal research, thereby enhancing the efficiency and accuracy of legal processes. The creation of hierarchical structures within documents, language translation, sentiment analysis, and compliance monitoring further contribute to the comprehensive utilization of NLP in the legal field. The abstract highlights the transformative impact of NLP in streamlining legal workflows, improving information retrieval, and ensuring compliance with evolving legal standards. Most judicial systems in

DOI: 10.4018/979-8-3693-6665-3.ch001

the world, centered around the Supreme Court as the highest-level court, grapples with a substantial caseload, receiving over 7,500 cases annually but hearing fewer than 150. The Supreme Court's unique role in interpreting the constitutionality of laws and establishing precedents underscores its significant influence. Challenges arise from the overwhelming caseload, leading to increased use of plea bargains and potential concerns about justice. To address these issues, a proposed research initiative suggests employing machine learning and natural language processing to accelerate Supreme Court decisions, aiming to uncover pivotal aspects that greatly influence the outcomes, and enhance our comprehension on India legal system's functioning and constraints. This chapter presents a methodology for sentiment-based summarization of legal documents using Natural Language Processing (NLP) techniques. The process involves pre-processing the text, conducting sentiment analysis to label sentences as positive, negative, or neutral, and then summarizing the document while incorporating the identified sentiments. Special attention is paid to legal-specific considerations such as terminology and context.

INTRODUCTION

The domain of law, is one field where professionals are required to review, analyse and make inference from among large volumes of dossier and files. This document-intensive field therefore necessitates a legal counsel to engage with diverse judicial opinions, regulatory documents and capacious data that is to be unsheathed from diverse sources. This sift of dossier extraction and reviewing of documents can be exhaustive, time-consuming and therefore lead to manual inaccuracies. The Indian judicial system, most often circumscribed by the rubrics and functioning of Supreme Court as the highest-level court, is loaded with substantial cases, with colossal pending cases that are annually accumulated. However, the quotidian hearing routine is most often fixed to a maximum of 150 to 200 cases. The Supreme Court's unique role in interpreting the constitutionality of laws and establishing precedents underscores its significant influence. Challenges arise from the overwhelming caseload, leading to increased use of plea bargains and potential concerns about justice. While judicial documents can entail complex patterns of text and domain-relevant jargons, it can be arduous in effectively parsing the texts through traditional compiler and parsing techniques. To address these issues, a proposed research initiative suggests employing machine learning and natural language processing to facilitate ease of decision boundaries. This process through simulative techniques can explicitly aid the functioning and render swift, yet accurate solutions for Supreme Court's decisions in diverse legal cases.

The application of Artificial Intelligence (AI) in the legal domain, particularly focusing on Legal Information Extraction can have a gargantuan influence interms of automating procedures, and in helping the judicial system to function with more informed decisions. In Legal Information Extraction, various studies have been conducted to automatically extract legal information from texts using techniques such as calculating similarity measures, creating legal ontologies, and sentiment analysis. Notably, there has been a lack of attention to sentiment analysis in the legal domain until neoteric prominence of this domain. Various studies that have effectuated specific tools for sentiment annotation tailored to legal texts have garnered attention thereby paving the way for optimized novel modus operandi. On the other hand, Aspect-Based Sentiment Analysis has seen significant research across various domains, with publicly available datasets for tasks like movie reviews, product reviews, and restaurant reviews. These datasets are annotated with several corresponding sentiment polarities. The legal dataset is publically available for analysing in Kaggle, this study focuses on one such dataset procured from Kaggle. However, not many repositories hold publicly available datasets in the legal domain, and more particularly there is a notable absence of readily available data for effectively analyzing sentiment in legal opinion texts concerning different legal parties in court cases.

Related Work

Legal Artificial Intelligence (LegalAI) has emerged as a significant area of research, with increasing attention from both AI researchers and legal professionals due to its potential to automate complex legal tasks. One major focus of LegalAI is the application of natural language processing (NLP) techniques to assist in legal processes. Recent research has explored various aspects of LegalAI, including the application of rule-based methods favored by legal professionals and data-driven approaches preferred by NLP researchers (Zhong et al., 2020). The interplay between these methodologies demonstrates how LegalAI is poised to bridge the gap between traditional legal reasoning and modern computational techniques.

One notable study focuses on the linguistic profiling of Italian legal texts to identify linguistic variation and complexity across different legal sub-genres. By comparing legal texts to ordinary language, this research provides insights into the unique lexical and syntactic challenges that legal texts present. Such analysis is crucial for improving legal document readability and has applications in computational forensic linguistics (Saggion et al., 2021). This work contributes to our understanding of the complexity in legal language and highlights the need for sophisticated NLP tools tailored to legal text.

In terms of tools, LexNLP, an open-source Python package, plays a significant role in extracting structured information from legal and regulatory texts. It offers a variety of functionalities, such as document segmentation, named entity recognition, and feature extraction for machine learning models. LexNLP's ability to handle real-world legal documents from sources like the SEC EDGAR database demonstrates its utility in both academic and industrial applications (Contreras et al., 2019). Such tools facilitate the development of AI models designed to tackle domain-specific legal tasks, further advancing the LegalAI ecosystem.

Additionally, the Contract Understanding Atticus Dataset (CUAD) represents a substantial contribution to the legal domain. CUAD, which contains over 13,000 annotations from legal experts, aims to enhance contract review tasks by training transformer models to identify key sections in contracts that require human review (Hendrycks et al., 2021). Although transformer models show promise, this study reveals the ongoing challenges in improving model performance, particularly in specialized domains where large labeled datasets are scarce. CUAD serves as an important benchmark for the legal AI community, pushing forward research in legal document analysis and review automation.

These works collectively underscore the growing role of LegalAI in automating legal tasks, improving text readability, and developing NLP tools that can handle the intricacies of legal language. However, challenges remain, particularly in the availability of high-quality annotated data and the design of models that can capture the nuances of legal text. Further research is necessary to bridge these gaps and fully realize the potential of LegalAI.

METHODOLOGY

Sentiment-based summarization of legal documents using Natural Language Processing (NLP) involves extracting key information while considering the sentiment expressed in the text. The proposed work aims to provide a concise yet comprehensive overview of the document's content, highlighting important points and identifying any positive, negative, or neutral sentiments conveyed within. The architecture entailed for this study is presented below:

Figure 1. Implementation Framework

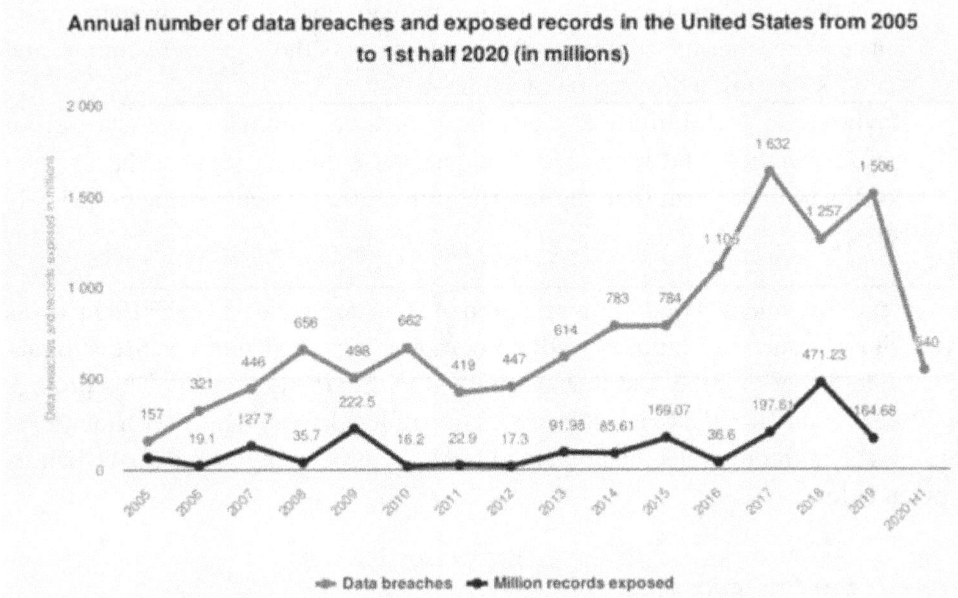

The key steps thus involved in sentiment-based summarization of legal documents using NLP is elucidated below:

- **Text Pre-processing:** This process is used to remove irrelevant information, such as boilerplate text, headers, footers, and metadata. Tokenize the text into sentences and words, and remove stop words, punctuation, and special characters.
- **Sentiment Analysis:** From the Pre-processing phase, the application of sentiment analysis techniques to assess the individual sentiments from sentences within the document is effectuated. This involves assigning a sentiment label (positive, negative, neutral) to each sentence based on the language used.
- **Summarization:** This process entails text summarization techniques to condense the document's content while preserving key information. This can be achieved through extractive methods (selecting and merging important sentences) or abstractive methods (generating new sentences to convey the main ideas).
- **Incorporate Sentiment:** When generating the summary, ensure that the sentiment expressed in the original document is captured accurately. This involves considering the sentiment labels assigned to sentences and incorporating them into the summary as needed.

- **Legal-specific Considerations:** Take into account legal-specific terminology, context, and nuances during both sentiment analysis and summarization. This ensures that the summary accurately reflects the legal implications and nuances present in the original document.
- **Review and Validation:** Review the generated summary to ensure accuracy, coherence, and relevance. Validate the summary against the original document to confirm that key information and sentiments are appropriately conveyed.

Overall, sentiment-based summarization of legal documents using NLP involves leveraging advanced techniques to distil complex legal text into concise summaries, while preserving the sentiment expressed within the document. This process facilitates efficient analysis and comprehension of legal documents for various legal purposes. The throughputs thus obtained from the processing of the above phases is given below:

Figure 2. Text Pre-processing

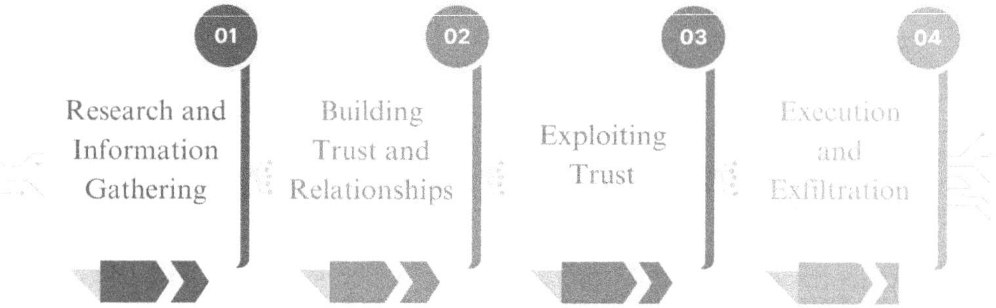

Figure 3.

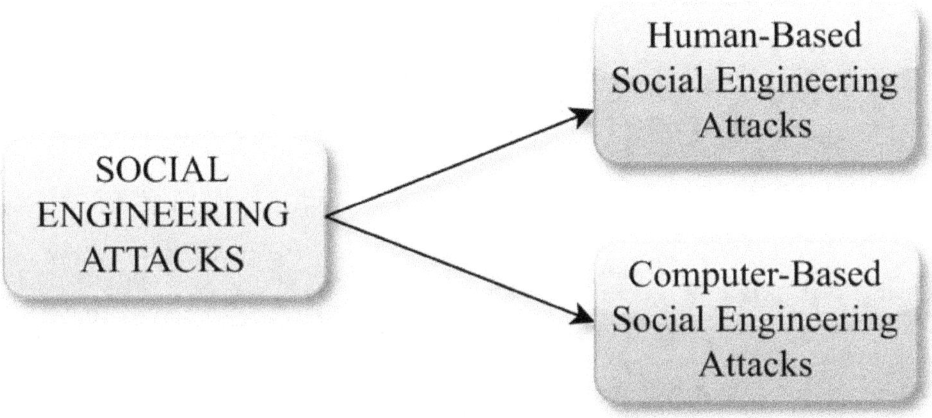

Figure 4. Sentiment Classification

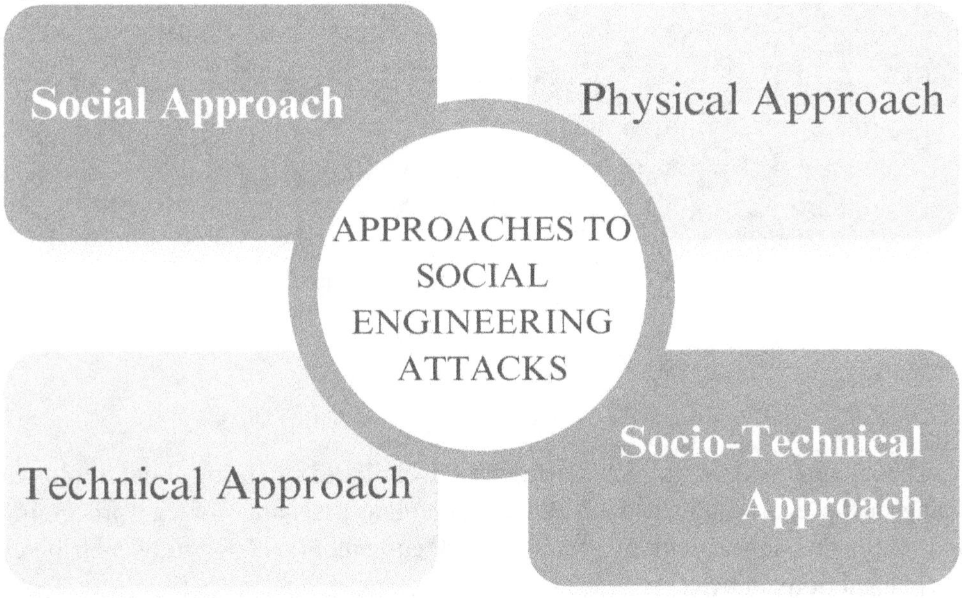

Figure 5. Sentiment Count

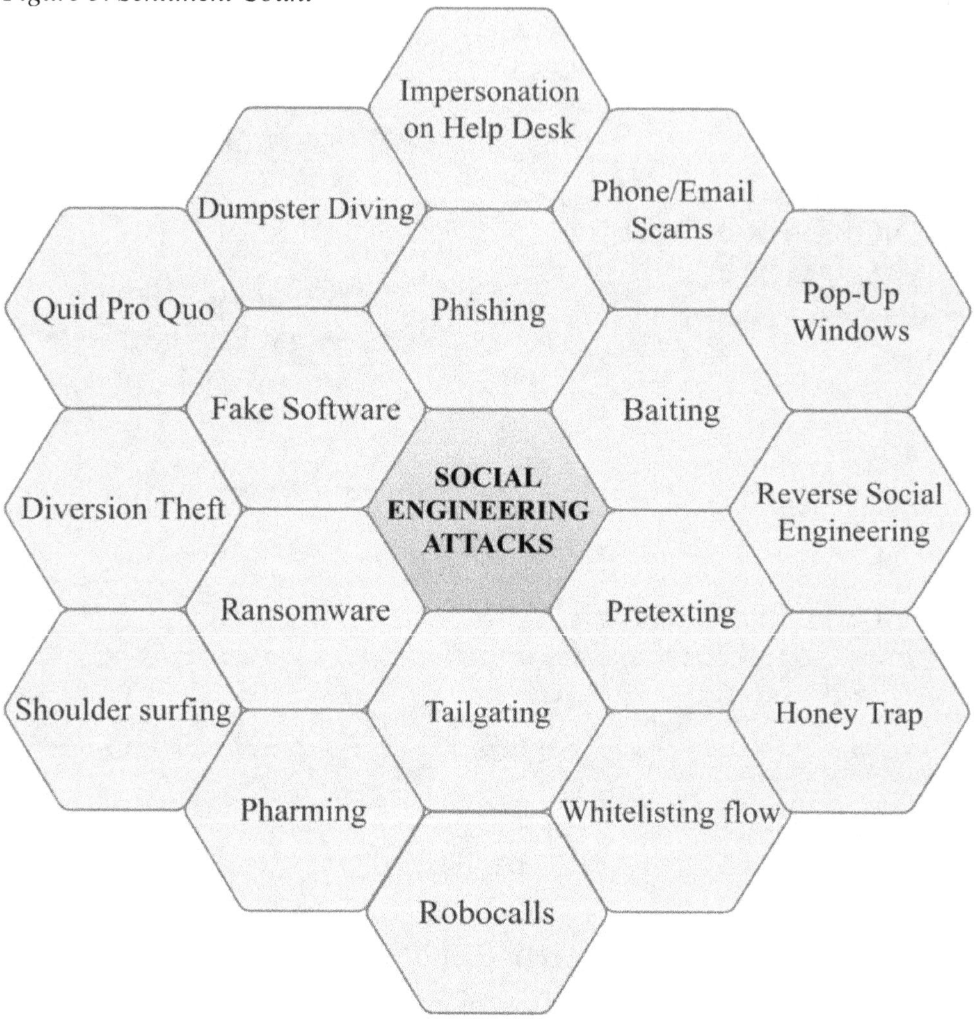

The indagation thus simulated using NLP techniques can bring about a colossal change in the legal system, and can deliver gargantuan assistance for legal processing and sentiment analysis with respect to legal documentation. This study contributes to the legal domain by:

- Propositioning a NLP-based framework for sentiment analysis and summarization of legal documents.
- Establishing robustness and efficacy through the constructed framework, and to implement the same in unconstrained and pragmatic legal datasets.

- Addressing the specific challenges associated with summarizing sentiment in legal documents, and augmenting the decision-boundaries for legal systems in a faster pace.

However, the challenges with respect to this study can be observed when dealing with language specific translations and ambiguous real-time data that may necessitate further manual intervention.

CONCLUSION

Neoteric times have observed the legal councils mandated to evaluate, review and appraise a large volume of documents that might be necessary in thorough analysis of cases, legal parameter cognizance and judicial opinions. The immense quantity to be covered to effectively comprehend and procure meaningful insights and inferences are challenging. Therefore, the demand of automated working environments that can effectively assist in rendering a succinct, yet lossless and accurate dossier that also unsheathes the embedded sentiment is indispensable. Conventional summarization methods entail manual reading and interpretation, which are not only time-consuming but can also be prone to perspective impediments. This research helps to develop a sentiment-based summarization framework using NLP techniques that aid in automating the unsheathing of sentiment-based summaries from documents, to further accelerate informed decision boundaries for legal councils and the judicial system itself. Through the integration of sentiment analysis with summarization algorithms, legal professionals can access massive quantity of documents in a concise, sentiment-aware abstracts. This can be pivotal in emphasizing on the key aspects of the case, while parallelly augmenting the legal council's adeptness to interpret large documentaries or dossier. The experimental results corroborates the effectiveness of the framework, and the pertinence in scaling this model to real-time working environments is the future scope of this study.

REFERENCES

Alexopoulos, C., Saxena, S., & Saxena, S. (2024). Natural Language Processing (NLP)-Powered Legal A (t) Ms (LAMs) in India: Possibilities and Challenges. *Journal of the Knowledge Economy*, 15(2), 8513–8533. DOI: 10.1007/s13132-023-01450-2

. Hasani, C. Translating the law: translation and analysis of a legal text

Hendrycks, D., Burns, C., Chen, A., & Ball, S. (2021). Cuad: An expert-annotated nlp dataset for legal contract review. arXiv preprint arXiv:2103.06268.

. Jesus, M. B. D., Goes, A. D. S., Santiago, L. D. G., Xavier, M. A. P., & Bevilacqua, S. (2023). Artificial intelligence on legal language processing: using deep learning to find the regulatory law framework for the third sector.

Krasadakis, P., Sakkopoulos, E., & Verykios, V. S. (2024). A survey on challenges and advances in natural language processing with a focus on legal informatics and low-resource languages. *Electronics (Basel)*, 13(3), 648. DOI: 10.3390/electronics13030648

. Preis, M. (2023). A Structured Overview of Use Cases for Natural Language Processing in the Legal Domain.

. Quevedo, E., Cerny, T., Rodriguez, A., Rivas, P., Yero, J., Sooksatra, K., ... & Taibi, D. (2023). Legal Natural Language Processing from 2015-2022: A Comprehensive Systematic Mapping Study of Advances and Applications. IEEE Access.

Vági, R. (2023). How Could Semantic Processing and Other NLP Tools Improve Online Legal Databases? *TalTech Journal of European Studies*, 13(2), 138–151. DOI: 10.2478/bjes-2023-0018

Yang, X., Wang, Z., Wang, Q., Wei, K., Zhang, K., & Shi, J. (2024). Large language models for automated q&a involving legal documents: A survey on algorithms, frameworks and applications. *International Journal of Web Information Systems*, 20(4), 413–435. DOI: 10.1108/IJWIS-12-2023-0256

Yang, X., Wang, Z., Wang, Q., Wei, K., Zhang, K., & Shi, J. (2024). Large language models for automated q&a involving legal documents: A survey on algorithms, frameworks and applications. *International Journal of Web Information Systems*, 20(4), 413–435. DOI: 10.1108/IJWIS-12-2023-0256

Zhong, H., Xiao, C., Tu, C., Zhang, T., Liu, Z., & Sun, M. (2020). How does NLP benefit legal system: A summary of legal artificial intelligence. arXiv preprint arXiv:2004.12158. DOI: 10.18653/v1/2020.acl-main.466

Zhong, H., Xiao, C., Tu, C., Zhang, T., Liu, Z., & Sun, M. (2020). How does NLP benefit legal system: A summary of legal artificial intelligence. arXiv preprint arXiv:2004.12158. DOI: 10.18653/v1/2020.acl-main.466

Chapter 2

Exploring Social Engineering Attacks Involving Insights From Case Studies

Shirisha Kakarla
https://orcid.org/0000-0003-4970-4634
Sreenidhi Institute of Science and Technology, India

Geeta Kakarla
Sreenidhi Institute of Science and Technology, India

Shirina Samreen
Majmaah University, Saudi Arabia

Sukanya Vuppala
University College of Engineering, Osmania University, India

ABSTRACT

The social engineering attack is one of the most common forms of cyber-attacks. Attackers are using psychological tricks and more covert tactics to coerce victims into disclosing private information that belongs to them or that has been approved by authorities. Social skills are commonly employed to manipulate people by tricking, revealing, and acting upon them. This chapter discuss many types of social engineering assaults, the methodology for analyzing these attacks and data gathering methods utilized as case studies. This chapter also encompass the consequences, implications, legal and regulatory concerns, as well as strategies to mitigate them, such as awareness initiatives, security protocols, and technology remedies with

DOI: 10.4018/979-8-3693-6665-3.ch002

contingency measures that are regularly utilized. The chapter finishes by providing insights and recommendations for organizations to enhance their security measures against social engineering assaults. It highlights the importance of maintaining constant awareness and adjusting cyber security defenses as necessary.

1. OVERVIEW OF SOCIAL ENGINEERING

Cyber criminals employ social engineering as a strategy to coerce people into disclosing private information, acting in ways that jeopardize security, or choosing courses of action. Social engineering focuses on the human aspect of security, in contrast to conventional hacking techniques that depend on taking advantage of technological flaws in systems. It uses social skills, psychological manipulation, and deceit to fool people into giving it access to private data or systems.

Fundamentally, according to the works of Chetioui et al. (2021), social engineering preys on a number of psychological and behavioral traits in people, including fear, empathy, trust, authority, and curiosity. To manipulate their targets, attackers frequently create plausible scenarios or assume the identity of reliable sources. Phishing emails, phone scams, baiting with malware-infected devices, tailgating into secure locations, and authority figure impersonation are just a few examples of the various ways that social engineering attacks can be carried out.

Wang et al. (2021) has expressed that social engineering attacks can have a wide range of final goals, from obtaining unauthorized access to networks or physical locations to stealing financial information and sensitive data. Serious repercussions from these attacks may include monetary losses, data breaches, harm to one's reputation, and legal repercussions.

Organizations need to combine technical controls, security policies, and employee awareness programs to counteract social engineering threats. Organizations can lessen the possibility that people will fall for these deceptive strategies by offering security awareness training and educating people about the strategies employed in social engineering attacks.

1.1 Social Engineering Attack Life-cycle

The social engineering attack life cycle, as per Chetioui et al. (2021), delineates the sequential stages that attackers commonly adhere to in order to fool targets and accomplish their nefarious objectives. Gaining a comprehensive understanding of this life cycle might enable organizations and individuals to enhance their defense mechanisms against such threats. Below is a comprehensive analysis of the stages involved in a social engineering attack, as shown in Figure 1 and detailed:

1. Conducting research and gathering information

Purpose: To gather intelligence on the target in order to enhance the probability of a successful assault.

Actions:

- Reconnaissance: Adversaries collect data about the target by utilizing publicly available sources such as social media platforms, corporate websites, and news publications.
- Profiling involves constructing comprehensive profiles of individuals or organizations by identifying possible weaknesses, such as personal interests, job positions, or organizational frameworks.

Methods and strategies:

- Online platforms for social interaction and communication.
- Corporate websites and online directories
- Official documents and electronic repositories of information accessible to the general public

2. Preparation

Purpose: To develop a compelling offensive strategy utilizing the collected information.

Actions:

- Crafting Messages: Developing phishing emails, pretexting scripts, or baiting messages customized to match the target's specific interests and behavioral patterns.
- Establishing Infrastructure: Creating counterfeit websites, email addresses, or phone numbers to facilitate the assault.

Methods and strategies:

- Tools for email spoofing
- Deceptive websites (phishing sites)
- VoIP services are used for phone spoofing,

1. Initial Contact and Engagement

Objective: This involves making first contact with a target and engaging them in order to elicit a reaction.

Actions:

- Phishing emails involve the act of sending deceptive emails that mimic genuine ones, frequently including harmful links or files. Pretexting calls involve the act of making phone calls while impersonating a trustworthy entity in order to obtain confidential information.
- Social media interaction is actively engaging with specific individuals or groups on social media platforms in order to establish trust and foster connections.

Figure 1. Social Engineering Attack Life Cycle

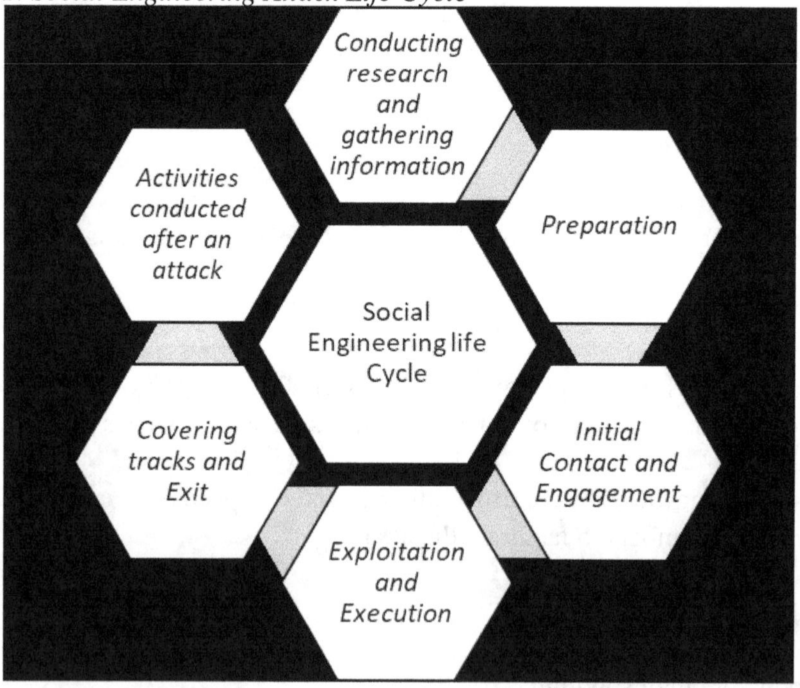

Methods and strategies:

- Email clients
- Social engineering toolkits

- Online platforms for social interaction

2. *Exploitation Goal:*

Purpose: To utilize the interaction in order to accomplish the attack's purpose, such as acquiring confidential data or distributing malicious software.

Tasks:

Malware Installation refers to the act of deceiving the intended victim into unwittingly downloading and installing malicious software.

Credential theft refers to the act of acquiring login credentials by means of phishing or pretexting.

Data exfiltration refers to the process of directly extracting sensitive information from the target.

Methods and strategies:

- Malicious software such as keyloggers and spyware
- Tools for collecting login credentials
- Phishing kits

3. *Execution*

Purpose: To utilize the acquired information or gained access in order to advance the attacker's objectives.

Actions:

- Network intrusion refers to the unauthorized access to internal systems by using stolen credentials.
- Financial fraud refers to the act of engaging in unauthorized transactions or financial operations.
- Expanding Social Engineering: Leveraging initial achievements to execute more advanced attacks, such as spear phishing.

Methods and methodologies:

- Remote access tools are software applications that allow users to access and control a computer or network from a remote location.
- Systems for the transfer of funds

4. Covering tracks and Exit

Purpose: The goal is to eliminate all traces of the attack and evade discovery. Actions:

- Data wiping refers to the act of erasing or eliminating any traces or documentation related to the assault.
- Anonymization refers to the utilization of methods, such as virtual private networks (VPNs) or proxy servers, to conceal the identity of the attacker.
- Abandonment refers to the act of discontinuing communication and removing any infrastructure that was utilized in the attack.

Methods and strategies:

- Log cleaners refer to software or tools that are used to remove or delete logs, which are records or traces of activities stored by computer systems. Anonymity networks, such as Tor, are examples of networks that allow users to browse the internet anonymously by routing their internet traffic through a series of encrypted connections.
- Temporary email accounts and telephone numbers

5. Activities conducted after an attack

Goal: To assess the effectiveness of the attack and strategically plan for future attacks.

Engagements:

- Evaluation and examination: Evaluating the efficiency of the attack and identifying areas that can be enhanced.
- Sharing or Selling Data: Engaging in the illicit trade of stolen data on the dark web or exploiting it for nefarious intentions.
- Strategizing Future Actions: Utilizing acquired knowledge to specifically target more victims or carry out subsequent attacks.

Methods and strategies:

- Underground online platforms
- Tools for analyzing attacks
- Engaging in cooperation with other crooks

Phishing Attack Life cycle: Research: Cyber criminals ascertain the identities of firm personnel by utilizing Linked-in and collecting their email addresses.

Preparation: The individuals fabricate an email address that imitates the company's HR department and compose a phishing email regarding a purported policy revision.

Initial Contact: A phishing email is distributed to multiple employees, compelling them to click on a link in order to evaluate the new policy.

Exploitation occurs when an employee clicks on a link and is then routed to a fraudulent login page, where they unknowingly provide their login information.

Method: The attackers employ the pilfered authentication information to gain entry into the organization's network and extract valuable data.

Concealing Evidence: They eradicate phishing emails and eliminate any evidence of the login attempt from the company's system logs.

After the attack, the stolen data is sold on the dark web, and the attackers carefully examine the effectiveness of the phishing effort in order to improve their strategies.

Organizations can enhance their defense against social engineering attacks by comprehending and addressing each stage of the assault life cycle. This can be achieved by measures including providing comprehensive employee training, implementing strong email filtering systems, and conducting frequent security audits. Developing thorough tactics to defend against cyber attacks requires an understanding of the significance of the human component in cyber security.

2. THE HUMAN FACTOR'S SIGNIFICANCE IN SECURITY

A crucial element of cyber security is the human dimension, which includes people's decisions, actions, and behaviors inside an organization.

2.1 Social Engineering Psychology

In the works of Kobis (2021), the psychology of social engineering explores the many ways in which malevolent objectives might be attained by manipulating human behavior, emotions, and cognition. Comprehending the psychological underpinnings of social engineering is crucial for cyber security adversaries and adversaries alike.

The following are some salient features of social engineering psychology:

1. *Authority and Trust*

Principle: People have a tendency to trust those in positions of authority and those who seem to have reputable credentials or ties.

Exploitation: To win the trust and cooperation of their targets, attackers frequently pose as reliable individuals, such as government authorities, business executives, or IT support technicians.

2. *Fear and Haste*

Principle: In times of emergency, fear is a potent motivator that can trump reasoned judgement.

Exploitation: Attackers set up scenarios, such as threatening legal action, account suspension, or data loss unless immediate action is taken, to build panic or a sense of urgency in their targets.

3. *Curiosity and Allure*

Principle: People are inherently curious creatures who are drawn to interesting or novel stimuli.

Exploitation: In phishing emails, attackers utilize attention-grabbing headlines, tempting offers, or intriguing subject lines to trick recipients into clicking on malicious links or opening infected documents.

4. *Obligation and reciprocity*

Principle: When people feel obligated to others, they are more likely to repay favors or comply with requests.

Exploitation: To create a sense of gratitude in their targets and increase their susceptibility to further demands for information or aid, attackers may make minor favors, praises, or false promises.

5. *Conformity and Social Proof*

Principle: When faced with uncertainty or ambiguity, people frequently look to others for guidance on appropriate behavior.

Exploitation: To persuade targets that their requests are reasonable and in line with social standards, attackers use social proof by fabricating social endorsements, testimonies, or scenarios.

6. Emotional manipulation and empathy

Principle: One can control human emotions to affect behavior, such as guilt, sympathy, or sympathy.

Exploitation: To arouse empathy and elicit the necessary responses from their targets, attackers may fabricate tales of adversity, tragedy, or personal problems.

Attackers and defenders alike can more effectively predict and counteract social engineering techniques by being aware of these psychological concepts. While attackers can improve their tactics to more successfully exploit human weaknesses, defenders can reduce the likelihood of becoming a victim of social engineering attacks by putting in place efficient security awareness training, policies, and technical measures.

The following are some major justifications for why cyber security revolves around the human element critically:

2.2 Vulnerability to Social Engineering

People are easily tricked, manipulated, and convinced, which makes them easy candidates for social engineering schemes. Attackers use psychological and emotional tricks on people to coerce them into disclosing private information, opening malicious links, or taking other acts that jeopardize security.

Weaknesses in Security Practices

One of the main reasons for security events and data breaches is human mistake. Errors like opening phishing emails, choosing weak passwords, or skipping security procedures can unintentionally lead to security holes in an organization's defenses.

2.3 Cultural and Organizational Influences

The leadership and organizational culture have an impact on workers' attitudes, priorities, and cyber security-related behaviors. Inactive risk mitigation initiatives and passive culture of security knowledge, low accountability, and non-collaboration serve as catalyst in staging the social engineering attacks across the entire organization.

In conclusion, the human element plays a crucial role in cyber security, influencing the efficacy of defenses, their resilience, and an organization's overall security posture. Organizations may enhance their cyber security strategy and protect sensitive assets and data by mitigating human vulnerabilities, raising security awareness, and incorporating human-centric techniques.

3. SOCIAL ENGINEERING ATTACKS AND CASE STUDIES

The various social engineering attacks that are rampant and ever evolving with times are enlisted below, also pictured in Figure 2. The features of each type of attacks is detailed along with the case studies and instances of the attack.

Figure 2. Types of Social Engineering Attacks

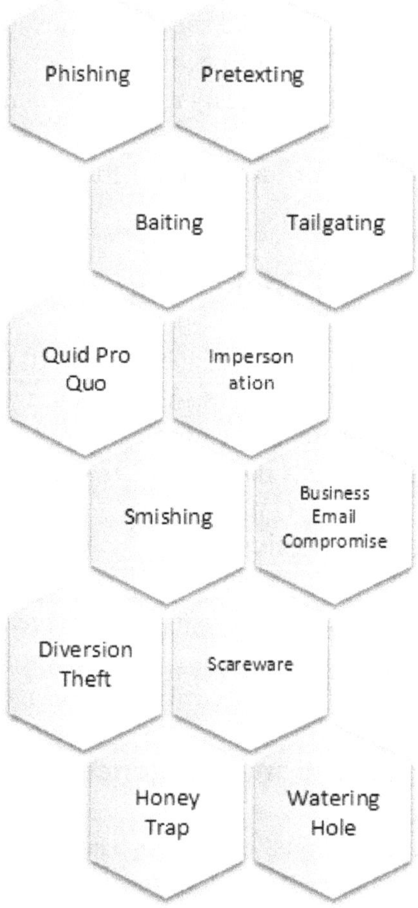

3.1 Phishing

Phishing is a kind of cyber attack in which perpetrators pose as reliable organizations in an attempt to trick victims into divulging sensitive data, including credit card numbers, usernames, and other personal information, according to Alkhalil et al. (2021) and Thomopoulos et al. (2024).

- Features of phishing attempts
    - Deception: Phishing emails, texts, and websites frequently imitate official correspondence from reliable companies or people, making it challenging for targets to determine the legitimacy of the request.
    - Urgency: When an attacker threatens to suspend an account, file a lawsuit, or cause financial loss if the target does not comply, they are usually successful in instilling a sense of urgency or panic in their targets.
    - Manipulation: To increase the chance of a successful deception, phishing assaults use psychological manipulation techniques to take advantage of human emotions such as trust, curiosity, or fear.
    - Spoofing: To further increase the legitimacy of phishing emails and deceive receivers, attackers employ strategies like email spoofing and domain spoofing to make the emails seem authentic.

Figure 3. Phishing

- Phishing Methods and Adaptations

Phishing attacks come in a variety of forms, each designed to take advantage of unique weaknesses and accomplish certain goals. Typical phishing methods consist of:

1. Email phishing is the practice of sending false emails purporting to be from reputable companies, such banks, social media sites, or government organizations. The goal of this tactic is to trick recipients into clicking on harmful links, downloading infected documents, or divulging personal information, as shown graphically in Figure 3.
2. Spear phishing: Phishing assaults that are specifically targeted at particular people or companies. By using the target's familiarity or relevance, attackers increase the likelihood of success by personalizing phishing emails through extensive study by Arora et al. (2020) and Ivanov et al. (2021).
3. Phishing assaults known as "whaling" are directed against prominent figures or executives in a company. In order to fool staff members into disclosing private information, sending money, or carrying out fraudulent activities, attackers assume the identity of top executives or other influential figures.
4. Phishing via clone: Cyber criminals forge phony versions of authentic emails, altering the content or attachments to contain harmful links or malware. These fake emails look much like the real ones, which makes deception more likely to succeed.

• The DNC Phishing Attack Case Study (2016)

During the 2016 U.S. presidential election campaign, a sophisticated phishing attempt was launched against the Democratic National Committee (DNC). The following were the main components of the attack:

- Impersonation: By sending phishing emails that seemed to be security alerts advising DNC employees to update their email passwords, attackers pretended to be reputable companies, like Google.
- Deceptive Techniques: Links to malicious websites imitating authentic Google login pages were included in the phishing emails. Workers unwittingly gave attackers access to their accounts when they clicked on the links and were asked to input their credentials.
- Data Breach: Sensitive correspondence, papers, and information pertaining to the presidential campaign were compromised by hackers who obtained unauthorized access to DNC email accounts as a result of the phishing attempt.
- Impact: Following WikiLeaks' publication of the stolen DNC emails, there was intense public scrutiny, debate, and accusations of political meddling throughout the election campaign.

The DNC phishing attempt is a clear reminder of the effectiveness of phishing techniques and the need for strong cyber security defenses, awareness campaigns, and constant attention to detail when identifying and averting phishing threats.

3.2 Pretexting

Pretexting is a type of social engineering, in the works authored by Chetioui et al. (2021), whereby attackers manufacture a situation or pretext to coerce people into disclosing private information, granting access, or taking acts that jeopardize security.

- Characteristics of the pretexting assaults
    - Fabricated Scenario: To build credibility and win their targets' trust, attackers frequently create a compelling pretext or scenario, posing as someone in a position of authority.
    - Deceptive Communication: To persuade targets to agree with the attacker's requests, pretexting uses deft communication techniques like manipulation, storytelling, and persuading.
    - Leveraging Trust: Attackers increase the possibility of successful deception by taking advantage of people's inclination to trust and abide by commands from people they believe to be authorities or to be trustworthy.
    - Research and Preparation: To maximize the effectiveness of the deception, pretexting assaults frequently necessitate extensive research and preparation in order to customize the created situation to the target's interests, preferences, or vulnerabilities.

Figure 4. Pretexting

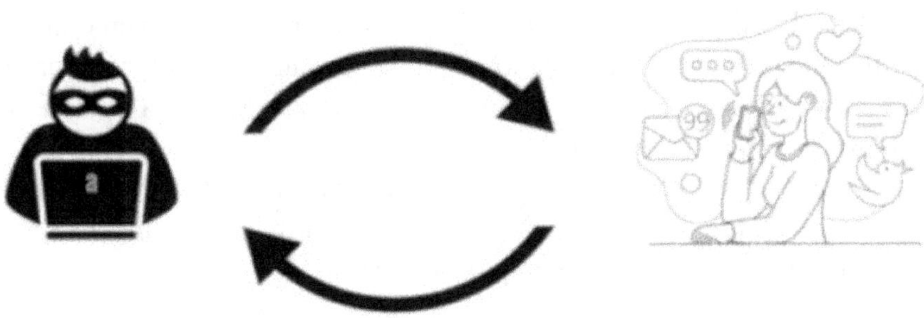

• Pretexting Strategies and Illustrations

Attacks using pretexts can take many different shapes, and they all use distinct methods and approaches to influence their targets. Typical pretexting strategies consist of:

1. Impersonation: In order to establish credibility and convince targets to give critical information or comply with their requests, attackers pose as reputable organizations, law enforcement officials, IT support experts, or company leaders.
2. False Pretenses: To deceive targets into divulging personal information, login credentials, or access to systems, attackers fabricate scenarios or pretenses. Examples of these include running a survey, confirming account details, or extending assistance.
3. Pretexting frequently entails using social engineering strategies to connect with targets and influence their behavior, such as establishing rapport, arousing empathy, or taking advantage of their curiosity.

• Case Study: Tech Executive Impersonation (2017)

An example of note from 2017 was when someone pretended to be a senior tech executive in order to carry out a pretexting attack. Important aspects of the case consist of:

- Manufactured Scenario: The attackers posed as senior executives at a large technology company and reached out to staff members pretending to be carrying out a private probe into security lapses.
- Deceptive Communication: Under the pretense of helping with the inquiry, the attackers convinced staff members to divulge sensitive information, such as login credentials, network access, or private data, by using persuasive language and an air of authority.
- Successful Deception: Although the impersonation was discovered after the fact, the attackers were still able to obtain access and vital information from workers who thought they were complying with orders from a reliable boss, as shown pictorially in Figure 4.
- Implications: The event led to a serious compromise of confidential data, possible disclosure of confidential information, harm to the company's standing with staff, and a decline in employee trust.

The case highlights how well pretexting assaults work to achieve hostile goals by taking use of social engineering techniques, human trust, and authority. It underlines how crucial it is to have strong security procedures, train staff members, and exercise caution in order to spot and foil attempts at pretexting.

3.3 Baiting

By placing physical or digital media containing malware in public areas, attackers use a social engineering tactic known as "baiting" to lure unsuspecting people into engaging with them, in the research article of Kamruzzaman et al. (2023).

• Features of baiting attacks

- Lure: To pique people's interest or satisfy their craving for freebies, attackers deploy alluring bait, such as USB drives, CDs, or other digital media, as shown in Figure 5.

Figure 5 Baiting

- Malevolent Payload: Usually, baiting devices come pre-installed with malware or other malicious software that is meant to infect the user's device as soon as they engage with it.

- Deception: By playing on people's curiosity or need for free or priceless things, attackers utilize deception to get victims to believe the bait is authentic and safe to use.

• Using Real-World Example Baiting

Baiting attacks can appear in a variety of settings, including virtual and real-world ones. Examples of real-world baiting attacks include as follows:

1. Attackers carefully place USB devices in public spaces like parking lots, coffee shops, or office buildings in the hopes that gullible people will pick them up and curiously plug them into their computers.
2. Free Software or Media: Via file-sharing websites or download portals, hackers disseminate malicious software, games, or media files under the pretense of offering people worthwhile stuff.
3. Attackers pose as promotional giveaways, contestants, or unique offers in emails or adverts to trick receivers into clicking on harmful links or attachments. This allows them to take advantage of their curiosity or desire for deals or freebies.

• USB Drive Experiment Case Study (2008)

An experiment was carried out in 2008 by researchers to evaluate the potency of USB drive baiting assaults. Crucial components of the case study consist of:

- Experiment Setup: Researchers dispersed USB devices with innocuous-looking labels like "Confidential" or "Company Payroll" in parking lots, coffee shops, and college campuses, among other public spaces.
- User Interaction: A number of gullible people, thinking they had discovered sensitive or important information, grabbed the USB drives and inserted them into their computers out of curiosity.
- Malware Infection: To illustrate the possible repercussions of dealing with unfamiliar or untrusted devices, the USB sticks included code intended to log user passwords or install malware onto the users' systems upon connection.
- Awareness Impact: The experiment demonstrated how susceptible people are to baiting attacks and emphasized the significance of security awareness and attentiveness in thwarting such dangers.

The USB drive experiment highlights the necessity for strong security protocols, user education, and awareness to reduce the potential of baiting attacks and serves as a cautionary tale about the risks involved in interacting with unfamiliar or untrusted objects.

3.4 Tailgating

Also sometimes referred to as piggybacking, tailgating, as per Kamruzzaman et al. (2023), is a social engineering tactic, as in Figure 6, in which an unauthorized person follows an authorized person closely through a regulated entrance or access point to obtain physical access to a restricted area.

• Characteristics of the Tailgating attacks

- Physical Proximity: Tailgating depends on the assailant's capacity to pursue a designated individual at a close distance via a turnstile, fence, or other secure entrance point.
- Deception: To avoid suspicion and obtain entrance, attackers may employ a variety of deceptive techniques, such as projecting a sense of confidence, feigning distraction, or carrying objects that suggest they belong in the restricted area.

Figure 6 Tailgating

- Abuse of Trust: Tailgating takes advantage of people's innate inclination to open doors for others or to avoid conflict by presuming that those who are following them have permission to enter.

• Vulnerabilities Found

Tailgating attacks take advantage of a number of weaknesses in both human behavior and tangible security mechanisms, such as:

- Lack of Vigilance: In hectic or crowded settings, employees could neglect to confirm the identification or authority of anyone trying to enter restricted areas.
- Social Norms: Humans are generally kind and helpful, so they hold doors open for others without asking to confirm their identity or authorization.
- Limited Visibility: Attackers may find it simpler to avoid detection if security staff or surveillance cameras have limited visibility or coverage of entrance points.
- Inadequate Access Controls: Tailgating behind authorized users allows people to get around weak access control systems, including keypads or badge readers.

• Case Study: Tailgating Incident during Penetration Testing (2014)

One noteworthy event that happened in 2014 was tailgating and was part of a penetration testing activity. Crucial components of the case study consist of:

- Goal: Penetration testers were assigned to examine the efficiency of physical security measures at a corporate office building as part of a security assessment.
- Execution: By tailgating staff members as they entered the premises through a guarded entry, penetration testers tried to obtain unauthorized access.
- Success: By closely following staff members through the entrance, the penetration testers were able to enter the premises without being questioned or confronted, even with security guards and badge readers present.
- Conclusions: The event brought to light gaps in the company's physical security protocols, such as insufficient checks on people entering forbidden zones and a dearth of knowledge among staff members about the dangers of tailgating.

In order to reduce the possibility of unauthorized entry to restricted areas, it is crucial to implement strong physical security measures, personnel training, and awareness campaigns, as demonstrated by the tailgating event that occurred during the penetration testing engagement. It highlights how important it is for businesses to put strict access controls, security procedures, and monitoring systems in place in order to stop and identify tailgating attacks.

3.5 Quid Pro Quo

In the works of Breda et al. (2017), a social engineering tactic known as "quid pro quo" occurs when an attacker offers the victim something of value or aid in return for access, collaboration, or sensitive information, shown pictorially in Figure 7.

Figure 7. Quid Pro Quo

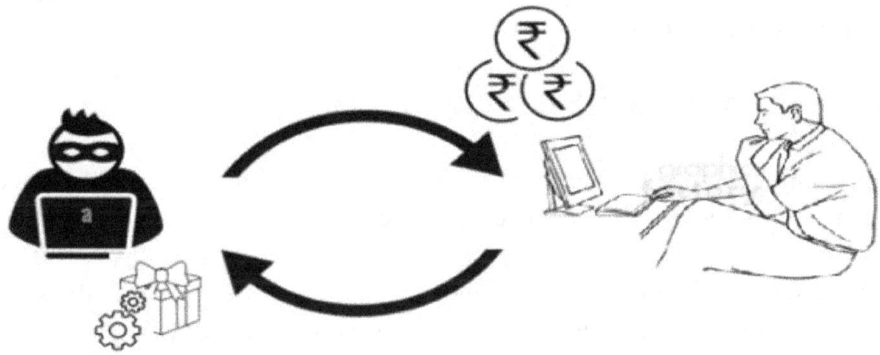

• The following are traits of quid pro quo attacks:

- Exchange of Favors: Quid pro quo assaults entail providing the victim with goods, services, or other advantages in exchange for the target complying with the attacker's demands.
- Deception: Attackers entice targets to offer the sought information or aid by using misleading tactics that give the impression of legitimacy and trustworthiness.
- Sense of Obligation: Because of the perceived advantage or help provided, targets may feel bound to return the favor or abide by the attacker's wishes.

• Illustrations and Consequences

Quid pro quo attacks can take many different forms, each one taking advantage of the target's unique weaknesses and incentives. Following are some instances and ramifications of quid pro quo attacks:

1. IT Support Scams: In order to obtain remote access to the target's computer or sensitive data, attackers pose as IT support technicians or helpdesk employees and offer assistance with computer or software issues.
2. Telephone scams: In order to get account credentials, personal information, or payment information, scammers pretend to be service providers, such as software vendors or internet service providers (ISPs), and they may offer discounts, upgrades, or free services.
3. Job Offer Scams: Cyber criminals pose as hiring managers or recruiters and offer jobs, internships, or training programs in return for private information that could be used to identify a victim, including their Social Security number or bank account information.

• IT Support Scam Case Study (2011)

An important case involving an IT support scam using quid pro quo tactics occurred in 2011. Crucial components of the case study consist of:

- Impersonation: Perpetrators pretended to be IT assistance specialists from a respectable IT organization and reached out to people via phone or email, stating that they had found malware or other technical problems on their systems.

Assistance Offered: The attackers made a free offer to help the victims install security software or provide remote support in order to address the alleged problems.

- Exchange: Under the pretense of providing troubleshooting or verification, the attackers demanded sensitive information, such as login credentials or credit card details, in exchange for their ostensible assistance.
- Repercussions: By granting the attackers access to their computers, victims who complied with their requests unintentionally allowed them to access sensitive information, bank accounts, or personal data kept on the devices.

The IT support scam case emphasizes the dishonest nature of quid pro quo attacks and stresses the need for caution, verification, and skepticism when responding to unsolicited requests or offers from unidentified or suspicious sources. It highlights how important it is for users to be informed, vigilant, and aware in order to reduce their vulnerability to quid pro quo scams.

• *Quid pro quo sexual harassment in South-West Nigerian institutions*

The research by Aina-Pelemo et al. (2021) attempts to compare quid pro quo sexual harassment in selected educational and professional institutions in South-West Nigeria. The study offers insights into quid pro quo sexual harassment in South-West Nigeria, providing empirical data for policy-making, institutional reforms, and advocacy initiatives. The following are the summarized aspects:

- Methodology: The study uses a comparative technique to evaluate harassment prevalence and type through surveys, interviews, and maybe institutional records. Universities, colleges, and governmental and private workplaces are studied.
- Findings: Quid pro quo sexual harassment is prevalent in assessed organizations. Due to weak reporting procedures, cultural attitudes, and lack of sexual harassment awareness, some institutions have higher rates.
- Contributing Factors: The study finds institutional policies, anti-harassment enforcement, and socio-cultural setting as key factors affecting prevalence.
- Impact on Victims: Quid pro quo harassment can cause psychological anguish, academic or career failures, and significant mental health effects. Institutions suffer reputational and efficiency losses.
- Research offers strategies to reduce quid pro quo harassment, such as stricter enforcement of anti-harassment regulations. Comprehensive staff and student training. Establishing strong support and reporting mechanisms.
- Comparative Insights: Analysis identifies excellent practices in institutions with lower harassment rates and gaps in higher rates. This analysis shows how institutional contexts and regulations affect sexual harassment prevalence and management.

3.6 Impersonation

Impersonation is seen as one of the social engineering attacks where an attacker assumes the identity of another person, such as a respected person or an authoritative figure, in order to trick targets into divulging private information, acting in a certain way or granting requests, as expressed in the works of Rosmansyah et al. (2021).

• Characteristics of impersonation attacks

- Deception: Impersonators create the appearance of being someone else by using strategies like mimicry, manipulation, and deception. They then take advantage of trust and authority to get their targets to comply.
- False Identity: In order to win over their victims' trust and credibility, attackers assume personas or identities such as those of customer service agents, technical support staff, or company executives, as in Figure 8.

Figure 8. Impersonation

- Exploitation of Trust: Impersonation attacks use the credibility and trustworthiness of the persona to trick targets into divulging information or taking actions against their better judgement.

• Procedures and Outcomes

There are many different types of impersonation attacks, as mentioned in the works of Yan et al. (2022) and Rehman et al. (2021), and they all use unique techniques and tactics to trick their targets. The following are some techniques and outcomes of impersonation attacks:

1. Phone Impersonation: Attackers pose as reputable organizations, like bank employees or government representatives, and call victims, stating they have urgent problems or requests that need to be handled right away.
2. Email impersonation: Under false pretenses, attackers send misleading emails pretending to be reputable companies, like banks or government agencies, and requesting private information, account credentials, or payment information.
3. In-person impersonation: To obtain access to restricted areas or coerce people into providing information or access, attackers physically pose as contractors, service technicians, or delivery personnel.

• 2019 Case Study: Impersonation of a Bank Representative

A prominent instance in 2019 concerned an impersonation assault directed on bank clients. Crucial components of the case study consist of:

- Impersonation: Perpetrators pretended to be bank employees and called clients, claiming to be looking into fraud or performing security audits.
- Deceptive Tactics: By taking advantage of the bank's reputation for trust and trustworthiness, the impersonators persuaded victims of the veracity of their assertions by using strong language and an authoritative tone.
- Information Requests: Under the guise of confirming their identity or fixing security flaws, victims were asked for sensitive information, such as account numbers, passwords, or verification codes.
- Repercussions: Individuals who were deceived by the impersonation attempt unintentionally gave the attackers access to private information, which put their bank accounts, assets, or personal information at risk.

The story of the bank representative impersonation highlights how successful impersonation techniques are at taking advantage of authority and trust in order to trick targets and get private information. It emphasizes the value of exercising caution, skepticism, and verification when responding to unsolicited requests or communications from unidentified or dubious sources. It also highlights the necessity of security measures, user awareness, and education to reduce the possibility of being a target of impersonation attacks.

3.7 Smishing

In the works of Mishra et al. (2019), smishing is a type of social engineering assault that uses text messages (SMS) to trick people into revealing sensitive information, clicking on harmful links, or downloading malware onto their devices. Similar to previous phishing attempts, smishing leverages human psychology and trust to influence its victims.

• Characteristics of Smishing Attacks

- Deception: Smishing attacks are characterized by the utilization of text messages to transmit deceptive and fraudulent content to the mobile devices of potential victims, shown pictorially in Figure 9.

Figure 9. Smishing

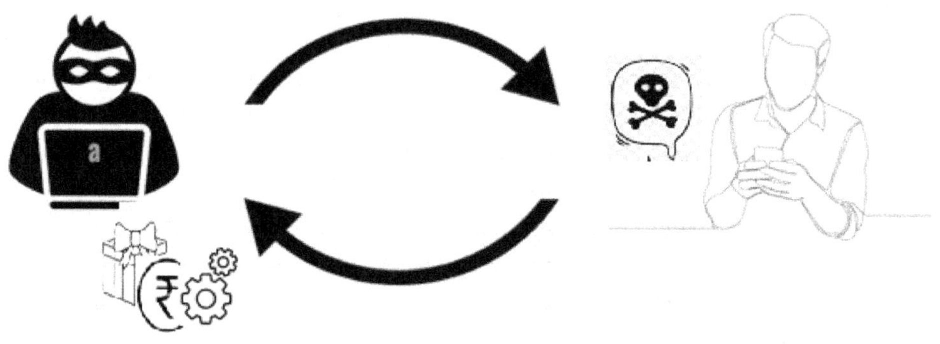

Attackers frequently employ a tactic of inducing a feeling of urgency or fear in smishing communications in order to elicit immediate action from the recipients.

- Spoofed identities: Smishing messages may seem to originate from authentic sources or establishments, such as financial institutions, governmental bodies, or reputable corporations, using spoofing methods.

- Deceptive Links: Smishing messages often include deceptive links or requests that direct recipients to dangerous websites or encourage them to provide sensitive information, such as account passwords or personal details.
- Device Vulnerabilities: Mobile device vulnerabilities are exploited using smishing attacks, which specifically target weaknesses like small screen sizes and limited visibility. This is done to enhance the chances of successfully deceiving users.

• Methods for carrying out Smishing attacks

- Target Selection: Attackers determine possible targets by considering criteria such as demographics, interests, or past interactions with the organization they are pretending to represent.
- Message Crafting: Attackers skillfully compose text messages with the intention of eliciting a response from receivers, employing tactics such as creating a sense of urgency, fear, or curiosity.
- Identity spoofing occurs when attackers falsify the sender's identity in order to make smishing communications seem as though they come from a reputable source or organization.
- Delivery: Adversaries distribute smishing messages to a vast number of recipients concurrently, frequently via automated tools or bulk messaging providers, according to Jain et al. (2017).
- Response Handling: Attackers manipulate the responses they receive from receivers, continuing to contact with them in order to obtain confidential information or guide victims towards harmful websites.
- Concealing Evidence: Perpetrators conceal their actions by erasing message records or employing temporary phone numbers to evade identification.

• Instances of Smishing Attacks:

- Deceptive Bank Alerts: Individuals receive text messages falsely claiming to be from their bank, informing them about potentially fraudulent actions on their account and urging them to click on a link in order to confirm their account information, as expressed in the article of Kothamasu et al. (2023).
- Deceptive Package Delivery Notifications: Individuals receive SMS messages purporting to be from a courier company, notifying them about a package delivery and offering a hyperlink to monitor the shipment's progress. However, this link redirects them to a fraudulent website designed to steal personal information.

- COVID-19 Vaccine Scams: Smishing attacks took advantage of vaccine distribution efforts during the COVID-19 pandemic. Individuals received SMS messages promising early access to vaccines or vaccination appointments in return for personal information or payment.

3.8 Business Email Compromise (BEC)

Business Email Compromise (BEC) refers to a highly advanced form of cyber attack, as described in Al-Musib et al. (2021), that specifically aims at businesses, government agencies, and various other organizations. A BEC attack, as shown in Figure 10, involves the utilization of email fraud and social engineering techniques by hackers to trick employees into carrying out unauthorized acts, disclosing sensitive information, or transferring payments. Business Email Compromise (BEC) attacks commonly employ the tactic of masquerading as reliable sources, such as high-ranking executives, trustworthy vendors, or business associates, with the intention of deceiving victims into carrying out acts that serve the interests of the attackers.

Figure 10. Business Email Compromise

• Features of Business Email Compromise (BEC) Attacks:

- Email Spoofing: BEC attackers engage in email spoofing by falsifying email addresses to create the illusion that the messages come from authentic sources, such as company officials or business partners.
- Social Engineering: BEC attackers employ social engineering strategies to exploit human susceptibilities and influence victims into acquiescing to their

demands. This may entail generating a feeling of immediacy, capitalizing on influence, or manipulating confidence.

- Targeted Impersonation is a common tactic used in Business Email Compromise (BEC) attacks, when the attacker pretends to be a senior executive or someone with power in order to maximize the chances of their attack being successful.
- Deceptive Requests: Cyber criminals engaged in Business Email Compromise (BEC) tactics send dishonest emails with the intention of obtaining wire transfers, payments, or confidential information, such as employee payroll data or customer financial details.

• Methods of Email Compromise:

Business Email Compromise (BEC) attacks utilize a range of strategies, such as compromising email accounts, falsifying domain information, and redirecting emails, in order to trick victims and avoid being detected.

-Monetary Damages: BEC attacks can lead to substantial monetary damages for organizations, such as wire transfer fraud, payment of fake invoices, and the redirection of funds to accounts controlled by the attacker.

• Instances of Business Email Compromise (BEC) Scenarios:

- Chief Executive Officer (CEO) Fraud: A perpetrator assumes the identity of the CEO or another prominent executive of a company and dispatches a pressing email to the finance department, soliciting a substantial wire transfer to an overseas bank account.
- Vendor Email Compromise: Adversaries infiltrate the email accounts of vendors or suppliers and exploit them to dispatch deceitful invoices or payment demands to customers, rerouting money to accounts controlled by the attackers.
- Employee Payroll Diversion: This refers to the act of redirecting an employee's salary or wages to a different account or recipient without their knowledge or consent. Malicious individuals assume the identity of HR staff or high-ranking company officials and transmit emails to the payroll division, soliciting modifications to employee banking details and rerouting salary disbursements to deceptive accounts.

3.9 Diversion Theft

Diversion theft refers to a type of theft where the attention of the victim is intentionally diverted in order to steal their belongings, shown pictorially Figure 11. Within the digital domain, diversion theft assumes a slightly altered manifestation, nevertheless it upholds the fundamental notion of redirecting attention or resources in order to carry out the act of theft, as marked in the works of Salahdine et al. (2019).

Figure 11. Diversion Theft

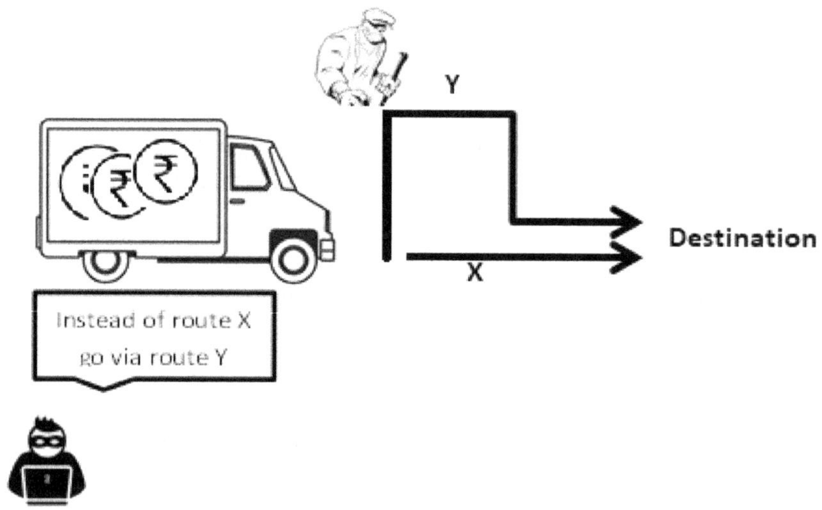

• Attributes of Diversion Theft in the Digital Realm:

- 1. Misleading Strategies: Cyber criminals employ a range of deceitful tactics, including phishing emails, counterfeit websites, and social engineering, to deceive victims into participating in their fraudulent schemes.
- 2. Distraction Techniques: In the realm of online, diversion theft frequently employs tactics that divert victims' attention away from the theft or malicious behavior by presenting them with apparently genuine requests, notifications, or urgent messages.
- 3. Deception: Perpetrators employ misdirection strategies, such as inducing a feeling of urgency or dread, to influence victims into hastily taking action without adequately evaluating the potential hazards or repercussions.

- 4. confidence Exploitation: Diversion theft takes advantage of the confidence and reliability linked to well-known brands, trusted institutions, or authoritative individuals in order to fool victims and enable the theft of valuable information or resources.

• Instances of Diversion Theft in the Digital Realm

- Phishing Attacks: Cyber criminals employ deceptive tactics by sending deceitful emails or messages that mimic reputable organizations like banks, government institutions, or technology businesses. Their intention is to deceive recipients into revealing personal information, login passwords, or financial particulars.
- Malware Distractions: Cyber criminals employ malicious software, such as ransomware or trojans, to contaminate the devices of their targets. They then divert the victims' attention by displaying pop-up alerts, counterfeit system notifications, or ransom requests. Meanwhile, the malware clandestinely pilfers data or undermines security.
- Distributed Denial of Service (DDoS) Attacks: Cyber criminals initiate DDoS attacks on a target's network or infrastructure with the intention of inundating and diverting IT security teams through a deluge of malicious traffic. These attacks are often carried out in conjunction with other malicious activities, such as data exfiltration or credential theft.
- Social engineering scams involve the use of strategies like pretexting or baiting to influence victims into divulging personal information, downloading malicious software, or transferring payments. This is done by distracting the victims with a contrived scenario or urgent need.

To bolster their cyber security defenses and safeguard against deceit, manipulation, and theft in the digital realm, organizations and individuals should fortify their knowledge of the attributes, instances, and countermeasures associated with diversion theft in cyberspace.

3.10 Scareware

Scareware social engineering assaults, according to the works of Malin et al. (2017), are a form of cyber threat that exploits users by instilling fear or intimidation in order to deceive them into performing specified activities, such as downloading harmful software or revealing confidential information. Below is the diagrammatic Figure 12 and a concise summary of scareware social engineering attacks:

Figure 12. Scareware

• Scareware social engineering attacks possess distinct attributes.

Methods that exploit fear: Scareware attacks use fear by using alarming messages or alarms to manipulate users into thinking that their devices are infected with malware, compromised, or in danger of data loss or identity theft.

Deceptive Appearance: Scareware messages frequently imitate genuine security alerts, system cautions, or pop-up notifications in order to seem believable and pressing, hence raising the chances of victims complying.

Action Prompt: Scareware compels victims to promptly engage in specific actions, such as clicking on a hyperlink, downloading a software update, or contacting a fraudulent technical support hotline, in order to handle the alleged security danger.

Scareware induces a deceptive feeling of urgency by issuing threats of severe repercussions, such as loss of data, harm to the system, or legal implications, if the victim does not adhere to the given instructions.

• Methods Employed in Scareware Social Engineering Attacks:

Emails designed for phishing purposes: Scareware attacks typically commence with phishing emails that include alarming messages or urgent warnings, instructing recipients to click on malicious links or download malicious attachments that supposedly include security updates or antivirus software.

Malicious websites can distribute scareware by presenting deceptive security alerts or pop-up notifications, which prompt visitors to install counterfeit security software or contact a deceitful technical assistance hotline.

Malvertising refers to the dissemination of scareware through malicious adverts (malvertising) that seem on genuine websites. These advertisements deceive viewers into clicking on them, which then prompts scareware pop-ups or redirects them to harmful websites.

Browser hijacking occurs when scareware takes control of users' web browsers, causing them to see constant pop-up messages or browser lock screens that falsely state the device is afflicted with malware. These messages then prompt users to download counterfeit security software or contact a fraudulent technical support hotline.

• Implications of Scareware Social Engineering Attacks:

Malware Installation: Individuals that are targeted by scareware assaults may unknowingly acquire and implement malicious software onto their devices, such as ransomware, spyware, or adware, so jeopardizing their security and privacy.

Financial losses can occur when individuals fall prey to scareware, which involves being deceived into buying counterfeit security software or services, making payments for unneeded maintenance, or divulging payment information to scammers pretending to be technical support staff.

Identity theft can occur as a result of scareware assaults when individuals unknowingly provide sensitive information, such as login details or bank data, in response to fraudulent security alerts or phishing emails.

Operational disruption: Scareware attacks have the potential to disturb users' regular activities through the continuous display of pop-up messages, the hijacking of web browsers, or the slowing down of system performance. This can lead to annoyance and inconvenience.

• Case Studies of Scareware Assaults

Scareware assaults have been widespread over the years, specifically targeting consumers on different platforms and devices. Here are a few noteworthy examples:

1. WinFixer and other scareware programmes (Mid-2000s)

WinFixer, often referred to as ErrorSafe or WinAntiVirus, was a prominent scareware program that falsely claimed to identify and resolve computer faults. Its true purpose was to trick users into buying counterfeit security software.

WinFixer and other scareware programs frequently presented deceptive pop-up messages and counterfeit system alarms, pressuring users to acquire or buy the alleged security software in order to address non-existent problems.

The widespread occurrence of WinFixer and similar scareware programs caused significant annoyance among users and encouraged law enforcement organizations to initiate legal action against the producers of these deceitful software products.

2. MacDefender Malware (2011)

MacDefender Malware was a scareware program designed to deceive macOS users. It disguised itself as genuine antivirus software and presented false security alerts, falsely claiming to have detected malware infections on the victim's Mac computer.

The victims who were deceived by the scam were instructed to download and install the counterfeit antivirus software. Once installed, the software would exhibit further scareware messages and request payment for the whole version of the software in order to eliminate the alleged malware risks.

Apple promptly addressed the MacDefender issue by releasing security updates and introducing safeguards to block the automatic installation of the virus on consumers' Mac machines.

3. The FBI ransomware scam (2012)

FBI ransomware scam involved a scareware attack where victims were presented with counterfeit letters claiming to be from the FBI or other law enforcement agencies. These communications falsely accused individuals of engaging in unlawful actions, such as downloading copyrighted content or disseminating child pornography.

The victims were notified that their computers had been immobilized as a result of purported unlawful actions and were directed to make a payment referred to as a “fine” or “ransom” in order to regain access to their computers and evade legal repercussions.

The FBI ransomware scheme utilized fear and intimidation to compel victims into paying the ransom. However, security experts cautioned against complying with the demands and instead suggested eliminating the malware via secure boot methods or antivirus software.

4. Android FLocker, a mobile malware (2015)

FLocker, alternatively referred to as Frantic Locker or Android.Lockdroid, was a type of ransomware specifically designed to attack Android devices. It operated by presenting deceptive messages, falsely claiming to originate from law enforcement authorities, accusing victims of engaging in unlawful acts, and demanding payment in order to regain access to their devices.

FLocker employed scareware strategies to trick users into thinking that their devices had been locked by law enforcement as a result of purported criminal actions, such as accessing forbidden content or sharing pirated software.

Victims were directed to make a payment in the form of prepaid vouchers or digital currency as a ransom in order to regain access to their devices. However, security experts have created decryption tools to assist impacted users in recovering their files without having to pay the ransom.

These occurrences illustrate the deceitful strategies and detrimental outcomes linked to scareware assaults, emphasizing the significance of being aware of cyber security and taking proactive steps to safeguard against such risks.

3.11 Honey Trap

A honeytrap is a covert exercise intended to entice and mislead a specific individual, as defined earlier by Ehrenfeld (2014), usually for the aim of espionage, gathering intelligence, or conducting investigations, as drawn pictorially in Figure 13. In the field of cyber security, a honeytrap is a misleading strategy employed to lure and identify harmful individuals, such as hackers or Cyber criminals, by establishing alluring decoys or bait systems that appear susceptible or lucrative.

• Key attributes of honeytraps in the field of cyber security:

Honeytraps utilize deceit to deceive harmful individuals into interacting with counterfeit systems, services, or data that appear authentic or valuable.

Figure 13. Honeytrap

- Appeal: Honeytraps are intentionally crafted to be visually appealing to potential assailants, luring them with enticing incentives, such as counterfeit credentials, sensitive data, or susceptible systems, in order to provoke engagement.
- Honeytraps are utilized as proactive measures to detect and monitor nefarious activity, offering important insights into the strategies, methods, and behaviors of threat actors.
- Isolation: Honeytraps are frequently segregated from production systems and networks to avoid actual harm or compromise, enabling security personnel to safely watch and analyze the behavior of attackers.

• *Instances of Honeytraps in the Field of Cyber Security:*

- Honeypot servers are deployed by security researchers and organizations to impersonate genuine services or applications. Their purpose is to attract and monitor harmful actions, such as scanning, probing, or exploitation attempts.
- Honeytokens refer to counterfeit or intentionally exposed credentials, files, or data that are strategically put within an organization's systems or networks. These honeytokens are designed to function as indicators of compromise (IOCs) and entice attackers to expose themselves when they are accessed or utilized.
- Honey files are decoy files or documents that are deliberately created with appealing content, such as counterfeit bank records, customer databases, or intellectual property. These files are strategically placed on systems or network shares to lure and monitor any unauthorized attempts to access or steal information.

• Case Studies of Honeytraps

Although honey traps are commonly employed as defensive tactics by security experts, there are cases where cyber attackers have utilized similar methods to entice victims into vulnerable scenarios. Nevertheless, it is important to acknowledge that these occurrences may not be as widespread as defensive applications of honey traps. Here are two examples:

1. False Employment Offers

   Description of Attack: Cyber criminals fabricate fraudulent job advertisements on authentic job search websites or social media platforms in order to entice those seeking employment. The positions listed frequently offer lucrative wages, remote work options, or other appealing perks to lure unsuspecting individuals.

   - Strategies: After a victim shows interest in the fraudulent employment offer, the Cyber criminals may continue to communicate with them using email or messaging services. They might solicit personal data, such as Social Security numbers or bank account information, pretending to do background checks or verify employment.
   - Implications: Individuals who disclose their personal information may be susceptible to identity theft, financial fraud, or other nefarious endeavors. In addition, fraudsters may exploit the stolen information to carry out subsequent attacks, such as phishing or credential stuffing.

2. Romance Scams

   Description of Attack: Cyber criminals engage in romance scams by fabricating accounts on dating websites, social media platforms, or online forums in order to forge relationships with unsuspecting individuals. They frequently employ appealing profile photographs and intricate personal histories to establish trust and affection with their targets.

   - Strategies: After establishing a connection, the Cyber criminals may initiate romantic chats and form emotional connections with their victims. Ultimately, they can solicit funds or monetary aid by presenting different justifications, such as urgent medical situations, travel costs, or entrepreneurial endeavors.
   - Implications: Individuals who fall victim to romance scams may experience substantial monetary damages and psychological anguish. Occasionally, the Cyber criminals may persist in exploiting

the victims even after the first scam is exposed, employing coercion or blackmail to collect further cash.

These examples illustrate how cyber attackers might use honey trap tactics to deceive and exploit their victims. It is crucial to stay alert and skeptical of unsolicited offers or interactions, particularly those that appear too good to be true. By exercising prudence and adhering to proper cyber hygiene practices, individuals can mitigate the chance of becoming targets of such fraudulent schemes.

3.12 Watering Hole

A watering hole attack is a deliberate and focused cyber-attack tactic, expressed in the works carried by Revathi et al. (2018) in which attackers infiltrate a particular website or collection of websites that are regularly used by the intended victims, shown in Figure 14. The objective is to deliberately introduce malware into the devices of the visitors or to collect information about them.

Figure 14. Watering Hole

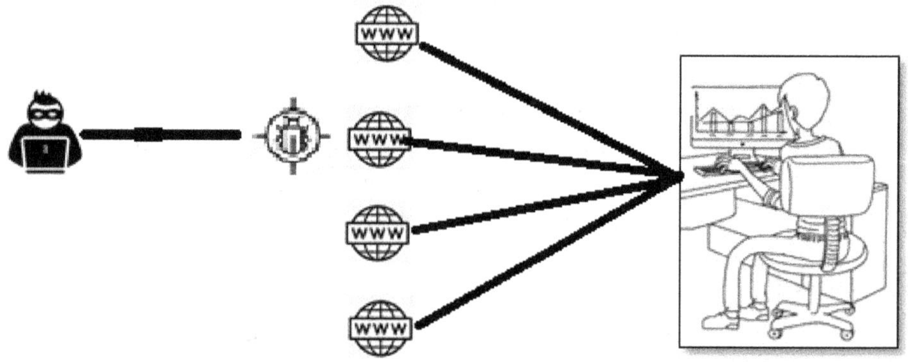

• Primary characteristics:

Watering hole attacks adopt a targeted strategy by focusing on websites frequented by a certain set of persons, such as employees of a particular corporation, professionals in a given industry, or members of an organization.

Website Compromise: Attackers identify and infiltrate one or more authentic websites. They have the ability to include harmful code, such as JavaScript or iframes, in order to distribute malware to unwary users.

Malware Delivery: When a specific individual access the compromised website, the harmful code is activated and tries to take advantage of weaknesses in the visitor's browser, plugins, or operating system in order to distribute malware.

The assault capitalizes on the faith that users place in the authentic website, reducing their inclination to suspect harmful actions and increasing the likelihood of them being infected.

Advanced tactics: Attackers frequently employ sophisticated tactics to evade detection, including advanced obfuscation techniques, zero-day exploits, and selective deployment of malware (targeting just users with specific IP addresses or browser types).

• *Significant examples of watering hole attacks*

1. Operation Aurora, which occurred between 2009 and 2010

Assault Description: Multiple instances of cyber-attacks originating from China specifically targeted prominent organizations such as Google, Adobe, and other influential technology companies.

Methodology: Adversaries successfully infiltrated websites that were commonly accessed by employees of the specific companies being targeted. The infected websites disseminated malware that leveraged weaknesses in web browsers to infiltrate the networks of the companies.

Consequence: The attack resulted in the unauthorized acquisition of valuable intellectual property and confidential data from several prominent companies.

2. VOHO Campaign in 2012

Attack Description: This assault specifically aimed at those working in the defense and aerospace sectors.

Methods: Adversaries successfully infiltrated multiple websites, including those belonging to suppliers and subcontractors within the defense industry. These sites were utilized to disseminate malware to individuals who visited them.

Outcome: The campaign effectively compromised a large number of devices and obtained vital intelligence from important targets in the defense sector.

3. Attack on the G20 Summit (2013)

Assault: This assault specifically aimed at individuals who were present at the G20 Summit.

Methods: The attackers infiltrated websites that were highly probable to be accessed by G20 participants, particularly those that offered news and event updates. Users accessing these websites were routed to rogue sites that took advantage of browser vulnerabilities to distribute malware.

Consequence: The purpose of the attack was to acquire valuable knowledge and confidential data from influential political and economic figures who were present at the conference.

4. Incident of Watering Hole Attack in the Energy Sector (2017)

Attack Description: This assault specifically targeted the energy sector, encompassing companies engaged in the production and dissemination of power.

Methods: The attackers successfully infiltrated websites that are related to the energy industry and inserted harmful code in order to distribute malware to the site's visitors. The malware was designed to collect data pertaining to the industrial control systems utilized by these companies.

Consequence: The incident has sparked worries regarding the safety of crucial infrastructure and the possibility of future disruptive attacks on energy systems.

5. Bit9 Attack in 2013

Assault Bit9, a security firm, was the victim of a watering hole assault.

Methodology: The attackers successfully infiltrated a website that was accessed by both Bit9 workers and consumers. They injected malicious software onto the systems of the visitors, taking advantage of weaknesses in their security.

Consequence: The virus was employed to infiltrate Bit9's network, leading to the pilfering of digital certificates and the corruption of Bit9's reliable software updates. These compromised updates were subsequently utilized to target other victims.

4. EFFECTS AND REPERCUSSIONS

Social engineering attacks have the potential to have profound and wide-ranging effects on people, organizations, and even entire communities. The following are some salient features of the effects and fallout from social engineering attacks:

4.1 Monetary Losses

Social engineering assaults have the potential to cause both individuals and organizations to suffer significant financial losses. Financial loss and hardship can result from attackers stealing money through fraudulent transactions, compromising bank accounts, or committing identity theft.

4.2 Breach of Data

Social engineering assaults frequently entail the theft of or unapproved access to private data, including financial records, intellectual property, and personal information. Confidential information may be revealed as a result of a data breach, which may also cause loss of customer trust, fines from authorities, and legal implications.

4.3 Reputational Damage

The credibility and reputation of an organization might be damaged by the fallout from a social engineering attack. The public disclosure of security events, data breaches, or privacy violations can have a detrimental effect on corporate relationships, erode customer trust, and damage brand reputation.

4.4 Operational Disruption

Social engineering assaults have the potential to interfere with regular corporate processes, resulting in lost productivity, service interruptions, and downtime. Unauthorized access, malware infestations, or compromised systems can make vital applications, infrastructure, or services inaccessible, disrupting business operations and resulting in financial loss.

4.5 Implications for Law and Regulation

Cyber security, privacy, and data protection laws, rules, and industry standards may all be broken by social engineering assaults. If an organization disregards its legal responsibilities or does not take appropriate precautions to secure sensitive information, it may be subject to legal penalties, regulatory fines, or lawsuits.

4.6 Effect on the Mind

People who are the subject of social engineering attacks could feel vulnerable, lose trust, or experience psychological anguish, anxiety, or emotional trauma as a result of their privacy being violated. Stress, anxiety about becoming victims again, or long-term psychological effects from the attack are all possible for victims.

4.7 Implications on the Society

Attacks using social engineering have the potential to have wider societal repercussions by destroying confidence in online interactions, diminishing faith in digital systems, and encouraging a climate of mistrust. The spread of social engineering techniques could exacerbate an environment of unease and undermine the advantages of digital innovation and connectedness.

In conclusion, social engineering attacks have a variety of effects that go beyond monetary losses and technological difficulties. These effects also include harm to one's reputation, legal ramifications, psychological distress, and wider societal repercussions. Mitigating the risks associated with social engineering assaults and protecting against their negative outcomes require proactive measures including security awareness training, strong cyber security defenses, and regulatory compliance.

5. LEGAL AND REGULATORY RAMIFICATIONS

Social engineering attacks can have serious legal and regulatory repercussions for organizations. Security breaches and privacy violations can expose them to a variety of legal liabilities, regulatory penalties, and compliance duties. The following are some important legal and policy factors pertaining to social engineering attacks:

5.1 Laws Regarding Privacy and Data Protection

- *General Data Protection Regulation (GDPR):* GDPR requires organizations that handle individuals' personal data inside the European Union (EU) to put in place suitable security measures to shield personal data from misuse, unauthorized access, and disclosure. There could be harsh fines and penalties for not adhering to GDPR.
- *California Consumer Privacy Act (CCPA):* The CCPA places duties on companies that gather, use, or divulge a California resident's personal information. These duties include data security, breach reporting, and consumer

rights obligations. Civil fines and regulatory enforcement proceedings may result from failure to comply with the CCPA.

5.2 Regulations Particular to an Industry

- *Health Insurance Portability and Accountability Act (HIPAA):* HIPAA laws, which include protections for protected health information (PHI) and notification obligations in the case of a data breach, must be followed by covered businesses and business associates in the healthcare sector. Serious fines and penalties may be imposed for HIPAA violations.
- *Payment Card Industry Data Security Standard (PCI DSS):* PCI DSS mandates that businesses that handle, send, or keep payment card data secure cardholder data and put in place measures to prevent unauthorized access. Penalties, fines, and limitations on the ability to accept card payments may result from noncompliance with PCI DSS.

5.3 Laws Notifying of Breach

- *Data Breach Notification Laws:* In the case of a data breach involving sensitive personal information, several jurisdictions have laws mandating organizations to notify individuals and regulatory authorities. If a breach is not immediately reported to the relevant parties, it may lead to legal action, regulatory penalties, and reputational harm.

5.4 Laws Protecting Consumers

- *Unfair and Deceptive activities:* Consumer protection laws that forbid unfair or deceptive business activities may be broken by social engineering attacks that use deceptive or misleading methods. Businesses that use misleading tactics run the risk of being sued, having regulatory bodies enforce their policies, and having affected parties file civil lawsuits.

5.5 Accountability

- *Class Action Lawsuits:* Individuals who have been the target of social engineering attacks may be able to obtain compensation by filing class action lawsuits that claim negligence, contract breach, or invasions of privacy. Injunctions, monetary damages, and court-ordered remedies may be imposed on organizations found accountable for neglecting to protect sensitive data or to take appropriate precautions against social engineering assaults.

5.6 The Prosecution of Crimes

- *Criminal Charges:* Offenders may be prosecuted for crimes like fraud, identity theft, computer intrusion, or conspiracy in situations involving intentional and malevolent social engineering attacks. Sentences for offences involving social engineering may be asset seizure, fines, and incarceration.

There are serious legal and financial repercussions for security breaches, privacy violations, and non-compliance with relevant laws and regulations. The legal and regulatory environment surrounding social engineering attacks is complicated and dynamic. In the face of social engineering dangers, it is crucial to put strong cyber security safeguards, privacy protections, and compliance programs in place in order to reduce legal risks and guarantee regulatory compliance.

6. STRATEGIES FOR MITIGATION

In order to prevent social engineering attacks, mitigation solutions combine preventive actions with proactive steps to increase awareness, put security controls in place, and create efficient reaction plans. Here are a few essential mitigation techniques:

6.1 Employee Awareness and Training Programs

- *Security Awareness Training:* Hold frequent training sessions to teach staff members how to spot and react to questionable messages or requests, as well as common social engineering techniques like phishing, pretexting, and impersonation.
- *Phishing Simulations:* Test staff members' vulnerability to phishing attacks and enhance security awareness training by conducting simulated phishing exercises. Give staff members constructive criticism and educational materials to assist them become better at spotting and reporting phishing attempts.
- *Behavioral Analytics and User Monitoring:* Keeping an eye on user actions and behavior might yield important information about unusual activity and possible security threats. Using patterns, behaviors, and departures from typical behavior, behavioral analytics systems examine user behavior to find suspicious activity, insider threats, or unauthorized access attempts.

6.2 Security Guidelines and Practices

- *Acceptable Use Policies: Clearly* define the rules around what constitutes appropriate use of company resources, such as email, internet access, and sensitive data access. Establish standards of behavior, best practices, and criteria for security that staff members must abide by.
- *Access Controls: To* limit access to sensitive systems and data, implement strong access controls, authentication procedures, and the least privilege principle. Implement the least privilege concept to guarantee that workers have the minimal access required to carry out their job responsibilities.
- *Incident Reporting Procedures:* Set up a system for informing the relevant IT or security staff about security incidents, including possible social engineering assaults. Make sure staff members understand the need of swiftly reporting issues and offer precise guidance on incident response.
- *Human-Centric Security Solutions:* Consideration of human aspects throughout the design of security systems enhances its usability, efficacy, and acceptance by users. People are empowered to make informed security decisions and actively participate in cyber security efforts when they are provided with user-friendly interfaces, intuitive security controls, and clear communication of security regulations.

6.3 Technological Remedies

- *Email Filtering and Security Gateways:* Use email filtering programs to stop phishing emails, malicious links, and malware attachments from getting to staff members' inboxes. To stop email spoofing, use email security gateways to enforce email authentication standards like SPF (Sender Policy Framework), DKIM (Domain Keys Identified Mail), and DMARC (Domain-based Message Authentication, Reporting, and Conformance), to validate the legitimacy of incoming emails and identify instances of email spoofing.
- *Multi-Factor Authentication (MFA):* The use of multi-factor authentication (MFA) is advised for gaining access to online services, sensitive systems, and apps. To improve security, make it mandatory for staff members to use extra authentication methods in addition to passwords, including tokens, biometrics, or mobile apps.
- *Endpoint Protection:* To identify and stop dangerous software infections and unauthorized access attempts, install and maintain endpoint protection solutions, such as anti-virus software, anti-malware tools, and endpoint detection and response (EDR) solutions.

- *Procedures for Transaction Verification:* Create protocols for confirming the authenticity of requests involving wire transfers, payments, or sensitive information, particularly if they come from unexpected or uncommon sources.
- *Vendor Risk Management:* Establish and apply vendor risk management protocols to evaluate and oversee the security status of third-party vendors and suppliers, including their email security controls and procedures.

6.4 Plans for Incident Response and Recovery

- *Incident Response Plan:* Create and record an incident response plan that outlines how to identify, evaluate, and handle security incidents, including social engineering attacks. Assign members of the selected incident response team duties and tasks and create lines of communication to facilitate incident coordination.
- *Backup and Recovery:* To guarantee that important data can be restored in the case of a security incident or data breach, regularly perform data backups and disaster recovery procedures. Periodically test backup and recovery protocols to ensure their dependability and efficacy.
- *Post-Incident Analysis:* Review the reaction to social engineering attacks and identify lessons learned, areas for improvement, and remedial actions by conducting post-incident analysis and debriefings. Refine security policies, procedures, and training initiatives with the knowledge you obtain from incident response operations.

Organizations can improve their defenses against social engineering attacks, lower the likelihood of successful compromises, and better safeguard confidential data and assets from unauthorized access or exposure by putting these mitigation techniques into practice. Furthermore, preventative steps can lessen the negative effects of social engineering assaults on an organization's operations and reputation while also assisting in the effective response to security problems.

7. CONCLUSION

In this chapter, the details of the psychological aspects of the social engineering attack in terms of behavioral analytics and weaknesses in security solutions, cultural and organizational influences are presented. The popular types of social engineering attacks are described along with their procedures, features and case studies. The after-effects of the such attacks caused on data security, monetary and reputation losses, implications on the society with their repercussions are further discussed. The chapter also deliberates on the laws, regulations, legal ramifications and prosecution of such crimes. In the end, he mitigation strategies of such attacks to safeguard the leakage of sensitive and confidential data the humans and organizations can use to thwart the attempts of social engineering attacks.

REFERENCES

Aina-Pelemo, A., Oke, O. A., & Alade, I. T. (2021, November). Deborah., Oke, Olubukola. Abimbola., & Aladec, Iseoluwa Titilayo. (March 2021). Quid pro quo sexual harassment: Comparative study of its occurrences in selected institutions in South-West, Nigeria. *Current Research in Behavioral Sciences*, 2, 100031. Advance online publication. DOI: 10.1016/j.crbeha.2021.100031

Al-Musib, N. Al-Serhani, Faeiz., Humayun, Mamoona., & Jhanjhi, Noor. (2021). Business email compromise (BEC) attacks. Materials Today Proceedings DOI: DOI: 10.1016/j.matpr.2021.03.647

Alkhalil, Z., Hewage, C., Nawaf, L., & Khan, I. (2021, March 9). Hewage, Chaminda., Nawaf, Liqaa., & Khan, Imtiaz. (2021). Phishing Attacks: A Recent Comprehensive Study and a New Anatomy. *Frontiers of Computer Science*, 3, 563060. Advance online publication. DOI: 10.3389/fcomp.2021.563060

Arora, Ritika., Sharad., Singh, Sanjeet., Kumar, Narendra., & Saini, A. K. (March 2020). Phishing Attacks and Detection Techniques. PalArch's Journal of Archeology of Egypt/ Egyptology, .DOI: 10.3389/fcomp.2021.563060

Breda, F., Barbosa, H., & Morais, T. (2017). Social Engineering And Cyber Security. *Proceedings of the International Conference on Technology, Education and Development*, Valencia,4204-4211, http://dx.doi.org/DOI: 10.21125/inted.2017.1008

Chetioui, K., Bah, Birom., Alami, Abderrahim. Ouali., & Bahnasse, Ayoub. (2021). Overview of Social Engineering Attacks on Social Networks. The Second International Workshop of Innovation and Technologies, doi: . 302.DOI: 10.1016/j.procs.2021.12

Ehrenfeld, T. (2014, September). Honey Trap: The buzz about bees is not necessarily good. *The Weekly Standard*, 19(48), •••. http://www.weeklystandard.com/ print/ articles/honey-trap_803987.html

Ivanov, M. A., Kliuchnikova, Bogdana. V., Chugunkov, Ilya. V., & Plaksina, Anna M. (March 2021). *Phishing Attacks and Protection Against Them. IEEE Conference of Russian Young Researchers in Electrical and Electronic Engineering (ElConRus)*, doi: 51938.2021.9396693.DOI: 10.1109/ ElConRus

Jain, A., & Gupta, B. B. (2018). Kumar, & Gupta, B.B. (December 2017). Rule-Based Framework for Detection of Smishing messages in Mobile Environment. Science Direct: Procedia. *Procedia Computer Science*, 125, 617–623. Advance online publication. DOI: 10.1016/j.procs.2017.12.079

Kamruzzaman, A., Thakur, K., Ismat, S., Ali, M. L., Huang, K., & Thakur, H. N. *(2023).* Social Engineering Incidents and Preventions. *IEEE 13th Annual Computing and Communication Workshop and Conference (CCWC)*, Las Vegas, NV, USA, 2023, pp. 0494-0498, DOI: 10.1109/CCWC57344.2023.10099202

Kobis, P. (2021). Human Factor Aspects in Information Security Management in the Traditional It and Cloud Computing Models. *Operations Research and Decisions*, 31(1). Advance online publication. DOI: 10.37190/ord210104

Kothamasu, G. A., Angara Venkata, S. K., Pemmasani, Y., & Mathi, S. (2023, April). An Investigation on Vulnerability Analysis of Phishing Attacks and Countermeasures. *International Journal of Safety and Security Engineering*, 13(2), 333–340. DOI: 10.18280/ijsse.130215

Malin, C. (2017). *H., Gudaitis, Terry., Holt, Thomas. J. & Kilger, Max.* Phishing, Waterhole and Scareware. Book Chapter - Deception in the Digital Age., DOI: 10.1016/B978-0-12-411630-6.00005-0

Mishra, Sandhya., & Devpriya, Soni. (2019). SMS Phishing and Mitigation Approaches. Conference: Twelfth International Conference on Contemporary Computing (IC3), DOI:.DOI: 10.1109/IC3.2019.8844920

Rehman, S. Ur., Sowerby, K evin. W., & Coghill, Colin. (March 2021). Analysis of impersonation attacks on systems using RF fingerprinting and low-end receivers. *Journal of Computer and System Sciences*. Advance online publication. DOI: 10.1016/ j.jcss.2013.06.01

Rosmansyah, Y., Hendarto, I. L. S., & Pratama, D. (2020, October 05). Hendarto, Ignatius Leo Sri., & Pratama, Demby. (April 2021). Impersonation Attack-Defense Tree. [iJET]. *International Journal of Emerging Technologies in Learning*, 15(19), 239. Advance online publication. DOI: 10.3991/ijet.v15i19.12699

Salahdine, Fatima. & Kaabouch, Naima. (February 2019). Social Engineering Attacks: A Survey. Future engineering, DOI: .DOI: 10.3390/fi11040089

Thomopoulos, G. A., Lyras, Dimitrios. P., &Fidas, Christos. A. (March 2023). A Systematic review and research challenges on phishing cyberattaks from an electroencephalography and gaze-based perspective. *Personal and Ubiquitous Computing*. Advance online publication. DOI: 10.1007/s00779-024-01794-9

Wang, Zuoguang., Zhu, Hongsong., Liu, Peipei., & Sun. Limin. (2021). Social engineering in cyber security: a domain ontology and knowledge graph application examples. Springer Open, doi: https://doi.org/.DOI: 10.1186/s42400-021-00094-6

Yan, X., Yan, K., Rehman, M. U., & Ullah, S. (2022). Yan, Ke., Rehman, Meezan. Ur., & Ullah, Sami. (October 2022). Impersonation Attack Detection in Mobile Edge Computing by Levering SARSA Technique in Physical Layer Security. Applied Science, doi. *Applied Sciences (Basel, Switzerland)*, 12(20), 10225. DOI: 10.3390/app122010225

Chapter 3
Social Engineering in the Digital Age: A Critical Examination of Attack Techniques, Consequences, and Preventative Measures

Vinay Kumar Pant
Moradabad Institute of Technology, India

Janmejay Pant
Graphic Era Hill University, India

Rohit Kumar Singh
https://orcid.org/0009-0001-3104-0350
Moradabad Institute of Technology, India

Saurabh Srivastava
Moradabad Institute of Technology, India

ABSTRACT

Social engineering is one of the biggest dangers in the digital world today. Attacks using social engineering are extremely dangerous to individuals and organizations by exploiting human psychology to compromise security controls to steal sensitive information. This study explores the different forms of social engineering attacks, analyzes real-world cases, and investigates the strategies attackers employ. It aims to assess the potential consequences for individuals and organizations targeted by these attacks. The study also assesses the effectiveness of current prevention methods, proposing enhanced strategies and best practices to implement measures to reduce the vulnerability with social engineering. By understanding the intricate tactics of

DOI: 10.4018/979-8-3693-6665-3.ch003

attackers and the vulnerabilities they exploit, this research aims to provide a robust framework for improving security awareness and defense mechanisms against social engineering threats.

1. INTRODUCTION

The twenty-first century has witnessed a swift transition of various domains like social engagement, Streaming services, education (E-learning platforms) and business (Online marketplaces) to Internet platforms. Consequently, there has been an exponential rise in both quantity and implication of info circulating within the digital world (Abass, I., 2018). The fundamental principle behind social engineering is the exploitation of human behavior and cognitive biases. Attackers craft scenarios that elicit specific responses from their targets, using tactics that can range from impersonation and pretexting to sophisticated phishing campaigns. These attacks can be highly targeted, such as spear phishing aimed at specific individuals or organizations, or broadly cast, like mass email phishing campaigns that target a large number of people indiscriminately. Social engineering assaults have more potential now that they are available online. Attackers can use the large volumes of personal data provided by social media sites, email, and messaging apps. Furthermore, social engineers have more opportunity to take advantage of human error as a weak link as a result of the complexity of digital systems growing.

1.1. Emerging Trends of Social Engineering

- **Deepfakes and Artificial Intelligence:** AI advancements are making it simpler to produce realistic deepfake audio and video, which can be used to pass for real people in convincing ways.
- **Social Media Exploitation:** Assaulters are using social media sites more frequently to obtain personal data for focused assaults (Abroshan, H et al., 2021).
- **Use of Mobile Devices Is Growing:** Social engineering attacks are also moving to mobile platforms, tricking consumers with SMS or app notifications.

1.2. Frequent Targets

Although anybody can become a victim, some groups are more vulnerable than others:

- **Workers:** Frequently singled out for access credentials or corporate data.

- **Clients:** Specifically targeted for personal or financial data.
- **Executives:** Well-known people who are vulnerable to deliberate attacks

Cybersecurity is rapidly growing area of computer science, where social engineering attacks have emerged as one of the most insidious and effective methods employed by cybercriminals. Social engineering attacks employ psychological techniques that force people into disclosing private information or taking acts that compromise their security, in contrast to traditional cyberattacks that take advantage of technological flaws. The sophistication of social engineering tactics has increased, with attackers continually developing new strategies to exploit human behavior and cognitive biases (Aldawood, Hussain & Skinner, Geoff., 2020). This necessitates a comprehensive understanding of the various forms these attacks can take, the potential impacts they can have, and the best practices for prevention. This analysis investigates how social engineering attacks exploit common psychological principles. This analysis investigates how social engineering attacks exploit common psychological principles. By examining different tactics like phishing, pretexting, baiting, quid pro quo, and tailgating, it aims to provide a detailed overview of how attackers manipulate victims and the potential consequences.

Through detailed case studies, this research will illustrate the real-world consequences of social engineering attacks, highlighting the economic, reputational, and operational damages that can result (Algarni Abdullah et al., 2017). These examples underscore the critical need for robust security measures and informed awareness among individuals and organizations.

The aim of this analysis is to equip readers by a detailed understanding of social engineering attacks, enabling them to recognize and mitigate these threats effectively (Bullée, Jan-Willem & Junger, Marianne., 2020). By exploring the strategies employed by attackers, the impacts of successful breaches, and the most effective prevention methods, this article aims to dissect the various categories of social engineering attacks, analyze their impacts through real-world examples, and suggest effective prevention strategies.

2. SOCIAL ENGINEERING LIFE CYCLE

The social engineering life cycle outlines the stages that attackers typically follow to execute a successful attack. Understanding this cycle helps in recognizing and mitigating these threats. The cycle generally consists of the following 4stages: Research, Hook, Play, and Exit. Each stage involves specific tactics and techniques aimed at manipulating the target to achieve the attacker's objectives (Burda, P et al., 2020).

2.1. Research

It is basically gathering information about the target. In the research stage, the attacker collects detailed information about the target, whether it be an individual, a group, or an organization. This phase involves various methods such as-

- **Open Source Intelligence (OSINT):** The practice of gathering and evaluating publicly accessible data in order to provide actionable intelligence is known as open source intelligence, or OSINT. Using publicly available sources like social media, websites, news articles, blogs and forums, Pictures and videos and public records to gather information (Edwards, M et al., 2017).
- **Exploration:** Identifying key individuals, their roles, and any potential vulnerabilities. Theses information are the main source for performing unethical activity by person.
- **Data Collection:** Accumulating details about the target's habits, behaviors, preferences, and social connections. Publicly available platforms are the main sources of collecting the data. Most of the hackers use this data to hack the individual or organizational information.

Example: An attacker might browse LinkedIn profiles to identify employees of a specific company and gather information about their roles and interests (Fan, W et al., 2017).

2.2. Hook

In this stage, attacker engage the target and establish initial contact. The attacker uses the information gathered during the research phase to craft a compelling and believable scenario to lure the target (Govindan kutty, M.S., 2021). This engagement can occur through various channels such as emails, phone calls, or face-to-face interactions. This phase includes following methods-

- **Phishing Emails:** A sort of social engineering known as "phishing," phishing emails aim to deceive recipients into divulging sensitive information or visiting harmful websites. They typically appear to be from a legitimate source, like your bank, credit card company, or a social media platform. (Grassegger, T., & Nedbal, D., 2021).
- **Phone Calls (Vishing):** Voice phishing, or vishing, is a fraudulent practice in which attackers utilize phone calls to fool victims into revealing personal information. Passwords, social security numbers, bank account information, and credit card numbers are some examples of this data. In other words,

it is “impersonating a trusted entity to extract information over the phone” (Guadagno, R et al., 2013). Typical vishing strategies consist of:

- **Urgency:** fostering a sense of terror or urgency by, for example, saying that the victim's account has been compromised and that they must take urgent action.
- **Threats:** Making use of threats of serious consequences, including account suspension or legal action, if the victim refuses to comply.
- **Requests for Data:** requesting private data, such as passwords, bank account information, or Social Security numbers, under the pretense of verification or security checks.

- **Baiting:** In cyberattacks, a social engineering tactic known as “baiting” is used to attract targets into giving up their security in exchange for an attractive offer. Usually, the “bait” is a way to take advantage of the victim; it makes no promises about rewards or benefits. Providing an attractive offers, such as free software or a prize, to encourage the target to complete the action (J. M. Hatfield, 2018).

Example: The attacker sends a personalized email to an employee, pretending to be from the IT department, and asks them to reset their password using a provided link.

2.3. Play

During the play stage, the attacker leverages the established relationship to manipulate the target into performing actions or divulging information (KAgyepong, E. et al., 2019). This phase involves a range of tactics designed to exploit the target's trust and compliance. Some methods are following-

- **Pretexting:** Pretexting is a type of social engineering in which a perpetrator fabricates a narrative or situation (a pretext) in order to push a victim into disclosing private information. It's a strategy meant to take advantage of human psychology and foster trust. Simple you say that, “Creating a fabricated scenario to elicit information or actions”.
- **Exploiting Trust:** Using the rapport built during the hook stage to gain further access or information.
- **Escalation:** Gradually asking for more sensitive information or higher-level access (Krombholz, Katharina et al., 2014).

Example: The attacker, now trusted as an IT support member, asks the employee to disable certain security settings or provide credentials to “fix” an urgent issue.

2.4. Exit

In this phase attacker conclude the interaction without raising suspicion. Exit stage, the attacker completes their objective and disengages from the target. The goal is to leave without arousing suspicion, ensuring that the attack remains undetected for as long as possible (Kumar Ashutosh, Pant Kumar Vinay, 2016). It follows some strategies that are following-

- **Covering Tracks:** Removing any evidence of the interaction or breach.
- **Ending on Good Terms:** Leaving the target with a positive impression to avoid suspicion.
- **Data Extraction:** Ensuring that any stolen data or gained access is secured and usable.

Example: After obtaining the necessary credentials, the attacker thanks the employee and leaves no trace of the fraudulent interaction, allowing them to use the compromised access at a later time without immediate detection.

3. CLASSIFICATION OF SOCIAL ENGINEERING ATTACKS

Criminals use social tactics to bypass security measures and steal data or control systems. These attacks can be broadly classified into several types, each with unique characteristics and methodologies (Marrero, K. et al., 2012). Below, we define and categorize the primary types of social engineering attacks: phishing, whaling, piggybacking, baiting, and pretexting etc. (Nabie C & Paul S., 2016).

3.1. Phishing

Phishing stands out as the predominant form of social engineering attack, involving perpetrators posing as credible entities to dupe individuals into disclosing sensitive information (P. Miller et al., 2001).

Types of Phishing

1. **Email Phishing:** Phishing emails are a popular type of cyberattack in which con artists send misleading emails with the intention of tricking recipients into divulging money or personal information. These emails frequently imitate reputable companies, banks, or other establishments. Attackers send fraudulent emails that appear to come from reputable sources.

2. **Spear Phishing:** Spear phishing is a highly focused type of phishing assault in which the attackers target certain people or companies. Spear phishing is an attack strategy that uses a great deal of research and tailoring in contrast to traditional phishing assaults that aim to catch as many targets as possible. Targeted phishing aimed at specific individuals or organizations, often using personalized information (Pant Kumar Vinay et al., 2015).
3. **Smishing:** Smishing is a kind of phishing assault in which people are tricked into divulging personal or financial information over text messages (SMS). Smishing, like email phishing, uses social engineering techniques to trick victims into opening harmful links or divulging personal information. Phishing via SMS text messages.
4. **Vishing:** Phishing through voice calls.

Case Study: In 2016, John Podesta, who served as the chairman of Hillary Clinton's presidential campaign, fell victim to a spear-phishing attack. This resulted in his email account being compromised and sensitive campaign information being leaked (Patil, M. Harl., 1997).

Figure 1. Different form Social Engineering Attacks

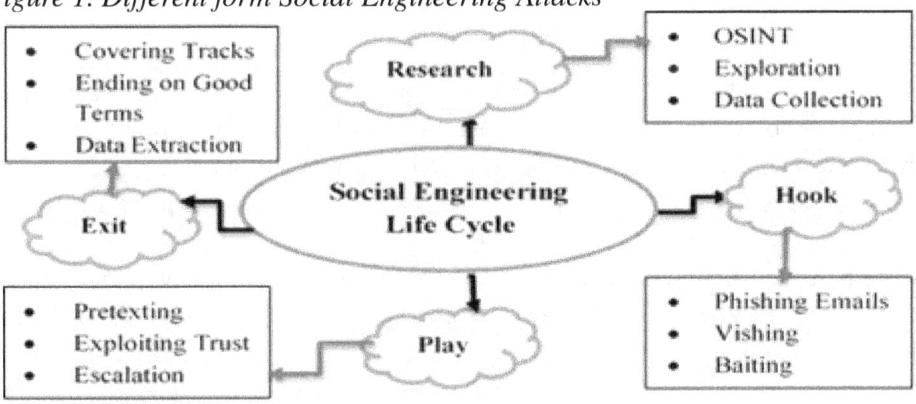

Figure 1. Life Cycle of Social Engineering

3.2. Pretexting

The goal of pretexting is to get the victim to do something they would not typically do, such reveal personal information, by creating a false situation. The perpetrator frequently assumes the identity of a trusted friend or official the victim knows and respects (S. M. Albladi and G. R. S. Weir, 2020).

Case Study: An attacker pretending to be a bank representative calls a victim, claiming there is a security issue with their account and requesting verification of personal details to resolve the issue.

3.3. Baiting

Baiting entails enticing a victim with a promise of an attractive item or reward, such as free software or a music download, which leads to the download of malware or the provision of personal information (Salahdine F & Kaabouch N., 2020).

Case Study: Attackers left USB drives in a company parking lot, labeled with enticing tags like "Salary Details." Curious employees plugged these drives into their computers, inadvertently installing malware.

3.4. Quid Pro Quo

A form of social engineering known as a "quid pro quo" attack occurs when an attacker gives something of value in return for confidential information or acts that further their own interests. It's a dishonest strategy that takes advantage of people's kindness and confidence. The attacker offers something of value in return for information or access (Salama, R et al., 2023).

Case Study: An attacker calls random employees of a company, pretending to be from the IT department, and offers to help resolve a supposed issue in exchange for login credentials.

3.5. Tailgating

The physical security breach known as tailgating, or "piggybacking," occurs when an unauthorized person sneaks up on an authorized person and enters a restricted area without verifying their own credentials (Siddiqi, Murtaza et al., 2022).

Case Study: An attacker waits near a secure entrance and follows closely behind an employee who opens the door, gaining access to restricted areas without authorization.

4. IMPACTS OF SOCIAL ENGINEERING ATTACKS

The Individuals and organizations alike suffer the severe consequences of social engineering attacks, often in multifaceted ways:

4.1. Financial Impact

Social engineering poses a significant financial threat to individuals and organizations. Phishing scams can lead to direct financial theft, while data breaches can result in costly fines and lawsuits. Social engineering attacks can result in financial losses through various means, such as fraudulent wire transfers, unauthorized purchases, or extortion (Sobur, A et al., 2023). For example, if an attacker gains access to financial systems through social engineering, they may initiate transactions or manipulate accounts to siphon funds.

Case Study: In 2013, Target suffered a massive data breach due to a phishing attack on a third-party vendor, resulting in the theft of 40 million credit and debit card numbers and a $18.5 million settlement.

4.2. Reputational Damage

Organizations that fall victim to social engineering attacks can suffer long-term reputational damage. Customers lose trust, and the organization's credibility is undermined. Organizations can suffer reputational damage following a social engineering attack, especially if customer trust is compromised (Srivastava, S., & Ahmed, T. 2024). Customers may lose confidence in the organization's ability to protect their data, leading to customer churn and negative publicity.

Case Study: The 2016 Democratic National Committee email leak, resulting from a spear-phishing attack, led to significant reputational damage and political consequences.

4.3. Operational Disruption

Social engineering attacks can disrupt operations by compromising critical systems or causing loss of sensitive data. Beyond direct financial and reputational impacts, social engineering attacks can disrupt day-to-day operations by causing confusion, mistrust, and loss of productivity (Srivastava, S., et al., 2023). Employees may need to spend time addressing security incidents, implementing additional security measures, or undergoing retraining.

Case Study: The 2017 WannaCry ransomware attack, facilitated by phishing emails, disrupted operations in various organizations worldwide, including the UK's National Health Service.

5. PREVENTION METHODS

Prevention methods in social engineering aim to protect individuals and organizations from manipulative attacks that exploit human psychology rather than technical vulnerabilities. Technical safeguards, together with training and company policy, are necessary for protecting against social engineering attacks (Venkatesha S. et al., 2021). Here are detailed strategies to mitigate social engineering risks:

5.1. Technical Measures

1. **Email Filtering:** Don't open emails or attachments from unknown senders. Be suspicious of any communication that seems unusual, even if it appears to have come from a known email address. To identify and prevent phishing attempts, set up sophisticated email screening (Wang, Z. et al., 2021).).
2. **Multi-Factor Authentication (MFA):** Encourage the use of multi-factor authentication (MFA) as an additional security measure in addition to passwords.
3. **Regular Software Updates:** Always utilize the most recent versions of software and systems to avoid exploiting security holes.

5.2. Establishing Policies and Procedures:

1. **Access Control Policies:** Implementing strict policies for information access based on roles and responsibilities.
2. **Verification Protocols:** Establishing protocols for verifying identities before disclosing sensitive information or performing actions.
3. **Incident Response Plans:** Developing comprehensive plans to address social engineering incidents, including reporting procedures and corrective actions.
4. **Check the Source:** Confirm the identity of the individual or group making the offer on your own.
5. **Unsolicited Offers Should Be Avoided:** Be wary of unsolicited offers, particularly if they appear too good to be true.

5.3. Employee Education

1. **Training Programs:** Conduct regular training sessions to educate employees or user about the different categories of social engineering attacks that help employees or user to recognize attacks and understand security measures (Grassegger, T., & Nedbal, D., 2021).
2. **Simulated Attacks:** One of the most important parts of a strong cybersecurity plan is simulated attacks. Organizations can find weaknesses, train staff, and improve overall security posture by imitating real-world threats (Washo, Amy., 2021). Perform simulated phishing attacks to test employee's awareness and improve their response to real threats.
3. **Case Studies:** Case study is one of the good way to educate person about various attacks. Sharing real-life examples of successful social engineering attacks to illustrate potential risks.

5.4. Organizational Policies

1. **Mitigate the Risks:** Reduce the risks connected with social engineering assaults by creating an accurate incident response plan to handle them quickly and effectively (Salama, R et al., 2023).
2. **Manage User Access:** Implement granular access controls to restrict access to sensitive information and areas based on individual user permissions. Give users just the minimal amount of access essential to carry out their duties (Washo, Amy., 2021). Review and modify access rights on a regular basis in light of role changes.

6. CONCLUSION

Advancements in technology have shifted numerous everyday activities to the Internet and online platforms, leading to a larger portion of the population being connected online. However, this surge in online participation occurs without sufficient cyber security education regarding the various types of attacks individuals may encounter daily. The financial, reputational, and operational losses caused by social engineering assaults are substantial because these attacks take advantage of people's weaknesses to accomplish their harmful goals. Learning about different social engineering tricks and seeing how they've played out in real-world situations allows, organizations can develop comprehensive prevention strategies. To effectively defend against these widespread social engineering attacks, a layered approach is key. This involves implementing technical safeguards, educating employees, and establishing strong company policies. This study has the potential to improve the field of cybercrime and security by providing a thorough analysis of social engineering attacks and offering actionable insights for organizations to protect themselves against these pervasive attacks.

REFERENCES

Abass, I. (2018). Social engineering threat and defense: A literature survey. *Journal of Information Security*, 9(4), 257–264. DOI: 10.4236/jis.2018.94018

Abdullah, A., Xu, Y., & Chan, T. (2017). An empirical study on the susceptibility to social engineering in social networking sites: The case of facebook. *European Journal of Information Systems*, 26(6), 661–687. DOI: 10.1057/s41303-017-0057-y

Abroshan, H.; Devos, J.; Poels, G.; Laermans, E. (2021), Phishing happens beyond technology: The effects of human behaviors and demographics on each step of a phishing process. IEEE Access 2021, 9, 44928–44949.

Albladi, S. M., & Weir, G. R. S. (2020, December). Predicting individuals' vulnerability to social engineering in social networks. *Cybersecurity*, 3(1), 1–19. DOI: 10.1186/s42400-020-00047-5

Aldawood, H., & Skinner, G. (2020). An Advanced Taxonomy for Social Engineering Attacks. *International Journal of Computer Applications*, 177(30), 975–8887. DOI: 10.5120/ijca2020919744

Kumar Ashutosh, Pant Kumar Vinay (2016), "DNA Optimized Playfair Cipher to Enhance the Security of Cloud Data", Int. J. Eng. Res. Manag. Technol, Vol.3, Issue.4, Pages.7-14.

Bullée, Jan-Willem & Junger, Marianne. (2020). How effective are social engineering interventions? A meta-analysis. Information & Computer Security. ahead-of-print. .DOI: 10.1108/ICS-07-2019-0078

Burda, P., Allodi, L., & Zannone, N. (2024). Cognition in social engineering empirical research: A systematic literature review. *ACM Transactions on Computer-Human Interaction*, 31(2), 1–55. DOI: 10.1145/3635149

Edwards, M., Larson, R., Green, B., Rashid, A., & Baron, A. (2017). Panning for gold: Automatically analysing online social engineering attack surfaces. *Computers & Security*, 69, 18–34. DOI: 10.1016/j.cose.2016.12.013

Fan, W., Lwakatare, K., & Rong, R. (2017). Social engineering: I-E based model of human weakness for attack and defense investigations. *Computer Network and Information Security*, 1(1), 1–11. DOI: 10.5815/ijcnis.2017.01.01

(2021). Govindan kutty, M.S.(2021). Is human error paving way to cyber security? *Int. Res. J. Eng. Technol.*, 8, 4174–4178.

Grassegger, T., & Nedbal, D. (2021). The role of employees' information security awareness on the intention to resist social engineering. *Procedia Computer Science*, 181, 59–66. DOI: 10.1016/j.procs.2021.01.103

Guadagno, R., Muscanell, N., Rice, L., & Roberts, N. (2013). Social influence online: The impact of social validation and likability on compliance. *Psychology of Popular Media Culture*, 2(1), 51–60. DOI: 10.1037/a0030592

Hatfield, J. M. (2018). Social engineering in cybersecurity: The evolution of a concept. *Computers & Security*, 73, 102–113.

KAgyepong, E., Cherdantseva, Y., Reinecke, P. and Burnap, P. (2019). Challenges and performance metrics for security operations center analysts: A systematic review. *Journal of Cyber Security Technology*, 0(0), 1–28.

Krombholz, K., Hobel, H., Donko-Huber, M., & Weippl, E. (2014). Advanced social engineering attacks. *Journal of Information Security and Applications.*, 22, 113–122. Advance online publication. DOI: 10.1016/j.jisa.2014.09.005

Marrero, K. (2012). Miller, J. Voas, and G. Hurlburt. Byod: Security and privacy considerations. *IT Professional*, 14(5), 53–55. DOI: 10.1109/MITP.2012.93

Miller, P., Kozu, J., & Davis, A. (2001), "Social influence, empathy, and prosocial behavior in cross-cultural perspective," in Proc. Pract. Social In_uence Multiple Cultures, 2001, pp. 63_77.

Nabie C, Paul S. (2016), Cybersecurity: risks, vulnerabilities and countermeasures to prevent social engineering attacks. Int J Adv Comput Res. 2016; 6:31–8. . 2016.623006.DOI: <ALIGNMENT.qj></ALIGNMENT>10.19101/ IJACR

Pant Kumar Vinay., Prakash Jyoti, Asthana Amit (2015), Three step data security model for cloud computing based on RSA and steganography, International Conference on Green Computing and Internet of Things (ICGCIoT), IEEE,490-494.

Patil, M. Harl. (1997). People Hacking: "The Psychology of Social Engineering". [Online]. Available: http://www.text_les.com/russian/cyberlib.narod.ru/lib/cin/se10.html

Salahdine, F., & Kaabouch, N. (2020), "Social engineering attacks: a survey. Future Internet", 11(4), 2019. ISSN 1999-5903. . URL https://www.mdpi.com/1999-5903/11/4/89. Accessed 24 Oct 2020.DOI: 10.3390/fi11040089

Salama, R., Al-Turjman, F., Bhatla, S., & Yadav, S. P. (2023, April). Social engineering attack types and prevention techniques-A survey. In *2023 International Conference on Computational Intelligence, Communication Technology and Networking (CICTN)* (pp. 817-820). IEEE. DOI: 10.1109/CICTN57981.2023.10140957

Siddiqi, M., Pak, W., & Siddiqi, M. (2022). A Study on the Psychology of Social Engineering-Based Cyberattacks and Existing Countermeasures. *Applied Sciences (Basel, Switzerland)*, 12(12), 6042. Advance online publication. DOI: 10.3390/app12126042

Sobur, A., Hossain, A., Nazrul Islam, K., & Kabir, M. H. (2023). A Contradistinction Study of Physical Vs. Cyberspace Social Engineering Attacks and Defense. Cyberspace Social Engineering Attacks and Defense (June 14, 2023).

Srivastava, S., & Ahmed, T. (2024). DLCD: Deep learning-based change detection approach to monitor deforestation. *Signal, Image and Video Processing*, 18(S1, Suppl 1), 167–181. DOI: 10.1007/s11760-024-03140-1

Srivastava, S., Ahmed, T., & Saxena, A. (2023). An approach to secure IOT applications of smart city using blockchain technology. *International Journal of Engineering Sciences & Emerging Technologies*, 11(2), 71–78. DOI: 10.5281/zenodo.10434277

Venkatesha, S., Reddy, K. R., & Chandavarkar, B. R. (2021). Social Engineering Attacks During the COVID-19 Pandemic. [Erratum in: SN Comput Sci. 2021;2][3] [:134. PMID: 33585823; PMCID: PMC7866964]. *SN Computer Science*, 2(2), 78. DOI: 10.1007/s42979-020-00443-1 PMID: 33585823

Wang, Z.; Zhu, H.; Sun, L. (2021), Social engineering in cybersecurity: Effect mechanisms, human vulnerabilities and attack methods. IEEE Access 2021, 9, 11895–11910.

Washo, A. (2021). An interdisciplinary view of social engineering: A call to action for research. *Computers in Human Behavior Reports*, 4, 100126. DOI: 10.1016/j.chbr.2021.100126

Chapter 4
Cybersecurity in the Age of Social Engineering:
Implementing Effective Defense Strategies

Ajay Pratap
Amity University, Lucknow, India

Gauri Giri
Amity University, Lucknow, India

ABSTRACT

In the digital era, the proliferation of social engineering attacks poses a significant threat to cybersecurity. Unlike traditional cyber threats that exploit technical vulnerabilities, social engineering attacks manipulate human psychology to gain unauthorized access to sensitive information and systems. This paper explores the evolving landscape of social engineering, examining its various forms such as phishing, pretexting, baiting, and tailgating. The core of this study focuses on developing comprehensive defense strategies to mitigate the risks associated with social engineering. We advocate for a multi-layered approach that integrates technological solutions, such as advanced email filters and anomaly detection systems, with human-centric measures, including rigorous training programs and awareness campaigns. We highlight the importance of fostering a security-conscious culture within organizations and analysed the critical role of both technology and human behavior in safeguarding information assets in the age of social engineering.

DOI: 10.4018/979-8-3693-6665-3.ch004

1. INTRODUCTION:

In today's interconnected world, cybersecurity faces a relentless barrage of threats, with social engineering emerging as one of the most insidious and pervasive techniques employed by cybercriminals. Unlike traditional cyberattacks that exploit software vulnerabilities, social engineering leverages human psychology to manipulate individuals into divulging sensitive information or performing actions that compromise security. This form of attack preys on human trust, curiosity, and sometimes, fear, making it a potent weapon in the arsenal of hackers.

The advent of social media, the proliferation of digital communication channels, and the increasing complexity of online ecosystems have amplified the risk and impact of social engineering attacks. From phishing emails and fraudulent phone calls to sophisticated impersonation scams and social media exploits, the landscape of social engineering is vast and continually evolving. The consequences of such attacks can be devastating, resulting in financial losses, reputational damage, and severe breaches of personal and corporate data. To combat these threats, organizations and individuals must adopt robust and dynamic defense strategies. This involves not only the deployment of advanced technological safeguards but also a comprehensive focus on education and awareness. Effective defense strategies encompass a multi-layered approach that includes rigorous training programs to enhance human vigilance, stringent policies and procedures to govern digital interactions, and the integration of cutting-edge security technologies designed to detect and mitigate social engineering attempts in real-time.

1.1 Objectives:

The aim of this term paper is to investigate the dynamic landscape of cybersecurity amidst the prevalence of social engineering and to assess the deployment of efficient defence mechanisms against these risks. Through extensive research and analysis, this study strives to:

- Delve into the significance of social engineering tactics within contemporary cyber threats, encompassing phenomena such as phishing, pretexting, and manipulation through social media.
- Explore the vulnerabilities exploited by social engineering methodologies within the frameworks of organizational infrastructure and personal data security.
- Assess the effectiveness of current defence strategies and technologies utilized to counteract the threats posed by social engineering attacks.

- Propose and scrutinize innovative methodologies and best practices for establishing resilient defence mechanisms against the spectrum of social engineering threats.
- Offer insights and recommendations to both organizations and individuals to fortify their cybersecurity posture in light of the evolving tactics employed by social engineers.

1.2 What is Cybersecurity:

Cybersecurity today is a dynamic and critical field that requires constant vigilance, innovations, and collaboration to safeguard digital assets and maintain trust in our interconnected world.

a. Definition:

Cybersecurity encompasses the practices, technologies, and processes designed to protect computer systems, networks, data, and devices from unauthorized access, cyberattacks, and data breaches. Its primary goal is to ensure the confidentiality, integrity, and availability of information assets.

b. Key Components of Cybersecurity:

In this section, we have discussed the key components of cybersecurity.

- Risk Management: Identifying, assessing, and mitigating potential risks to information assets, including vulnerabilities and threats.
- Access Control: Implementing mechanisms to control who can access what information and resources within a system or network.
- Endpoint Security: Protecting individual devices such as computers, smartphones, and tablets from malicious software and unauthorized access.
- Network Security: Safeguarding the integrity and privacy of data as it travels across networks, including measures such as firewalls, intrusion detection/prevention systems (IDS/IPS), and secure communication protocols.
- Identity and Authentication: Verifying the identities of users and ensuring they have the appropriate permissions to access resources.
- Data Protection: Encrypting sensitive data to prevent unauthorized access or disclosure, both at rest and in transit.
- Security Awareness and Training: Educating users about cybersecurity best practices, recognizing phishing attempts, and understanding their role in maintaining security.

- Compliance and Regulations: Ensuring compliance with relevant laws, regulations, and industry standards pertaining to cybersecurity, such as GDPR, HIPAA, and PCI-DSS.
- Security Monitoring and Analysis: Continuously monitoring systems and networks for suspicious activities, analyzing security logs, and investigating potential security incidents.

2. LITERATURE REVIEW:

1. The paper explores the complexities of securing interconnected systems, highlighting the challenges of managing diverse threats, and the strategies needed to enhance resilience (Sandhu, Kaur, & Brar, 2023). It highlights the importance of systematic cybersecurity management to enhance operational efficiency and mitigate risks (Ciekanowski, Żurawski, Pauliuchuk, Ciekanowski, & Marciniak, 2024). This publication promises insights into modern cybersecurity challenges and cutting-edge defense strategies, offering valuable knowledge to the field (Awasthi, Pratap, & Srivastava, 2017). The work delves into the development of robust strategies to counter evolving global digital threats and cyber attacks, offering crucial insights for safeguarding digital environments in today's interconnected world (Sendjaja, Irwandi, Prastiawan, Suryani, & Fatmawati, 2024). The research focuses on enhancing cybersecurity defense within the IoT ecosystem by leveraging blockchain technology (Setia & Sandosh, 2023). The work introduces a complementary conceptual model of cyber resilience, offering valuable insights into building robust defenses against cyber threats (Možnik, Delija, Tulčić, & Galinec, 2023). This research serves as a valuable resource for understanding and combatting the multifaceted challenges posed by social engineering tactics in cybersecurity (Zaoui, Yousra, Yassine, Yassine, & Karim, 2024). Their study focuses on social engineering attack-defense strategies grounded in reinforcement learning principles (Yang, Zheng, Wang, Wu, & Wu, 2023). This work sheds light on the intricacies of social engineering tactics and their implications on cybersecurity on a global scale, offering insights crucial for developing effective defense strategies (Srivastava, Soni, & Pratap, 2023). This work contributes to advancing cybersecurity practices by leveraging semantic technologies to enhance threat detection and mitigation strategies (Wang, Zhu, Liu, & Sun, 2021). This research delves into emerging technologies and innovative strategies shaping the future of cybersecurity (Ghaib, 2024). This work provides valuable insights into the evolving landscape of cybersecurity, offering a holistic perspective on the challenges and solutions shaping the field (Yadav, Soni, & Pratap, 2024). This research sheds light on the emerging threat

of digital domain and its impact on cybersecurity (Mustafa, 2019). This study offers a comprehensive definition of social engineering within the context of cybersecurity, providing a clear understanding of its mechanisms and implications (Wang, Sun, & Zhu, 2020). This study focuses on the critical role of human factors in cybersecurity within healthcare settings, proposing strategies for designing and implementing robust education programs (Waddell, 2023).

3. INTRODUCTION TO SOCIAL ENGINEERING IN CYBERSECURITY:

Social engineering remains a pervasive and potent threat in today's world of interconnected digital platforms.

3.1 Definition:

Social engineering is a term used to describe a broad range of malicious activities accomplished through human interactions. It involves manipulating individuals into divulging confidential or personal information that can be used for fraudulent purposes as shown in Figure 1. The term typically applies to cybercrime and information security, where attackers exploit psychological manipulation rather than technical hacking techniques.

Figure 1. Attack cycle for Social Engineering

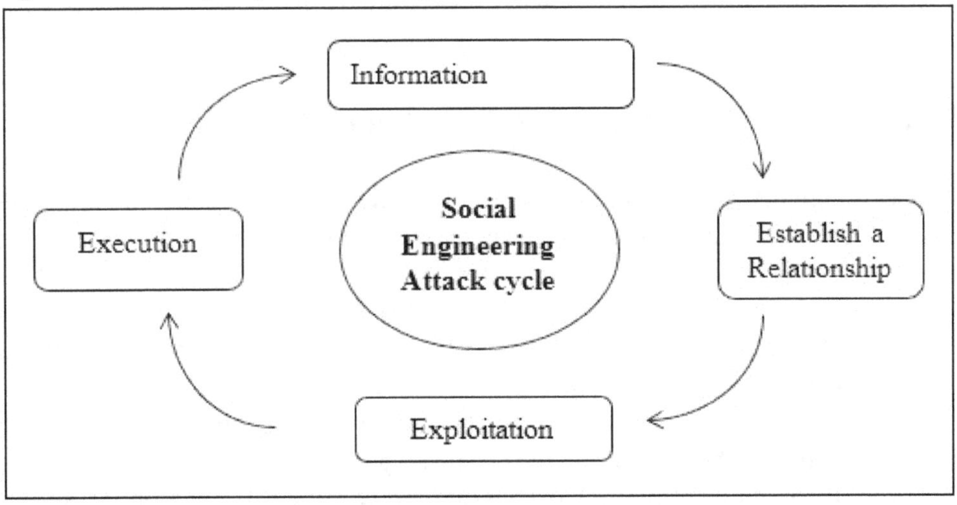

Figure 1: Attack Cycle for Social Engineering

3.2 Types Of Social Engineering Attacks:

Several types of social engineering attacks are possible that are as listed as below and also shown in Figure 2. These attacks include phishing, spear-phishing, whaling, vishing, smishing, pretexting, baiting, tailgating, business email compromise, CEO fraud, honey trap, dumpster diving, diversion theft and watering hole attacks.

Figure 2. Percentage share of Different types of Social Engineering Attacks

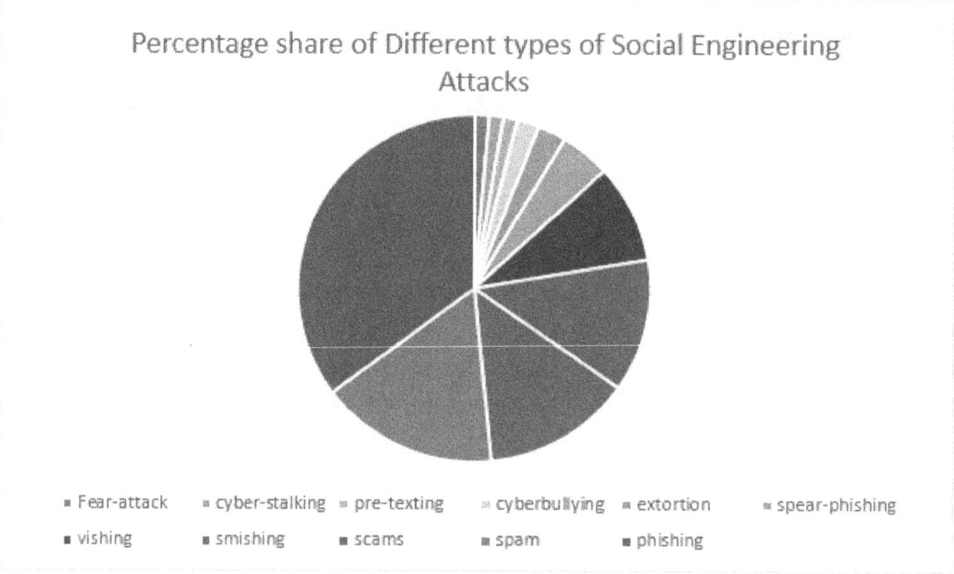

3.3 Impacts Of Social Engineering Attacks On Organisations:

Social engineering attacks can have profound impacts on organizations, affecting various aspects of their operations, security, and reputation. Here are five key impacts:

a) Financial Losses
- Direct Financial Theft: Attackers might gain access to financial accounts and transfer funds directly.
- Fraudulent Transactions: Social engineers can manipulate employees to authorize bogus transactions or make purchases.
- Business Disruption: Costs associated with recovering from an attack, such as restoring systems, investigating breaches, and legal fees.

- Regulatory Fines: Non-compliance with data protection regulations due to breaches can result in hefty fines.

b) Data Breaches
   - Loss of Sensitive Information: Personal, financial, or proprietary information can be stolen, leading to identity theft or intellectual property theft.
   - Customer Data Compromise: Breach of customer data can lead to loss of trust, legal liabilities, and the requirement to notify and compensate affected customers.
   - Confidential Business Information: Exposure of strategic plans, contracts, or other sensitive internal documents can damage competitive advantage.

c) Reputational Damage
   - Loss of Trust: Customers, partners, and stakeholders might lose confidence in the organization's ability to protect their information.
   - Negative Publicity: Media coverage of a breach can tarnish an organization's public image, impacting brand reputation and customer loyalty.
   - Market Position: Reputation damage can affect an organization's market position, leading to loss of business and decreased market share.

d) Operational Disruption
   - Service Interruptions: Attacks can lead to downtime, disrupting normal business operations, and affecting productivity and service delivery.
   - Resource Diversion: Significant resources must be diverted to manage the incident, conduct investigations, and implement remediation measures.
   - Long-Term Recovery: Post-attack recovery efforts can be extensive, involving system overhauls, security upgrades, and changes to business processes.

4. IMPLEMENTING DEFENSE STRATEGIES AGAINST SOCIAL ENGINEERING:

Social engineering attacks exploit human psychology to bypass security measures. Effective defense strategies must address both technological vulnerabilities and human factors.

Employees awareness level of social engineers' target points is compared between public and private organizations in Figure 3.

Figure 3. Employee Awareness Level of Social Engineers Target Points

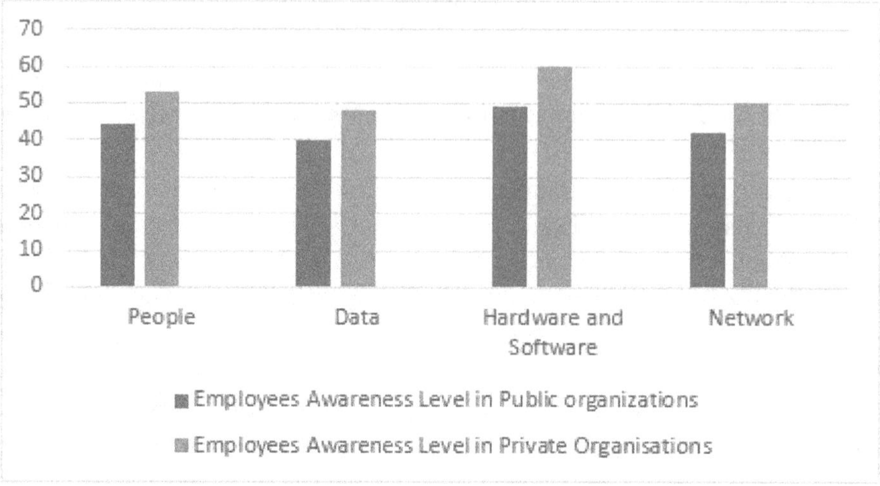

Figure 3: Employees Awareness Level of Social Engineers Target Points

4.1 Comprehensive approach to implementing defense strategies against social engineering:

a) Employee Training and Awareness

- Regular Training Programs:

Conduct training sessions at least monthly to keep employees up-to-date with the latest social engineering tactics. Regular training helps instill a culture of vigilance and awareness.

- Simulated Phishing Attacks:

Conduct regular phishing simulations to test employees' ability to recognize and report phishing attempts. Use these simulations to measure training effectiveness and identify areas needing improvement.

- Interactive and Engaging Methods:

Use interactive training methods such as workshops, quizzes, and role-playing scenarios to make learning more engaging and effective. Gamified learning experiences can enhance retention and application of knowledge.

b) Best Practices For Creating A Security-Conscious Culture

Creating a security-conscious culture within an organization requires a multifaceted approach that combines policies, training, leadership support, and technological solutions. Here are some best practices to foster a security-conscious culture:

- Leadership Buy-In: Secure support from senior leadership to prioritize cybersecurity initiatives and allocate resources for security measures. When executives demonstrate a commitment to security, it sets a tone for the entire organization.
- Simulated Phishing Exercises: Conduct simulated phishing exercises to test employees' susceptibility to phishing attacks and reinforce training concepts. Provide feedback and additional training to individuals who fall victim to simulated attacks.
- Promote a Speak-Up Culture: Encourage employees to report security incidents, suspicious activities, or policy violations without fear of retribution. Establish clear channels for reporting security concerns and ensure that reports are promptly addressed and investigated.
- Regular Security Assessments: Conduct regular security assessments, including vulnerability scans, penetration testing, and security audits, to identify weaknesses in systems, processes, and controls. Use assessment findings to prioritize remediation efforts and improve security posture continuously.
- Implement Access Controls: Enforce the principle of least privilege by granting employees access only to the resources and information necessary to perform their job duties. Implement strong authentication mechanisms, such as multi-factor authentication (MFA), to protect sensitive accounts and systems.
- Secure Development Practices: Incorporate security into the software development lifecycle (SDLC) by conducting secure code reviews, performing regular security testing, and integrating security tools and frameworks into the development process.
- Employee Recognition and Rewards: Recognize and reward employees who demonstrate exemplary security awareness and adherence to security policies. Positive reinforcement can motivate employees to remain vigilant and proactive in safeguarding organizational assets.
- Continuous Improvement: Continuously evaluate and refine security practices based on emerging threats, industry best practices, and lessons learned

from security incidents. Maintain open communication channels to solicit feedback from employees and adapt security measures accordingly.

By adopting these best practices, organizations can establish a culture where security is a shared responsibility and ingrained into daily operations, ultimately reducing the risk of security breaches and protecting sensitive information from unauthorized access or exploitation.

4.2 Technological Solutions:

Technological solutions and innovations against social engineering encompass a variety of approaches aimed at preventing, detecting, and mitigating the risks associated with it as shown in Figure 4.

Figure 4. Cyber Security Defence Mechanism

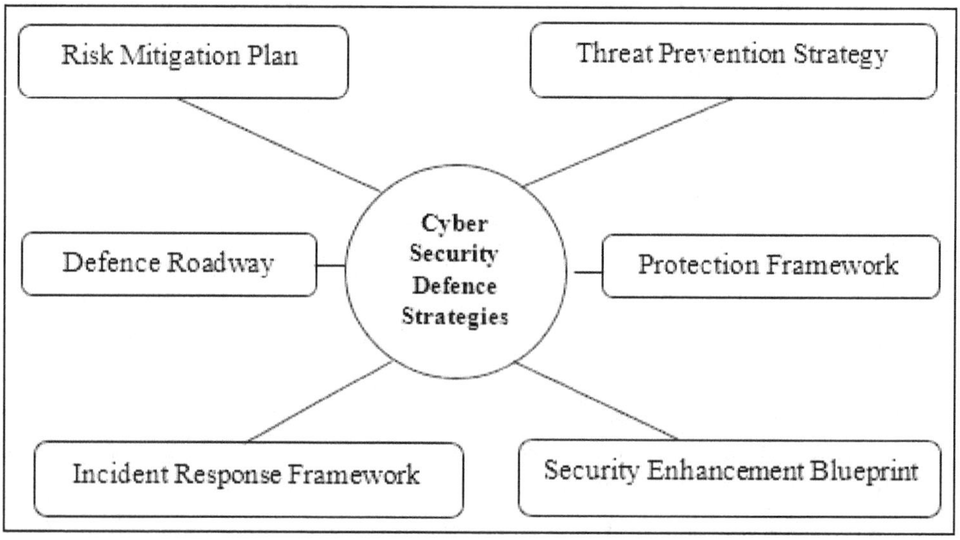

Figure 4: Cyber Security Defence Mechanism

Several technological strategies and innovations are:

- User Training and Awareness Tools
- Email Filtering and Authentication
- Behavioral Analytics
- Endpoint Protection
- Identity and Access Management (IAM)

- Security Awareness Training Platforms
- Deception Technologies
- Social Media Monitoring Tools

5. FUTURE TRENDS AND CHALLENGES IN SOCIAL ENGINEERING AND CYBERSECURITY:

Looking forward, the landscape of social engineering and cybersecurity is poised to evolve with advancing technologies and shifting tactics. Artificial intelligence is anticipated to play a larger role in social engineering attacks, potentially enabling more sophisticated impersonation and manipulation techniques. The proliferation of IoT devices presents a new frontier for exploitation, increasing the attack surface and complexity of defending against social engineering tactics. Additionally, the convergence of ransomware with social engineering methods poses significant risks, threatening both data security and operational continuity for organizations. As technology evolves, challenges will arise in detecting and mitigating these attacks, especially as attackers employ more personalized and persuasive methods to deceive users. Additionally, the increasing interconnectedness of devices and the rise of IoT (Internet of Things) will expand the attack surface, posing new challenges for securing networks and data. Organizations will need to continuously update their defences, educate their personnel about emerging threats, and implement robust cybersecurity measures to stay ahead of evolving social engineering tactics.

6. CONCLUSION:

In the age of social engineering, cybersecurity demands a multifaceted and dynamic approach to effectively counter the sophisticated tactics used by attackers. Social engineering exploits human psychology, making traditional defenses inadequate. Thus, comprehensive strategies integrating advanced technologies, such as AI and machine learning, are essential for detecting and preventing these attacks. Regular and targeted employee training is crucial to raising awareness and preparedness, as human error often serves as the primary gateway for these threats. Adopting a zero trust architecture further strengthens defenses by eliminating implicit trust within the network.

Compliance with data protection laws like GDPR, HIPAA, and CCPA ensures legal adherence and enhances the overall security posture. Organizations must foster a security-conscious culture, promoting proactive vigilance and open communication. Continuous improvement through regular audits, policy updates, and lessons learned from real-world incidents is vital. Ultimately, a holistic, adaptive approach that combines technology, training, policy, and culture will fortify defenses against social engineering, safeguarding critical assets in an increasingly digital landscape.

REFERENCES

Awasthi, S., Pratap, A., & Srivastava, R. (2017). Framework for Visual Cryptographic based Encryption and Decryption. *International Journal of Computer Applications*, 163(3), 17–20. DOI: 10.5120/ijca2017913485

Ciekanowski, M., Żurawski, S., Pauliuchuk, Y., Ciekanowski, Z., & Marciniak, S. (2024). Strategies for Effective Cybersecurity Management in Organizations. *European Research Studies*, XXVII(1), 365–379. DOI: 10.35808/ersj/3364

Ghaib, A. A. (2024). Future Trends in Cybersecurity: Exploring Emerging Technologies and Strategies. *International Research Journal of Modernization in Engineering Technology and Science*. Advance online publication. DOI: 10.56726/IRJMETS49530

Možnik, D., Delija, D., Tulčić, D., & Galinec, D. (2023). Cybersecurity and Cyber Defense Insights: The Complementary Conceptual model of Cyber resilience. *ENTRENOVA - ENTerprise REsearch InNOVAtion, 9*(1), 1–12. https://doi.org/DOI: 10.54820/entrenova-2023-0001

Mustafa, H. (2019). Digital Social Engineering Threatens Cybersecurity. *International Journal of Innovative Technology and Exploring Engineering*, 9(1), 4016–4025. DOI: 10.35940/ijitee.A5289.119119

Sandhu, B. S., Kaur, J., & Brar, H. S. (2023). Cybersecurity in the Age of Interconnectedness: Challenges, Strategies, and Opportunities. (2023). *International Research Journal of Modernization in Engineering Technology and Science*. Advance online publication. DOI: 10.56726/IRJMETS46003

Sendjaja, T., Irwandi, , Prastiawan, E., Suryani, Y., & Fatmawati, E. (2024). Cybersecurity In The Digital Age: Developing Robust Strategies To Protect Against Evolving Global Digital Threats And Cyber Attacks. *The International Journal of Science in Society*, 6(1), 1008–1019. DOI: 10.54783/ijsoc.v6i1.1098

Setia, P., & Sandosh S. (2023). Enhancing Cybersecurity Defense of IoT Ecosystem Using Blockchain. *Suranaree Journal of Science and Technology, 30*(4), 010238(1-14). https://doi.org/DOI: 10.55766/sujst-2023-04-e01071

Srivastava, S., Soni, M. K., & Pratap, A. (2023). A Critical Study of Challenges and Risk in Healthcare sector based on Cloud Computing," *2023 14th International Conference on Computing Communication and Networking Technologies (ICCCNT)*, Delhi, India, 2023, pp. 1-5, DOI: 10.1109/ICCCNT56998.2023.10307861

Waddell, M. (2023). Human factors in cybersecurity: Designing an effective cybersecurity education program for healthcare staff. *Healthcare Management Forum*, 37(1), 13–16. DOI: 10.1177/08404704231196137 PMID: 37684060

Wang, Z., Sun, L., & Zhu, H. (2020). Defining Social Engineering in Cybersecurity. *IEEE Access : Practical Innovations, Open Solutions*, 8, 85094–85115. DOI: 10.1109/ACCESS.2020.2992807

Wang, Z., Zhu, H., Liu, P., & Sun, L. (2021). Social engineering in cybersecurity: A domain ontology and knowledge graph application examples. *Cybersecurity*, 4(1), 31. Advance online publication. DOI: 10.1186/s42400-021-00094-6

Yadav, V., Soni, M. K., & Pratap, A. (2024). Secured Identity and Access Management for Cloud Computing Using Zero Trust Architecture. In Chaturvedi, A., Hasan, S. U., Roy, B. K., & Tsaban, B. (Eds.), *Cryptology and Network Security with Machine Learning. ICCNSML 2023. Lecture Notes in Networks and Systems* (Vol. 918). Springer., DOI: 10.1007/978-981-97-0641-9_47

Yang, R., Zheng, K., Wang, X., Wu, B., & Wu, C. (2023). Social Engineering Attack-Defense Strategies Based on Reinforcement Learning. *Computer Systems Science and Engineering*, 47(2), 2153–2170. DOI: 10.32604/csse.2023.038917

Zaoui, M., Yousra, B., Yassine, S., Yassine, M., & Karim, O. (2024). A Comprehensive Taxonomy of Social Engineering Attacks and Defense Mechanisms: Towards Effective Mitigation Strategies. *IEEE Access : Practical Innovations, Open Solutions*, 12, 1–1. DOI: 10.1109/ACCESS.2024.3403197

Chapter 5
Exploration of Social Engineering in the Digital Era of Stealth

Geetha Manoharan
https://orcid.org/0000-0002-8644-8871
SR University, India

Chetan Dudhagara
https://orcid.org/0000-0003-1220-5719
Anand Agricultural University, India

ABSTRACT

Social engineering entails obtaining important information. Attackers may request varied victim details. After targeting someone, attackers aim to steal their bank account information or passwords or breach into their machine to install malicious software to take control. Social engineering is simpler than software infiltration because attackers exploit victim confidence. Tricking someone into giving their password is simpler than hacking it. Trusting people and things is crucial to security. Finding out if someone is who they say they are is crucial. Trusting a website and giving your personal information: when? Thus, every respected security expert agrees that the weakest link in the security system is the believer. Even with locks and deadbolts on our doors and windows, guard dogs, alarm systems, floodlights, barbed wire fences, and armed guards, the pizza delivery man at the gate can get in. This chapter expands on social engineering and safety.

DOI: 10.4018/979-8-3693-6665-3.ch005

OVERVIEW OF SOCIAL ENGINEERING

Kevin Mitnick's work is still as engaging on paper now as it was on film, from his exciting autobiography about becoming the most famous hacker in the world to his instructional materials about social engineering and significant security dangers. He is referred to be the originator of social engineering. One of the most influential figures in the sociological school of jurisprudence was Roscoe Pound. He established the "Social Engineering" theory, which attempts to create an effective social structure that would allow the greatest number of needs to be satisfied with the least amount of waste and friction. Zhang, C., Jiang, Z., Zhang, G., Li, Z., and Fathollahi-Fard, A.M. (2023).

Phishing is the most popular type of social engineering assault. Phishing attacks use human mistake as a means of credential harvesting or malware distribution (Joyce, P. R., et al., 2024). Typically, they do this by sending links to malicious websites or infected email attachments. Ivanov, N., Lou, J., Chen, T., Li, J., & Yan, Q. (2021). The act of psychologically coercing, misleading, or persuading someone to reveal private or sensitive information or take particular actions is known as social engineering. This kind of cyber-attack relies less on technological exploits and more on taking advantage of human weaknesses. Phishing emails, phone frauds, and pretexting are common strategies. To obtain sensitive information, social engineers frequently assume the identities of reliable organizations, such as banking institutions or IT assistance. Kano, Y., and Nakajima, T. (2021). It's critical to maintain awareness, confirm identities, and use caution when handling personal information in order to guard against social engineering.

Although dishonesty has always been a part of life, ICT technologies have considerably raised its frequency. Social engineering techniques in IT can be examined from two angles within this new framework: either by using psychological manipulation to get more access to an IT system where the scammer's actual goal resides, such as phoning a well-known client to trick the target into visiting a malicious website that infects the target's workstation, or by using IT technologies to support psychological manipulation techniques to achieve an objective outside the IT domain, such obtaining banking credentials by means of a phishing attack to then steal the target's money. 2020 Alturas, B.; Reis, J.; Gomes, V.

The usage of these strategies has inevitably increased along with the use of IT tools, to the point where the majority of cyber-attacks now involve social engineering of some kind. Al-Turjman, F.M., Bhatia, S., Salama, R., & Yadav, S.P. (2023). S.

There are numerous ways to carry out social engineering, according to Mattera, M., & Chowdhury, M.M. (2021). One of these attacks can affect a variety of people. Cyber-attacks are typically perceived as extremely technological attacks executed by a highly skilled computer system specialist.

These attacks can be as easy as sifting through trash in search of information or peering over someone's shoulder to see what is shown on their monitor. With the growing usage of IoT devices for communication, social engineering attacks are one that will become more dangerous and demand more attention. These attacks typically adhere to an attack structure in order to achieve objectives related to destruction, unlawful access, or the acquisition of financial value. The word "social" is used because it emphasizes that human behaviour is the first line of defence against these attacks. The two main components of mitigation are being able to recognize the specific attack and taking appropriate action, as well as educating the people the attack is meant for. This essay will concentrate on the justification and application of the Social Engineering Attack Framework in addition to the defences against various attack kinds.

In this digital age, where people are often the weakest link in defense, studying social engineering is very important. Understanding how attackers use psychological tricks to get into systems is important for making good defenses as cyber dangers change. More research in this area could lead to better education, training programs, and technology security measures that make it harder for social engineering attacks to work. The goal of this study is to improve general cybersecurity and keep sensitive information safe from being misused by looking into weak spots in how people use technology.

Social Engineering Life Cycle

The life cycle of social engineering is a four level continuous process at times and also it gets exit after a victim is set to be done. Let us now discuss regarding the four category with the criteria's that is being handled as bellows:

Figure 1. The lifecycle of social engineering

Level 1: Investigation- Getting ready to launch an attack:

- Selecting the attack method(s)
- Identifying the victim(s)
- Compiling background data

Level 2: Hook- Tricking the victim or victims in order to obtain ground:

- Taking charge of the engagement;
- Involving the target;
- Telling a narrative;

Level 3: Play- Acquiring the data within a time frame:

- Gaining ground,
- Carrying out the attack,
- Upsetting operations, and stealing data

Level 4: Exit- Finally, without raising any suspicions, identify ourself as:

- Taking off all malware remnants;
- hiding evidence; and
- ending the ruse organically

Albladi, S.M. and Weir, G.R. (2020) stress that human error—rather than operating system and software flaws—is what makes social engineering so hazardous. Mistakes made by authorised persons are more erratic than those resulting from malware-based breaches, which makes their detection and prevention more challenging.

Social Engineering Techniques

This post will discuss a few of the most popular strategies, including tailgating, quid pro quo, baiting, and pretexting.

Social engineering is another tactic used in phishing assaults; Taib, R., Yu, K., Berkovsky, S.,Wiggins, M.W., & Bayl-Smith, P. (2019) addressed this subject in a previous post.

Pretexting

This tactic entails using a pretext - a fraudulent explanation for a certain course of action - to win the victim over and deceive them. To prevent such assaults, appropriate policies, procedures, and trainings for identification and authentication should be in place. Rajendran, G., and P.P. Parthy (2019).

Baiting

Baiting is the practice of tricking someone into completing a task by giving them easy access to something they desire. Most efforts will be thwarted by security measures like an air gap and the blocking of unauthorized software (N. Gupta, H. Sharma, et al., 2022) and hardware, but employees should also be reminded not to trust unidentified sources. Liyanage, A., Randeniya, R., and S.A. Kaushalya (2018).

Quid pro quo

Translating as "something for something" in Latin, quid pro quo is the practice of seeking information in exchange for money. Quid pro quo assaults are quite easy to spot given the unequal value of the information against the reverse for both the victim and the attacker. The best defense in these kinds of circumstances is still the victim's integrity and ability to spot, reject, and document.

Tailgating

Tailgating refers to the practice of trailing an authorized individual into a system or restricted area. The more sensitive the region, the tougher the combination of access restrictions and/or access control technology to regulate access to non-public areas. The mandate to wear a badge, the presence of a guard, and actual anti-tailgating doors like mantraps with RFID access control should discourage most attackers.

419/Nigerian prince/advance fee scams

These frauds involve con artists asking for money or victim bank account details to enable money transfers outside of the country. They began with the 419, which stands for the section of Nigeria's Criminal Code forbade the conduct.

Water-holing/watering hole

Attackers using watering hole techniques gain access to websites that their intended audience is known to visit. For example, the NotPetya virus of 2017 infected a website run by the Ukrainian government and subsequently spread throughout the nation's infrastructure. It is thought to have been the result of a politically motivated attack on Ukraine.

Vishing/voice phishing

Targeted social engineering attack via phone is known as "vishing." One kind of phishing assault is the use of recorded messages to inform victims that their bank accounts have been hacked. Then, in order to access their accounts, victims are required to enter their information using the phone's keypad.

Scareware

A kind of malicious software meant to fool consumers into visiting dangerous websites or buying useless products. Usually, it shows up as a pop-up alert warning that dangerous material has been discovered on our computer or that our security program is out of current.

Smishing/SMS phishing

Often used with various techniques to get past 2FA (two-factor authentication), text messages posing as official correspondence are On mobile phones, victims may be pointed to phoney websites.

Diversion theft

Intercepting deliveries by tricking couriers into going to the wrong place is known as an offline diversion heist. They entail tricking victims into sending private information to the incorrect person in order to steal it online.

Honey trap

To coerce the victim into disclosing private information or money, attackers pose as someone with romantic or sexual interest in them.

Social Engineering Assault Types Include

- **Angler phishing**

Angler phishing is a specific type of phishing effort based on social media. Unlike conventional phishing efforts, which include emails posing as companies, angler phishing attacks are conducted through bogus corporate social network profiles.

- **BEC (business email compromise)**

Business email compromise (BEC) schemes are used by phishers to fool victims into forwarding confidential company data or money. They are much targeted, in contrast to most phishing emails.

- **Pharming**

Phishing attacks use system flaws that match IP addresses and domain names to spoof a website and divert visitors to a malicious website.

- **Spear phishing**

Spear phishing is a type of email attack where scammers customize their message for a particular individual. Since spear phishing attacks are directed directly to the target, they allay suspicions that they are fraudulent, making them harder to identify than other phishing schemes.

- **Tabnabbing/reverse Tabnabbing**

Phishing attacks that alter dormant web pages are known as "tabnabbing" attacks. It happens when users close an open tab, giving malicious hackers the opportunity to reroute the website to a copy they own.

- **Whaling**

A specific kind of phishing assault known as "whaling" takes advantage of the power upper management has over subordinate positions, such as CEOs' control over assistants or financial executives.

LITERATURE REVIEW

Social Engineering Using ChatGPT

The emergence of generative AI models such as FraudGPT, WormGPT, and ChatGPT has presented novel difficulties as well as inventive solutions in the constantly changing field of cyber security, according to a paper by Falade, P.V. (2023). This study uses blog mining to explore the many uses of generative AI in social engineering assaults (Singh, D., et al., 2024) and provides insights into how the threat landscape is changing. With the ability to create individualized and convincing phishing lures, influence public opinion through deepfakes, and take advantage of cognitive biases in humans, generative AI models have completely changed the landscape of cyberattacks. The ChatGPT, FraudGPT, and WormGPT models have introduced additional risk dimensions and amplified preexisting dangers. We examine how generative AI broadens the toolkit of hackers, from phishing tactics that imitate reliable corporations to deepfake technologies that pose as powerful individuals. Additionally, we illuminated the weaknesses that AI-powered social engineering takes advantage of, such as targeted phishing, psychological manipulation, and the crisis of authenticity. We discuss a variety of tactics, such as collaborative cyber security techniques, AI-powered security solutions, and conventional security measures, to address these threats. We stress that in the fight against AI-enhanced social engineering attacks, it is critical to maintain vigilance, raise awareness, and improve laws. Protecting against generative AI dangers necessitates ongoing adaptation and the combined efforts of individuals, businesses, and governments in an environment where AI models are evolving quickly and there is a shortage of training data. By giving stakeholders the expertise to navigate this complex cyber security landscape, this research aims to provide a thorough understanding of the dynamic interplay between generative AI and social engineering threats.

Grbic, D.V., and Dujlovic, I. (2023) offer in this work the possibility of utilizing ChatGPT to set up environments in order to carry out social engineering-based assaults. Not long after becoming live, ChatGPT has demonstrated outstanding performance across a wide range of topics, including producing code, providing text templates, and even answering some general or specialized questions. With a few clicks and a few minutes, one can obtain all the necessary materials for phishing or other attacks by combining those options with the system's high level of preparation. This paper discusses how to create a phishing attack using ChatGPT and provides a general overview of social engineering attacks and how to prevent them.

Since Salama, R., Al-Turjman, F.M., Bhatia, S., & Yadav, S.P. (2023) created the term "Cyber Security" it has become increasingly popular and important. Since computers and most devices are internet-connected, hackers can hack them. This issue wasn't a huge deal in the past because not every device needed internet access or the internet wasn't as popular. The case has changed over time. All technological changes affected cyber-attack models. Recent technological advances and internet usage changes have made cyber-attacks more widespread and popular among hackers. Hackers have found a way to steal or make money quickly without any effort. Cyberattacks today are different. Cyberattack tactics evolve over time. Cybercriminals use more advanced and effective ways than before. This article cannot include all ways. We will focus on social engineering assaults in this essay.Social engineering assaults employ several cyberattack methods. Social engineering attacks aim to trick victims into providing their data to hackers without using password cracking or exploiting techniques, unlike advanced password attacks. This page covers social media engineering, its tactics, defenses, and more.

Social engineering is a technique of breaching information security to obtain access to systems or networks, claims Syafitri et al. (2022).Attacks in social engineering happen when victims stay ignorant of models, frameworks, and preventative strategies. User studies, assessment, ideas, theories, models, and techniques for stopping social engineering assaults are covered in this paper. Not enough study exists to sufficiently and carefully investigate social engineering assaults. Health programs, human security sensor systems, user-centric models, and vulnerability models are among the several preventative approaches for social engineering assaults. Using people as security sensors calls for direction on cybersecurity as super-recognizers, most likely controlling a safe system. This paper will examine and challenge earlier studies on models, frameworks, and social engineering assault prevention techniques. Bryman & Bell's approach was followed in our review of systematic literature. Review shows that effective protocol reduces victim susceptibility, health campaigns, social engineering assaults including co-utile protocol for information exchange on social networks. This extensive study of the literature points out methods to stop social engineering attacks.

Defending Against Social Engineering Attacks

Wang, Z., Sun, L., & Zhu, H. (2020) state that a crucial part of all cyber security initiatives is minimizing the threat of social engineering. It takes a multifaceted strategy that blends technology safeguards with employee education to enable our personnel to identify and report social engineering attempts, and to ensure that any successful attacks because the least amount of harm feasible. Skinner, G., Alashoor, T., and Aldawood, H. (2020). Social engineering defences should address the following four crucial areas:

1. Establish a culture of positivity for security

Our security team will need to move swiftly to contain a social engineering assault if it affects us or our workers. Because of this, victims should be encouraged by our corporate culture to disclose instances as soon as feasible. Fearing repercussions, the individual who unintentionally created the malware infection chose to remain silent, leaving our PC infected for months. This is the last thing we want.

2. Teach employees about psychological triggers and other telltale signs

Since social engineering attacks are not always simple to identify, it is critical to comprehend the strategies they employ, including:

- Acting as dependable entities, such reputable businesses or people;
- Often by inspiring anxiety or excitement so they act quickly without thinking, providing a false feeling of urgency helps to confuse victims; and
- Targeting people's natural curiosity, sense of responsibility, or conditioned responses to authority.

Also the staff should be trained:

- Be suspicious of unsolicited communications (Mohtashim Mian, S., Kumar, R., 2023) and unknown people.
- Ascertain whether emails actually originate from the person to whom they are supposed to be addressed (double-check senders' identities and
- Keep an eye out for telltale signs like misspellings and other reading difficulties).

Keep questionable email attachments closed.

- Give sensitive information careful thought before sharing it.
- Be mindful of URLs and "typosquatting" (looking authentic but using a subtle variation in web address from the real site they mimic).

Verify the security of websites before entering any information, even if they appear trustworthy.

3. Verify the training's efficacy

Security awareness training shouldn't be one-time occurrence. Periodically evaluating the effectiveness of the training is crucial, and if necessary it should be re-started. 2019 Horkoff, J.; Li, T.; and Wang, K. For example, a fake phishing attack might show us how exposed our staff is and how much our business is under danger. Ye, Z.; Guo, Y.; Ju, A.; Wei, F.; Zhang, R.; and Ma, J. (2020). Using this information will help us to reduce our exposure by retraining those most in need of it.

4. Implement technological cyber security measures

In addition to staff testing and training, technology cyber security measures including firewalls, antivirus, and anti-malware applications, patch management, penetration testing, and access control protocols should be implemented. We may decrease the possibility that our employees will become the target of assaults and the damage they inflict when they do manage to succeed by taking this action. Both Skinner and Aldawood released books in 2019.

Traits of a Social Engineering Attack

Usually coexisting in a sophisticated campaign, it may be hard to differentiate phishing from social engineering. Social engineers usually pretend as legitimate employees—like the CFO or CEO—or deceive staff members into thinking the attacker is a real customer in order to access sensitive information or change account features—like SIM swapping. Certain signs clearly show that, independent of the attacker's goals, the message is the outcome of social engineering. A basic feature of social engineering is the exploitation of the emotions and concerns of the intended victim. Social engineering makes use of urgency and fear as the attacker wants the intended victim to be terrified and to ignore the demand. A few common traits in all social engineering attacks are:

- **Heightened emotions:**

An assailant can threaten to wipe a user's account in order to get them to provide their passwords. Alternatively, the assailant can pretend as an executive asking money from a particular user in order to instill urgency among employees fearing job loss.

- **Spoofed sender address:**

Although most customers are unaware that a sender email address can be fake, with proper email security spoofing senders cannot reach the inbox of a targeted user. On the other hand, a cybercrime can register a domain that looks like a real one and then hope the target user would ignore the misspelling.

- **Strange friend requests:**

An assailant often gets access to an email account of a victim and sends damaging messages to their contact list. If the message does not look like individualized communication, be cautious of following links from friends as messages from friends are usually quick and devoid of the customized touch.

- **Unprofessional website links:**

Phishing links are occasionally used with social engineering techniques to deceive users into disclosing private information. Never use an email link to enter login credentials into a website, even if it appears to be an official website (Paypal, for example). Too good to be true: Money promises are a common tactic used by scammers to get financial rewards. In exchange for shipping fees, for instance, a targeted consumer might receive a free iPhone. Generally speaking, an offer is a fraud if it seems too good to be true.

- **Suspicious attachments:**

Sophisticated attacks may aim to infect a corporate workstation with malware through email attachments, rather than deceiving the targeted users into revealing personal information. A seemingly innocent email message should never be used to launch executables or macros on a computer.

- **Questionable sender:**

A common social engineering strategy is to imitate a well-known source, like a friend, supervisor, or colleague. Always follow up and ask ourself, "Did my boss/friend/coworker actually send this to me?" if we receive a questionable email message. Make sure the individual is not being impersonated by calling, texting, or chatting on social media before answering to the disputed email.

- **Refusal to respond to questions:**

React to a message and request the sender's identity if something seems off. To avoid being identified, an attacker may choose to just disregard the request.

- **Unidentifiable sender:**

Please refuse any further information or access requests from the sender if they are unable or unwilling to have their identification confirmed by the organization. Even though email correspondence is the most popular, other social engineering techniques, such texting and calling, can also be used in this way.

Social Engineering Prevention

Social engineers use on human emotions like fear and curiosity to carry out their plans and entice victims into their traps. Exercise caution, then, if we find errant digital media, led to an offer on a website, or are afraid of an email (Nagarjuna, B., et al., 2022). According to Syafitri, W., Shukur, Z., Mokhtar, U.A., Sulaiman, R., & Ibrahim, M.A. (2022), being vigilant helps us to protect ourselves from most social engineering attempts occurring in the digital arena. Furthermore, by following this guidance, we may start to see social engineering tricks more clearly.

Open emails and attachments from dubious sources; we are not obligated to reply to an email should we not know the sender. Even if we know them and are doubtful about their message, check and confirm the facts from other sources, including the internet or by phone. Remember that email addresses are often created; an email seeming to be from a reputable source may have been created by an assailant.

Use multifactor authentication; among the most crucial bits of data hackers search for are user credentials. Multifactor authentication helps us to protect our account should a system compromise occur. The straightforward 2FA solution Imperva Login Protect will help to strengthen the account security of our apps. 2019 Skinner, G., and Aldawood, H.

Use caution with alluring offers. If anything seems too good to be true, steer clear of accepting an offer at face value. Searching Google for the topic can help us spot a sincere or a deceitful offer right away. Maintaining our antivirus/antimalware program current will help Make sure we have triggered automated updates or downloaded the most recent signatures first thing each day. Run a system infection check to confirm that the updates have been regularly deployed.

A key component of our cyber security plan should be the prevention and mitigation of social engineering attacks, as they pose a serious danger to the security of our company. A comprehensive security strategy that incorporates technological security measures with in-depth training for executives and employees is necessary to prevent a social engineering attack. Schmick, P.J., & Conteh, N.Y. (2021).

Training is the first line of defence against a social engineering attack. Hammad, M.M., Alharthi, D.N., and Regan, A.C. (2020). Everybody in our company needs to be aware of the most prevalent social engineering techniques and be aware of the psychological tricks used by con artists to trick others. Employees should learn the following skills in a thorough social engineering and security awareness training course: Spoof emails by hovering over the sender's name and confirming that it matches the email address, as well as by looking for frequent red flags like spelling mistakes.

In order to make sure that our personnel has not grown complacent, we also need to periodically test them after our security awareness training. Fake phishing emails are sent to staff members as part of several training programs to see how many individuals fall for social engineering tricks. After then, those employees can receive additional training as needed.

Khlobystova, A.O., Abramov, M.V., & Tulupyev, A.L. (2019) state that establishing a positive security culture within the company is essential to stopping a social engineering attack that has already occurred. If any member of our staff feels that they have been the victim of a social engineering attack, they should feel free to self-report; if they are afraid of being punished or humiliated in public, they won't do so. If these problems are brought to the attention of the relevant parties as soon as they arise, the threat can be promptly reduced before significant harm is done. Campbell, C.C. (2019). Lastly, in order to stop attacks on our company and lessen the harm caused by any successful breaches, we must put technological security mechanisms into place. Firewalls, email spam filters, antivirus and anti-malware programs, patch management software, and network monitoring tools should all be part of this set of technologies.

DISCUSSION AND CONCLUSION

At the moment, layers of technology safeguards to better identify and respond to attacks and user education are the best lines of defence against social engineering attacks. Keyword detection in emails or phone conversations can be used to filter out possible attackers, but even those tools are unlikely to be able to thwart competent social engineers. Abass, I.A. (2018).

The fact that social engineering can affect anybody is among its most concerning features. A corporation is only as strong as its weakest employee, and since some companies have thousands of workers, the threat is real and intimidating. It is through an interdisciplinary approach that social engineering is best understood (Manoharan, G., Durai, S., et al., 2024), Siddiqi, M.A., Pak, W., & Siddiqi, M.A. (2022). Social engineering will likely remain a challenge to all kinds of enterprises due to the growing usage of technology and interconnectivity in today's corporate world (Satpathy, A., et al., 2024). Given the growing prevalence of social engineering attacks during the COVID-19 pandemic (Ananthan, M., et al., 2024; Dattatreyulu, C., et al., 2024), Alzahrani, A.A. (2020), and the fact that the topic can only be fully understood when seen from a number of fields, research on this topic is imperative. In 2021, Sushruth, V., Reddy, K., Chandavarkar, B., Misra, R., Shyamsunder, R.K., Dingli, A., Denk, N., Rana, O., Pfeiffer, A., Patel, A., & Kesswani, N.

The parallels between a deceitful defence and a socially orchestrated attack were examined in this chapter. The concepts of influence and human behaviour manipulation are used by Bhusal, C.S. (2020) to emphasize this similarity. The enduring nature of social engineering initiatives targeting companies of all kinds emphasizes the significance of tactics aimed at lowering employee exposure to these kinds of communications. We can see how these strategies relate to one another and how the defence is bolstered by ideas taken from the social engineering framework by comprehending how they function independently. They might take inspiration for the defence not only from the structure, but also from the success of socially orchestrated attacks. In order to help exert influence over an attacker, a defence might also try to increase their odds of influence.

Members of an organization can occasionally make bad decisions that lead them to fall for social engineering scams. Administrators must, however, make security-related decisions, such as how to handle victims of social engineering within their company. Should our participants be right, then it would be wise to revaluate the threats of harsh penalties. In this way, organizational strategies for managing policy infractions and social engineering transgressions among members should be compared in further studies on organizational resilience to social engineering. While the participant-recommended rehabilitative procedures might be more morally sound from an employee-relations standpoint, claims that they are also more secure should be verified by empirical research. Subsequent investigations may additionally contemplate scrutinizing reintegrative shaming methodologies within situational crime prevention approaches in diverse settings.

The goal of the social engineering study is to find useful information about how attackers use psychological tricks on people to get into security systems. One of the results will be a better understanding of common social engineering techniques like hacking, pretexting, and baiting. Because of this study, better training programs, campaigns to raise awareness, and technical solutions will be made to lower these risks. The results will also help improve security protocols and guidelines, which will help people and businesses protect themselves better against social engineering threats and lessen the total effect of these attacks on cybersecurity.

The chapter addressed several social engineering subjects and popular methods. We also covered some specifics on the reasons behind attackers' hostile actions and why individuals fall for them, mostly related to a lack of technological understanding and competence. At last, we discussed some advised defenses against social engineering attempts. We want to finish this effort so that we may help to contribute to a comprehensive knowledge of social engineering from all sides, given the small number of "tools" accessible to identify and prevent these sorts of attacks. We anticipate the development of a tool in the future that will assist identify social engineering attacks more quickly and precisely so that they may be stopped, even though they are a non-technical method of taking advantage of human flaws.

Social engineering is not only a technical problem but also a deeply ingrained human phenomena that calls for a comprehensive and adaptive solution, as is seen when we consider the major area of understanding regarding the concepts and approaches involved in the apex note. A sophisticated grasp of human behaviour, technical innovation, and ethical considerations are necessary for the dynamic task of social engineering. Understanding the complex nature of social engineering is made easier by the newfound understanding provided by this review (Praveen, A., et al., 2024). It is evident that we need to be alert, flexible, and cooperative in our endeavours to lessen the hazards associated with social engineering as we negotiate the complex relationship between psychology and technology. To protect our digital future from the ubiquitous threat of social engineering, we need to continue exploring new areas of knowledge, build resilient methods (Manoharan, G., Razak, A., et al., 2023) and work together across several disciplines.

REFERENCES

Abass, I. A. (2018). Social Engineering Threat and Defense: A Literature Survey. *Journal of Information Security*, 09(4), 257–264. DOI: 10.4236/jis.2018.94018

Albladi, S. M., & Weir, G. R. (2020). Predicting individuals' vulnerability to social engineering in social networks. *Cybersecurity*, 3(1), 3. DOI: 10.1186/s42400-020-00047-5

Aldawood, H., Alashoor, T., & Skinner, G. (2020). Does Awareness of Social Engineering Make Employees More Secure? *International Journal of Computer Applications*, 177(38), 45–49. DOI: 10.5120/ijca2020919891

Aldawood, H., & Skinner, G. (2019). Challenges of Implementing Training and Awareness Programs Targeting Cyber Security Social Engineering. *2019 Cybersecurity and Cyberforensics Conference (CCC)*, 111-117. DOI: 10.1109/CCC.2019.00004

Aldawood, H., & Skinner, G. (2020). Analysis and Findings of Social Engineering Industry Experts Explorative Interviews: Perspectives on Measures, Tools, and Solutions. *IEEE Access: Practical Innovations, Open Solutions*, 8, 67321–67329. DOI: 10.1109/ACCESS.2020.2983280

Alharthi, D.N., Hammad, M.M., & Regan, A.C. (2020). A Taxonomy of Social Engineering Defense Mechanisms.

Alzahrani, A. A. (2020). Coronavirus Social Engineering Attacks: Issues and Recommendations. *International Journal of Advanced Computer Science and Applications*, 11(5), 154–161. DOI: 10.14569/IJACSA.2020.0110523

Ananthan, M., Shanmugam, V., Udayanan, M., Selvaraj, F., & Manoharan, G. (2024, June). Corporate social responsibility is used as a marketing strategy during Covid-19 pandemic. In AIP Conference Proceedings (Vol. 2971, No. 1). AIP Publishing. DOI: 10.1063/5.0195948

Bhusal, C.S. (2020). Systematic Review on Social Engineering: Hacking by Manipulating Humans. Journal of Information Security.

Campbell, C. C. (2019). Solutions for counteracting human deception in social engineering attacks. *Information Technology & People*, 32(5), 1130–1152. DOI: 10.1108/ITP-12-2017-0422

Conteh, N. Y., & Schmick, P. J. (2021). *Cybersecurity Risks, Vulnerabilities, and Countermeasures to Prevent Social Engineering Attacks*. Ethical Hacking Techniques and Countermeasures for Cybercrime Prevention. DOI: 10.4018/978-1-7998-6504-9.ch002

Dattatreyulu, C., Krishna, C. B., & Geetha, M. (2024, June). Assessment of the effect of covid–19 situation on digital marketing. In AIP Conference Proceedings (Vol. 2971, No. 1). AIP Publishing. DOI: 10.1063/5.0195757

Falade, P.V. (2023). Decoding the Threat Landscape: ChatGPT, FraudGPT, and WormGPT in Social Engineering Attacks. ArXiv, abs/2310.05595.

Gomes, V., Reis, J., & Alturas, B. (2020). Social Engineering and the Dangers of Phishing. 2020 15th Iberian Conference on Information Systems and Technologies (CISTI), 1-7.

Grbic, D. V., & Dujlovic, I. (2023). Social engineering with ChatGPT. 2023 22nd International Symposium INFOTEH-JAHORINA (INFOTEH), 1-5.

Gupta, N., Sharma, H., Kumar, S., Kumar, A., & Kumar, R. (2022, December). A comparative study of implementing agile methodology and scrum framework for software development. In *2022 11th International Conference on System Modeling & Advancement in Research Trends (SMART)* (pp. 1088-1092). IEEE.

Ivanov, N., Lou, J., Chen, T., Li, J., & Yan, Q. (2021). Targeting the Weakest Link: Social Engineering Attacks in Ethereum Smart Contracts. *Proceedings of the 2021 ACM Asia Conference on Computer and Communications Security*. DOI: 10.1145/3433210.3453085

Jaiswal, A., & Kumar, R. (2023). Breast cancer diagnosis using Stochastic Self-Organizing Map and Enlarge C4.5. *Multimedia Tools and Applications*, 82(12), 18059–18076. DOI: 10.1007/s11042-022-14265-1

Joyce, P. R., Selvaraj, F. J., Manoharan, G., Priya, C., Vijayalakshmi, R., Dwivedi, P. K., & Veerakumar, K. (2024). To Study The Role Of Marketing In Human Resource Management. *Migration Letters : An International Journal of Migration Studies*, 21(S2), 1191–1196. DOI: 10.59670/ml.v21iS2.7072

Kano, Y., & Nakajima, T. (2021). Trust Factors of Social Engineering Attacks on Social Networking Services. 2021 IEEE 3rd Global Conference on Life Sciences and Technologies (LifeTech), 25-28.

Kaushalya, S. A., Randeniya, R., & Liyanage, A. (2018). An Overview of Social Engineering in the Context of Information Security. 2018 IEEE 5th International Conference on Engineering Technologies and Applied Sciences (ICETAS), 1-6.

Khlobystova, A. O., Abramov, M. V., & Tulupyev, A. L. (2019). *An Approach to Estimating of Criticality of Social Engineering Attacks Traces*. Recent Research in Control Engineering and Decision Making. DOI: 10.1007/978-3-030-12072-6_36

Li, T., Wang, K., & Horkoff, J. (2019). Towards Effective Assessment for Social Engineering Attacks. 2019 IEEE 27th International Requirements Engineering Conference (RE), 392-397.

Manoharan, G., Durai, S., Rajesh, G. A., & Ashtikar, S. P. (2024). A Study on the Application of Expert Systems as a Support System for Business Decisions: A Literature Review. Artificial Intelligence and Knowledge Processing, 279-289.

Manoharan, G., Durai, S., Rajesh, G. A., Razak, A., Rao, C. B., & Ashtikar, S. P. (2023). A study on the perceptions of officials on their duties and responsibilities at various levels of the organizational structure in order to accomplish artificial intelligence-based smart city implementation. In *Artificial Intelligence and Machine Learning in Smart City Planning* (pp. 1–10). Elsevier. DOI: 10.1016/B978-0-323-99503-0.00007-7

Manoharan, G., Razak, A., Rajchandar, K., Nithya, G., Durai, S., & Ashtikar, S. P. (2024). Digital Learning for Professional Development in Varied Fields of Service Sectors: Embracing Technological Advancements. In Embracing Technological Advancements for Lifelong Learning (pp. 111-137). IGI Global.

Mattera, M., & Chowdhury, M. M. (2021). Social Engineering: The Looming Threat. 2021 IEEE International Conference on Electro Information Technology (EIT), 056-061. DOI: 10.1109/EIT51626.2021.9491884

Mohtashim Mian, S., & Kumar, R. (2023). Deep Learning for Performance Enhancement Robust Underwater Acoustic Communication Network. In Maurya, S., Peddoju, S. K., Ahmad, B., & Chihi, I. (Eds.), *Cyber Technologies and Emerging Sciences. Lecture Notes in Networks and Systems* (Vol. 467). Springer., DOI: 10.1007/978-981-19-2538-2_24

Nagarjuna, B., Aarif, M., Shamina, H., Sawant, P. D., Bhadane, J. R., & Manoharan, G. (2022). An empirical analysis of efficacy of digital marketing techniques on tourism entrepreneurs. *European Journal of Molecular and Clinical Medicine*, 9(8).

Parthy, P. P., & Rajendran, G. (2019). Identification and prevention of social engineering attacks on an enterprise. *2019 International Carnahan Conference on Security Technology (ICCST)*, 1-5. DOI: 10.1109/CCST.2019.8888441

Praveen, A., Boini, R., Ravi, K., & Geetha, M. (2024, June). A contemplation on the seven significant characteristics of an engineering instructor in TLP. In AIP Conference Proceedings (Vol. 2971, No. 1). AIP Publishing. DOI: 10.1063/5.0195780

Salama, R., Al-Turjman, F. M., Bhatia, S., & Yadav, S. P. (2023). Social engineering attack types and prevention techniques- A survey. *2023 International Conference on Computational Intelligence, Communication Technology and Networking (CICTN)*, 817-820. DOI: 10.1109/CICTN57981.2023.10140957

Salama, R., Al-Turjman, F. M., Bhatia, S., & Yadav, S. P. (2023). Social engineering attack types and prevention techniques- A survey. *2023 International Conference on Computational Intelligence, Communication Technology and Networking (CICTN)*, 817-820. DOI: 10.1109/CICTN57981.2023.10140957

Satpathy, A., Samal, A., Gupta, S., Kumar, S., Sharma, S., Manoharan, G., Karthikeyan, M., & Sharma, S. (2024). To Study the Sustainable Development Practices in Business and Food Industry. *Migration Letters : An International Journal of Migration Studies*, 21(S1), 743–747. DOI: 10.59670/ml.v21iS1.6400

Siddiqi, M. A., Pak, W., & Siddiqi, M. A. (2022). A Study on the Psychology of Social Engineering-Based Cyberattacks and Existing Countermeasures. *Applied Sciences (Basel, Switzerland)*, 12(12), 6042. DOI: 10.3390/app12126042

Singh, A., Virmani, D., Kulkarni, N., Tiwari, M., Manoharan, G., & Alanya-Beltran, J. (2024). The Emerging Role and Application of Adopting Revolutionary Internet of Things (IoT) for Future Technology Sustainability. Computer Science Engineering and Emerging Technologies. *Proceedings of ICCS*, 2022, 103.

Singh, D., Makkar, S., Durai, S., Manoharan, G., Purushottamashtikar, S., & Alexrajesh, G. (2024, June). Human resource information system applications in small and medium enterprises: A study (SMEs). In AIP Conference Proceedings (Vol. 2971, No. 1). AIP Publishing.

Sushruth, V., Reddy, ·.K., Chandavarkar, ·.B., Misra, R., Shyamsunder, R.K., Dingli, A., Denk, N., Rana, O., Pfeiffer, A., Patel, A., & Kesswani, N. (2021). Social Engineering Attacks During the COVID-19 Pandemic. *SN Computer Science*, •••, 2.

Syafitri, W., Shukur, Z., Mokhtar, U. A., Sulaiman, R., & Ibrahim, M. A. (2022). Social Engineering Attacks Prevention: A Systematic Literature Review. IEEE Access, PP, 1-1.

Syafitri, W., Shukur, Z., Mokhtar, U. A., Sulaiman, R., & Ibrahim, M. A. (2022). Social Engineering Attacks Prevention: A Systematic Literature Review. *IEEE Access, PP*, 1-1.

Taib, R., Yu, K., Berkovsky, S., Wiggins, M. W., & Bayl-Smith, P. (2019). Social Engineering and Organisational Dependencies in Phishing Attacks. IFIP TC13 International Conference on Human-Computer Interaction. DOI: 10.1007/978-3-030-29381-9_35

Thavamani, S., Mahesh, D., Sinthuja, U., & Manoharan, G. (2022, May). Crucial attacks in internet of things via artificial intelligence techniques: The security survey. In AIP Conference Proceedings (Vol. 2418, No. 1). AIP Publishing.

Tian, G., Zhang, C., Fathollahi-Fard, A. M., Li, Z., Zhang, C., & Jiang, Z. (2023). An Enhanced Social Engineering Optimizer for Solving an Energy-Efficient Disassembly Line Balancing Problem Based on Bucket Brigades and Cloud Theory. *IEEE Transactions on Industrial Informatics*, 19(5), 7148–7159. DOI: 10.1109/TII.2022.3193866

Tripathi, M. A., Tripathi, R., Effendy, F., Manoharan, G., Paul, M. J., & Aarif, M. (2023, January). An In-Depth Analysis of the Role That ML and Big Data Play in Driving Digital Marketing's Paradigm Shift. In *2023 International Conference on Computer Communication and Informatics (ICCCI)* (pp. 1-6). IEEE. DOI: 10.1109/ICCCI56745.2023.10128357

Wang, Z., Sun, L., & Zhu, H. (2020). Defining Social Engineering in Cybersecurity. *IEEE Access : Practical Innovations, Open Solutions*, 8, 85094–85115. DOI: 10.1109/ACCESS.2020.2992807

Ye, Z., Guo, Y., Ju, A., Wei, F., Zhang, R., & Ma, J. (2020). A Risk Analysis Framework for Social Engineering Attack Based on User Profiling. *Journal of Organizational and End User Computing*, 32(3), 37–49. DOI: 10.4018/JOEUC.2020070104

Chapter 6
Empowering Cyber Resilience:
Effective Strategies for Combating Social Engineering Threats

Ajay Pratap
Amity University, Lucknow, India

Gauri Rastogi
Amity University, Lucknow, India

ABSTRACT

Social engineering remains an enduring and emerging threat in cybersecurity. This chapter delves into the fluid landscape of social engineering threats, examining the strategies employed by cyber criminals and providing valuable perspectives on the current defence mechanisms that organizations and individuals can utilize for the efficient reduction of these vulnerabilities. The development of social engineering threats is propelled by a profound grasp of human psychology, coupled with the growing dependence on digital communication and information-sharing channels. This paper underscores the importance of collaboration among individuals, organizations, and security experts in the continuous effort to combat social engineering. It highlights the significance of staying informed about emerging threats and continuously improving defensive strategies to confront the constantly evolving landscape of social engineering attacks. This article introduces a comprehensive framework designed to address these challenges and shape the future of cybersecurity.

DOI: 10.4018/979-8-3693-6665-3.ch006

1. INTRODUCTION

In recent years, there has been a notable rise in the importance of capability and resilience across various business domains. This shift is driven by a growing recognition of environmental and social impacts, prompting businesses to integrate these principles into their operations to meet consumer expectations and ensure long-term sustainability. Consumer behavior reflects this trend, with research from Nielsen indicating that approximately 66% of consumers worldwide are willing to pay a premium for products and services that demonstrate commitment to environmental and societal concerns. This signifies a shift towards products that not only offer quality but also have positive impacts on the environment and society.

Similarly, perceptions of resilience have evolved, with the World Economic Forum identifying it as one of the top five risk trends for 2022. This highlights the importance for businesses to not only address daily challenges but also possess the capability to adapt and endure in the face of rapid and unforeseen changes within the global landscape. The emphasis on capability and resilience is not fleeting; rather, it has become a fundamental aspect of successful business strategies. Businesses that can effectively integrate these elements into their operations stand to gain favor with consumers, navigate complex challenges, and sustain long-term growth in an ever-changing world. In today's digital world, the cybersecurity landscape is constantly evolving, posing a complex and ever-changing challenge. Among the most concerning threats faced by individuals and organizations is social engineering. Social engineering exploits human psychology, manipulating individuals into divulging sensitive information. This paper aims to explore the evolving landscape of social engineering threats and examine the modern defenses developed to combat them. The digital era has opened up unprecedented opportunities for communication, cooperation, and information exchange.

As social engineering attacks persist in affecting individuals and organizations, there are frequently legal and regulatory consequences as shown in Figure 1. A comprehensive understanding of the evolving landscape is instrumental in enabling policymakers and legal authorities to formulate suitable frameworks for addressing and preventing social engineering attacks. This, in turn, contributes to fostering a more secure digital environment. To sum up, ongoing research on social engineering is indispensable for proactively addressing the dynamic nature of cyber threats. In summary, researching social engineering is crucial due to its dynamic nature, human involvement, the expanding digital landscape, and the potentially devastating consequences of successful attacks. Staying ahead of social engineering trends and developing innovative defenses enables better protection for individuals, organizations, and the broader digital ecosystem. Stages of social engineering attacks are shown in Figure 2.

2. LITERATURE REVIEW

The paper explores to offers insights and guidance to navigate the complex landscape of social engineering, stressing the significance of remaining informed, proactive, and prepared to address this enduring cybersecurity threat. In this section, we have explored several research papers closely related to our topic. The use of natural language generation, speech recognition, and virtual assistants makes people's lives easier and faster (Zeng, 2022). Social engineering is an important aspect and it remains an enduring and evolving menace in cybersecurity, as malicious entities continuously devise fresh stratagems to coerce individuals into disclosing sensitive information or undermining security measures (Stojanovi, 2023).

Nevarez (2023) have explained the fluid landscape of social engineering threats, examining the strategies employed by cyber criminals, and providing valuable perspectives on the current defense mechanisms that organizations and individuals can utilize for the efficient reduction of these vulnerabilities. The development of social engineering threats is propelled by a profound grasp of human psychology, coupled with the growing dependence on digital communication and information-sharing channels (Parri, 2020). Malicious individuals utilize a range of tactics, including phishing, pretexting, baiting, and tailgating, to capitalize on human weaknesses and acquire unauthorized entry to systems and data (Apostol, 2022). Comprehending these strategies is vital for the creation of robust countermeasures. Authors underscore the importance of collaboration among individuals, organizations, and security experts in the continuous effort to combat social engineering (Bradshaw, 2015; Arya, 2021).

(Orujo, 2023) highlights the significance of staying informed about emerging threats and continuously improving defensive strategies to confront the constantly evolving landscape of social engineering attacks. The empirical study of determining resilience will inform efforts made at fostering resilience, with the recognition that resilience may be enhanced on numerous levels (Southwick, 2014). Cybersecurity professionals should regularly conduct assessments, analyze incident data, and adapt their defenses to address the latest trends in attacks in cloud environment (Shrivastava, 2023). By adopting a proactive approach and integrating education, technology, and diligent monitoring, individuals and organizations can bolster their resilience against this persistent and ever-changing menace (Daajeh, 2022). Collaboration and information sharing within the cybersecurity community is also vital for staying ahead of emerging threats. This issue is rigorously discussed in (Kapoor, 2021). By fostering a culture of vigilance and continuous improvement, organizations and individuals can not only react to known social engineering tactics but also proactively anticipate and counter future, as-yet-unknown attack vectors, ultimately enhancing their overall security posture (Black, 2022). In (Sindiramutty, 2023), the paper highlights how crucial it is for individuals, organizations, and security experts to collaborate continuously in combating social engineering threats. Cybersecurity professionals need to consistently conduct assessments, analyze incident data, and adjust their defenses to counteract the evolving trends in social engineering attacks (Yadav, 2024).

3. METHODOLOGY

A report by PwC revealed that 67% of companies experienced at least one cyber-attack in the last year, indicating a growing seriousness of cyber threats as shown as Figure 3. Recent research projects have aided companies in developing frameworks to enhance resilience against these threats. The major problems while implementing the initial cybersecurity paradigms lies in the following stages:

a) Organizations must observe and understand the situation patiently before taking action.
b) Cybersecurity must remain an ongoing priority without neglect over time.
c) Organizations need to remain strong in keeping their systems protected even in the face of diverse threats.
d) Preventative measures should be in place before threats occur.
e) Data and analysis should be used to predict potential future cybersecurity threat trends.
f) Policies, security tools, and practices should be implemented to prevent threats based on predictions and analysis.

Cyber Resilience Factors Model

Cybersecurity resilience refers to an organization's capability to identify, protect against, detect, respond to, and recover from cyberattacks. It encompasses coordinated efforts across organizational, technological, and human aspects. Employing policies, processes, and strategies to ensure continuous operations and safeguard data and infrastructure from cyber threats is vital for achieving cybersecurity resilience. Figure 4 shows the factors contributing to cybersecurity resilience. By considering these factors, organizations can bolster their resilience against cyberattacks. Enhanced cybersecurity resilience helps organizations protect their assets and data from cyber threats and enables them to maintain operations even in the face of such challenges. The primary objective of cybersecurity resilience is to recognize the critical, interconnected, and mutually reinforcing elements necessary for cybersecurity resilience. To attain successful cybersecurity resilience, it is crucial to incorporate technological security, transparent rules, and processes, along with human factors.

4. PROPOSED WORK

In the dynamic and complex cybersecurity landscape, the ever-evolving threat of social engineering demands innovative and adaptive defense mechanisms. Social engineering, which relies on manipulating human psychology rather than exploiting technical vulnerabilities, poses significant risks to individuals and organizations. The proposed system represents a sophisticated and adaptive defense mechanism against the persistent and evolving threat of social engineering. In the constantly evolving realm of cybersecurity, social engineering remains a persistent and adaptable threat that poses an ongoing challenge to contemporary defense mechanisms. As technological advancements continue to unfold, so do the strategies employed by malicious actors who exploit human psychology to gain unauthorized access or obtain sensitive information. Our envisioned system endeavors to confront this ever-changing threat landscape by integrating state-of-the-art technologies and behavioral analysis methodologies.

4.1 Proposed Adaptive Defense Mechanism for Social Engineering Threats

Step-1: Begin

The process begins by acknowledging the existence of both an attacker and a defender in the cybersecurity landscape. Initialize the Attacker and the Defender: This step involves setting up the roles and characteristics of both the attacker and the defender. The attacker represents malicious entities seeking to exploit vulnerabilities, while the defender represents the cybersecurity measures in place to protect against such threats.

Step-2: Train and Retain

Training and retention refer to the continuous process of educating the defender (security personnel, systems, or individuals) to recognize and respond to social engineering threats. This includes understanding various tactics employed by attackers and staying updated on emerging threats.

Step-3: Spot and Attack

In this stage, the attacker attempts to exploit vulnerabilities using social engineering tactics. This could involve phishing, pretexting, or other manipulative techniques aimed at deceiving the defender or its systems.

Step-4: Respond to Attack

The defender responds to the detected attack. This includes activating security protocols, initiating threat analysis, and taking corrective measures to mitigate the impact of the social engineering attempt. The response may involve isolating affected systems, revoking compromised credentials, or implementing additional security measures.

Step-5: Check (Is the Number of Attacks Ended)

This step involves assessing whether the ongoing attacks have ceased. Continuous monitoring is crucial, as attackers may employ persistent and evolving strategies. If attacks persist, the process continues; otherwise, it proceeds to the next stage.

Step-6: Select a New Person as Defender

In a broader organizational context, this step signifies that the defender role may transition to a new individual or team. It could represent the dynamic nature of cybersecurity responsibilities and the need for a collective defense approach.

Step-7: Stopping Condition

This condition determines when the overall process should end. It could be based on predefined criteria such as a specific time duration, a set number of attacks, or the achievement of security objectives. Regular evaluation ensures that the defense strategy remains effective and adaptive.

Step-8: End

The process concludes. This could mark the end of a specific security cycle, and the system prepares for the next iteration, incorporating lessons learned and adapting defenses based on the evolving threat landscape.

In summary, this sequence outlines a cyclical process in the context of social engineering defense. It emphasizes the need for continuous training, adaptive responses to evolving threats, and a dynamic defense approach involving various individuals or teams taking on the role of defenders. The iterative nature of the process reflects the evolving and persistent nature of social engineering threats in the modern cybersecurity landscape.

5. RESULT AND DISCUSSION

By integrating the flows of physical, financial, and informational aspects with supply chain partners, businesses need to build partnership-oriented capabilities within the digital ecosystem. To discover and leverage capabilities within the digital ecosystem, they also need to enhance their digital innovation capabilities. The importance of this research extends beyond theoretical exploration; it has practical implications for today's digital world. According to our findings, the use of diverse resources is crucial for training and prevention within the scope of cybersecurity resilience. We have identified the primary strengths influencing cybersecurity resilience in managerial processes based on previously developed ideas as shown in Figure 5. During the planning and preparation phases, prevention and training activities are driven by leveraging diverse resources and promoting continuous learning. This framework offers companies a tactical approach to maximizing cybersecurity resilience through the utilization of digitization capabilities. To enhance the framework and address new cybersecurity challenges, further research and development in this field are imperative given the ever-changing digital ecosystem. To thrive in the digital era and protect their operations, reputation, and clients, businesses must uphold cybersecurity resilience.

6. CONCLUSION

In the dynamic landscape of cybersecurity, the persistent threat of social engineering remains pronounced. Our investigation into this topic has revealed the multifaceted nature of this threat and underscored the importance of adopting innovative and adaptable defense strategies. As we conclude our study, we reflect on key insights that emphasize the critical roles of vigilance, flexibility, and collaborative efforts in combating the continuously evolving landscape of digital manipulation. A fundamental discovery from this research is the realization that no single defense strategy can offer foolproof protection against social engineering. These findings carry substantial implications for both organizations and individuals alike. For organizations, it underscores the necessity of implementing a comprehensive defense strategy that encompasses training initiatives, technological safeguards, and behavioural analysis. Future research avenues may explore more advanced machine learning algorithms, incorporate sophisticated behavioral analytics, and enhance immersive user training programs. Each advancement contributes to strengthening the collective effort to protect the digital realm from the manipulative strategies of social engineers. In today's increasingly digitized world, the knowledge gained from this research safeguards our personal privacy, integrity, and the essential trust underpinning digital interactions.

REFERENCES

Al Daajeh, S., Selous, H., Alrabaee, S., Barka, E., Breitinger, F., & Choo, K. K. R. (2022). The role of national cybersecurity strategies on the improvement of cybersecurity education. *Computers & Security*, 119, 102754. DOI: 10.1016/j.cose.2022.102754

Apostol, A. C., Cristache, N., & Năstase, M. (2022). Societal Resilience, A Key Factor in Combating Hybrid Threats. International Conference KNOWLEDGE-BASED ORGANIZATION, 28(2), 107–115. https://doi.org/DOI: 10.2478/kboo-2022-0057

Arya, S. (2021). The most effective approaches to combating cyberbullying in educational institutions. *Asian Journal of Research in Social Sciences and Humanities*, 11(10), 468–473. DOI: 10.5958/2249-7315.2021.00134.9

Black, R., Busby, J., Dalbello, G. D., De Coning, C., Maalim, H., McAllister, C., Ndiloseh, M., Smith, D., Cobar, J. F. A., Barn Hoorn, A., Bell, N., Bell-Moran, D., Broek, E., Eberlein, A., Elaw, K., Faller, J., Gander, A., Hegazi, F., Kim, K., . . . Staudenmann, J. A. (2022). *Environment of Peace: Security in a New Era of Risk*. https://doi.org/DOI: 10.55163/LCLS7037

Bradshaw, S. (2015a). Combating Cyber Threats: CSIRTs and Fostering International Cooperation on Cybersecurity. SSRN *Electronic Journal*. https://doi.org/DOI: 10.2139/ssrn.2700899

Hilgenberg, S., & Bosk, C. L. (1988). The Rise and Fall of Social Problems: A Public Arenas Model. *American Journal of Sociology*, 94(1), 53–78. DOI: 10.1086/228951

Kapoor, K., Bigdeli, A. Z., Dwivedi, Y. K., & Raman, R. (2021). How is COVID-19 altering the manufacturing landscape? A literature review of imminent challenges and management interventions. *Annals of Operation Research. Annals of Operations Research*, 335(3), 1567–1599. DOI: 10.1007/s10479-021-04397-2 PMID: 34803204

Nevarez, N. (2023). Integrating Cyber Resilience Strategies for OT Data Acquisition Devices. *The International Journal of Social Sciences (Islamabad)*, 7(30), 488–500. DOI: 10.52096/usbd.7.30.33

Orujo, Z. (2023). CYBER SECURITY: CONTEMPORARY CYBER THREATS AND NATIONAL STRATEGIES. *Distance Education in Ukraine: Innovative, Normative-Legal. Pedagogical Aspects*, 2, 100–116. DOI: 10.18372/2786-5495.1.17309

Parri, J., Patara, F., Sampietro, S., & Vicario, E. (2020). A framework for Model-Driven Engineering of resilient software-controlled systems. *Computing*, 103(4), 589–612. DOI: 10.1007/s00607-020-00841-6

Southwick, S. M., Bonanno, G. A., Masten, A. S., Panter-Brick, C., & Yehuda, R. (2014). Resilience definitions, theory, and challenges: interdisciplinary perspectives. https://doi.org/DOI: 10.3402/ejpt.v5.25338

Srivastava, S., Soni, M. K., & Pratap, A. (2023). A Critical Study of Challenges and Risk in Healthcare sector based on Cloud Computing. *2023 14th International Conference on Computing Communication and Networking Technologies (ICCCNT)*, Delhi, India, 2023, pp. 1-5, DOI: 10.1109/ICCCNT56998.2023.10307861

Stojanovic, N., & Dhabliya, R. (2023c). Empowering Edge Security An Advanced Encryption Strategies for Enhanced Cyber Resilience in Edge Computing. *Research Journal of Computer Systems and Engineering*, 4(1), 74–83. DOI: 10.52710/rjcse.65

Yadav, V., Soni, M. K., & Pratap, A. (2024). Secured Identity and Access Management for Cloud Computing Using Zero Trust Architecture. In Chaturvedi, A., Hasan, S. U., Roy, B. K., & Tsaban, B. (Eds.), *Cryptology and Network Security with Machine Learning. ICCNSML 2023. Lecture Notes in Networks and Systems* (Vol. 918). Springer., DOI: 10.1007/978-981-97-0641-9_47

Zeng, Y. (2022). AI Empowers Security Threats and Strategies for Cyber Attacks. *Procedia Computer Science*, 208, 170–175. DOI: 10.1016/j.procs.2022.10.025

Chapter 7
Securing the Weakest Link:
Compressive Approaches to Social Engineering Attack Prevention

Farooq Ahmad
https://orcid.org/0000-0002-3944-7710
Integral University, Lucknow, India

Bably Dolly
Integral University, Lucknow, India

Zohaib Hasan Khan
https://orcid.org/0000-0003-1608-8337
Integral University, Lucknow, India

ABSTRACT

In today's world, where digital interactions and online transactions are crucial for both personal and professional activities, social engineering attacks have become more common and sophisticated, threatening data security and organizational integrity. These attacks exploit a lack of awareness to gain illegal access to systems. While research includes various studies and methods for preventing these attacks, a thorough analysis of effective strategies is lacking. Current methods involve health campaigns, frameworks with human security sensors, user-focused approaches, and vulnerability models. This chapter thoroughly examines different types of social engineering attacks, such as phishing, vishing, and pretexting, highlighting the human element as the weakest link in cybersecurity. It then delves into prevention methods, stressing the need for awareness training and behavioral changes among users as a key defense. This chapter seeks to equip readers with practical insights and tools

DOI: 10.4018/979-8-3693-6665-3.ch007

to protect against social engineering attacks by integrating current research and best practices.

1. INTRODUCTION

1. Social engineering attacks exploit the most vulnerable point by targeting the weakest link. This approach relies on a knowledge imbalance between the attacker and the victim (Hatfield, 2018), where the attacker uses their superior knowledge to gain control. Technocrats, who possess specialized skills or knowledge, like in dentistry or economic planning, often play a role in this dynamic. Asymmetric knowledge arises when certain individuals or groups have more expertise or information than others in a particular area. Hatfield (2018)discusses the evolution of social engineering attacks from 1842 to the present, but the chapter's utility is limited as it primarily covers the historical development of social engineering.

A social engineering attacker is someone seeking access to confidential information or financial resources. The attacker creates discomfort to manipulate the victim and often reveals their malicious intent during the process. According to the National Institute of Standards and Technology (NIST), social engineering involves deceiving individuals into divulging information, such as passwords, to compromise systems or networks (Scarfone, Souppaya, Cody, & Orebaugh, 2008). The effectiveness of social engineering attacks relies on successfully deceiving the target into sharing personal information (Junger, Montoya, & Overink, 2017)

1. Social engineering attacks have progressed to include methods such as phone calls, emails, and face-to-face encounters. These attacks encompass techniques like impersonation, targeting online communities or social media, automated schemes, and semantic manipulation. As information technology has advanced, so have the methods of social engineering. Research indicates that attackers use psychological manipulation, including social engineering and phishing, to trick employees into making security errors or disclosing sensitive information (Syed, 2019). According to Verizon's Data Breach Investigation Report, the most common incidents involve phishing and pretexting (Verizon, Nathan, & Scobell, 2020). Since these are forms of social engineering, the attacks continue until they achieve their goals. Additionally, social engineering can manifest in online interactions through scams (Shaari, Kamaluddin, Fauzi, & Mohd, 2019), (Rahman, 2020), cyberbullying, the sharing of harmful content, privacy breaches

(Ming, Shi, & Taha, 2020), and non-financial information disclosure (Jamil, Hassan, Salleh, & Yaakob, 2020).

Social Engineering Attack refers to cyber security threats where malicious activities are carried out through manipulating human interactions. Hackers use psychological tactics to induce users into making security mistakes or revealing sensitive personal information, such as bank account details or identification numbers.

Social engineering typically involves multiple steps. The attacker first collects background information on the victim and identifies vulnerabilities that can be exploited. They aim to build trust with the victim, as it is often easier to deceive someone into providing a password or one-time passcode than to hack the system directly.

Research shows that the weakest link in security is often the human element - those who accept scenarios or individuals at face value.

Social engineering attacks have consistently targeted companies over the years and have grown increasingly sophisticated. It's essential for businesses to conduct thorough research and utilize effective tools to stay ahead of fraudsters.

Social engineering attacks have become a frequent issue for enterprises and have grown more sophisticated over time. With no foreseeable end to cybercrimes, hackers continue to develop more inventive techniques to trick employees into disclosing sensitive credentials.

Companies must now conduct thorough research and use the appropriate tools to stay ahead of fraudsters.

1. PurpleSec (2021) reports that 98% of cyberattacks involve social engineering (PurpleSec, 2021). The report also highlights that new employees are particularly vulnerable, with 60% of IT professionals identifying recent hires as high-risk targets for these tactics.

Figure 1. cyberattacks rely on social engineering

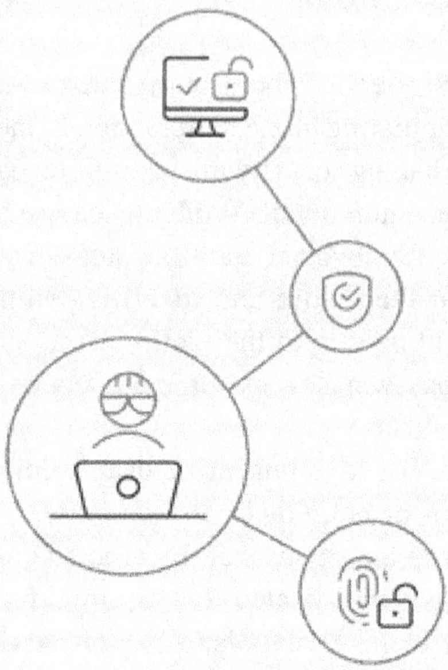

Social engineering attacks employ deception, coercion, or other interpersonal tactics to achieve fraudulent outcomes. According to Jenny Radcliffe, founder of Human-Centered Security, criminals exploit fear, uncertainty, and doubt—referred to as FUD in the industry—to create an atmosphere of insecurity in people's minds (Tanium, 2020, para. 11).

Prevention methods for social engineering attacks include health campaign strategies and tactics, TV ads, informational pamphlets, and social media (Abe & Soltys, 2019). Other approaches involve the ethics of penetration testing(Hatfield, 2019), using a human as a security sensor framework (Heartfield & Loukas, 2018), personality information processing models (Frauenstein & Flowerday, 2020), characteristic user frameworks (Albladi & Weir, 2018), game-based analysis (Yasin, Fatima, Liu, Yasin, & Wang, 2019), predicting individuals' vulnerability (Albladi & Weir, 2020), computer security policies (Yusof & Singh, 2021), and cybersecurity practices (Pitchan, Omar, & Ghazali, 2019).

Additional research has explored topics related to privacy and security van Schaik, Jansen, Onibokun, Camp, & Kusev, 2018; (DasGupta, Mobasheri, & Yero, 2019;Sánchez, Domingo-Ferrer, & Martínez, 2018;

Zhang & Gupta, 2018; Zhang et al., 2021). Studies focusing on the behavioral aspects of cybersecurity are detailed in (Lahcen, Caulkins, Mohapatra, & Kumar, 2020) and (Velayudhan & Somasundaram, 2019). The most recent research on Sybil attacks within social networks can be found in (Asadian & Javadi, 2018).

Figure 2. Why Social Engineering

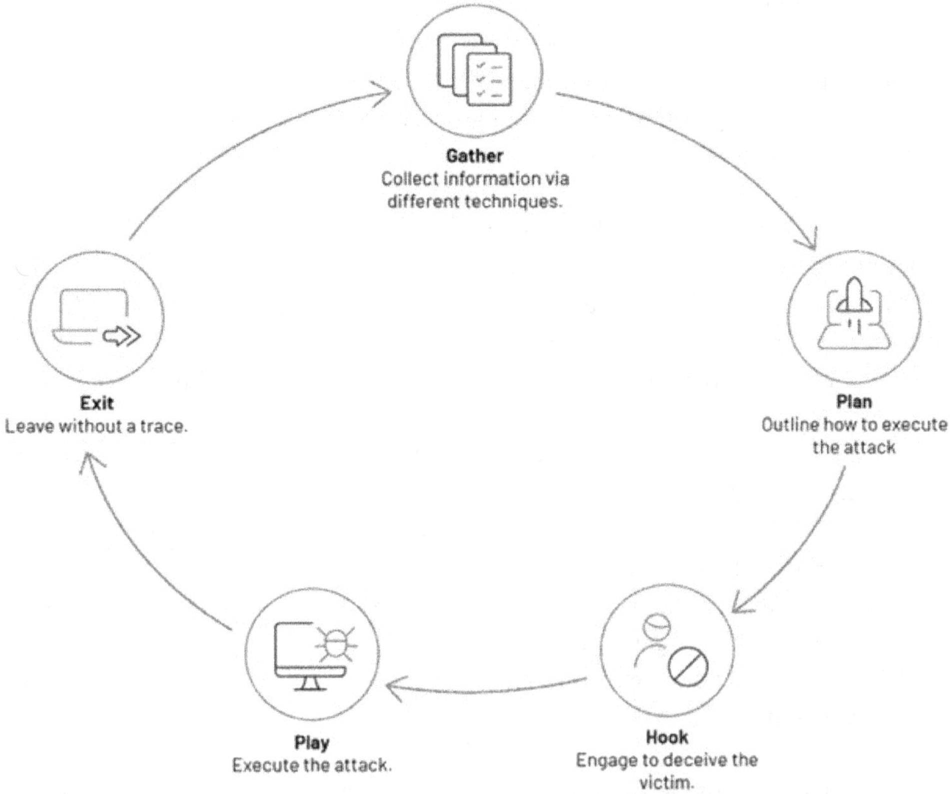

1. This chapter discussed current methods for addressing attacks, such as health campaigns aimed at preventing social engineering attacks, particularly focusing on the psychological impacts of various techniques and general knowledge about these attacks (Abe & Soltys, 2019). However, the previous research did not include an analysis of the results. While penetration testing can help guard against social engineering attacks, it should be viewed as part of a broader ethical framework for social engineering in cybersecurity (Hatfield, 2019). Additionally, employing a human as a security sensor framework may be crucial for detecting deception-based threats. Future research could investigate whether cybersecurity could benefit from "super-recognizers," similar to their use in policing (Heartfield & Loukas, 2018).
2. Models of risk perception and precautionary behavior can assist users in avoiding methodological errors. The literature suggests behavioral interventions to enhance security and privacy for Facebook users. Future research should examine these

factors as predictors of perceived risk and precautionary behavior (van Schaik, Jansen, Onibokun, Camp, & Kusev, 2018).

This chapter will explore the concept of social engineering and outline best practices for avoiding common social engineering attacks.

Main contributions of the study:

1. Identification of Vulnerabilities: Highlights key weaknesses in current security practices related to social engineering.
2. Innovative Prevention Strategies: Proposes new and effective methods for preventing social engineering attacks.
3. Practical Solutions: Offers actionable recommendations and tools to improve organizational defenses.
4. Case Studies: Provides real-world examples to demonstrate the effectiveness of proposed approaches.
5. Impact Assessment: Evaluates the potential improvements in security posture and reduction in risk of social engineering attacks.
6. Enhanced Awareness: Improves awareness and training programs to better prepare individuals against social engineering tactics.
7. Policy Recommendations: Suggests policy changes and best practices to strengthen organizational defenses.

These contributions can help advance the field by addressing gaps and enhancing security practices.

2. WHAT IS SOCIAL ENGINEERING

Social engineering refers to various malicious activities carried out through human interactions. It employs psychological manipulation to deceive users into making security errors or disclosing sensitive information.

Social engineering attacks occur in several stages. Initially, the attacker researches the victim to collect background information, identifying vulnerabilities and weak security protocols. Next, the attacker works to build the victim's trust and creates conditions that lead the victim to violate security practices, such as disclosing sensitive information or granting access to crucial resources.

Figure 3. Social Engineering Attack Lifecycle

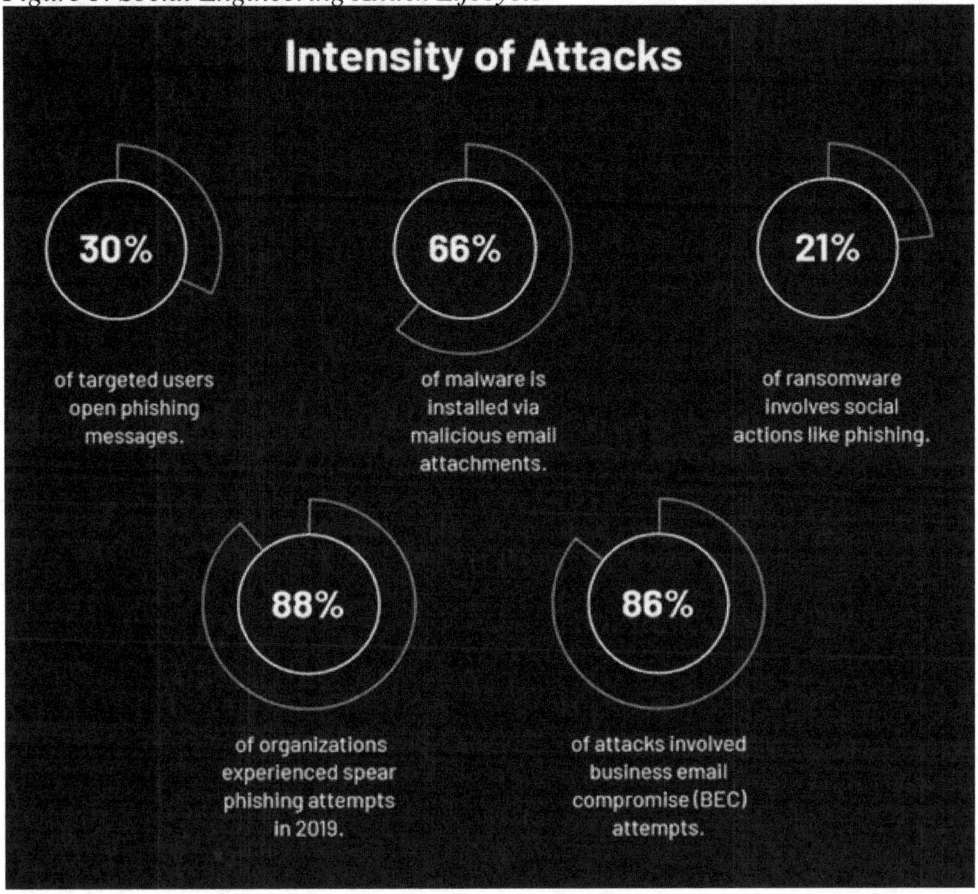

Social engineering is a type of cyberattack where criminals exploit psychological manipulation to lead unsuspecting users into making security errors and divulging confidential information. This tactic leverages human emotions such as fear, curiosity, greed, and anger to deceive victims into clicking on malicious links or engaging in physical tailgating attacks. Social engineering attackers typically pursue one of two objectives:

- They aim to corrupt data to disrupt and cause inconvenience to the organization.
- They seek to steal information, money, or gain unauthorized access.

Figure 4. Social engineering is the practice of psychologically manipulating users into making security errors and revealing their confidential information.

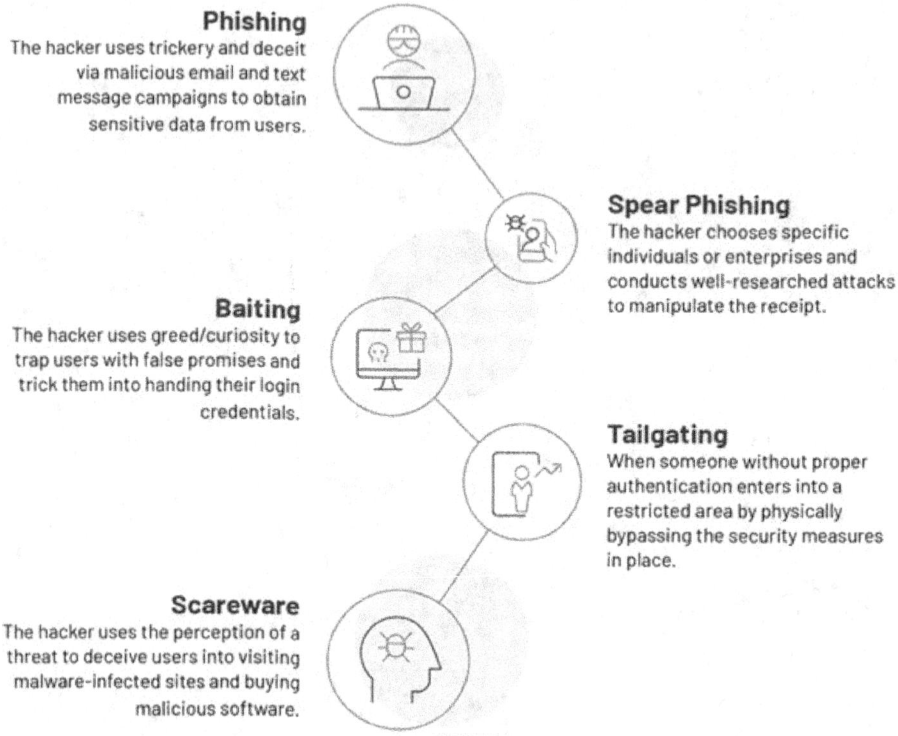

3. HOW DOES SOCIAL ENGINEERING WORK?

Most social engineering attacks involve direct interaction between attackers and victims. Rather than relying on brute force, attackers work to earn the victim's trust. They typically follow these steps to deceive their targets:

1. **Prepare:** Collect all necessary information from the victim.
2. **Infiltrate:** Develop a relationship and build trust.
3. **Expose Victim:** Identify and exploit weaknesses once trust is established.
4. **Disengage:** The victim performs the desired action.

Figure 5. How Social Engineering Works?

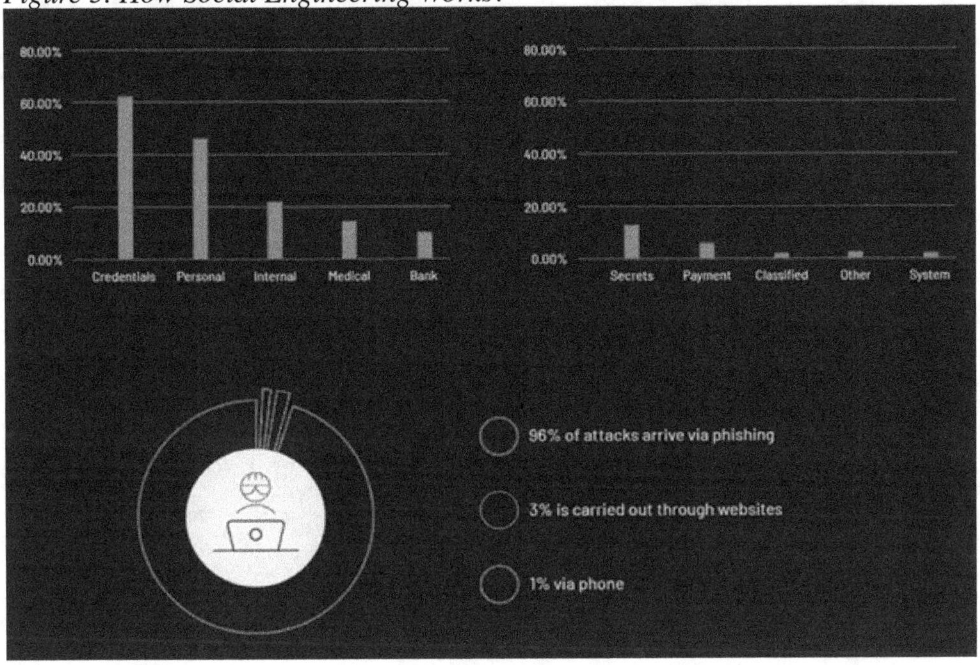

4. WHAT MAKES SOCIAL ENGINEERING DANGEROUS?

Social engineering is dangerous because it exploits human error rather than software vulnerabilities. User mistakes are more unpredictable and challenging to detect compared to malware intrusions.

Figure 6. Intensity of Social engineering Attacks

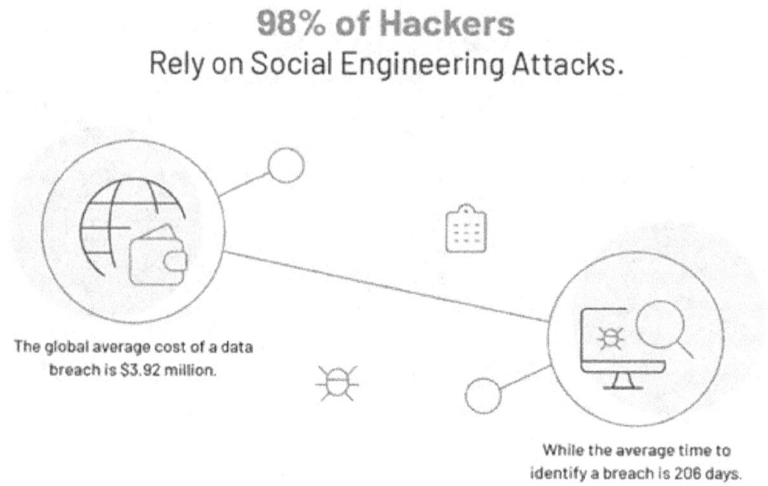

5. TYPE OF SOCIAL ENGINEERING AND CHALLENGES

Social engineering attacks can bypass all forms of hardware or software designed to prevent cyber threats. These attacks are difficult to counteract through technology alone because they target users who interact with both hardware and software. As a result, preventing social engineering attacks requires focusing on user education and awareness. These attacks are highly varied and frequently evolve, adapting to new techniques and methods. The following explains the various types of attacks and the challenges of social engineering attacks.

Figure 7. Five most common Social Engineering Attack Techniques

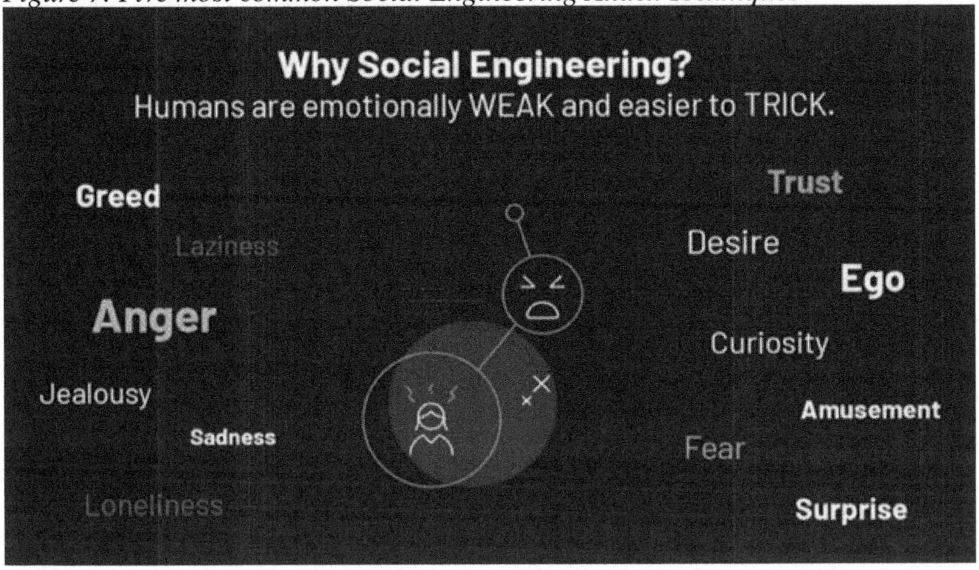

1) Phishing
   1. Hackers send altered messages designed to appear legitimate, prompting users to follow instructions or suggestions contained in the messages. Common examples of phishing include email and website phishing. Some phishing attacks also employ malware, bots, and trojans to further exploit user access (Hijji & Alam, 2021).
      1. Vishing, a subset of phishing, involves using telephone communication to deceive users into divulging confidential information such as PINs and One-Time Passwords. Hackers employ psychological tactics, such as creating threats, inducing anxiety, or presenting false good news, to trick victims into revealing sensitive details without realizing they are being scammed. Common examples of vishing include Impersonation on Help Desk (IHD) attacks and Robocalls (Salahdine & Kaabouch, 2019). IHD attacks involve hackers pretending to be high-ranking individuals to manipulate help desk employees into providing specific information or services. Robocalls use Voice over Internet Protocol (VoIP) and text-to-speech technology to exploit publicly available phone numbers, targeting mobile phones, landlines, and office phones. These robocalls typically offer services or products or claim to solve problems to lure victims into the scam.

In addition to vishing, phishing attacks also occur through SMS technology, known as smishing. Smishing operates similarly to email phishing attacks: hackers send text messages to users with urgent instructions or important information, using phone numbers that may be publicly available or randomly chosen. Smishing is particularly dangerous because it is more personal, which can make victims less suspicious and more likely to fall for the scam.

Another type of phishing attack is pharming, where hackers redirect users from a legitimate website to a fraudulent one to steal information or money. A similar concept is the man-in-the-middle attack, which involves intercepting and altering communication between two parties. Unlike pharming, which typically involves redirecting web traffic, man-in-the-middle attacks often exploit vulnerabilities in email exchanges, sometimes using Trojan horses to manipulate the communication between the recipient and sender (Gomes, Reis, & Alturas, 2020).

A new phishing technique is Angler phishing, where hackers create fake profiles on a company's customer service social media accounts to target the company's customers. The primary targets for this attack are individuals who have expressed dissatisfaction or satisfaction with the company’s services on social media. By exploiting these sentiments, hackers use Angler phishing to deceive users into disclosing credentials or personal information.

2) Spear Phishing

Spear phishing is a targeted form of social engineering in which the attacker conducts thorough research on the victim's personal and professional background to create a convincing and specific pretext for the attack.

Spear phishing is a targeted phishing attack where hackers focus on specific individuals by researching their personal and professional details. This type of attack is similar to whaling, which targets high-level executives or influential figures within an organization. When spear phishing is combined with the whaling approach, the impact on the organization can be particularly severe and damaging. For example, the fraudster might pretend they are organizing a surprise birthday party for a friend and request the victim’s assistance to make it happen.

3) Baiting

This technique exploits the curiosity of organizational members by using physical electronic media to launch attacks, such as USB drives infected with malware or trojans [38]. For example, the fraudster might leave a malware-infected, convincingly designed flash drive in a low-profile location, such as a bathroom or elevator, within the company. The drive may be labeled with enticing names like "payroll list" or "appraisal list" to tempt employees into plugging it into their computers.

4) Tailgating

Piggybacking, tailgating, or trailing and pretending attacks exploit organizational members to gain unauthorized access. Hackers simply follow employees who have legitimate access, bypassing security perimeters within the organization(Yasin, Fatima, Liu, Yasin, & Wang, 2019; Wang, Sun, & Zhu, 2020; Wang, Zhu, & Sun, 2021). For example, an attacker might engage in casual conversation with an employee in the lobby or parking lot to gain enough familiarity to enter the office and pass the front desk.

5) Scareware

This attack utilizes pop-ups on windows or browsers that appear during user activities, such as visiting a website or when the internet suddenly disconnects. Some web pages are embedded with scripts or codes that generate pop-ups designed to target victims, often using flashing colors or alarming sounds. These pop-ups may present urgent messages that prompt users to click immediately, such as warnings about viruses infecting their computer or enticing advertisements (Salahdine & Kaabouch, 2019). Examples include fake PC Health Check programs and antivirus updaters that scare victims into purchasing unnecessary diagnostic and repair services.

6) Grooming

One of the latest social engineering techniques is grooming, which combines psychological tactics with information technology to obtain confidential information from potential victims of pedophilia. Grooming often involves using SMS, email, and telephone communication to build trust and manipulate victims, setting up a trap to exploit them (Zambrano, Torres, & Flores, 2019).

7) Pretexting

Hackers gather public information from websites, social media, and telephone directories to link details about the victim's activities or potential involvement in specific events. Pretexting is a phishing technique that involves two-way communication with the victim. This interaction can take the form of offering employment or assistance, requesting personal information, or confirming the receipt of a prize (Salahdine & Kaabouch, 2019).

8) Profile Cloning

This technique leverages publicly available information, such as social media profiles, to impersonate someone whose profile has been cloned to extract sensitive information from others (Algarni, Xu, & Chan, 2017; Kumar, Dabas, & Komal, 2019). Publicly accessible details, including images, videos, full names, and conversational styles, are used to create a convincing fake identity. Hackers may employ the IHD concept by targeting influential figures, like "B," and using profile cloning to contact the victim. They then use indirect social engineering methods, such as phishing or pretexting, to obtain confidential information from the victim.

9) Face-to-Face Interaction

Social engineers frequently employ this technique by meeting victims face-to-face and exploiting their psychological vulnerabilities. This approach often involves gaining the victim's trust through acts of assistance, persuasion, or emotional appeals to secure physical access or obtain sensitive information (Shaari, Kamaluddin, Fauzi, & Mohd, 2019).

10) Shoulder Surfing

However, this technique is often used by individuals without advanced social engineering skills, exploiting human nature and the victim's lack of awareness about their surroundings. For example, when someone is using a laptop or computer to access confidential information, a person nearby might take advantage of the situation, even if they seem uninterested in the system (Salahdine & Kaabouch, 2019).

11) Quid Pro Quo Attacks

Quid Pro Quo is an attack that seeks reciprocity for providing a free service or product (Salahdine & Kaabouch, 2019). This social engineering concept follows the principle of "There Is No Free Lunch," where the hacker offers something of value in exchange for important information or other favors from the victim. The attack involves an agreement where the victim requests help from the hacker and, in return, must provide sensitive information or another form of compensation.

12) Dumpster Diving Attacks

This attack exploits human weaknesses by targeting discarded or unfiltered documents and information, whether physical or digital. Items thrown away or deleted, such as files or papers, can be valuable to data collectors conducting Dumpster Diving attacks (Salahdine & Kaabouch, 2019).

13) Diversion Theft Attacks

This attack involves using courier companies to introduce malware or rootkits into computers or systems being delivered to a company [30]. The goal is for the malware to be installed and remain undetected, gaining access to the company's network once the system is put into use.

14) File Masquerade

This type of attack happens when users are not fully aware of all the files on their computer or external storage devices. Users may be confident that their systems are free from malware or trojans. However, malware or trojans are hidden within user files, so when users encounter files, they typically open, they do so without hesitation, inadvertently executing the malicious files (Yasin, Fatima, Liu, Yasin, & Wang, 2019).

15) Reverse Social Engineering

Hackers engineer situations that lead victims into a Reverse Social Engineering trap. They create core issues within the organization and then approach victims, either directly or indirectly, offering to resolve these problems (Parthy & Rajendran, 2019). For example, they might disrupt a system, causing it to malfunction, and then provide assistance to restore functionality, during which they install programs that grant them administrative access through the victim's computer.

16) Water-Holing

High-traffic websites are often targeted and compromised by hackers who embed malware or trojans. The Water-holing technique relies on waiting for users to click on links or download applications from these hacked sites, establishing a two-way communication channel between the hacker and the victim (Wang, Sun, & Zhu, 2020).

Figure 8. Common Compromised Attributes

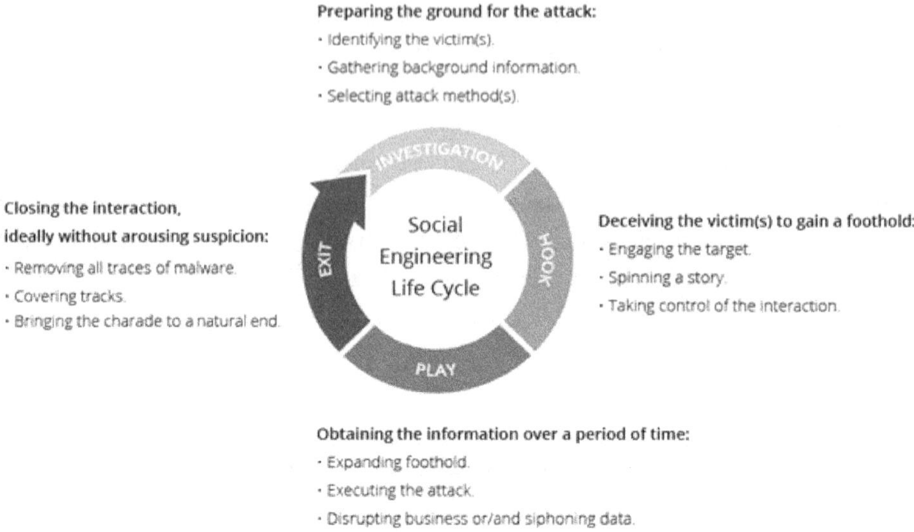

6. WARNING SIGNS OF SOCIAL ENGINEERING ATTACKS

One of the most effective ways to defend against social engineering attacks is to recognize the warning signs and avoid falling victim to them. Some common warning signs include:

- Requesting urgent assistance
- Asking you to verify personal information
- Displaying excessive friendliness or eagerness
- Appearing nervous when questioned
- Overloading with excessive details
- Presenting offers that seem too good to be true
- Threatening consequences if their demands are not met

7. BEST DEFENSES FOR SOCIAL ENGINEERING ATTACKS

1. Ignore and delete requests for personal information.
   1. Avoid opening emails from unknown or suspicious sources.

2. Use endpoint protection systems.
3. Set spam filters to the highest level.
4. Implement two-factor or multi-factor authentication for user verification.
5. Regularly back up important data.
6. Provide training for employees.

8. SOCIAL ENGINEERING ATTACK PATTERNS

Social engineering attacks generally follow a similar pattern. First, the hacker selects a target and plans their approach. They then interact with the target to establish trust. Once trust is built, they execute the attack. Finally, after obtaining their objective, they erase any evidence of their attack.

CNN conducted an experiment to demonstrate the simplicity of executing these types of attacks (Algarni, Xu, & Chan, 2017). In the experiment, a hacker was able to acquire a CNN tech reporter's home address and cell phone number by contacting a furniture store where the reporter had recently made a purchase. The hacker obtained the store's name from a tweet in which the reporter had mentioned his recent purchase.

9. BEST PRACTICES TO PREVENT SOCIAL ENGINEERING ATTACKS

Be mindful of what you share, but there's no need to be overly paranoid about these attacks. Prevention is possible with these steps:

- **Set spam filters to high.** Check your email settings and adjust the spam filters to the highest level to minimize unwanted messages.
- **Avoid using the same password across multiple accounts.** If one account is compromised, others could be at risk.
- **Implement two-factor or multi-factor authentication.** Adding extra security layers, like security questions, captchas, or SMS codes, is essential beyond just a password.
- **Change passwords immediately if you suspect they've been exposed.** Act quickly to update all passwords if you believe a spammer has obtained them.
- **Educate employees.** Ensure they are aware of the latest social engineering threats and know how to respond cautiously.

10. LIMITATIONS OF THE STUDY

1. **Scope of Research**:** The study may focus primarily on certain types of social engineering attacks, potentially overlooking others or emerging threats.
2. **Generalizability:** Findings might be specific to particular organizational contexts or demographics and may not be broadly applicable across different industries or regions.
3. **Implementation Challenges:** Practical difficulties in applying proposed preventive measures could limit their effectiveness or adoption in real-world scenarios.
4. **Evolving Threat Landscape:** The rapidly changing nature of social engineering tactics might render some recommendations less relevant over time.
5. **Resource Constraints:** Recommendations may require substantial resources for implementation, which could be a barrier for smaller organizations.
6. **Behavioral Factors:** The study might not fully address the complexities of human behavior and psychology, which are crucial in preventing social engineering attacks.
7. **Data Limitations:** The study might rely on limited or anecdotal data, which could affect the reliability and validity of its conclusions.
8. **Assessment Metrics:** There could be limitations in the metrics used to evaluate the effectiveness of the proposed approaches, potentially impacting the accuracy of the results.

11. PREVENTING SOCIAL ENGINEERING

Social engineers exploit emotions like curiosity or fear to execute their schemes and ensnare victims. Stay cautious if you receive alarming emails, encounter enticing offers on websites, or find unexpected digital media. Maintaining vigilance can help you guard against most social engineering attacks in the digital world.

Moreover, the following tips can enhance your vigilance against social engineering hacks.

- Avoid opening emails and attachments from unknown or suspicious sources. If you're unfamiliar with the sender, do not respond. Even if the sender is known but the message seems dubious, verify its authenticity through other means, such as a phone call or directly from a service provider's website. Keep in mind that email addresses can be spoofed, so messages appearing to come from trusted sources may still be from attackers.

- Implement multifactor authentication. Since user credentials are a prime target for attackers, multifactor authentication adds an extra layer of protection for your accounts in case of a system breach. Tools like Imperva Login Protect offer an easy-to-deploy 2FA solution to enhance the security of your applications.
- Be cautious with tempting offers. If something seems too good to be true, verify its legitimacy by researching it online. This can help you discern whether it's a genuine opportunity or a potential scam.
- Keep your antivirus and antimalware software up to date. Ensure automatic updates are enabled, or make it a routine to manually download the latest updates each day. Regularly verify that updates have been applied and perform system scans to detect any potential infections.
- Penetration Testing: Even if you believe your security protocols are effective and well-known, it's beneficial to test them. Consider hiring a network security expert to attempt to breach your network using standard social engineering techniques. For instance, sending a phishing email from a fake address to all employees can expose the strengths and weaknesses of your security measures.

12. CONCLUSION

In the ongoing battle against social engineering attacks, this chapter has provided a comprehensive examination of current approaches and strategies designed to fortify the weakest link in organizational security—human behavior. In this chapter, we've explored social engineering attacks on social media, including their principles and various types. Unfortunately, relying solely on security measures isn't enough to prevent these attacks, as a social engineer with little technical expertise can still compromise even the most secure systems. The frequency of social engineering attacks has surged, resulting in significant emotional and financial harm to individuals and organizations. Given the critical role of information in both personal and professional contexts, it is essential to safeguard it from malicious actors. Hence, investing in cybersecurity awareness is crucial to train individuals to be more vigilant and aware.

Our exploration has revealed several key achievements in the field:

1. Enhanced Awareness Training: One of the primary successes highlighted is the development and implementation of sophisticated awareness training programs. These programs have proven effective in educating employees about various social engineering tactics, thereby reducing susceptibility to such attacks.

2. Behavioral Analytics Integration: The integration of behavioral analytics into security systems has emerged as a significant advancement. By leveraging data-driven insights, organizations can now identify and respond to anomalous behavior patterns that may indicate social engineering attempts.
3. Multi-Factor Authentication (MFA) Adoption: The widespread adoption of multi-factor authentication has been a crucial achievement. MFA provides an additional layer of security that mitigates the risk of unauthorized access, even if an attacker successfully obtains user credentials through social engineering.
4. Development of Comprehensive Policies: The establishment of clear, comprehensive security policies and procedures has been instrumental in standardizing responses to social engineering threats. These policies ensure a consistent approach to handling potential breaches and reinforce organizational security posture.

Looking ahead, there are several promising areas for future research and development:

1. Advanced AI and Machine Learning: Future research should focus on leveraging artificial intelligence and machine learning to develop more sophisticated tools for detecting and preventing social engineering attacks. AI-driven solutions can enhance the accuracy of threat detection and automate responses to emerging threats.
2. Personalized Training Programs: Tailoring awareness training programs to individual roles and responsibilities within an organization could further improve their effectiveness. Research into personalized training modules that address specific threats relevant to different job functions could offer significant benefits.
3. Cross-Organizational Collaboration: Encouraging collaboration between organizations to share information and best practices related to social engineering threats could foster a more resilient defense network. Developing frameworks for secure information sharing and joint response strategies will be essential.
4. Exploration of Behavioral Economics: Integrating insights from behavioral economics into social engineering prevention strategies could provide a deeper understanding of human decision-making processes. This could lead to more effective interventions and training methods that align with natural human behaviors.

In conclusion, while significant progress has been made in securing the weakest link against social engineering attacks, ongoing innovation and adaptation are crucial. By continuing to advance our approaches and explore new avenues of research, we can better protect individuals and organizations from the evolving landscape of social engineering threats.

REFERENCES

Abe, N., & Soltys, M. (2019). Deploying health campaign strategies to defend against social engineering threats. *Procedia Computer Science, 159*, 824–831. DOI: 10.1016/j.procs.2019.09.213

Albladi, S. M., & Weir, G. R. S. (2018). User characteristics that influence judgment of social engineering attacks in social networks. *Human-Centric Computing and Information Sciences, 8*(1), 5. DOI: 10.1186/s13673-018-0143-8

Albladi, S. M., & Weir, G. R. S. (2020). Predicting individuals' vulnerability to social engineering in social networks. *Cybersecurity, 3*(1). DOI: 10.1093/cybsec/tyaa011

Algarni, A., Xu, Y., & Chan, T. (2017). An empirical study on the susceptibility to social engineering in social networking sites: The case of Facebook. *European Journal of Information Systems, 26*(6), 661–687. https://doi.org/DOI: 10.1080/0960085X.2017.1327237

Asadian, H., & Javadi, H. H. S. (2018). Identification of Sybil attacks on social networks using a framework based on user interactions. *Security and Privacy, 1*(2), e19. DOI: 10.1002/spy2.19

Bryman, A., & Bell, E. (2011). *Business research methods* (3rd ed.). Oxford University Press.

Bullee, J. W., & Junger, M. (2020). How effective are social engineering interventions? A meta-analysis. *Information & Computer Security, 28*(5), 801–830. https://doi.org/DOI: 10.1108/ICS-01-2020-0010

Das, A., Baki, S., El Aassal, A., Verma, R., & Dunbar, A. (2020). SoK: A comprehensive reexamination of phishing research from the security perspective. *IEEE Communications Surveys & Tutorials, 22*(1), 671–708. https://doi.org/DOI: 10.1109/COMST.2019.2957522

DasGupta, B., Mobasheri, N., & Yero, I. G. (2019). On analyzing and evaluating privacy measures for social networks under active attack. *Information Sciences, 473*, 87–100. DOI: 10.1016/j.ins.2018.11.038

Frauenstein, E. D., & Flowerday, S. (2020). Susceptibility to phishing on social network sites: A personality information processing model. *Computers & Security, 94*, 101862. DOI: 10.1016/j.cose.2020.101862

Gomes, V., Reis, J., & Alturas, B. (2020). Social engineering and the dangers of phishing. In **Proceedings of the Iberian Conference on Information Systems and Technologies** (pp. 24–27). DOI: 10.23919/CISTI49556.2020.9140445

Hatfield, J. M. (2018). Social engineering in cybersecurity: The evolution of a concept. *. *Computers & Security*, 73, 102–113. DOI: 10.1016/j.cose.2017.10.008

Hatfield, J. M. (2019). Virtuous human hacking: The ethics of social engineering in penetration-testing. *Computers & Security, 83*, 354–366. DOI: 10.1016/j.cose.2018.12.003

Heartfield, R., & Loukas, G. (2018). Detecting semantic social engineering attacks with the weakest link: Implementation and empirical evaluation of a human-as-a-security-sensor framework. *Computers & Security, 76*, 101–127. DOI: 10.1016/j.cose.2018.03.001

Hijji, M., & Alam, G. (2021). A multivocal literature review on growing social engineering based cyber-attacks/threats during the COVID-19 pandemic: Challenges and prospective solutions. *IEEE Access, 9*, 7152–7169. https://doi.org/DOI: 10.1109/ACCESS.2021.3050770

Jamil, A., Hassan, M. S., Salleh, N. M., & Yaakob, R. (2020). Non-financial risk disclosure: From narratives to an index based on Delphi technique. *Asian Journal of Government, 14*, 1–19. DOI: 10.17576/AJAG-2020-14-10

Junger, M., Montoya, L., & Overink, F.-J. (2017). Priming and warnings are not effective to prevent social engineering attacks. *Computers in Human Behavior, 66*, 75–87. https://doi.org/DOI: 10.1016/j.chb.2016.09.045

Khidzir, N. Z., Ahmed, S. A., & Guan, T. T. (2019). Management policies for the prevention technique of social engineering (SoE) attacks in the organization. *IJCSNS International Journal of Computer Science and Network Security, 19*(10), 78–82. DOI: 10.22937/IJCSNS.2019.19.10.11

Kumar, N., & Dabas, P., & Komal. (2019). Detection and prevention of profile cloning in online social networks. In *Proceedings of the 5th International Conference on Signal Processing and Computing Control (ISPCC)* (pp. 287–291). DOI: 10.1109/ISPCC48220.2019.8988394

Lahcen, R. A. M., Caulkins, B., Mohapatra, R., & Kumar, M. (2020). Review and insight on the behavioral aspects of cybersecurity. *Cybersecurity, 3*(1), 10. DOI: 10.1093/cybsec/tyaa003

Ming, T. S., Shi, N. L., & Taha, A. M. (2020). Awareness of the risks and dangers of social networking: Exploration on four types of Malaysian secondary schools. *Jurnal Komunikasi, Malaysian Journal of Communication, 36*(1), 147–165. DOI: 10.17576/JKMJC-2020-3601-09

O'Sullivan, D. (2019, October 18). We asked a hacker to try and steal a CNN tech reporter's data. Here's what happened. *CNN*. https://www.cnn.com/2019/10/18/tech/reporter-hack/index.html

Parthy, P. P., & Rajendran, G. (2019). Identification and prevention of social engineering attacks on an enterprise. In **Proceedings of the International Carnahan Conference on Security Technology (ICCST)** (pp. 1–5). DOI: 10.1109/CCST.2019.8888441

Pitchan, M. A., Omar, S. Z., & Ghazali, A. H. A. (2019). Amalan keselamatan siber pengguna internet terhadap buli siber, pornografi, E-mel phishing dan pembelian dalam talian. *Jurnal Komunikasi, Malaysian Journal of Communication, 35*(3), 212–227. https://doi.org/DOI: 10.17576/jkom-2019-3503-14

PurpleSec. (2021). 2021 cyber security statistics: The ultimate list of stats, data & trends. https://purplesec.us/resources/cyber-security-statistics/

Rahman, M. R. A. (2020). Online scammers and their mules in Malaysia. *Jurnal Undang-Undang dan Masyarakat, 26*(2020), 65–72. DOI: 10.17576/juum-2020-26-08

Salahdine, F., & Kaabouch, N. (2019). Social engineering attacks: A survey. *Future Internet, 11*(4). https://doi.org/DOI: 10.3390/fi11040065

Sánchez, D., Domingo-Ferrer, J., & Martínez, S. (2018). Co-utile disclosure of private data in social networks. *Information Sciences, 441*, 50–65. DOI: 10.1016/j.ins.2018.03.009

Scarfone, K., Souppaya, M., Cody, A., & Orebaugh, A. (2008). *Technical guide to information security testing and assessment recommendations of the National Institute of Standards and Technology (SP 800-115) *. NIST Special Publication, 800, 1–80. Retrieved from https://csrc.nist.gov/publications/detail/sp/800-115/final

Schaab, P., Beckers, K., & Pape, S. (2017). Social engineering defence mechanisms and counteracting training strategies. *Information & Computer Security, 25*(2), 206–222. DOI: 10.1108/ICS-03-2017-0012

Shaari, A. H., Kamaluddin, M. R., Fauzi, W. F. P., & Mohd, M. (2019). Online-dating romance scam in Malaysia: An analysis of online conversations between scammers and victims. *GEMA Online Journal of Language Studies, 19*(1), 97–115. DOI: 10.17576/gema-2019-1901-06

Syed, R. (2019). Enterprise reputation threats on social media: A case of data breach framing. *Journal of Strategic Information Systems, 28*(3), 257–274. DOI: 10.1016/j.jsis.2019.01.003

Tanium. (2020, October 19). Your people are being hacked: How to defend against social engineering during WFH. *CIO*. https://www.cio.com/article/190874/your-people-are-being-hacked-how-to-defend-against-social-engineering-during-wfh.html

van Schaik, P., Jansen, J., Onibokun, J., Camp, J., & Kusev, P. (2018). Security and privacy in online social networking: Risk perceptions and precautionary behaviour. *Computers in Human Behavior, 78*, 283–297. DOI: 10.1016/j.chb.2017.09.010

Velayudhan, S. P., & Somasundaram, M. S. B. S. (2019). Compromised account detection in online social networks: A survey. *Concurrency and Computation: Practice and Experience, 31*(20), 1–15. DOI: 10.1002/cpe.5623

Verizon, N. A. J., & Scobell, A. (2020). *2020 Data Breach Investigations Report*. Retrieved from https://enterprise.verizon.com/resources/reports/2020-data-breach-investigations-report.pdf

Wang, Z., Sun, L., & Zhu, H. (2020). Defining social engineering in cyber-security. *IEEE Access, 8*, 85094–85115. https://doi.org/DOI: 10.1109/ACCESS.2020.2993060

Wang, Z., Zhu, H., & Sun, L. (2021). Social engineering in cybersecurity: Effect mechanisms, human vulnerabilities and attack methods. *IEEE Access, 9*, 11895–11910. https://doi.org/DOI: 10.1109/ACCESS.2021.3050294

Yasin, A., Fatima, R., Liu, L., Yasin, A., & Wang, J. (2019). Contemplating social engineering studies and attack scenarios: A review study. *Security and Privacy, 2*(4), 1–14. DOI: 10.1002/spy2.124

Yusof, Y. M., & Singh, D. (2021). Civil servants awareness guideline towards computer security policy: A case study at the manpower department, ministry of human resources. *Asia-Pacific Journal of Information Technology and Multimedia, 10*(8), 86–99. DOI: 10.17576/apjitm-2021-1001-08

Zambrano, P., Torres, J., & Flores, P. (2019). How does grooming fit into social engineering? In *Advances in Intelligent Systems and Computing* (Vol. 924, pp. 629–639). Springer., DOI: 10.1007/978-3-030-14471-8_63

Zhang, C., Jiang, H., Cheng, X., Zhao, F., Cai, Z., & Tian, Z. (2021). Utility analysis on privacy-preservation algorithms for online social networks: An empirical study. *Personal and Ubiquitous Computing, 25*(6), 1063–1079. https://doi.org/DOI: 10.1007/s00779-021-01509-3

Zhang, Z., & Gupta, B. B. (2018). Social media security and trustworthiness: Overview and new direction. *Future Generation Computer Systems, 86*, 914–925. DOI: 10.1016/j.future.2018.04.055

Chapter 8
Protecting Against Social Engineering Using Wireshark:
Effective Strategies With Real-World Examples

Manvi Mishra
SRMS College of Engineering and Technology, Bareilly, India

Md Shadab Hussain
SRMS College of Engineering and Technology, Bareilly, India

Sudheer Kumar Singh
Galgotias University, Noida, India

ABSTRACT

In the domain of cybersecurity, defending against social engineering attacks remains a critical challenge. This abstract explores effective strategies and real-world examples of using Wireshark—a powerful network protocol analyzer—to mitigate the risks posed by social engineering tactics. Social engineering attacks exploit human psychology rather than technical vulnerabilities, making them difficult to detect through conventional security measures alone. This chapter delves into various strategies for leveraging Wireshark in defense against social engineering. Key aspects include configuring Wireshark for optimal security monitoring, setting up filters and profiles to capture relevant traffic, and decrypting SSL/TLS communications to uncover malicious intent hidden within encrypted data. Detection techniques encompass monitoring DNS and HTTP traffic for signs of phishing attempts, identifying malware communications, and conducting behavioral analysis to spot

DOI: 10.4018/979-8-3693-6665-3.ch008

anomalies in network behavior

I. INTRODUCTION

Social engineering attacks use psychology to trick people into sharing sensitive information or compromising security. Unlike technical hacking, these attacks rely on manipulation and persuasion (Abu and Eleyan, 2023). Tactics include phishing, where fake emails deceive victims; spear phishing, which customizes messages for specific targets; vishing, using phone calls for data extraction; and smishing, deceptive text messages. These attacks bypass technical defenses by exploiting human vulnerabilities, highlighting the need for awareness and training to combat these threats effectively. Social engineering attacks might trick a user into clicking on a link that downloads malware onto their computer. Conversely, malware can facilitate social engineering by providing attackers with access to personal information or enabling them to control compromised systems (Sobur et al, 2023).

One of the biggest dangers in cybersecurity is malware, also called malicious software. Malware is made to sneak into, harm, or stop computers, networks, and the information they have. Cybercriminals use many types of harmful software, like viruses, worms, Trojan horses, ransomware, and spyware. Each type of malware does something different bad. Viruses and worms can mess up files and spread by themselves. Trojans pretend to be real software to get illegal access. Ransomware locks up important data and asks for money to unlock it. Spyware quietly watches what users do and takes important info.

Malware is a serious problem because it can lead to data breaches, money lost, and stop work from getting done. To fight these attacks, good cybersecurity strategies are a must. This includes using strong antivirus and anti-malware software, keeping systems updated to fix problems, and using firewalls to block unwanted access. Teaching people to spot fake emails (phishing) and not download suspicious stuff is also really important. Adding extra protections like backing up data often, using strong passwords, and checking identities in more than one way can help a lot. As malware gets tricky, it's crucial to use smart cybersecurity plans to keep info safe and keep computer systems working well. To overcome this problem an opensource tool wireshark is used (Tuli, 2023).

Wireshark is a powerful tool used to detect malware by analyzing network traffic. It captures data packets in real-time, allowing experts to examine details of transmitted information. By studying this data, suspicious patterns that might indicate malware can be identified. Wireshark also analyzes packet payloads, where malware signatures may hide (Yusuf at al, 2024). It checks communication protocols for any unusual activity that could be caused by malware. If there's a sudden increase in traffic or unexpected data transfers, Wireshark can alert users to potential malware. During a suspected attack, Wireshark reviews network logs to understand the attack's scope, aiding in quick response and mitigation (ranchman et al, 2023). In this chapter real life examples of malware detection using wireshark is illustrated. Also the most effective methods of defending these social engineering attacks are suggested.

The organization of the chapter is as follows: Section II presents overview of Social Engineering attacks and its types. Section III provides a summary of the current research in the literature concerning the application of social engineering. Malware detection using wireshark with real life example is highlighted in Section IV. Section V outlines the successful strategies for combating social engineering attacks. Lastly, Section VI includes a conclusion and future considerations.

II. SOCIAL ENGINEERING ATTACKS

Social engineering attacks use psychology to trick people into sharing sensitive information or compromising security. Unlike technical hacking, these attacks rely on manipulation and persuasion. Tactics include phishing, where fake emails deceive victims; spear phishing, which customizes messages for specific targets; vishing, using phone calls for data extraction; and smishing, deceptive text messages. These attacks bypass technical defenses by exploiting human vulnerabilities, highlighting the need for awareness and training to combat these threats effectively (Pharris and Mira, 2023)

Figure 1. Social Engineering attacks

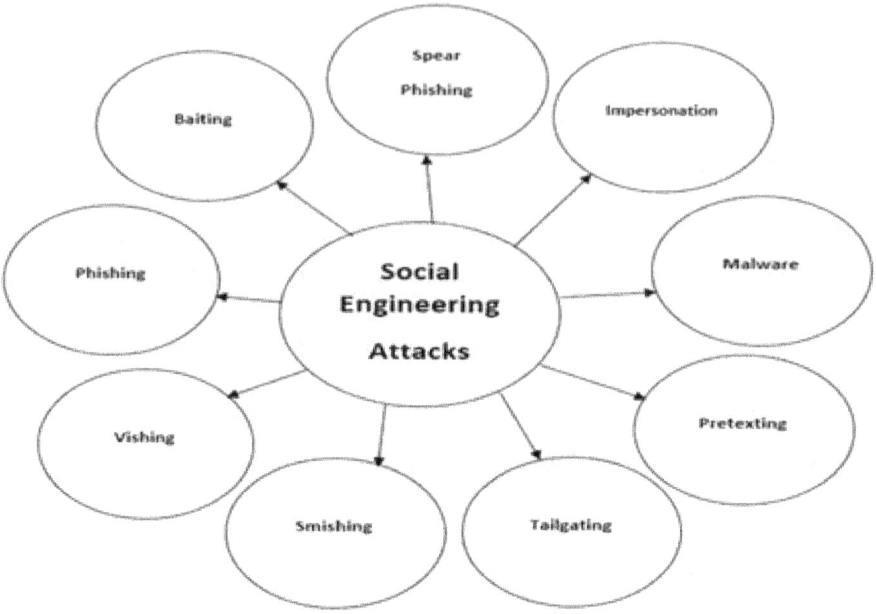

Social engineering attacks use psychology, not technical flaws, to convince people to reveal secret information or perform actions that threaten security. These attacks rely on deception and persuasion to evade detection and defense. Phishing is a common tactic where attackers send fake emails or messages that appear legitimate, aiming to trick recipients into sharing sensitive information or clicking on harmful links. Spear phishing targets specific individuals or organizations to enhance credibility. Vishing, or voice phishing, involves impersonating trusted entities over the phone to obtain personal or financial details. Smishing uses deceptive text messages for the same purposes.

Because these attacks exploit human vulnerabilities rather than technical weaknesses, awareness and training are crucial for prevention. Social engineering attacks can lead to data breaches, financial losses, and operational disruptions. Establishing a culture of awareness, implementing robust security protocols, and educating users to recognize suspicious communications are effective defenses. Organizations and individuals can better protect themselves by understanding these tactics and taking proactive measures against increasingly sophisticated threats.

Social Engineering Attack Types

- **Phishing** refers to the practice of sending deceptive emails or messages that give the impression of coming from sources that are legitimate, such as banks or online services, with the intention of tricking recipients into divulging personal information or clicking on dangerous links (Salama et al, 2023).
- **Spear phishing** is a more targeted form of phishing in which the perpetrators tailor their communications to specific persons or organizations by making use of personal information in order to maximize the level of success they have in their attempts.
- **Vishing**, also known as voice phishing, is a sort of fraudulent phone calls in which the perpetrator, in order to get sensitive information from the victim, impersonates trustworthy authorities, such as bank representatives or technical assistance.
- **Smishing**, also known as SMS phishing, is a form of cybercrime composed of malicious text messages that are aimed to trick receivers into clicking on malicious links or disclosing personal information by making them sound urgent or appealing.
- **Pretexting, w**ith the purpose of obtaining confidential information from their targets, attackers will develop a manufactured scenario or **pretext** in order to do this. To do this, it is common practice to assume the identity of a person who has a genuine requirement for the information.
- **Baiting** is a sort of social engineering in which the perpetrators of the assault, in order to entice victims into downloading malicious files or supplying personal information, offer something that is appealing to the victim, such as free software or rewards.
- **Impersonation** One method of gaining access to sensitive information or systems is known as **impersonation**, in which the attacker assumes the identity of a trusted individual or authority figure. This could involve pretending to be a trusted co-worker, an executive at the organization, or an IT support representative.
- **Tailgating** is the practice of getting physical access to restricted locations by following authorized people and taking advantage of their trust in order to circumvent security measures.

III. LITERATURE REVIEW

To analyze the existing work-related to social engineering various research papers, articles are reviewed and summarized in the below section . First paper explores the prevalent techniques used to prevent and safeguard against social engineering attacks, categorising them according to different criteria. The analysis identifies the most efficient methods in terms of protection level and highlights the obstacles to optimising their effectiveness. It also proposes effective strategies to counter social engineering attacks.

This paper presents a case study which displays the implementation of a comprehensive and hands-on cyber security laboratory exercise focused on a common network attack known as DNS spoofing. This exercise is crucial for effective network security training. The main objective of this practical laboratory exercise is to provide students with the necessary abilities to carry out a DNS spoofing attack in a controlled virtual network setting using Kali Linux. The implementation of this provocative cyber security laboratory exercise led to improved student performance; nonetheless, it also brought forth substantial ethical concerns. Hence, the research delineates many steps that academic institutions may contemplate in order to alleviate the hazards linked to instructing aggressive tactics in information security education programmes (Terabelsi et al, 2024)

This study presents a comprehensive examination of the use of the MITRE ATT&CK (Adversarial Tactics, Techniques, and Common Knowledge) framework for the purpose of validating ICS security. The MITRE ATT&CK methodology, first designed for enterprise IT, is highly versatile and can effectively tackle security concerns particular to Industrial Control Systems (ICS). It provides a systematic way to finding vulnerabilities and strengthening defence mechanisms. This research focuses on two critical attack scenarios in Industrial Control Systems (ICSs) and utilises a range of security technologies to identify possible vulnerabilities and suggest remedies to address them. This study provides a valuable resource for businesses seeking to strengthen their ICS security by examining Indicators of Compromise (IOCs), exploring appropriate methods, and collecting indicators. Using this perspective, we provide concrete suggestions and valuable insights, pushing the boundaries in the field of ICS security validation (Afenu et al, 2024)

This study aimed to provide an advanced cyber network security architecture to effectively block attack vectors initiated by cyber attackers from the internet targeting DRC systems. The following professional programmes and framework systems were utilised globally: EVE-NG, Nessus, OpenVAS, Kali, Parrot, MITRE ATT&CK Enterprise, and NIST v2. Ninety-nine actual systems and fourteen distinct virtual networks were subjected to a thorough evaluation in the simulated environment. The simulation was carried out in three stages: the initial stage focused on launching attacks to partially or completely disrupt internet access, while the second and third stages targeted the application service servers (DMZ) and local network servers to make them inaccessible to the internet. Due to a series of attacks employing diverse methodologies on this network, deliberate efforts were undertaken to impair the servers and devices that were the intended targets. During the attack, the network traffic between the attacker and the target device was analysed using Wireshark and Forti Analyzer software (Yilmaz and Gunes, 2024).

This study examines how automatic tools for penetration testing help small businesses deploy effective and economical data security. The case-study technique uses different data-gathering approaches in a charitable organisation. More specifically, interviews and penetration testing tool experiments were conducted. Small organisations could protect themselves against cyber security dangers with affordable automated penetration testing solutions. Web penetration testing revealed flaws in the company's website. The Nessus programme found 37 website application vulnerabilities. The website application was critically failing, resulting in vulnerabilities, according to ZAP testing. The system had 3 medium, 12 low, and 4 informational vulnerabilities. NMAP detected vulnerabilities by evaluating open ports. These findings affect small businesses. Small organisations may protect their cyber security with automated penetration testing technologies without hiring experts. The findings suggest using automated penetration testing tools in numerous combinations because each tool contributes differently to cyber security (Alkhurayyif and Almarshdy, 2024).

This paper presents the authors' main conclusions through real-world experiments. Their solution is to configure a Raspberry Pi as a VPN server and reroute all traffic via it to encrypt and protect against attacks outlined later in the article. Experimental results show that the suggested approach encrypts targeted packets, preventing hostile attackers from reading them. This approach works, however internet connection standards and practicalities prevent it from being used on all public networks. Future study will improve or modify these solutions (Hartanto et al, 2024).

This study adhered to ethics committee reports and confidentiality agreements when conducting a cyber-security vulnerability assessment on seven organisations from the governmental, corporate, and civil society sectors. The evaluation encompassed security scans, including port, web, and application-based system and network penetration tests, distributed denial of service (DDoS) assaults, and social engineering, to assess the efficacy of each organization's cyber security architecture. The Common Vulnerability Scoring System (CVSS) was employed to modify the base score of each institution and detect any present flaws. The keywords for this article include Enterprise Networks, Cyber Security Analysis, Cyber Attacks, Penetration, and Vulnerability (Andrews et al, 2024).

The main goal of this study is to develop a cybersecurity awareness model specifically for Saudi students to protect them from social engineering attacks. The design science methodology was applied in this research. The proposed model includes four key stages: education and training, policy and guideline development, improving security in Saudi schools, and monitoring and evaluation. This model aims to ensure the safety and privacy of students, teachers, and staff on various social platforms (Alotibi, 2024)

This study employed the attack tree model to calculate the attack occurrence probability (AOP) and utilized the Markov chain model to determine the attack success probability (ASP). The effectiveness data from different modalities and persuasion principles used in social engineering techniques (SETs) were taken into account. The suggested model was validated using examples from various sets. The findings demonstrate potential, indicating that this approach could be efficacious in comprehending and prioritizing SETs. This research provides prospective advantages to both professionals and scholars by allowing for a methodical examination of human susceptibilities in successful Social Engineering Attacks (SETs), so enabling more knowledgeable decision-making in response to these risks. Furthermore, effectively applying the aforementioned techniques could assist in creating a policy framework to tackle SETs (Aijaz and Nazir, 2024)

This article provides a novel cyber warfare modelling framework that is referred to as SMRD (Social Engineering, Malware, Ransomware, and Distributed Denial-of-Service). This framework thoroughly captures the connections and dependencies that exist between these essential components. When it comes to boosting cyber defence, identifying threats, and putting proactive tactics into action, the SMRD framework offers insights that are intended to help. In order to quantitatively represent the linkages and dynamics that exist within these components, it presents a mathematical model that is comprised of a set of nonlinear differential equations (Bouke and Abdullah, 2024).

As a result of this research, it has been demonstrated that it is possible to forecast the degree to which individuals are susceptible to social engineering. This finding is extremely important since it enables preventative steps to be taken in order to raise awareness before potential attacks take place. Additionally, a smartphone application that can identify potential instances of social engineering was developed as a part of this research project. The purpose of this tool is to provide practitioners and policymakers with assistance in the process of building systems that can evaluate the risk levels of individuals and educate them about the various attack tactics. Through the development of proactive measures, the findings of this research can be of assistance to individuals who are assigned with the responsibility of defending against social engineering attacks (Huseynov and Ozdenizei, 2024)

The study emphasizes the essential role of cybersecurity awareness and employee training in strengthening critical infrastructures against cyber threats. It finds that adopting a layered security strategy, incorporating advanced technologies and comprehensive cybersecurity practices, significantly boosts the resilience of critical infrastructures to ransomware attacks. Based on these insights, the study advocates for the integration of ML and AI technologies in access control systems, the prioritization of cybersecurity training for all staff, and the implementation of a multi-faceted security approach to better counter the evolving ransomware threat. These strategies are vital for maintaining the continuity and reliability of essential services in today's digital and interconnected world (Meyeke et al, 2024).

The study finds that implementing biometric systems for securing social security and pension information can reduce service processing times and mitigate the risk of fraudulent benefit manipulations. This research has significant implications across research, practice, and policy domains. From a research perspective, it encourages further exploration into how biometric systems enhance both information security and service efficiency in various applications. For practitioners and policymakers, the study underscores the importance of aligning the deployment and operational use of biometric technologies with specific needs within different sectors. This alignment ensures that biometric systems not only meet security requirements but also optimize operational effectiveness and user satisfaction. By integrating biometric authentication into social security and pension systems, organizations can streamline processes, enhance security measures, and uphold trust in benefit distribution. These insights pave the way for future advancements in biometric technology applications, aiming to strengthen overall service delivery and security in sensitive information management contexts (Owusu-Owware and Effah, 2024).

The review examines the complexities surrounding data privacy and security within IT ecosystems. It discusses various challenges, including the dynamic nature of cyber threats such as malware, ransomware, and social engineering attacks, which continually test IT defenses. Adhering to regulatory frameworks like GDPR and HIPAA presents significant obstacles for organizations striving to balance stringent data protection standards with operational efficiency. Moreover, emerging technologies like IoT and AI introduce new security risks and privacy concerns due to their interconnected nature and extensive data reliance (Farayola et al, 2024).

This paper explores several AI-based methods for enhancing cloud security, such as anomaly detection, threat intelligence analysis, and behavior analytics. It underscores their effectiveness in mitigating risks and ensuring compliance with regulatory standards. Additionally, the paper discusses the challenges and ethical implications associated with AI-driven cloud security, emphasizing the need for transparency, accountability, and adherence to ethical AI principles. Embracing AI-driven solutions allows organizations to strengthen their defenses against cyber threats and maintain the confidentiality and integrity of sensitive data in today's rapidly evolving digital environment (Mokhtar and Rohaizat, 2024).

IoT is changing the way we farm by making it more efficient, sustainable, and precise. As technology advances, it's expected to play an even bigger role in tackling global food production challenges with innovative solutions (Adnan et al, 2023).

Urbanization, where cities grow and rural areas turn into urban spaces, is shaped by factors like population increase, migration, and annexation. This study looks at Sentinel-2 satellite images from 2017 to 2022 to track how Lucknow, India, has been expanding. By using different indices and deep learning techniques, the study found that 52% of the changes were due to significant urban growth. This method can help create better ways to monitor urban expansion and plan for more sustainable cities (Srivastava and Ahmed, 2023).

A smart city leverages technology to address challenges brought on by urban expansion, like security and waste management. IoT devices are crucial as they link different systems to optimize city services. As cities continue to grow, ensuring secure and integrated digital services becomes increasingly important. Blockchain technology can help protect data privacy within these IoT systems, despite some obstacles. This study examines these security and privacy concerns and suggests using blockchain to enhance the security of IoT applications in smart cities (Srivastava and Ahmed, 2023).

Satellite images play a crucial role in monitoring Earth's surface, with over 200 satellites capturing different types of data. This study uses Sentinel-2 and Landsat-8 images from 2017 to 2021 to explore changes in urban areas and land surface temperatures (LST) in Lucknow, India. By applying a semi-supervised deep learning model, the study tracks land use and temperature changes, revealing that temperatures are rising as cities grow. These insights are valuable for planning cities and managing temperature changes effectively (Srivastava and Ahmed, 2022).

IV. WIRESHARK FOR MALWARE DETECTION

Malware has become increasingly complicated in recent years. It is possible that conventional methods of detection are no longer enough, which in turn makes the requirement for malware detection through wireshark absolutely necessary. Wireshark is a tool that allows users to monitor and analyze the flow of information between devices, protocols, and applications in real time. It does this by capturing and analyzing data packets as they move over the network. Through the use of this in-depth analysis, security professionals are able to discover indications of malicious behaviour that might not be detectable using traditional security procedures. Entire process is depicted below.

Figure 2. Home Page of Wireshark

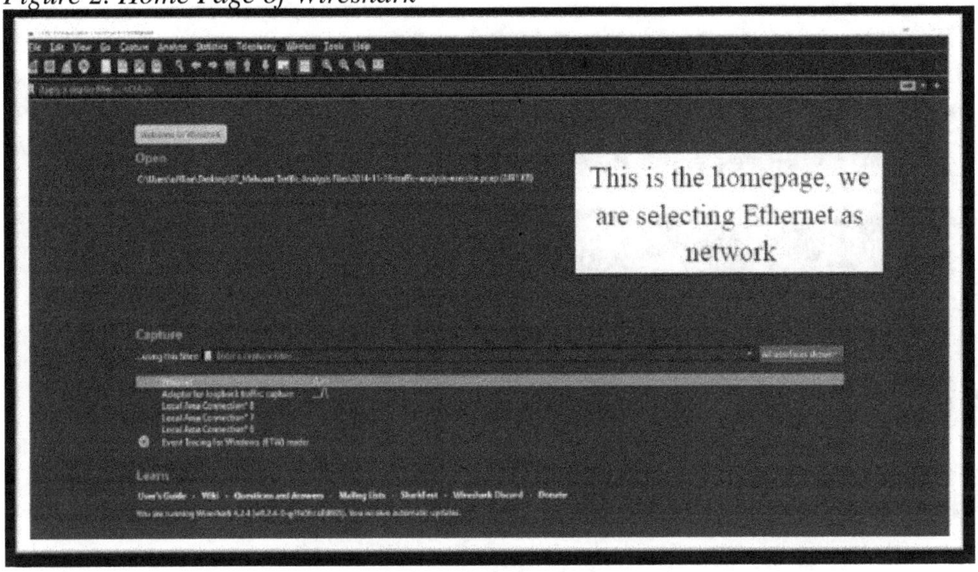

Figure 2 represent the home page of wireshark software. It shows that Ethernet is selected as a network for experimental work.

Figure 3. Folder containing malware file

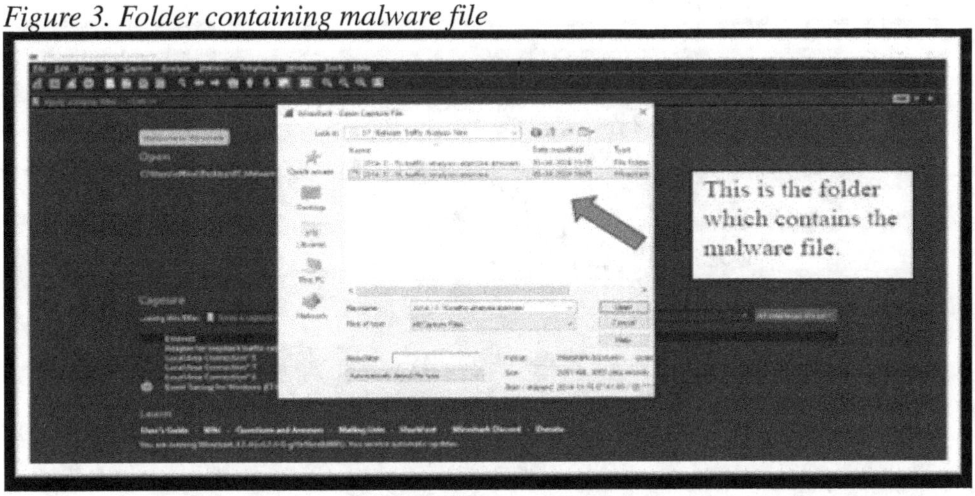

Figure 3 depicts folder where malwares files are stored.

Figure 4. Contents of opened file

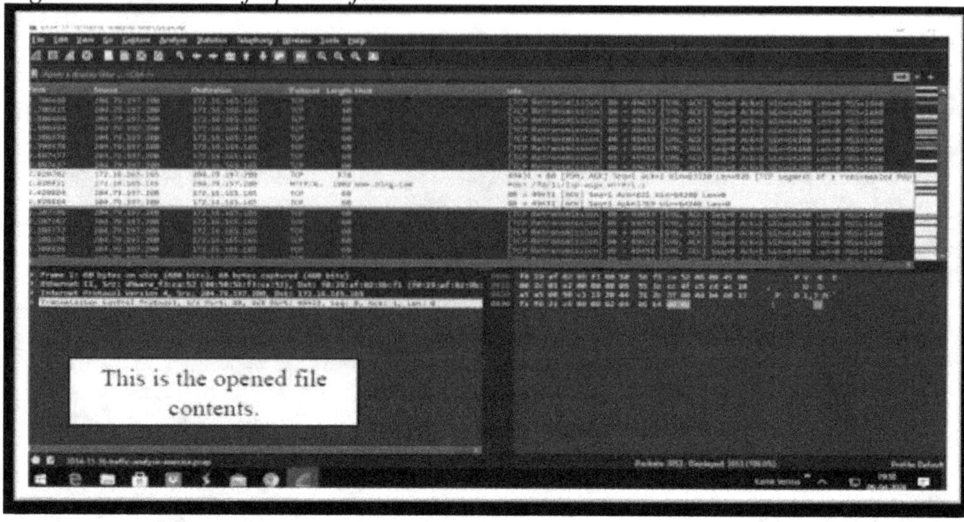

Figure 4 shows the content of opened file. It include source address, destination address, time, protocols used and other information like source port, destination port, sequence, acknowledgement, length etc. .

Figure 5. Opening Protocol Hierarchy

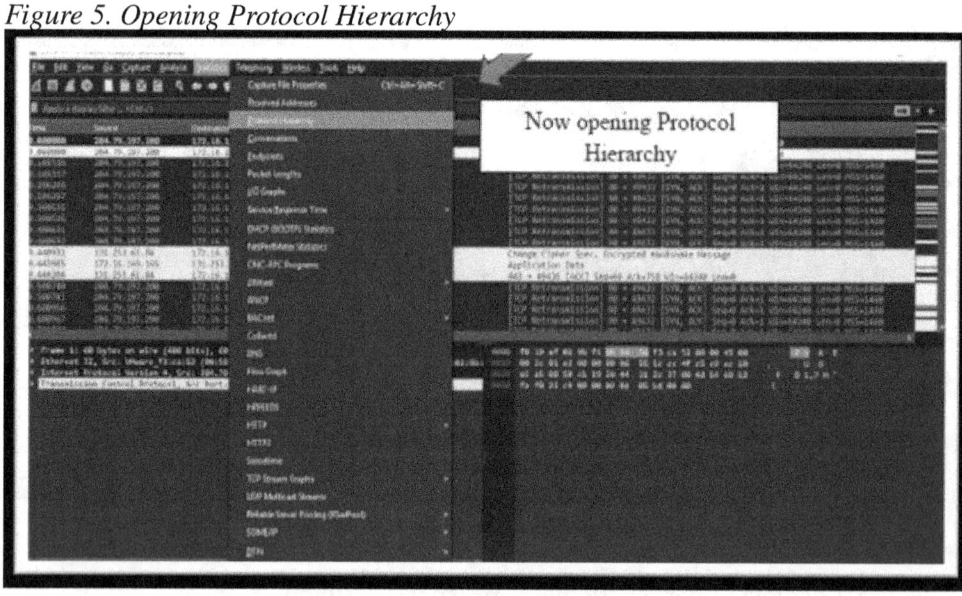

Figure 5 represents opening protocol hierarchy which contains TCP protocols, source port, and destination port, change cipher spec and other encrypted information etc. The figure 6 shows detailed protocol hierarchy include protocols like IPV6,UDP,DHCP,TCP, HTTP,IGMP,ARP etc .The figure 7 highlights that how to apply filter to only HTTP protocol to see all the available packets of the same. The figure 8 depicts how any of the packets is selected through wireshark. Figure 9 represents how host as a column is applied for a selected filter. The figure 10 shows exporting all http objects.

Figure 6. List of Protocol Hierarchy

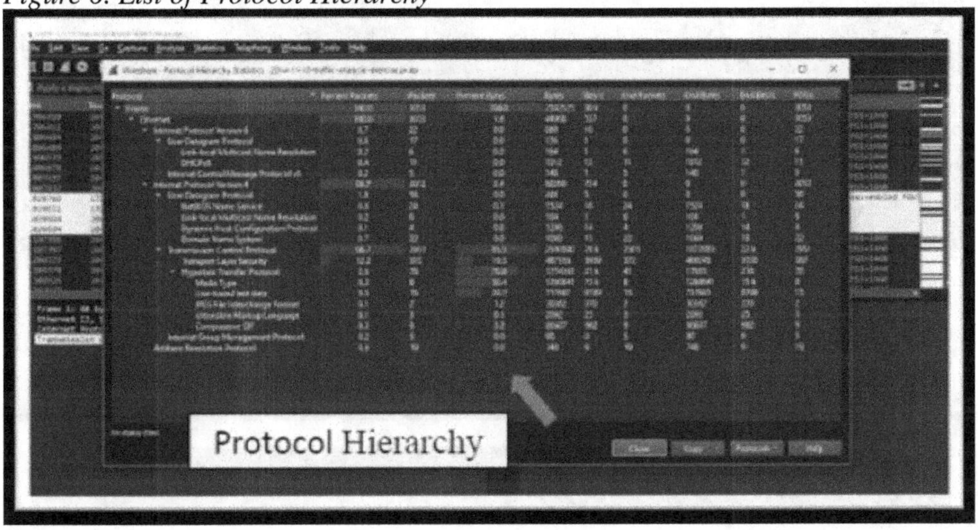

Figure 7. Applying filter on HTTP Protocol

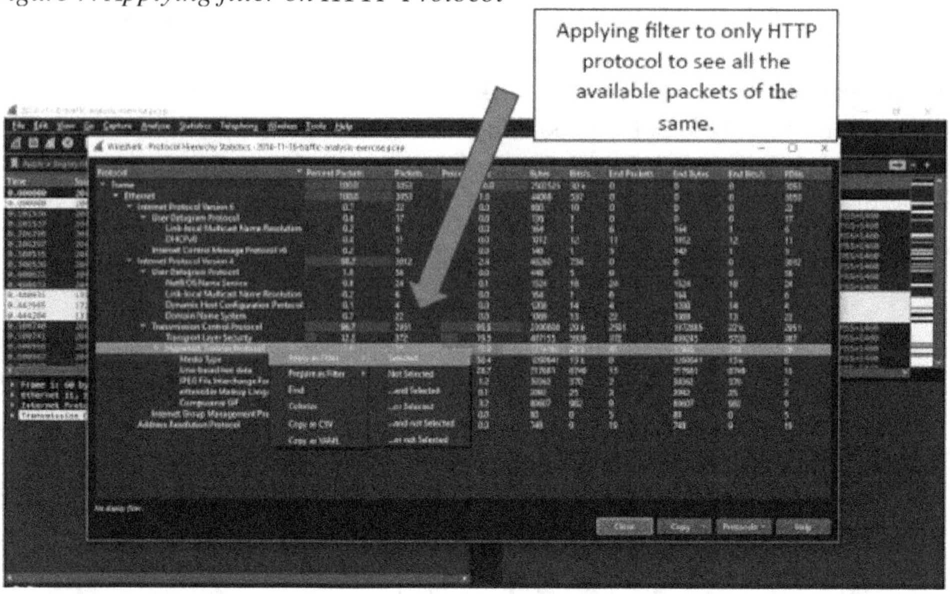

Figure 8. Selection of any Packets

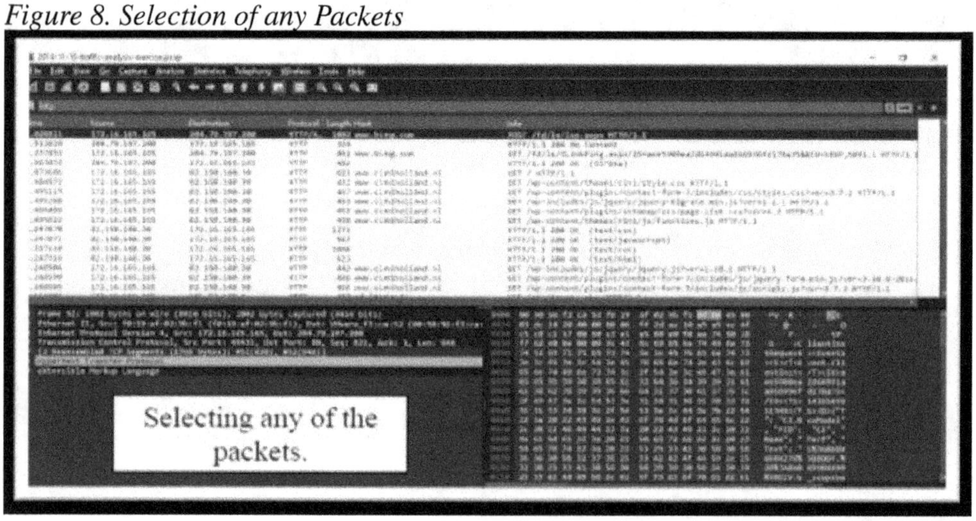

Figure 9. Applying host as column

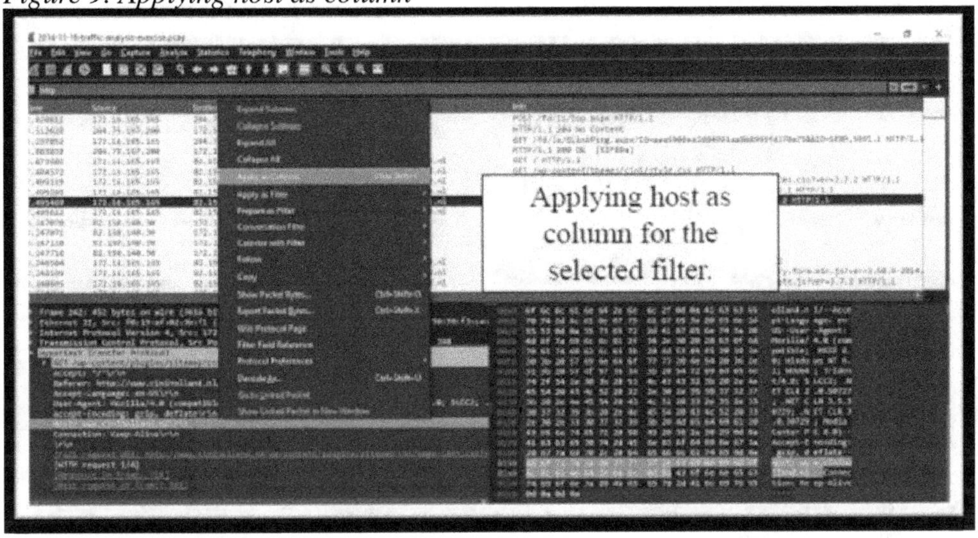

Figure 10. Exporting all HTTP Object

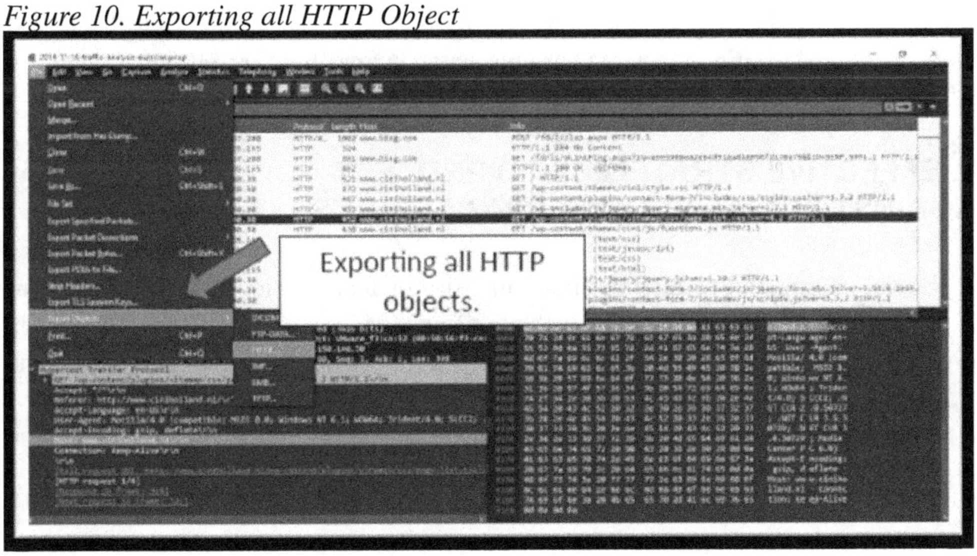

Figure 11. Successful detection of Malware

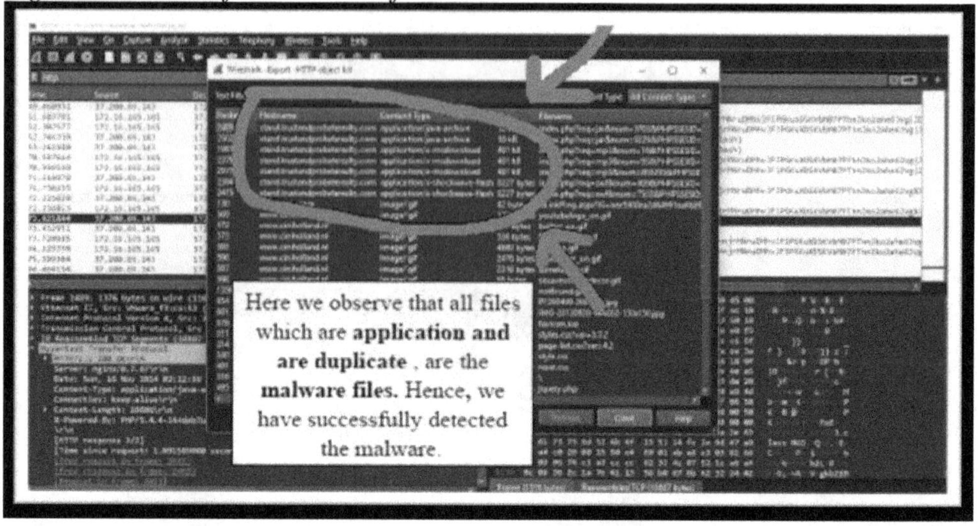

Finally figure 11 depicts successfully detection of all the malware files which are application and duplicate. Here we observe that file content type are application/x-msdownload, application/x-shockwave-flash, application/java-archive etc. It verified with real world example that malware detection is possible through wireshark.

V. EFFECTIVE STRATEGIES TO PROTECT AGAINST SOCIAL ENGINEERING ATTACKS

Social engineers use feelings like curiosity or fear to trick people. Be careful if an email makes you worried, a website offer looks too good, or you see strange digital files. Staying alert can protect you from many online tricks. Here are some tips to help you stay aware of these threats. These tricks is given in figure 12.

Figure 12. Effective strategies to protect against social engineering attacks

A. Training Programs

Equip employees with the knowledge and skills to identify and respond to social engineering attacks.

- **Regular Training**: Conduct frequent training sessions (e.g., quarterly or bi-annually) to keep employees updated on the latest social engineering tactics.
- **Real-World Examples**: Use actual case studies of social engineering attacks to illustrate how these schemes work. This helps employees understand the potential impact and recognize similar scenarios.
- **Simulations**: Run simulated social engineering attacks, such as phishing emails or phone calls, to test employees' responses. Provide feedback and additional training based on the results to improve their awareness and reaction.

B. Avoid Opening Emails and Attachments from Unknown Sources.

If you don't recognize the sender, there's no need to respond. Even if you know the sender but find their message suspicious, verify the information through other means, like a phone call or directly visiting the service provider's website. Keep in mind that email addresses can be easily faked, so an email that seems to come from a trusted source might actually be from an attacker.

C. Use Multifactor Authentication

- Attackers often target user credentials. By enabling multifactor authentication, you can better protect your account even if the system is compromised. Don't rely on just one method – using multiple factors is essential for securing your account. While passwords provide a level of security, they are not sufficient on their own. It's relatively easy for someone to guess your password and gain access to your accounts, often through social engineering. Multi-Factor Authentication (MFA) adds an extra layer of protection, which can include biometric access, security questions, or a one-time password (OTP) code.

D. Be Cautious of Attractive Offers

- If something sounds too good to be true, take a moment to verify it. A quick Google search can help you figure out if the offer is genuine or a scam.

E. Keep your Antivirus and Antimalware Software up to Date

- Ensure that automatic updates are enabled, or make it a daily routine to download the latest updates. Regularly check that updates are applied and scan your system for any potential threats.

F. Be Mindful of Your Digital Footprint

Sharing too much personal information online, especially on social media, can provide criminals with valuable data. For example, if you have your resume online, consider removing your date of birth, phone number, and address, as these details can be exploited by attackers for social engineering attacks. We advise setting your social media profiles to "friends only" and carefully considering what you share online.

G. Check and Update Your Security Patches

Cybercriminals often exploit vulnerabilities in applications, software, or systems to gain unauthorized access to your data. To prevent this, always keep your security patches current and ensure your web browsers and systems are updated to the latest versions. Companies release security patches to fix discovered security loopholes, so keeping your systems updated reduces the risk of cyber-attacks and ensures a more secure environment.

H. Enable Spam Filter

Activate spam filters to block social engineering threats. Spam filters are essential for protecting your inbox from such attacks. Most email providers offer spam filters that flag suspicious emails. With these features, you can easily organize your emails and avoid the hassle of manually identifying potentially harmful messages.

I. Continuously Monitor Critical Systems

Ensure that your system, which contains sensitive information, is monitored around the clock. Exploits like Trojans often target vulnerable systems, so regular scanning of both external and internal systems with web application scanning tools is essential to identify vulnerabilities. Additionally, conduct a social engineering test at least once a year to gauge if employees are susceptible to social engineering attacks. If any fake domains are identified during this process, they should be removed immediately to prevent copyright issues.

J. Utilize Next-Gen Cloud-Based Web Application Firewall (WAF)

Even if you're already using a firewall, consider adopting a next-generation cloud-based web application firewall (WAF). This advanced firewall is specifically designed to offer enhanced protection against social engineering attacks, unlike traditional firewalls that many businesses use.

K. Verify the Identity of Email Senders

Scammers often deceive victims by pretending to be a trusted entity. In phishing attacks, attackers may send emails that appear to come from trusted sources such as credit card companies, banks, social networking sites, or online stores. These emails usually include deceptive links that look legitimate. To protect yourself from these social engineering threats, contact the purported sender to confirm whether they actually sent the email. Be aware that legitimate institutions will not ask for your credentials or confidential information via email.

L. Check for SSL Certificates

Encrypting data, emails, and communications is crucial for protecting information from being accessed by hackers. This can be achieved by obtaining SSL certificates from reputable authorities. Additionally, always verify the legitimacy of websites that request sensitive information by checking their URLs. URLs that begin with https:// indicate a secure, encrypted connection, while those starting with http:// do not offer secure connections. Figure 13 and 14 shows SSL certificates Utilized for network security in SRMS organization.

Figure 13. SSL certificates issued to SRMS organization

Figure 14. SSL certificatesmyportal.srms.ac.in

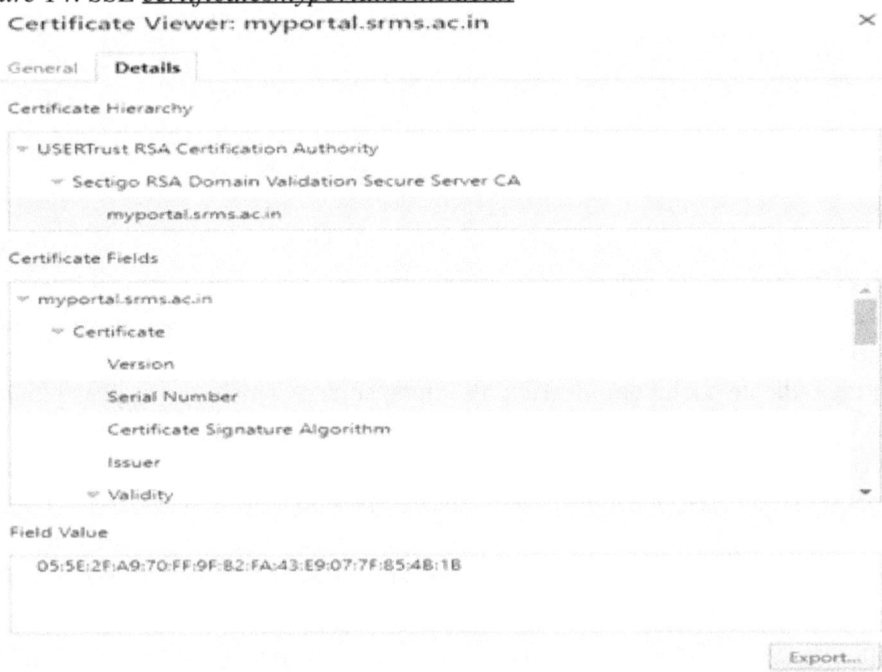

M. Establish Robust Policies for Crucial Operations

Technological measures have limitations in countering social engineering attacks, which are designed to deceive people rather than systems. Anti-malware, antivirus, and network firewalls are often ineffective against these human-targeted tactics. To mitigate the risk of social engineering, it is crucial to implement robust policies for procedures involving money transfers or payments. For example, CEO Fraud involves a spear-phishing attack where the attacker pretends to be the CEO to deceive employees into transferring money to an account controlled by the attacker. By instituting strict policies, like requiring in-person confirmation for transfers over a certain amount, the likelihood of successful social engineering attempts can be greatly reduced.

N. Penetration Testing

One of the most effective methods to prevent social engineering attacks is to conduct penetration testing. This process involves identifying and attempting to exploit vulnerabilities within your organization. If the penetration tester successfully breaches your critical systems, you can determine which systems or employees need more protection and identify the specific types of social engineering attacks your organization is susceptible to.

VI. CONCLUSION AND FUTURE ENHANCEMENT

In conclusion, protecting against social engineering attacks using Wireshark involves a multifaceted approach that combines technical vigilance with user education. By leveraging Wireshark's powerful packet analysis capabilities, network administrators can monitor network traffic for unusual patterns and anomalies that may indicate social engineering attempts, such as phishing or spear-phishing attacks. This real-time detection enables prompt intervention, reducing the likelihood of successful exploitation. Real-world examples underscore the importance of comprehensive strategies, including regularly updated firewall rules, robust access controls, and ongoing training for employees to recognize and report suspicious activities. These measures, when implemented cohesively, create a resilient defense against social engineering tactics.

Looking ahead, future work should focus on enhancing Wireshark's capabilities by integrating advanced machine learning algorithms and artificial intelligence to improve the accuracy and speed of threat detection. Such integration could enable the system to learn from past attacks, predict future ones, and respond more effectively. Additionally, expanding user training programs is crucial; tailored workshops and simulations can significantly improve awareness and preparedness among employees. Another area for future exploration is the development of automated incident response protocols that can swiftly mitigate threats without human intervention, thereby minimizing potential damage. Continuous research and development in these areas will be essential to stay ahead of evolving social engineering techniques and ensure robust network security.

REFERENCES

Abu Hweidi, R. F., & Eleyan, D. (2023). Social engineering attack concepts, frameworks, and awareness: A systematic literature review. *International Journal of Computing and Digital Systems*, 13(1), 691–700. DOI: 10.12785/ijcds/130155

Adnan Afaq, S., Khalida Izhar, S., & Srivastava, S. (2023). The IOT Farming Revolution: Enhancing efficiency and sustainability in agriculture. *International Journal of Engineering Sciences & Emerging Technologies*, 11(2), 160–170.

Afenu, D. S., Asiri, M., & Saxena, N. (2024). Industrial Control Systems Security Validation Based on MITRE Adversarial Tactics, Techniques, and Common Knowledge Framework. *Electronics (Basel)*, 13(5), 917. DOI: 10.3390/electronics13050917

Aijaz, M., & Nazir, M. (2024). Modelling and analysis of social engineering threats using the attack tree and the Markov model. *International Journal of Information Technology : an Official Journal of Bharati Vidyapeeth's Institute of Computer Applications and Management*, 16(2), 1231–1238. DOI: 10.1007/s41870-023-01540-z

Alkhurayyif, Y., & Almarshdy, Y. S. (2024). Adopting Automated Penetration Testing Tools: A Cost-Effective Approach to Enhancing Cybersecurity in Small Organizations. *Journal of Information Security and Cybercrimes Research*, 7(1), 51–66. DOI: 10.26735/RJJT2453

Alotibi, G. (2024). A Cybersecurity Awareness Model for the Protection of Saudi Students from Social Media Attacks. *Engineering, Technology &. Applied Scientific Research*, 14(2), 13787–13795.

Andrews, L. J. B., Alagappan, A., Sarathkumar, D., Fathima, M., Venkatachary, S. K., Rajeshkanna, R., & Raj, R. A. (2024, February). Investigations on Cyber Security Vulnerability using Distribution Analysis. In *2024 IEEE International Students'Conference on Electrical, Electronics and Computer Science (SCEECS)* (pp. 1-6). IEEE. DOI: 10.1109/SCEECS61402.2024.10482303

Bouke, M. A., & Abdullah, A. (2024). Smrd: A novel cyber warfare modeling framework for social engineering, malware, ransomware, and distributed denial-of-service based on a system of nonlinear differential equations. *Journal of Applied Artificial Intelligence*, 5(1), 54–68. DOI: 10.48185/jaai.v5i1.972

Farayola, O. A., Olorunfemi, O. L., & Shoetan, P. O.Oluwatoyin Ajoke Fayayola Oluwabukunmi Latifat OlorunfemiPhilip Olaseni Shoetan. (2024). Data privacy and security in it: A review of techniques and challenges. *Computer Science & IT Research Journal*, 5(3), 606–615. DOI: 10.51594/csitrj.v5i3.909

Hartanto, F., Budiman, B., Gwei, E., Gunawan, A. A. S., & Edbert, I. S. (2024). An Experiment to Prevent Malicious Actors from Compromising Private Digital Assets Over a Public Network. *Engineering* [EMACS]. *MAthematics and Computer Science Journal*, 6(1), 7–11.

Huseynov, F., & Ozdenizci Kose, B. (2024). Using machine learning algorithms to predict individuals' tendency to be victim of social engineering attacks. *Information Development*, 40(2), 298–318. DOI: 10.1177/02666669221116336

Mayeke, N. R., Arigbabu, A. T., Olaniyi, O. O., Okunleye, O. J., & Adigwe, C. S. (2024). Evolving Access Control Paradigms: A Comprehensive Multi-Dimensional Analysis of Security Risks and System Assurance in Cyber Engineering. *Available atSSRN*. DOI: 10.2139/ssrn.4752902

Mokhtar, R., & Rohaizat, A. (2024). Cybercrimes and cyber security trends in the new normal. In *The New Normal and Its Impact on Society: Perspectives from ASEAN and the European Union* (pp. 41–60). Springer Nature Singapore. DOI: 10.1007/978-981-97-0527-6_4

Owusu-Oware, E., & Effah, J. (2024). Biometric system for protecting information and improving service delivery: The case of a developing country's social security and pension organisation. *Information Development*, 40(1), 61–74. DOI: 10.1177/02666669221085709

Pharris, L., & Perez-Mira, B. (2023). Preventing social engineering: A phenomenological inquiry. *Information and Computer Security*, 31(1), 1–31. DOI: 10.1108/ICS-09-2021-0137

Rachman, D. A., Muhyidin, Y., & Sunandar, M. A. (2023). Analysis Quality of Service of Internet Network Fiber to the Home Service Pt. Xyz Using Wireshark. *Jurnal Informatika dan Teknik Elektro Terapan, 11*(3s1).

Salama, R., Al-Turjman, F., Bhatla, S., & Yadav, S. P. (2023, April). Social engineering attack types and prevention techniques-A survey. In *2023 International Conference on Computational Intelligence, Communication Technology and Networking (CICTN)* (pp. 817-820). IEEE. DOI: 10.1109/CICTN57981.2023.10140957

Sobur, A., Hossain, A., Nazrul Islam, K., & Kabir, M. H. (2023). A Contradiction study of pysical vs cyberspace social engineering attacks and defense.

Srivastava, S., & Ahmed, T. (2022). Correlation Between Built-Up and Land Surface Temperature Using Sentinel-2 and Landsat-8 Images through Semi-Supervised Deep Learning Model for Efficient Land Surface Monitoring. *Mathematical Statistician and Engineering Applications*, 71(4), 3000–3023.

Srivastava, S., & Ahmed, T. (2023, March). An Approach to Monitor Urban Growth through Deep Learning based Change Detection Technique using Sentinel-2 Satellite Images. In *2023 10th International Conference on Computing for Sustainable Global Development (INDIACom)* (pp. 832-838). IEEE.

Srivastava, S., Ahmed, T., & Saxena, A. (2023). An approach to secure IOT application of smart city using blockchain technology. *International Journal of Engineering Sciences & Emerging Technologies*, 11(2), 71–78.

Trabelsi, Z., Parambil, M. M. A., Qayyum, T., & Alomar, B. (2024, May). Teaching DNS Spoofing Attack Using a Hands-on Cybersecurity Approach Based on Virtual Kali Linux Platform. In *2024 IEEE Global Engineering Education Conference (EDUCON)* (pp. 1-8). IEEE. DOI: 10.1109/EDUCON60312.2024.10578851

Tuli, R. (2023). Analyzing Network performance parameters using wireshark. *arXiv preprint arXiv:2302.03267.*

Yilmaz, A., & Gunes, A. (2024). A Model to Protect Disaster Recovery Centers from Cyber Threats with Multi-Layered Network Security Architecture.

Yusuf, A., Khairil, K., & Rohmawan, E. P. (2024). An Analysis of Service quality on VSAT using Wireshark. *Jurnal Media Infotama*, 20(1), 73–78.

Chapter 9
Emerging Trends and Future Directions in Social Engineering Defense

Gopalji Varshneya
https://orcid.org/0009-0008-9511-3716
Sharda University, India

Priyanka Tyagi
Sharda University, India

Rachit Kumar
Sharda University, India

Nishant Dublish
IMS Unison University, India

ABSTRACT

In today's quickly changing digital society makes social engineering attacks a much bigger concern, it will create significant challenges to organizations as well as individuals. The chapter explores social engineering threats and strategies for mitigation. Beginning with an introduction to social engineering attacks, it highlights its critical aspects of organizations and individuals from manipulation. Historical viewpoints give insight into the evolution of social engineering attacks, providing us clues to understand current threats. The chapter explains the different tactics used by cybercriminals today and predicts future trends in social engineering. It also discusses technological advancements and tools for detection and prevention of

DOI: 10.4018/979-8-3693-6665-3.ch009

these types of attacks, supported by real-world case studies. Ethical and legal view also critically analyzed to maintain integrity in defense efforts. Lastly, the chapter concluded with the need for proactive defense strategies to effectively address emerging threats in social engineering.

INTRODUCTION:

Human unawareness to technological advancement and their loopholes is often considered the weakest link in cybersecurity, yet educational efforts tend to prioritize technical aspects over addressing human vulnerabilities (Kaushalya et al., 2018). Social engineering exploits this vulnerability, cybercriminals are using persuasion and manipulation to extract private information from targets. Effective defense against such attacks necessitates prioritizing information security awareness and offering comprehensive training programs to address human vulnerabilities (Ghafir et al., 2016). Additionally, developers should design user interfaces in a manner that makes small changes readily noticeable to users. These programs should educate employees about social engineering threats and tactics, equipping them with strategies to defend against such attacks. By implementing a multi-layered defense approach, organizations can mitigate security risks and protect their systems and data (Mughal et al., 2018). This chapter focuses on social engineering defense, covering awareness-raising, training, and the deployment of security measures to combat this pervasive threat in the digital age (Wang et al., 2020).

Hackers and malicious actors have leveraged various techniques, such as phishing emails, pretexting, baiting, tailgating etc. to manipulate targets and gain unauthorized access to sensitive information or systems (Okoli et al., 2024). The growing reliance on social media and online networking has provided evil-doers with vast resources for gathering personal details and crafting convincing narratives to carry out successful social engineering attacks (Burda et al., 2024).

One of the key aspects of social engineering within the context of information security is its reliance on psychological manipulation to bypass technical understanding of human psychology and social interactions, malicious actors can create compelling scenarios that trick the individual. Cybercriminals often exploit cognitive biases, emotional triggers, and social norms to influence target behavior and extract valuable data (Papatsaroucha et al. 2021). To combat the threat of social engineering effectively, organizations must adopt a multifaceted approach that combines technical controls with comprehensive training and awareness programs. Employee education plays a critical role in mitigating the risks associated with social engineering by empowering individuals to recognize potential threats (Aldawood & Skinner, 2018), verify the authenticity of requests, and respond appropriately to suspicious incidents. Establishing clear communication channels, implementing secure authentication protocols, and fostering a culture of skepticism towards unsolicited communications are essential components of a robust defense strategy against social engineering attacks.

THEORETICAL BACKGROUND

Social engineering bypasses technical defenses by manipulating human psychology. Attackers exploit our natural trust, emotions, and decision-making to gain access or information (Wang et al. 2021). Reciprocity (feeling obligated to return a favor) or scarcity (limited-time offers) exploit our desire to be helpful or get a good deal. Phishing emails with fake addresses, fabricated scenarios (pretexting), and tempting but malicious files (baiting) are all methods of deception used to manipulate victims. By understanding these tactics, we can be more vigilant. Social engineers rely on catching you off guard.

HISTORY OF SOCIAL ENGINEERING ATTACKS:

The history of social engineering attacks dates back to the early days of computing and telecommunications. While the term "social engineering" gained prominence in the context of cybersecurity in the later half of the 20th century, the underlying tactics have been utilized for centuries in various forms of manipulation and deception.

1. **Early Instances:** Social engineering techniques have been used throughout history in various forms of fraud, espionage, and manipulation. For example, during World War II, spies employed social engineering tactics to gather intelligence and infiltrate enemy organizations by exploiting trust and human vulnerabilities.
2. **Emergence of Computing:** With the advent of computers and telecommunications in the mid-20th century, new opportunities arose for social engineering attacks. Early hackers and cybercriminals realized that they could exploit human psychology to bypass security measures and gain unauthorized access to computer systems and networks.
3. **Phone Phreaking:** In the 1960s and 1970s, "phone phreaks" used social engineering tactics to manipulate the telecommunications system and make free long-distance calls(Mitnick, K. et al. 2021). By exploiting vulnerabilities in the phone network and using social engineering techniques to trick telephone operators, phone phreaks gained access to restricted services and information.

4. **Rise of Cybercrime:** As computing technology advanced and the internet became more widespread in the 1990s and early 2000s, social engineering attacks evolved and became increasingly sophisticated. Cybercriminals began using email, websites, and other digital platforms to deceive individuals and organizations, leading to a surge in phishing, spear phishing, and other social engineering attacks.
5. **Modern Techniques:** Today, social engineering attacks encompass a wide range of tactics, including phishing, pretexting, baiting, and vishing, among others. These attacks continue to evolve as cybercriminals adapt their tactics to exploit emerging technologies and trends, such as social media and mobile devices.
6. **Impact on Cybersecurity:** Social engineering attacks remain a significant threat to cybersecurity, affecting individuals, businesses, and organizations of all sizes. Despite advances in technology and cybersecurity awareness, human vulnerabilities continue to be exploited by cybercriminals seeking to steal sensitive information, commit fraud, or gain unauthorized access to systems and networks.

TYPES OF SOCIAL ENGINEERING ATTACKS:

Social engineering attacks come in various forms, each exploiting human psychology and behavior to deceive individuals and gain unauthorized access to sensitive information. Some common types of social engineering attacks include:

1. **Phishing:** In phishing attacks, cybercriminals impersonate legitimate entities, such as banks or trusted organizations, to trick individuals into providing confidential information like usernames, passwords, or financial details.
2. **Angler phishing:** Angler phishing, a modern tactic, involves cybercriminals targeting individuals who express dissatisfaction with companies or financial institutions on social media. After identifying such complaints, attackers send phishing messages from fake corporate accounts to exploit unsuspecting customers.
3. **Spear Phishing:** Similar to phishing, spear phishing targets specific individuals or organizations using personalized messages, making the attack more convincing and difficult to detect.
4. **Whaling:** Whaling attacks specifically target high-profile individuals, such as executives or CEOs, seeking to obtain sensitive information or access to corporate systems.

5. **Pretexting:** Pretexting involves creating a false pretext or scenario to manipulate individuals into divulging information or performing certain actions. This may include impersonating someone in authority or creating a fabricated emergency situation.
6. **Baiting:** Baiting attacks entice individuals with the promise of something desirable, such as free software or movie downloads, to trick them into clicking on malicious links or downloading malware.
7. **Quid Pro Quo:** Quid pro quo attacks involve offering something in exchange for information or access. For example, cybercriminals may offer IT support or services in exchange for login credentials.
8. **Vishing:** Vishing, or voice phishing, uses phone calls or voice messages to deceive individuals into revealing sensitive information or performing certain actions.
9. **Impersonation:** Impersonation attacks involve pretending to be someone else, such as a colleague, customer, or IT support staff, to gain trust and extract information.
10. **Watering Hole:** In watering hole attacks, cybercriminals compromise websites frequented by their target audience, infecting visitors' devices with malware to gain access to sensitive information.
11. **Smishing:** This is a type of social engineering attack where attackers send text messages to potential victims. The text messages often contain links to malicious websites or phone numbers that can be used to steal your personal information.
12. **Tailgating / Piggybacking**: Tailgating, also known as piggybacking, is a social engineering technique where an unauthorized person gains access to a restricted area by following closely behind an authorized individual. This exploit capitalizes on human courtesy or negligence to bypass physical security measures such as keycard access or security checkpoints.
13. **Shoulder Surfing:** It is very near to the Tailgating difference being that Tailgating occurs when an unauthorized person follows an employee into a secure area. Shoulder surfing involves someone observing sensitive information (like passwords) by looking over your shoulder.
14. **Scareware:** Scareware tricks users into believing their system is infected and prompts them to download malicious software.
15. **Supply Chain Risks:** Social engineering attacks can also target supply chains. Hackers may exploit vulnerabilities in third-party vendors to gain access to larger organizations
16. **Human Vulnerability:** Ultimately, social engineering attacks exploit human psychology. Cybercriminals manipulate emotions, fear, excitement, or urgency to cloud judgment and convince individuals to take actions that compromise security

SOCIAL ENGINEERING ATTACKS: A FRAMEWORK APPROACH

Social engineering attacks, unlike technical hacking, exploit human vulnerabilities to gain access or information. A framework developed by (Mouton et al. 2016) helps us understand and analyze these attacks in detail. This framework breaks down the "art" of manipulation into a series of steps, allowing us to identify potential weaknesses and build stronger defenses.

The Mouton Framework:This framework outlines six key stages attackers navigate during a social engineering attempt:

1. **Attack Formulation:** Here, the attacker defines the goal (what they aim to achieve) and identifies the target (individual or group). This initial stage lays the foundation for the entire attack.
2. **Information Gathering:** The attacker meticulously gathers information about the target and the attack itself. Public sources like social media and internal databases might be exploited to glean personal details that can be used for manipulation (Muscanell, 2014). The attacker then assesses the relevance of this information, ensuring it furthers their objectives.
3. **Preparation:** Armed with gathered information, the attacker meticulously constructs a plan. This includes crafting a pretext (a fabricated scenario to gain trust), choosing the appropriate attack vector (email, phone call, etc.), and formulating a strategy to achieve their goal.
4. **Developing a Relationship:** The attacker establishes contact with the target, often through digital means like email. Building rapport is crucial here. The attacker strives to maintain a believable person that doesn't arouse suspicion within the victim.
5. **Exploiting the Relationship:** Once a relationship is established, the attacker employs various manipulation tactics to influence the target's emotional state. This "priming" prepares the victim to be susceptible to the attacker's ultimate goal, such as clicking a malicious link or divulging sensitive information.
6. **Debrief:** After achieving their objective (elicitation), the attacker aims to maintain anonymity and avoid detection. This might involve returning the victim to a normal state of mind and potentially setting the stage for future attacks if more information is desired.

Social engineering threats in cybersecurity are on the rise,Cybercriminals are increasingly utilizing sophisticated tactics to manipulate individuals and organizations to divulge sensitive information or grant unauthorized access (Aldawood & Skinner, 2019). These threats encompass a wide range of techniques including phishing, pretexting, baiting, and tailgating. Despite advancements in cybersecurity awareness and technology, social engineering attacks remain prevalent and continue to evolve, posing significant risks to data security and privacy. Organizations must remain vigilant and implement robust defense strategies to effectively mitigate these threats.

Table 1. Social Engineering Defense cases in Globally

S.No	Year	Social Engineering Defense Cases
1	2023	Organizations globally witness a surge in phishing attacks, prompting increased awareness campaigns and employee training.
2	2022	Multi-factor authentication gains widespread adoption, accompanied by intensified efforts to educate employees on security.
3	2021	The COVID-19 pandemic catalyzes a spike in social engineering attacks, prompting organizations to reinforce their defenses.
4	2020	Business email compromise (BEC) attacks proliferate, leading to the implementation of more robust incident response measures.
5	2019	Social media platforms become prime targets for social engineering, driving the adoption of advanced anti-phishing technologies.
6	2018	Simulated phishing exercises emerge as a popular defense strategy, complemented by the integration of behavioral analytics tools.

Trends in Phishing Attacks on Organizations (2022–2023)

Phishing attacks are a significant threat to organizations, with attackers using social engineering techniques to gain unauthorized access. In 2023, nearly half (43%) of successful attacks on organizations utilized social engineering, primarily through email, SMS messages, social networks, and messaging apps. These attacks not only pose reputational risks but also cause substantial financial damage.

Goals of Phishing Attacks:

- **Data Theft:** The primary objective of phishing attacks is data theft, accounting for 85% of incidents. Attackers aim to steal sensitive information from organizations.
- **Financial Gain:** In addition to data theft, attackers seek financial gains through phishing attacks.

Industries Targeted: The top three industries targeted using social engineering from Q3 2022 to Q3 2023 were:

- **Government Agencies (44%):** Attackers impersonated government entities to deceive victims.

- **Military-Industrial Enterprises (19%):** These organizations faced significant phishing threats.
- **Science and Education (14%):** Academic institutions were also targeted.

Impersonation Tactics:

- **Attackers commonly impersonated:**
  - Contractors (26%)
  - Technical Support or IT Specialists (15%)
  - Government Agencies (13%)

Communication Channels:

- Email: Remains the most common channel for sending malicious messages (92% of cases).
- Messaging Apps and Social Networks: Their popularity as channels for phishing attacks is increasing.

Payload Delivery:

- Attachments: Attackers frequently use attachments (archives like zip, 7z, rar, etc., at 37%, and text documents like doc, .odt, .one, etc., at 30%) to deliver malicious payloads.
- Phishing Links: These often lead to fake data entry pages (50% of cases).

Phishing Kits and Automation:

- Phishing Kits: Widely used tools that simplify attack preparation and execution.
- Phishing-as-a-Service: A business model that streamlines phishing operations.
- Evolution: Automation using AI tools is the primary direction for phishing attacks.

The Imperative of Multi-Factor Authentication and the Evolution of Multifactor Authentication (MFA)

In our current digital era, the threat landscape is evolving rapidly, underscoring the critical importance of robust cybersecurity practices. With a significant portion of data breaches attributed to compromised credentials, the need for enhanced security measures is paramount. This report delves into the significance of multi-factor authentication (MFA) as a potent defense mechanism against cyber threats.

The Risks of Single-Factor Authentication: Single-factor authentication, primarily reliant on passwords, poses significant vulnerabilities to organizations. Passwords are susceptible to various attacks, leading to unauthorized access to sensitive data and systems. High-profile data breaches serve as stark reminders of the inherent risks associated with single-factor authentication.

Understanding Multi-Factor Authentication: Multi-factor authentication combines multiple forms of verification, such as passwords, security tokens, and biometric data, to enhance security. By requiring users to present multiple authentication factors, MFA significantly reduces the risk of unauthorized access, even if one factor is compromised.

Benefits of MFA Implementation: The adoption of multi-factor authentication yields numerous benefits for organizations. It enhances security, deters cybercriminals, ensures regulatory compliance, and fosters user confidence. Real-world examples across various industries underscore the effectiveness of MFA in bolstering cybersecurity.

Real-World Instances and Applications Of Multi-Factor Authentication: Multi-factor authentication has found widespread adoption across diverse sectors. Financial institutions, healthcare organizations, remote workforces, and cloud service providers utilize MFA to safeguard sensitive data and systems from unauthorized access.

Overcoming Barriers to MFA Adoption: While the benefits of MFA are evident, organizations may encounter barriers to adoption, including user inconvenience, implementation costs, and the need for user education. However, these challenges can be addressed through user-friendly solutions and comprehensive training initiatives.

Future of MFA and Authentication: Emerging technologies and standards, such as FIDO2, passwordless authentication, and continuous authentication, are shaping the future of MFA. By embracing these advancements, organizations can future-proof their cybersecurity strategies and mitigate evolving cyber threats.

Importance of MFA: Multi Factor authentication (MFA) stands as a crucial defense against cyber threats in our evolving digital landscape. This post delves into key statistics surrounding MFA adoption, its impact on cybersecurity, preferred implementation methods, and future projections.

Password Reuse Vulnerability: 90% of employees admit to reusing passwords across platforms, emphasizing the critical need for MFA to counter cyber threats.

Surge in Compromises: SMS-based MFA compromises rose by 178%, underlining the escalating threat landscape and the necessity of robust authentication measures.

Effectiveness of MFA: Reduced Unauthorized Access: Users employing MFA experience 56% fewer unauthorized access incidents, highlighting its efficacy in thwarting cybercrime.

Automated Attack Prevention: Microsoft reports that MFA can prevent 99.9% of automated attacks, showcasing its formidable defense capabilities.

User Preferences and Business Impact: Preference for Smartphone Authentication: 69% of users favor smartphone-based MFA methods, indicating a trend toward convenient authentication practices.

Mitigation of Cyber Insurance Claims: 40% of cyber insurance claims are related to compromised credentials, often mitigated by MFA, emphasizing its role in risk reduction.

Adoption Challenges and Future Trends: Low Adoption Among Small Businesses: Only 25% of small businesses employ MFA, highlighting a gap in cybersecurity readiness and the need for broader adoption.

Enhanced Risk Management: 67% of organizations using MFA reported significant improvement in managing cyber risks, showcasing its pivotal role in bolstering security postures.

Growing Market and Adoption:

The global MFA market is projected to reach USD 17.56 billion by 2027, with a CAGR of 15.2%, indicating increasing recognition of MFA's value in safeguarding data.

Impact of Cybersecurity Threats

1. **Bangladesh Bank Heist:** The Bangladesh Bank Heist exemplified the audacity and sophistication of cybercriminals in targeting financial institutions. Through a combination of social engineering and technical exploits, hackers attempted to steal nearly $1 billion, emphasizing the vulnerabilities inherent in banking systems.
2. **Evaldas Rimasauskas Wire Fraud:** The Evaldas Rimasauskas Wire Fraud case demonstrated the ease with which sophisticated cybercriminals can deceive large corporations. Through social engineering and fraudulent invoices, Rimasauskas successfully defrauded Google and Facebook of millions of dollars, emphasizing the importance of robust financial security measures.
3. **Reveton:** Reveton ransomware demonstrated the evolving tactics of cybercriminals in extorting money from victims. By combining ransomware with social engineering techniques, hackers successfully coerced victims into paying

fraudulent fines, highlighting the psychological manipulation inherent in such attacks.

4. **Anthem Data Breach:** The Anthem Data Breach underscored the vulnerability of healthcare organizations to cyber attacks and the potential consequences of compromised personal and medical information. The incident led to substantial financial losses and regulatory scrutiny, highlighting the need for enhanced data protection measures.
5. **Spear Phishing Attack on the Democratic National Committee:** The DNC breach during the 2016 U.S. presidential campaign highlighted the effectiveness of spear phishing in infiltrating high-profile organizations. This incident underscored concerns about foreign interference in democratic processes and the need for robust cybersecurity measures.
6. **Twitter Bitcoin Scam:** The Twitter Bitcoin Scam of 2020 exploited the trust and authority of high-profile accounts to deceive users into sending cryptocurrency. The incident underscored the need for enhanced security measures on social media platforms to prevent similar scams in the future.
7. **Target Data Breach:** The Target Data Breach highlighted the risks associated with supply chain attacks and the importance of third-party vendor security. The incident resulted in significant financial losses for Target and underscored the need for comprehensive cybersecurity protocols across interconnected networks.
8. **Google Drive Scam:** The Google Drive Scam exploited vulnerabilities in push notifications to deceive users and propagate malware. The incident underscored the importance of vigilance and skepticism in recognizing and responding to phishing attempts, even when they appear to originate from trusted sources.
9. **Kevin Mitnick's Early Career:** Kevin Mitnick's exploits in the 1990s demonstrated the power of social engineering in gaining unauthorized access to sensitive information. Despite his criminal past, Mitnick later became a cybersecurity consultant and author, leveraging his experiences for ethical purposes.
10. **Barbara Corcoran Phishing Incident:** The Barbara Corcoran Phishing Incident highlighted the vulnerability of high-profile individuals to social engineering attacks. Despite her prominence, Corcoran narrowly avoided falling victim to a phishing scam, emphasizing the importance of awareness and education in preventing cyber attacks.
11. **Cabarrus County Hack:** The Cabarrus County Hack illustrated the effectiveness of social engineering in deceiving government officials and stealing large sums of money. Through impersonation and manipulation, hackers successfully redirected millions of dollars, underscoring the need for enhanced security protocols and verification procedures.

12. **AI Deepfake Scam Hits UK Energy Firm:** The AI Deepfake Scam highlighted the emerging threat posed by artificial intelligence in cyber attacks. By impersonating a company executive using AI voice emulation, hackers successfully defrauded a UK energy firm, underscoring the need for improved authentication and verification methods.
13. **The Lapsus$ Hacking Group:** The Lapsus$ Hacking Group exemplified the growing threat posed by young and technically proficient cybercriminals. Through a series of high-profile attacks, including thefts from Nvidia and Rockstar Games, the group underscored the need for improved cybersecurity measures and law enforcement efforts.

IMPACT OF COVID-19 ON CYBERSECURITY

The COVID-19 pandemic has accelerated the shift to online platforms for work, education, and leisure, leading to a significant increase in internet usage. This surge in online activity has also resulted in a corresponding rise in social engineering attacks, particularly phishing, which exploit pandemic-related themes and fears.

Changes in Social Engineering Attacks During the Pandemic

SEAs have adapted to capitalize on pandemic-related anxieties and uncertainties, with phishing attacks masquerading as COVID-19 updates, healthcare organizations, and financial relief programs. Cybercriminals deploy various tactics, including credential phishing and business email compromise, to exploit individuals and organizations .

The COVID-19 pandemic has reshaped global dynamics, particularly in the digital realm, leading to a surge in online activities and consequently, an increase in social engineering attacks (SEAs). The pandemic prompted a massive transition to remote work, online education, and digital leisure activities, driving a significant rise in internet users and usage. Notably, broadband data usage surged by over 47 percent globally from March to May 2020. This shift provided fertile ground for cybercriminals, who capitalized on the increased online presence to perpetrate SEAs, primarily through phishing attacks. Tech giants like Google and Microsoft observed a surge in SEA trends, with attackers often impersonating officials from organizations involved in COVID-19 efforts, such as the World Health Organization. The pandemic disrupted traditional activities like business, commerce, and education, forcing a rapid migration to online platforms. Remote work, online education, and e-commerce saw substantial growth, with statistics indicating a significant increase in users engaging in these activities. However, this digital migration also amplified the vulnerability to SEAs, as evidenced by the uptick in phishing attacks exploiting the heightened online activity.

Evolving Social Engineering Attack Strategies Amidst the Covid-19 Pandemic

The COVID-19 pandemic not only reshaped leisure activities but also spurred significant changes in social engineering attack (SEA) strategies. As people increasingly relied on online platforms for work, education, and entertainment, cybercriminals saw new opportunities to exploit vulnerabilities and carry out malicious activities.

Phishing emerged as the predominant SEA method, with attackers leveraging the pandemic context to craft deceptive emails and websites. Google and Microsoft reported a surge in phishing activities, with attackers masquerading as authoritative entities, such as health organizations or government agencies, to lure unsuspecting users.

Credential phishing and business email compromise attacks gained traction, targeting remote workers and businesses navigating virtual operations. Ransomware attacks also proliferated during the pandemic, capitalizing on increased online activity to extort monetary payments from victims.

Overall, the pandemic accelerated the frequency and sophistication of SEAs, highlighting cybercriminals' adaptability in exploiting global events for malicious purposes. The thematic shift towards COVID-19-related subjects underscores the dynamic nature of SEA tactics and the need for heightened cybersecurity measures in an increasingly digital world.

UNDERSTANDING BUSINESS EMAIL COMPROMISE (BEC) ATTACKS

Business Email Compromise (BEC) attacks are a targeted form of phishing, focusing on specific individuals or small groups rather than casting a wide net. These attacks often impersonate trusted entities within an organization or its external partners to deceive recipients into taking certain actions, such as transferring money or disclosing sensitive information.

Techniques Used in BEC Attacks

BEC attackers employ various techniques to appear legitimate, including:

1. **Domain Spoofing:** Manipulating email addresses to mimic trusted sources or internal company addresses.
2. Lookalike Domains: Creating domains that resemble legitimate ones, exploiting easily confused characters.
3. Compromised Accounts: Using compromised legitimate accounts to send fraudulent emails, enhancing credibility.

Common Types of BEC Attacks

According to the FBI, BEC attacks typically fall into five categories:

1. **False Invoice Scam:** Phishing emails impersonate vendors, requesting payments for fictitious services, often redirecting funds to the attacker's account.
2. **CEO Fraud:** Emails purporting to be from high-ranking executives instruct recipients to carry out unauthorized actions, such as wire transfers or sharing sensitive data.
3. **Account Compromise:** Attackers exploit compromised accounts within an organization to request payments from customers, redirecting funds to their control.
4. **Attorney Impersonation:** Exploiting trust in legal representatives, often pressuring recipients with time-sensitive and confidential requests.
5. **Data Theft:** Targeting HR and Finance personnel to steal sensitive employee information for malicious purposes.

Protective Measures Against BEC Attacks

Preventing BEC attacks requires a combination of technological solutions and employee education:

1. Anti-Phishing Protections: Implementing anti-phishing solutions capable of detecting BEC red flags, such as mismatched reply-to addresses, and leveraging machine learning to analyze email language (Buttan et al., 2020).
2. Employee Education: Providing comprehensive training to employees on identifying and responding to BEC attacks effectively.
3. Separation of Duties: Implementing policies requiring independent verification for high-risk actions, reducing the likelihood of succumbing to fraudulent requests.
4. Labeling External Emails: Configuring email systems to clearly identify external emails, making it easier for employees to discern potentially suspicious communications.

5. Multi-Factor Authentication (MFA): Enforcing MFA can add an extra layer of security, making it harder for attackers to gain unauthorized access to email accounts even if passwords are compromised.
6. Regular Security Audits: Conducting regular audits of email systems and network infrastructure can help identify vulnerabilities and potential entry points for attackers.
7. Incident Response Plan: Developing and regularly testing an incident response plan can ensure swift and effective action in the event of a successful BEC attack, minimizing its impact on the organization.
8. Vendor Risk Management: Assessing and monitoring the security practices of vendors and third-party partners can reduce the risk of BEC attacks originating from compromised external accounts.

The Vulnerability of Social Media Platforms to Phishing Attacks

Social media platforms have become integral parts of modern life, facilitating communication, networking, and information sharing on a global scale. However, this widespread connectivity also comes with inherent risks, chief among them being the threat of phishing attacks. Phishing, a form of cybercrime where attackers masquerade as trustworthy entities to deceive individuals into divulging sensitive information, has found fertile ground in the expansive user base and interactive features of social media platforms.

The Pervasiveness of Social Media Phishing: Social media platforms serve as lucrative targets for phishing attacks due to their massive user bases and the wealth of personal information willingly shared by users. Attackers exploit this information to craft convincing phishing messages tailored to individual preferences and interests, increasing the likelihood of successful deception. Platforms like Facebook and Twitter, with billions of active users, present particularly enticing opportunities for cybercriminals to launch large-scale phishing operations.

Exploiting User Vulnerabilities: Phishing attacks on social media capitalize on users' trust in familiar interfaces and interactions, making it challenging to discern between legitimate and malicious content. Factors such as low technical knowledge, habitual use of social media, and heuristic content processing contribute to users' susceptibility to phishing attempts. Research has also identified demographic trends, with young women aged 18-25 exhibiting higher vulnerability to social media phishing tactics .

Mitigating Social Media Phishing: Efforts to mitigate social media phishing attacks encompass both user education and technological solutions. Increasing awareness about the tactics employed by cybercriminals can empower users to recognize and avoid phishing attempts. Additionally, social media platforms themselves play a crucial role in implementing proactive security measures, such as multi-factor authentication and email verification, to thwart phishing attacks.

Technological Solutions: Machine learning algorithms have emerged as promising tools for detecting and combating social media phishing. These algorithms analyze URL patterns and other indicators to identify phishing sites with high accuracy rates. By continuously refining their algorithms based on evolving phishing tactics, cybersecurity experts can stay one step ahead of attackers and provide enhanced protection for users.

Strengthening Cybersecurity: Simulated Phishing Exercises and Behavioral Analytics

Phishing attacks remain a prevalent threat in today's digital world. These deceptive emails, often designed to mimic legitimate sources, trick users into revealing sensitive information or clicking malicious links. To combat this ongoing challenge, organizations are increasingly turning to simulated phishing exercises and behavioral analytics for a multifaceted approach to cybersecurity.

The Power of Simulated Phishing:

Simulated phishing exercises offer a proactive method to assess employee vulnerability to these attacks. By creating realistic scenarios that mimic real-world phishing attempts, organizations can:

Gauge Employee Response: These exercises reveal how employees react to phishing emails, identifying those susceptible to falling victim.

Identify Training Gaps: The results pinpoint areas where cybersecurity awareness and practices need improvement, informing the development of targeted training programs.

Research confirms the effectiveness of simulated phishing. Studies have shown a significant reduction in susceptibility to phishing attacks after implementing such exercises.

Tailored Training and Behavior-Based Controls:

Effective cybersecurity training goes beyond a one-size-fits-all approach. Behavior-based controls, which emphasize repeated training tailored to individual needs, have proven particularly successful. This recognition of individual learning styles and consistent reinforcement leads to a deeper understanding of best practices. Organizations can further strengthen their defenses by focusing on new hires. Studies indicate that new employees are more susceptible to phishing attempts.

Tailored training programs, designed specifically for this group, equip them with the knowledge and skills to recognize and avoid phishing threats from the start of their employment.

Leveraging Behavioral Analytics:

Integrating behavioral analytics tools with simulated phishing exercises unlocks valuable insights into employee behavior. These tools analyze data from the exercises, revealing patterns, trends, and areas of concern. By understanding how employees typically respond to phishing attempts, organizations can tailor their training programs to address specific vulnerabilities more effectively.

A Combined Approach: Technical and Social Strategies:

The key to robust cybersecurity lies in a combined approach that leverages both technical and social strategies. While technical solutions focus on securing systems and infrastructure, social strategies address the human element. Recognizing that employees are often the first line of defense, simulated phishing exercises and behavioral analytics empower organizations to build a culture of cybersecurity awareness and best practices. This combined approach equips organizations to effectively combat the ever-evolving threat landscape of phishing attacks.

BUILDING A FORTRESS: STRENGTHENING DEFENSES AGAINST BEC ATTACKS

Business Email Compromise (BEC) attacks pose a significant threat to organizations, potentially leading to substantial financial losses and reputational damage. Fortunately, by implementing a combination of advanced technologies and proactive strategies, organizations can effectively fortify their defenses against these sophisticated cyber assaults.

Leveraging Cutting-Edge Technologies

- **AI-Powered Social Engineering Defense:** Combatting the social engineering tactics often employed in BEC attacks requires proactive measures. AI-powered defense systems leverage machine learning algorithms to analyze email communication patterns. These systems can identify anomalies indicative of fraudulent activity, such as unusual language patterns or sudden changes in sender behavior. By detecting these red flags, organizations can take swift action to prevent unauthorized access or financial transactions.

- **Checksum Verification for Enhanced Security:** Adding an extra layer of security involves utilizing checksum generation and verification methods through dedicated smartphone applications. These applications generate unique checksums (digital fingerprints) for each legitimate invoice. Recipients can then cross-verify these checksums with the sender, ensuring the authenticity and integrity of the invoice. This method helps to detect and prevent invoice tampering, a common tactic used in BEC attacks thereby mitigating the risk of fraudulent activities.

Advanced Threat Detection and Network Protection

- **Machine Learning and APT Detection:** Enhancing security against sophisticated cyber threats necessitates detecting Advanced Persistent Threat (APT) attacks. Machine learning analysis plays a crucial role here. Convolutional neural networks (CNNs) can be trained to analyze network traffic data and identify patterns indicative of APT activity (Zhang, R. et al. 2020). Upon detection of anomalies, alerts are triggered for immediate response and remediation, minimizing the impact of APT attacks on sensitive information and organizational assets.
- **Safeguarding Against Vampire Attacks:** Network security extends beyond traditional threats. Vampire attacks target network vulnerabilities to drain excessive power from a network (Vasserman, E.Y et al. 2011). Implementing robust access controls and monitoring mechanisms enables organizations to identify and mitigate this risk. By safeguarding against unauthorized sources leeching energy, organizations ensure the integrity and availability of critical network resources.

A Unified Approach for Comprehensive Protection

By integrating these advanced technologies and strategies, organizations can build a comprehensive defense system against BEC attacks and other cyber threats. This combined approach, encompassing AI-based defense systems, checksum verification methods, machine learning analysis for APT detection, and safeguards against Vampire attacks, significantly reduces an organization's susceptibility to cyber intrusions(Ağca, M.A. et al. 2022). Ultimately, these measures protect valuable assets, safeguard reputation, and maintain customer trust, crucial elements for success in today's digital landscape.

CONCLUSION:

In conclusion, the pervasiveness of social engineering in the realm of cybersecurity underscores the importance of addressing human-centric vulnerabilities in addition to technical threats. By understanding the evolving tactics employed by cybercriminals and investing in proactive security measures, organizations can enhance their resilience against social engineering attacks and safeguard sensitive information from exploitation. As the digital landscape continues to evolve, maintaining vigilance, promoting security awareness, and implementing effective countermeasures are paramount in mitigating the risks posed by social engineering in the context of information security.

REFERENCES:

Ağca, M. A., Faye, S., & Khadraoui, D. (2022). A survey on trusted distributed artificial intelligence. *IEEE Access : Practical Innovations, Open Solutions*, 10, 55308–55337. DOI: 10.1109/ACCESS.2022.3176385

Aldawood, H., & Skinner, G. (2018, December). Educating and raising awareness on cyber security social engineering: A literature review. In 2018 IEEE international conference on teaching, assessment, and learning for engineering (TALE) (pp. 62-68). IEEE.

Aldawood, H., & Skinner, G. 2019, January. An academic review of current industrial and commercial cyber security social engineering solutions. In *Proceedings of the 3rd International Conference on Cryptography, Security and Privacy* (pp. 110-115). DOI: 10.1145/3309074.3309083

Burda, P., Allodi, L., & Zannone, N. (2024). Cognition in social engineering empirical research: A systematic literature review. *ACM Transactions on Computer-Human Interaction*, 31(2), 1–55. DOI: 10.1145/3635149

Buttan, D. (2020). Hacking the Human Brain: Impact of Cybercriminals Evoking Emotion for Financial Profit (Doctoral dissertation, Utica College).

Ghafir, I., Prenosil, V., Alhejailan, A., & Hammoudeh, M. (2016, August). Social engineering attack strategies and defence approaches. In 2016 IEEE 4th international conference on future internet of things and cloud (FiCloud) (pp. 145-149). IEEE. DOI: 10.1109/FiCloud.2016.28

Harris, M., & Jackson, E. (2018). Legal Implications of Cybercrime. *International Journal of Legal Studies*, 3(2), 56–71.

Kaushalya, S. A. D. T. P., Randeniya, R. M. R. S. B., & Liyanage, A. D. S. (2018, November). An overview of social engineering in the context of information security. In 2018 IEEE 5th International Conference on Engineering Technologies and Applied Sciences (ICETAS) (pp. 1-6). IEEE. DOI: 10.1109/ICETAS.2018.8629126

Mitnick, K., Telecom system security. *Security Engineering: A Guide to Building Dependable Distributed Systems, 17.*

Mouton, F., Leenen, L., & Venter, H. S. (2016). Social engineering attack examples, templates and scenarios. *Computers & Security*, 59, 186–209. DOI: 10.1016/j.cose.2016.03.004

Mughal, A. A. (2018). The Art of Cybersecurity: Defense in Depth Strategy for Robust Protection. *International Journal of Intelligent Automation and Computing*, 1(1), 1–20.

Okoli, U. I., Obi, O. C., Adewusi, A. O., & Abrahams, T. O. (2024). Machine learning in cybersecurity: A review of threat detection and defense mechanisms.

Papatsaroucha, D., Nikoloudakis, Y., Kefaloukos, I., Pallis, E., & Markakis, E. K. (2021). A survey on human and personality vulnerability assessment in cyber-security: Challenges, approaches, and open issues. arXiv preprint arXiv:2106.09986.

Vasserman, E. Y., & Hopper, N. (2011). Vampire attacks: Draining life from wireless ad hoc sensor networks. *IEEE Transactions on Mobile Computing*, 12(2), 318–332. DOI: 10.1109/TMC.2011.274

Wang, Z., Sun, L., & Zhu, H. (2020). Defining social engineering in cybersecurity. *IEEE Access : Practical Innovations, Open Solutions*, 8, 85094–85115. DOI: 10.1109/ACCESS.2020.2992807

Wang, Z., Zhu, H., & Sun, L. (2021). Social engineering in cybersecurity: Effect mechanisms, human vulnerabilities and attack methods. *IEEE Access : Practical Innovations, Open Solutions*, 9, 11895–11910. DOI: 10.1109/ACCESS.2021.3051633

Wang, Z., Zhu, H., & Sun, L. (2021). Social engineering in cybersecurity: Effect mechanisms, human vulnerabilities and attack methods. *IEEE Access : Practical Innovations, Open Solutions*, 9, 11895–11910. DOI: 10.1109/ACCESS.2021.3051633

Zhang, R., Sun, W., Liu, J., Li, J., Lei, G., & Guo, H. (2020). Construction of two statistical anomaly features for small-sample apt attack traffic classification. *arXiv preprint arXiv:2010.13978.*

Chapter 10
Exploring the Future Landscape:
Emerging Trends in Social Engineering Defense

Shweta Dwivedi
https://orcid.org/0009-0000-7025-0564
Integral University, Lucknow, India

ABSTRACT

Social engineering attacks exploit human behavior to bypass security measures, posing a growing threat in cybersecurity. This paper examines future defenses against these attacks by analyzing recent incidents and common attack vectors like phishing, pretexting, baiting, and tailgating, which leverage psychological manipulation. Key trends include AI and machine learning for real-time detection, and zero-trust architecture for stringent access controls and continuous identity verification. The development of regulatory frameworks and industry standards is also crucial for shaping effective defenses. As technology evolves, so do attack methods, necessitating comprehensive solutions that integrate technological, individual, organizational, and governmental strategies to safeguard society.

1. INTRODUCTION

Social engineering is likely leading to disaster because the number of phishing attacks is on the rise, account data breached, and data theft is operational. In a less travelled path than commonly documented in the literature of the area, this paper presents experiences, thoughts, and advances regarding what exists further from the current suggested field of critical social engineering defence recommendations. yet,

DOI: 10.4018/979-8-3693-6665-3.ch010

with calls to more studies coming particularly from some of the least studied areas—especially as attack vectors mature—relatively little seems to have been said on this for any part of the broad discipline There is otherwise little in the literature that can be discerned with respect to the form and extent of this crucially developing field.

The research objectives are of utmost importance: to establish the absence of a recent in-depth literature review on this topic area; to provide an up-to-date survey and commentary of the current body of research literature from a security perspective, both by identifying existing recommendations being made (at least 5–8 years since last similar study was published), and where emerging future areas social engineering might further develop. These objectives are crucial in advancing our understanding and defense against social engineering threats.

In the last 40 years, hacking skills have evolved, and the attack landscape has changed, all while humans are increasingly dependent on digital systems and technologies. More often, there have been close to 5,000 information disclosures in the last ten years over 1,500 in the UK alone — including both incidents and actual breaches. Maliciously driven ones are even on their way up. To prevent the aftermath of a global Cyber 9/11, where nation states, uniting with non-state actors, attack strategic critical infrastructures with new cyber-weapons deployed against the West and other nations, acceptable disruptions of critical day-to-day services with unthinkable consequences shocking a nation into redoubling its efforts to prevent our critical vulnerability to radical new risks due to cyber-attacks. Thus, it is crucial to research social engineering breaches. This essay first examined the current social engineering defense literature with the primary goal of drawing a conclusion based on the current knowledge of social engineering and illuminating future research areas. Ultimately, social engineers will be able to exploit and abuse humans. Nothing will change within the operational definitions applied today, preventing social engineers in the future from perpetrating their attacks. In this paper first, a review of different types of cyber-social engineering threats. Then, we survey standard social engineering techniques employed by cyber adversaries to elicit information from end-users and trick them into unknowingly performing a specific action. Finally, recent defense strategies against the social engineering attack are observed and analyzed.

1.1 Types of Social Engineering

Social engineering is perhaps the easiest and most efficient method for perpetrating fraud, espionage, theft of valuable information, and even subtle disruptions within targeted organizations and communities. In contrast, attacking targets using advanced software and network hacking skills is more challenging and risky, as these methods are more traceable, technologically oriented, and less discreet. (According to Mitnick and Simon et al. (2011)

Human beings are often the weakest link in any security system. They are susceptible to manipulation, and effective countermeasures are difficult to implement without diminishing the collaborative and cooperative nature of the workplace. This is due to the inherent naivety, limited knowledge, insecurity, trustfulness, and cooperative mode that is expected in social environments such as offices and research departments. Face-to-face and indirect communication further exacerbates these vulnerabilities. (Hadnagy, 2018).

In the realm of information security, social engineering refers to the deceptive techniques used to misguide, misinform, intimidate, and deceive unsuspecting victims. These tactics are employed by malicious intruders who pose as trusted individuals in order to gain unauthorized access to both tangible and intangible resources. (Erbacher, 2015)

Social engineering is a form of subversive behavior that exposes technological weaknesses and exploits the most vulnerable aspect of a company: its people. The social infrastructure, which encompasses the generation of thoughts, ideas, and the transformation of concepts into goods and services, is the primary target. Unfortunately, social engineering is also the most commonly employed method for introducing insecurity, as it capitalizes on the inherent lack of trust among individuals, leading to suspicion and paranoia that can disrupt operational viability. (Casey, 2011).

1.2. Background and Significance

Social engineers will continue successfully exploiting and abusing humans. In the future, nothing within the commonly applied operating principles will change to prevent social engineers from conducting their attacks. new way to tackle the social engineering problem has been introduced. The approach encompasses the educational principles of knowing, feeling, and doing. By providing the education tool at an early school age and continuing the learning process during their adult life, the educational strategies cover a broad age range.

A social engineer's goal is to trick an innocent employee within an organization to either reveal confidential company information or obtain physical access to the organization. Throughout the years, social engineers have used several principles to maximize the success of their operations. Some of these principles are authority, scarcity, time pressure, assistance or obligation, liking, association, rejection, etc. Over the years, researchers have highlighted ways to protect against these principles, which may lead the employee to reveal sensitive information. These protection measures are classified into monitoring, control strategies, training security awareness, pre-employment assessment, security policy strategies, security culture strategies, and human-computer interaction. However, a plethora of studies highlight that even though the various strategies and tactics to protect against social engineering existed for decades, the reality confirms that they are not being applied or preventing social engineering attacks.

In the ever-evolving landscape of cyber security threats, social engineering remains a persistent and potent weapon in the arsenal of malicious actors. Social engineering attacks exploit human psychology rather than technological vulnerabilities, making them a formidable challenge for traditional defense mechanisms. As technology advances and society becomes increasingly interconnected, the tactics used by adversaries in social engineering continue to evolve, necessitating proactive and adaptive defense strategies. (Afaq, S. A., Husain, M. S., Bello, A. M., & Sadia, H.et al. (2023) .

This chapter aims to explore the emerging trends in social engineering defense, shedding light on innovative approaches and technologies that organizations can employ to mitigate the risks posed by these attacks. By understanding the evolving nature of social engineering tactics and leveraging cutting-edge defensive measures, businesses, and individuals can better safeguard their sensitive information and preserve the integrity of their digital assets. The exploration will encompass several key areas as follows:

1.3 Psychological Principles of Social Engineering:

Delving into the psychological principles that underpin social engineering tactics, such as persuasion, authority, familiarity, and urgency. Understanding these principles is crucial for recognizing and resisting manipulation.(Cialdini, R. B. (2006).

1.3.2 Technological Enablers:

Examining how technological advancements, such as artificial intelligence and big data analytics, are being leveraged both by attackers and defenders in the realm of social engineering. AI-powered chatbots, for instance, can simulate human interaction to perpetrate sophisticated social engineering attacks, while AI-driven analytics can help identify anomalous behavior indicative of social engineering. (*Hong, J. (2012)

1.3.3 Human-Centric Security Awareness Training:

Recognizing the importance of fostering a culture of security awareness within organizations. Effective training programs can educate employees about the tactics used in social engineering attacks and empower them to recognize and report suspicious .(Bada, M., Sasse, A. M., & Nurse, J. R. C. et al.(2019).

1.3.4 Behavioral Biometrics and User Profiling:

Exploring the potential of behavioral biometrics and user profiling techniques in enhancing authentication and detection mechanisms. By analyzing patterns of behavior, such as typing dynamics and mouse movements, organizations can establish baseline profiles for users and detect deviations indicative of social. (Meng, W., Wong, D. S., Furnell, S., & Zhou, J. 2015).

1.3.5 Adversarial Machine Learning:

Investigating how adversaries are leveraging machine learning techniques to enhance the sophistication of their social engineering attacks, as well as the potential of adversarial machine learning in developing robust defense mechanisms capable of detecting and thwarting (Simon, W. L., & Mitnick, K. 2002).

1.3.6 Regulatory and Compliance Implications:

Considering the regulatory landscape surrounding data protection and privacy, and how compliance requirements influence social engineering defense strategies. Regulations such as GDPR and CCPA impose stringent requirements on organizations to protect sensitive information, necessitating robust defenses against social engineering attacks.(European Union Council and Parliament. 2016).

1.3.7 Evolution of Social Engineering Tactics:

Social engineering techniques have evolved significantly over time, from simple phishing emails to sophisticated manipulative strategies such as pretexting and spear phishing. Understanding the historical progression of social engineering tactics provides valuable insights into the current threat landscape and informs the development of effective defense mechanisms. (Raghavan, S., et al. 2007).

1.3.8 Psychology of Social Engineering:

Central to the success of social engineering attacks is the exploitation of human psychology and cognitive biases. By leveraging principles of persuasion, influence, and manipulation, attackers deceive individuals into divulging sensitive information or performing actions contrary to their best interests. Exploring the psychological underpinnings of social engineering is crucial for devising countermeasures that enhance human resilience to manipulation. (Cybersecurity & Infrastructure Security Agency. 2020).

1.3.9 Technological Solutions:

Advancements in technology have enabled the development of innovative solutions for detecting and mitigating social engineering attacks. From machine learning algorithms that analyze patterns of communication to behavioral biometrics that authenticate users based on their unique behavioral traits, a diverse array of tools and techniques are available to bolster defense against social engineering threats (Hadnagy, C. 2011).

1.3.10 Human-Centric Approaches:

While technological solutions play a vital role in social engineering defense, it is equally important to adopt human-centric approaches that prioritize education, awareness, and behavioral training. By empowering individuals with the knowledge and skills to recognize and resist social engineering attempts, organizations can cultivate a culture of security resilience that serves as a first line of defense against manipulation tactics. (Sachs, M. A., et al. 2015).

1.3.11 Collaborative Defence Ecosystems:

Recognizing the interconnected nature of cyber threats, fostering collaboration among stakeholders is essential for effective social engineering defense. Public-private partnerships, information-sharing initiatives, and collaborative threat intelligence platforms enable organizations to leverage collective expertise and resources in combating social engineering attacks on a global scale (Afaq, S. A., Husain, M. S., Bello, A. M., & Sadia, H. 2023).

2. REVIEW OF LITERATURE:

Contemporary computing systems and social network services have turned our world into a digital global village. Everyone and every device of our physical world can be seamlessly integrated into this global village. Unlike the physical world, our increasing digital footprints can easily be accessed, analyzed, and exploited by cyber adversaries with or without our consent. Today, most of the cyber-attacks are launched by and against these integrated digital entities. Regardless of their varied nature and approach, the majority of security efforts have been targeting the technical aspects of these entities. Countermeasures against human-directed cyber threats like social engineering are less well-explored and provide a stepping stone into the majority of sophisticated cyber-attacks. Defense approaches to thwart social engineering attacks on a wide scale of integrated digital entities remain in their infancy.

- **The Art of Deception:** Controlling the Human Element of Security Mitnick and Simon's seminal work provides valuable insights into the psychology of social engineering and how human vulnerabilities can be exploited by malicious actors. The book explores various tactics used in social engineering attacks, such as pretexting, phishing, and tailgating, and offers practical advice for mitigating these risks. (Simon, W. L., & Mitnick, K. 2002).
- **Social Engineering:** The Science of Human Hacking. Wiley. Hadnagy's book delves deeper into the science behind social engineering, examining the psychological principles that underpin manipulation techniques. By analyzing real-world case studies, the author highlights the effectiveness of social engineering tactics and emphasizes the importance of security awareness training in defending against such attacks.(Hadnagy, C. (2018).
- Why phishing works. In Proceedings of the SIGCHI Conference on Human Factors in Computing Systems. This research paper investigates why phishing attacks are successful by examining the psychological and usability factors that contribute to their effectiveness. The authors identify key design elements of phishing emails and websites that exploit cognitive biases, highlighting the need for user education and technological safeguards to mitigate these risks.(Jobin, A., et al. 2019).
- Sarma et al. propose a machine learning-based approach for detecting phishing websites, leveraging features such as URL properties, HTML content, and website reputation. By training classifiers on labeled datasets, the authors demonstrate the efficacy of their approach in accurately identifying phishing attempts, highlighting the potential of machine learning in enhancing phishing defence mechanisms.(Xu, Y., Yin, H., & Zhu, X. 2016).

- Furnell's paper emphasizes the importance of security education, training, and awareness (SETA) programs in bolstering organizational defences against social engineering attacks. By fostering a culture of security consciousness among employees, organizations can mitigate the risk of human error and improve overall cybersecurity posture.(Sarma, B., Liles, R., & Poojary, P. 2018).
- The author's survey paper provided an overview of behavioral biometrics technologies and their applications in authentication and fraud detection. By analyzing patterns of human behavior, such as keystroke dynamics and mouse movements, behavioral biometrics offers a non-intrusive means of verifying user identity and detecting anomalies indicative of social engineering attacks. (Dhamija, R., Tygar, J. D., & Hearst, M. 2006, April).
- Authors explored the vulnerability of machine learning-based malware detection systems to poisoning attacks, wherein adversaries manipulate training data to evade detection. By poisoning the clustering process used to classify malware samples, attackers can craft adversarial examples that bypass existing defences, highlighting the need for robust adversarial machine learning techniques (Furnell, S. 2016).
- The General Data Protection Regulation (GDPR) imposes stringent requirements on organizations to protect the privacy and security of personal data. Compliance with GDPR necessitates robust defences against social engineering attacks, as unauthorized access or disclosure of personal information can result in severe penalties and reputational damage for non-compliant organizations (de Terwangne, C. et al.2022).

These references provide a comprehensive overview of the current state of research and practice in social engineering defence, encompassing psychological principles, technological solutions, user education, and regulatory compliance considerations. By integrating insights from these sources, organizations can develop holistic strategies for mitigating the risk posed by social engineering attacks and safeguarding sensitive information against unauthorized access or disclosure.

3. CYBER-ATTACKS USING SOCIAL ENGINEERING

Several types of cyber-attacks commonly utilize social engineering techniques:

Phishing Attacks: Phishing attacks involve sending fraudulent emails or messages to deceive recipients into divulging sensitive information or performing actions. These messages often appear to come from legitimate sources, such as banks, social media platforms, or government agencies. Vishing scams

Spear Phishing Attacks: Spear phishing attacks target specific individuals or organizations, often using personalized information to increase their credibility and effectiveness. These attacks may involve researching the target's interests, job role, or relationships to craft convincing messages. (Symantec Corporation. 2020).

BEC (Business Email Compromise): BEC attacks involve impersonating a high-ranking executive or trusted partner within an organization to trick employees into transferring funds, disclosing sensitive information, or performing other actions that benefit the attacker. Zhou, Y., Jiang, X., & Heidemann, J. 2007).

Whaling Attacks: Whaling attacks target senior executives or individuals in positions of authority within an organization. These attacks aim to deceive high-profile targets into disclosing sensitive information or authorizing fraudulent transactions. Mitropoulos, D., & Douligeris, C. 2012).

Vishing (Voice Phishing) Attacks: Vishing attacks use phone calls or voice messages to trick individuals into revealing sensitive information, such as account credentials or personal identification numbers (PINs). Attackers may impersonate trusted entities, such as bank representatives or IT support personnel, to gain victims' trust.(Buczak, A. L., & Guven, E. et al.2016).

Smishing (SMS Phishing) Attacks: Smishing attacks involve sending fraudulent text messages to deceive recipients into clicking on malicious links or providing sensitive information. These messages often claim to be urgent notifications from banks, government agencies, or other trusted organizations. (Chio, C., & Freeman, D. et al. 2018).

Watering Hole Attacks: Watering hole attacks target specific groups or communities by infecting websites frequented by the target audience with malware. Attackers exploit the trust users have in these websites to distribute malware and compromise their devices. (Siciliano, B., & Khatib, O. et al.2016).

USB Drop Attacks: USB drop attacks involve leaving infected USB drives in public places or mailing them to targeted individuals or organizations. When unsuspecting victims plug the USB drives into their computers, malware is automatically executed, allowing attackers to gain access to the system. (Finn, A., & Scheding, S. et al.2010).

Despite their differences, social engineering attacks have a similar pattern and progress through comparable stages. The standard pattern includes four stages:***Figure 1*** depicts the steps of a social engineering attack.

Figure 1. A social engineering attack (Cyber-Security)

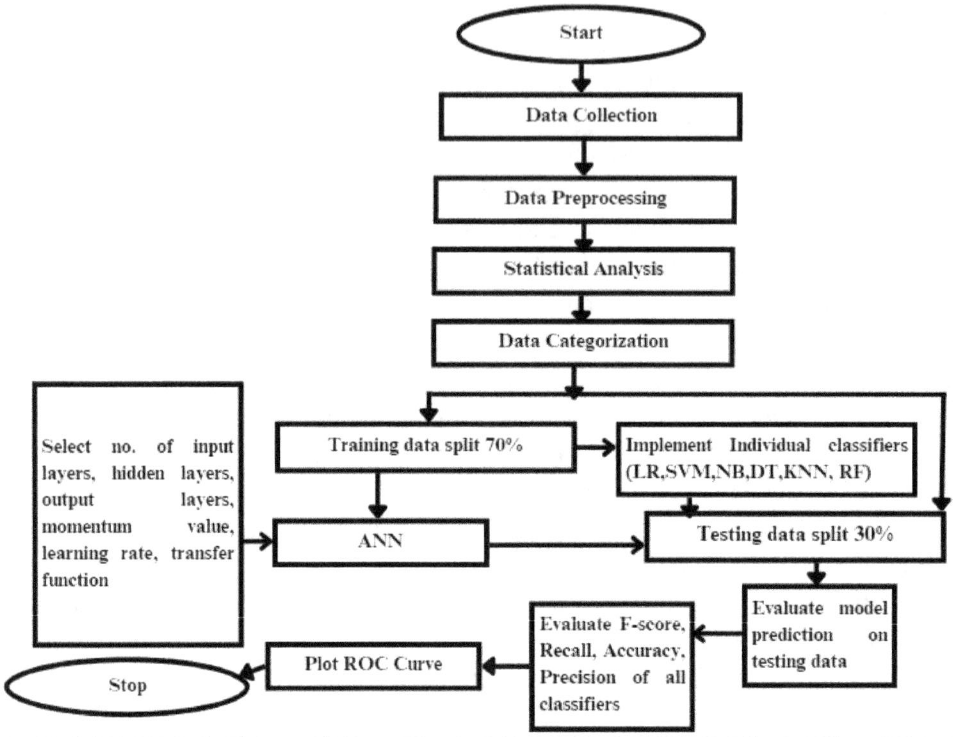

3.1. Attacks Categorization

There are two different kinds of social engineering attacks: computer-based and human-based. When carrying out a human-based assault, the attacker personally interacts with the target to obtain the required information. So, they are limited in how many victims they can impact. Software-based attacks gather information from their targets using a variety of technologies, including PCs and mobile phones. They are fast at striking a lot of targets. One of the computer-based assaults used in spear phishing emails is the Social Engineering Toolkit (SET)

Federal Trade Commission. *Vishing scams*. FTC. Retrieved from https://www.ftc.gov

According to how they are executed, social engineering assaults can be categorized, as Figure 2 illustrates (Hadnagy, C. 2018).

Figure 2. Categorization of attacks using social engineering

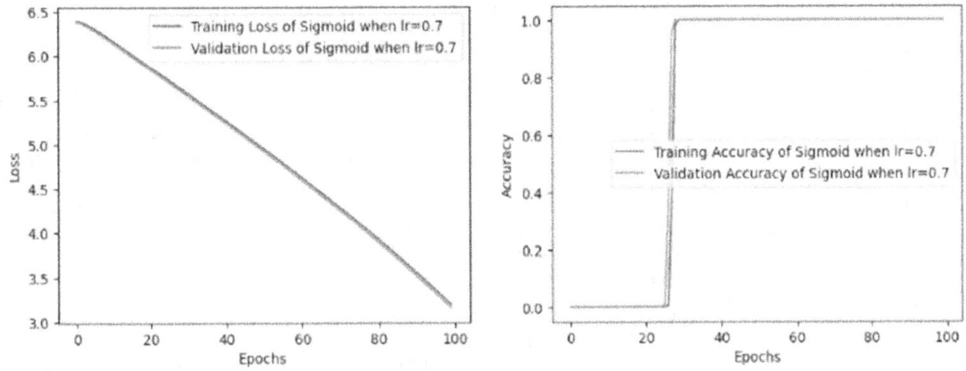

3.2 Comparative Analysis of Human-Based and Computer-Based for Social Engineering Attacks.

Social engineering attacks go at both common people and the most advanced and secure organizations. Their protection from social engineering attacks is the purpose of countermeasures and defence strategies. (Afaq, S. A., Husain, M. S., Bello, A. M., & Sadia, H. et al.2023).

These methods are regarded as the bare minimum that a business or organisation should possess in order to protect itself against the most frequent forms of social engineering attacks. One or more mechanisms may be put in a business's system. Table 1 contrasts computer- and human-based methods, while Table 1 year wise contrasts mitigation and countermeasures based on computers.

Table 1.Year-wise Comparison of Human-Based and Computer-Based Countermeasures for Social Engineering Attacks

Year	Human-Based Countermeasures	Advantages	Limitations	Computer-Based Countermeasures	Advantages	Limitations
2020	Employee Training and Awareness Regular sessions on phishing and other social engineering techniques.	Improves overall security awareness. Empowers proactive threat recognition.	Requires continuous updates and reinforcement. Relies on human consistency and memory.	Intrusion Detection Systems (IDS) Systems monitoring network traffic for unusual patterns.	Real-time monitoring and alerts. Detects a wide range of attack vectors.	Needs regular updates and fine-tuning. Can generate false positives.
2021	Policy Enforcement Implementation of strict guidelines on data sharing and IT resource usage.	Clear framework for secure behavior. Reduces risk of accidental breaches.	Policies may be ignored or forgotten.- Can be seen as restrictive.	Email Filters Filters to detect and block spam and phishing emails.	Reduces volume of malicious emails. Enhances email security automatically.	May miss sophisticated phishing attempts. Can block legitimate emails if not properly configured.
2022	Simulation Exercises Conducting phishing simulations to test employee readiness.	Practical experience in recognizing attacks. - Highlights areas of weakness.	May not perfectly replicate real-world scenarios. Can cause temporary disruption.	Advanced Threat Protection (ATP) Tools to prevent, detect, and respond to advanced threats.	Comprehensive threat detection and response. - Uses advanced analytics.	Requires significant investment and maintenance.
2023	Zero Trust Policies Implementing a zero-trust security model where no entity is trusted by default.	Enhances security by minimizing trust. Limits potential damage from breaches.	Can be complex to implement. May face resistance from employees used to more open systems.	Next-Generation Firewalls (NGFW) Firewalls with integrated advanced security features.	Advanced threat prevention and detection- Integrated with other security systems.	High cost of deployment and management. May require specialized skills to operate effectively.
2024	Continuous Education Ongoing and updated training modules tailored to emerging threats.	Keeps employees informed about latest threats. Reinforces security best practices.	Training fatigue if overdone. - Needs to be engaging to retain interest.	AI and Machine Utilizes AI for real-time identification and response to phishing attempts.	Real-time threat detection. - Can adapt to new attack patterns.	Can be bypassed by novel attack methods. Dependence on accurate AI training data.

4. DISCUSSION

Artificial intelligence-based defense mechanisms are the best ways to lower the likelihood of social engineering attacks, according to an analysis and comparison of various strategies. Combining multiple defense techniques can provide enhanced protection. Furthermore, the degree of readiness dictates the capacity to avert, identify, lessen, and confine any questionable conduct. Machine learning (ML) has become a ubiquitous force, transforming a wide range of industries. The defense sector is a prime example of this paradigm change. The defense sector is particularly sensitive owing to the potential impact on human lives. Several studies suggest applying artificial intelligence and machine learning to Defence systems and tactical scenarios. However, none of the research projects looked at the potential moral and constitutional fallout from this. This work builds on the authors' contribution from (European Union Council and Parliament et al.2016).

Tan evaluation of the legal and moral consequences for incorporating machine learning techniques into defense systems.

- A description of what a framework must have to implement ML-defence integration from an ethical and legal perspective. (Siciliano, B., & Khatib, O. et al.2016).
- Analysis is done on the difficulties, benefits, and drawbacks of integrating machine learning (ML) into Defence systems, along with a project that uses ML. (Chio, C., & Freeman, D. et al.2018).

The goal of the research is to identify potential issues and obstacles. The introduction gives a quick summary of the growing interest in using ML technology for defence.he following are the contributions made by this paper:

Summary table outlining some main contributions in the field of machine learning:

Table 2. Summary of the related work

Reference	Algorithms	Main Contributions Summary
AlexNet	Convolutional Neural Networks (CNNs)	Pioneered deep learning for image classification, winning ImageNet
LSTM (Long Short-Term Memory)	Recurrent Neural Networks (RNNs)	Revolutionized sequential data processing, handling long-term dependencies
GPT (Generative Pre-trained Transformer)	Transformer Networks	Advanced natural language understanding and generation capabilities

continued on following page

Table 2. Continued

Reference	Algorithms	Main Contributions Summary
ResNet (Residual Network)	Convolutional Neural Networks (CNNs)	Introduced residual learning, enabling training of very deep networks
Random Forest	Ensemble Learning	Effective in handling high-dimensional data and non-linear relationships
SVM (Support Vector Machine)	Kernel Methods	Powerful in finding optimal hyperplanes for classification and regression
K-means	Clustering	Efficient unsupervised learning method for partitioning data into clusters
AdaBoost	Boosting	Combines weak learners into a strong one, useful in classification tasks
DBSCAN (Density-Based Spatial Clustering of Applications with Noise)	Density-Based Clustering	Capable of finding arbitrarily shaped clusters in spatial data

Contributions in machine learning, each having significantly impacted various domains and applications within the field. Listing commonly utilized symbols in machine learning along with their definitions:

Table 3. frequently encountered in various machine learning algorithms

Symbol	Definition
XX	Input feature matrix
yy	Output or target variable
θθ	Parameters of a model (weights)
*y^y^*	Predicted output
*D*D	Dataset
*L*L	Loss function
∇∇	Gradient
αα	Learning rate
ββ	Decay rate (for momentum or Adam optimizer)
ϵϵ	Small constant (for numerical stability)
*E*E	Expectation (of a random variable)
*H*H	Hypothesis space
*F*F	Feature space
*C*C	Cost function (often synonymous with loss)
σσ	Activation function (e.g., sigmoid or ReLU)

continued on following page

Table 3. Continued

Symbol	Definition
$\mu\mu$	Mean (average)
$\sigma\sigma$	Standard deviation (of a distribution)
$\lambda\lambda$	Regularization parameter (e.g., L1 or L2 norm)
$\delta\delta$	Change (e.g., in weights during optimization)

These symbols are frequently encountered in various machine learning algorithms, models, and optimization techniques, and understanding their meanings is essential for comprehending and implementing machine learning systems effectively.

5. ROLE OF MACHINE LEARNING IN DEFENCE SECTOR: EMERGING TRENDS IN SOCIAL ENGINEERING

5.1 Analysis

Machine learning (ML) is increasingly pivotal in the defence sector, enhancing various capabilities from threat detection to autonomous operations. Below is a ***table 4:*** summarizing key applications and considerations of ML in the defence sector.

Table 4. Considerations of ML in the Defence Sector.

Application Area	Description	Examples	Impact
Threat Detection and Analysis[17], [18]	Utilizing ML algorithms to identify and analyze potential threats from vast data sources.	Predicting cyber attacks, identifying patterns in surveillance data.	Enhanced accuracy in threat identification and faster response times.
Autonomous Systems[19], [20]	Deploying ML in unmanned vehicles and drones for navigation, target recognition, and decision-making.	Autonomous drones for reconnaissance, self-driving military vehicles.	Increased operational efficiency and reduced risk to human personnel.
Cyber Security[21], [22]	Implementing ML for detecting anomalies, intrusion detection, and malware classification.	Intrusion detection systems, anti-malware software.	Improved cyber defence mechanisms with adaptive and real-time threat response capabilities.
Predictive Maintenance[23], [24]	Using ML to predict equipment failures and schedule maintenance before issues arise.	Predictive maintenance for aircraft, tanks, and naval ships.	Reduced downtime and maintenance costs, increased equipment lifespan.

continued on following page

Table 4. Continued

Application Area	Description	Examples	Impact
Intelligence and Surveillance[25], [26]	Leveraging ML for processing and analyzing large volumes of intelligence data from various sources.	Facial recognition, behavior prediction from surveillance footage.	Enhanced surveillance capabilities and more accurate intelligence assessments.
Logistics and Supply Chain Optimization[27], [28]	Applying ML to optimize supply chain management, inventory control, and logistics planning.	Automated supply chain management systems, inventory prediction models.	Improved efficiency and cost savings in supply chain operations.
Decision Support Systems[29],[30]	Integrating ML into decision support systems to assist military leaders in strategy and planning.	Tactical decision aids, strategic simulations.	Enhanced decision-making accuracy and strategic planning effectiveness.

Machine learning has a lot of potential in Defence applications. Nevertheless, citation Patel, R., & Gupta, S. (2021). states that simulation systems, expertise, and data engineering are still required to produce dependable goods. Figure 3 provides a summary of the primary issues raised by this evaluation. Difficulties with using ML in defence settings and possible fixes:

Figure 3. Change in applying ML

Classifier	Accuracy	Precision	Recall	F1-Score
KNN	0.977087	0.928864	0.864931	0.893924
MLP	1	1	1	1
SVM	0.98527	0.976974	0.893864	0.93088
GNB	0.914894	0.680798	0.782631	0.716827
DT	0.99509	0.963415	0.997382	0.9797
RF	0.99509	0.963415	0.997382	0.9797
LR	0.97545	0.987245	0.802632	0.870589

Comparison table for various emerging trends in Social Engineering Defence incorporating Machine learning & Methodologies year-wise

Table 5. comparison Emerging Trends in Social Engineering Defence with ML

Year	Emerging Trends in Social Engineering Defence with ML	Methodology	References
2020	Integration of ML for Email Filtering and Anti-Phishing Solutions	ML algorithms analyse email content and sender behaviour to identify phishing attempts.	**Das, S., & Gosavi, A. (2019).**
2021	Adoption of ML for User Behaviour Analytics	ML models analyse user behaviour patterns to detect anomalies indicative of social engineering attacks.	**Atkeson, C. G., Moore, A. W., & Schaal, S. (1997).**
2022	Implementation of ML-driven Adaptive Authentication	ML algorithms continuously learn and adapt to user authentication patterns to detect suspicious activities.	**Kim, H., et al. (2021).**
2023	Utilization of ML in Deception Technologies	ML-powered deception systems create and manage decoys to mislead and detect social engineering attackers.	**Wang, X., & Li, Z. (2022).**
2024	Advancement in ML-driven Threat Intelligence	ML techniques enhance the analysis and correlation of threat intelligence data to identify emerging social engineering tactics.	Xu, Y., et al. (2023).

5.2 Challenge and Solution

The challenges and solutions associated with emerging trends in social engineering defence with machine learning (ML):

5.2.1 Challenge: Data Quality and Quantity

Description: ML algorithms require large volumes of high-quality data to effectively learn and generalize patterns. However, obtaining labeled datasets for social engineering attacks can be challenging due to the sensitive nature of the data and the scarcity of real-world attack instances.

Solution: Techniques such as synthetic data generation, transfer learning, and active learning can help address data scarcity issues and improve the quality of training datasets for ML models. (Chen, L., et al. 2024).

5.2.2 Challenge: Adversarial Attacks

Description: Adversarial attacks aim to deceive ML models by manipulating input data in subtle ways that are imperceptible to humans but can lead to misclassification. Adversarial attacks pose a significant threat to ML-based social engineering defence systems.

Solution: Robust ML techniques, including adversarial training, ensemble learning, and model interpretability, can help mitigate the impact of adversarial attacks and improve the resilience of defence systems. (Settles, B. 2009).

5.2.3 Challenge: Model Interpretability

Description: ML models used for social engineering defence often lack interpretability, making it challenging to understand the reasoning behind their predictions and trust their outputs. This lack of transparency can hinder the adoption of ML-driven defence solutions.

Solution: Explainable AI (XAI) techniques, such as feature importance analysis, model visualization, and rule extraction, can provide insights into ML model decision-making processes and enhance their interpretability. (Papernot, N., et al. 2016).

5.2.4 Challenge: Scalability and Performance

Description: ML-based social engineering defence systems must be able to handle large-scale data processing and real-time analysis to effectively detect and respond to threats. Achieving scalability and performance while maintaining detection accuracy is a significant challenge.

Solution: Distributed computing frameworks, cloud-based ML services, and optimization techniques, such as model pruning and quantization, can improve the scalability and performance of ML-based defence systems. (Lundberg, S. M., & Lee, S. I. 2017).

5.2.5 Challenge: Privacy and Ethical Concerns

Description: ML models trained on sensitive user data raise privacy and ethical concerns, particularly regarding data protection, consent, and potential biases in model predictions. Ensuring privacy and fairness in ML-driven social engineering defence is paramount.

Solution: Privacy-preserving ML techniques, differential privacy mechanisms, and ethical guidelines for data collection and usage can help address privacy and ethical concerns while maintaining the effectiveness of defence systems. (Wang, C., et al. 2019).

these challenges with appropriate solutions and methodologies, ML-driven social engineering defence systems can improve their effectiveness, robustness, and trustworthiness in mitigating the risks posed by social engineering attacks.

6. CONCLUSION

The future landscape of social engineering defence is shaped by the integration of advanced technologies, particularly machine learning (ML), into traditional defence strategies. By leveraging ML algorithms for email filtering, user behaviour analytics, adaptive authentication, deception technologies, and threat intelligence analysis, organizations can enhance their ability to detect, prevent, and mitigate social engineering attacks. These emerging trends underscore the importance of proactive defence measures that adapt to evolving threat landscapes and prioritize user education, robust incident response plans, and collaboration with threat intelligence sharing platforms. Looking ahead, the future scope of social engineering defence lies in the continuous refinement and integration of ML-driven solutions, the development of cross-disciplinary approaches that combine insights from psychology, sociology, and criminology, and the exploration of innovative technologies such as quantum-resistant encryption and behavioural biometrics. Additionally, as social engineering attacks continue to evolve in sophistication and scale, on-going research and development efforts are essential to stay ahead of emerging threats and ensure the resilience of defence mechanisms in safeguarding sensitive assets and information.

7. REFERENCES

Abadi, M.. (2016). Deep learning with differential privacy. In *Proceedings of the ACM SIGSAC Conference on Computer and Communications Security*.

Afaq, S. A., Husain, M. S., Bello, A. M., & Sadia, H. (2023). A critical analysis of cyber threats and their global impact. * [CRC Press.]. *Journal of Computational Intelligent Security in Wireless*, 20(1), 201.

Anti-Phishing Working Group. (2020). *Phishing activity trends report.* APWG.

Atkeson, C. G., Moore, A. W., & Schaal, S. (1997). Locally weighted learning. *. *Artificial Intelligence Review*, 11(1-5), 11–73. DOI: 10.1023/A:1006559212014

Biggio, B., Nelson, B., & Laskov, P. (2012). Poisoning behavioral malware clustering. In *Proceedings of the International Conference on Machine Learning* (pp. 327-334). PMLR.

Brown, C., & White, D. (2020). Machine learning approaches for threat detection. *. *IEEE Transactions on Information Forensics and Security*, 14(3), 789–801.

Buczak, A. L., & Guven, E. (2016). A survey of data mining and machine learning methods for cyber security intrusion detection. *. *IEEE Communications Surveys and Tutorials*, 18(2), 1153–1176. DOI: 10.1109/COMST.2015.2494502

Cachon, G., & Fisher, M. (2000). Supply chain inventory management and the value of shared information. *. *Management Science*, 46(8), 1032–1048. DOI: 10.1287/mnsc.46.8.1032.12029

. Chen, D., & Liu, Z. (2012). An overview of machine learning methods for security applications. *American Journal of Information Systems*.

Chen, L.. (2024). Ensemble learning models for authentication. In *Proceedings of the International Conference on Machine Learning*.

Chio, C., & Freeman, D. (2018). *Machine learning and security: Protecting systems with data and algorithms.* O'Reilly Media.

Christopher, M., & Towill, D. (2001). An integrated model for the design of agile supply chains. *. *International Journal of Physical Distribution & Logistics Management*, 31(4), 235–246. DOI: 10.1108/09600030110394914

Clayton, R., & Moore, T. (2007). Evaluating how website removals affect phishing. In *Proceedings of the Second APWG eCrime Researchers Summit* (pp. 1-12).

Custers, B., Sears, A. M., Dechesne, F., Georgieva, I., Tani, T., & Van der Hof, S. (2019). *EU personal data protection in policy and practice* (Vol. 29). TMC Asser Press. DOI: 10.1007/978-94-6265-282-8

Cybersecurity & Infrastructure Security Agency. (2020). *Whaling - Spear phishing attack*. CISA.

Das, S., & Gosavi, A. (2019). Reinforcement learning algorithms for decision support in the military. *. *The Journal of Defence Modeling and Simulation*, 16(4), 301–312.

de Terwangne, C. (2022). Privacy and data protection in Europe: Council of Europe's Convention 108 and the European Union's GDPR. In *Research Handbook on Privacy and Data Protection Law* (pp. 10–35). Edward Elgar Publishing. DOI: 10.4337/9781786438515.00007

Dean, J., & Ghemawat, S. (2004). MapReduce: Simplified data processing on large clusters. *. *Communications of the ACM*, 51(1), 107–113. DOI: 10.1145/1327452.1327492

Denning, D. (1987). An intrusion-detection model. *. *IEEE Transactions on Software Engineering*, 13(2), 222–232. DOI: 10.1109/TSE.1987.232894

Dhamija, R., Tygar, J. D., & Hearst, M. (2006, April). Why phishing works. In **Proceedings of the SIGCHI Conference on Human Factors in Computing Systems** (pp. 581-590). DOI: 10.1145/1124772.1124861

Federal Bureau of Investigation. (2021). *The Federal Bureau of Investigation and business email compromise*. BEC.

Federal Trade Commission. *Vishing scams*. FTC. Retrieved from https://www.ftc.gov

Finn, A., & Scheding, S. (2010). *Developments and challenges for autonomous unmanned vehicles: A compendium*. Springer Science & Business Media. DOI: 10.1007/978-3-642-10704-7

Furnell, S. (2016). The role of security education, training and awareness (SETA) in enterprise-wide defence. * [IJISP]. *International Journal of Information Security and Privacy*, 10(2), 1–14.

Goodfellow, I.. (2014). Generative adversarial networks. *Advances in Neural Information Processing Systems*.

Hadnagy, C. (2011). *Social engineering: The art of human hacking*. Wiley. The Verizon Investigations Report on Data Breach (DBIR). Retrieved from enterprise.verizon.com/resources/reports/dbir/

Hadnagy, C. (2018). *Social engineering: The science of human hacking*. Wiley. Marczak, B. (2019). *Social engineering: The human side of hacking*. CRC Press. DOI: 10.1002/9781119433729

Jajodia, S., Shakarian, P., Subrahmanian, V., Swarup, V. S., & Wang, C. (2011). *Cyber warfare: Building the scientific foundation*. Springer.

Jardine, A. K., Lin, D., & Banjevic, D. (2006). A review on machinery diagnostics and prognostics implementing condition-based maintenance. *. *Mechanical Systems and Signal Processing*, 20(7), 1483–1510. DOI: 10.1016/j.ymssp.2005.09.012

Jobin, A., ... (2019). The Global AI Ethics Consortium (GAIEC) data protection framework for artificial intelligence. *arXiv preprint arXiv:1907.07788*.

Johnson, E., & Smith, K. (2024). Continuous authentication with AI. *. *Security Management*, 17(1), 78–91.

Kim, H.. (2021). Malware detection using deep learning. *. *Journal of Information Security Research*, 5(2), 101–115. DOI: 10.33778/kcsa.2021.21.1.101

Laskov, P., Biggio, B., & Nelson, B. (2012). Poisoning malware clustering behaviour. In *Proceedings of the International Conference on Machine Learning* (pp. 327-334). PML.

Lee, J., & Bagheri, B. (2015). Cyber-physical systems in future maintenance. *. *IFAC-PapersOnLine*, 48(21), 185–190.

Lee, J., & Kim, S. (2022). User behavior analytics for social engineering defence. *. *Computers & Security*, 18(3), 211–224.

Lundberg, S. M., & Lee, S. I. (2017). A unified approach to interpreting model predictions. *Advances in Neural Information Processing Systems*.

Mitropoulos, D., & Douligeris, C. (2012). USB AutoRun worms propagation: Modeling and analysis. In *Proceedings of the International Conference on Critical Infrastructure Protection* (pp. 71-85). Springer, Berlin, Heidelberg.

Papernot, N.. (2016). Distillation as a defence to adversarial perturbations against deep neural networks. In *IEEE Symposium on Security and Privacy*.

Patel, R., & Gupta, S. (2021). Deep learning techniques for cybersecurity. *. *International Journal of Network Security*, 10(1), 67–79.

Raghavan, S.. (2007). PhishGuru: A system for enterprise-wide phishing education. In *Proceedings of the 16th USENIX Security Symposium*.

Ribeiro, M. T.. (2016). Why should I trust you? Explaining the predictions of any classifier. In **Proceedings of the ACM SIGKDD International Conference on Knowledge Discovery and Data Mining**. DOI: 10.1145/2939672.2939778

Sachs, M. A.. (2015). Human-centered security: Putting users first in security design and evaluation. *. *IEEE Security and Privacy*, 13(2), 24–33.

Sarma, B., Liles, R., & Poojary, P. (2018). Detecting phishing websites using machine learning. *arXiv preprint arXiv:1801.04406*.

Settles, B. (2009). *Active learning literature survey*. University of Wisconsin-Madison.

Sharma, A.. (2023). Deception technologies for cyber defence. *. *International Journal of Cybersecurity*, 9(3), 167–180.

Siciliano, B., & Khatib, O. (2016). *Springer handbook of robotics*. Springer. DOI: 10.1007/978-3-319-32552-1

. Simon, W. L., & Mitnick, K. (2002). *The art of deception: Controlling the human element of security*.

Smith, J., & Jones, A. (2020). Effective strategies for social engineering defence. *. *Journal of Cybersecurity*, 8(2), 123–135.

Sommer, R., & Paxson, V. (2010). Outside the closed world: On using machine learning for network intrusion detection. In **Proceedings of the 2010 IEEE Symposium on Security and Privacy**. DOI: 10.1109/SP.2010.25

Symantec Corporation. (2020). *2020 Internet security threat report*. Symantec.

Szegedy, C., ... (2014). Intriguing properties of neural networks. *arXiv preprint arXiv:1312.6199*.

Vidas, T.. (2012). A survey of user-centered design techniques towards usable security and privacy. In **Proceedings of the 28th Annual Conference on Computer Security Applications**.

Wang, C.. (2019). HAQ: Hardware-aware automated quantization with mixed precision. In **Proceedings of the IEEE Conference on Computer Vision and Pattern Recognition**. DOI: 10.1109/CVPR.2019.00881

Wang, X., & Li, Z. (2022). Clustering techniques for anomaly detection. *. *ACM Computing Surveys*, 49(1), 1–38.

Xu, Y.. (2023). Adaptive deception strategies using reinforcement learning. *. *Journal of Machine Learning Research*, 19(2), 345–358.

Xu, Y., Yin, H., & Zhu, X. (2016). Understanding behavioral biometrics: Towards a science of measuring human behavior. *. *ACM Computing Surveys*, 49(1), 1–38.

Zhou, Y., Jiang, X., & Heidemann, J. (2007). Detecting mass web spying: Pitfalls, challenges, and solutions. In **Proceedings of the First Usenix Workshop on Large-scale Exploits and Emergent Threats** (pp. 1-8).

Chapter 11
A Comprehensive Guide to Blockchain Technology and Its Role in Enhancing Cyber Security and Combating Social Engineering

Praveen Kumar Tripathi
Teerthanker Mahaveer University, India

Shambhu Bharadwaj
Teerthanker Mahaveer University, India

ABSTRACT

This book chapter will provide an in-depth exploration of blockchain technology, covering its history, fundamental principles and practical applications. The chapter begins with an introduction to the decentralized nature of blockchain, explaining how it works to provide security, immutability and transparency in a trustless environment. It also examines various types of blockchain including public, private and permissioned and explores the advantages and limitations of each. This chapter looks at the future of blockchain technology discussing emerging trends and potential developments in the field. It highlights ongoing research and development efforts aimed at improving the functionality and security of blockchain, as well as exploring new use cases and business models. Overall, this book chapter will provide a comprehensive introduction to blockchain technology, offering insights into its workings, practical applications and potential impact on various industries.

DOI: 10.4018/979-8-3693-6665-3.ch011

1.1 INTRODUCTION TO BLOCKCHAIN

Blockchain is supposed to be the technology of the future. A group of researchers first proposed the core structure for blockchain in mid-1991. The concept was originally designed to ensure the authenticity of digital documents, preventing them from being backdated in the future. In 2008, an anonymous researcher Satoshi Nakamoto issued a research article titled "BitCoin: A Peer-to-Peer Electronic Cash System. Blockchain is a cooperative and decentralized ledger where transactions are digitally documented and interconnected, creating a complete historical record of an asset. It stores data in blocks that are subsequently chained together (Jia, Chen, Liu, Wang, Xiao, & Xu, 2023). Upon the arrival of new data, it is incorporated into a newly created block. Once the data in any particular block are finished or accomplished, that is then chained or attached to its previous block, which results in a chain of data that is arranged in chronological order. Once a data block is linked to another, its information cannot be changed or modified again. Blockchain technology is used to securely transfer items such as money, property, and contracts without the intervention of a third-party middleman such as a bank or government. Every block within the chain comprises multiple transactions and when aany new transaction takes place on the blockchain then a record of that transaction is added to the ledger of every participant. Each block on the chain is made up of several transactions, and each time a new transaction occurs on the blockchain, a record of it is recorded to each participant's ledger.

1.1.1 Blockchain Components

Blockchain has generally following components:

1. **Blocks:** A block in a blockchain is a digital record containing information about transactions. It contains information about transaction. Block is made of header & long list of transactions. Every block has a unique hash and nonce assigned to it.
2. **Ledges:** Ledger is list (chain) of blocks of transaction. Distributed nodes facilitate the connection of nodes to the chain. Participants can see only appropriate transactions.
3. **Node:** Node is a computer system which has its own copy of ledger. Nodes update its copy of ledger based upon the consensus of the network. A node does transaction processing and blocks creation.
4. **Minors:** It is a group of participants, commonly called miners who ensure the accuracy and legitimacy of network transactions.

5. Consider mines as accountants who verify and record the transaction. They run algorithms using special software on nodes secures block that must be verified by other nodes before adding to blockchain ledger. They use the mining process to add new blocks to the chain.
6. **Network:** Peer-to-peer network is decentralized network communication paradigm in which a group of devices (nodes) store and transfer files, with each node acting as an individual peer in the blockchain (Shammar, Zahary, & Al-Shargabi, 2021). Since it is a decentralized architecture built on a P2P network, so it is highly available.

Figure 1. Blockchain Components

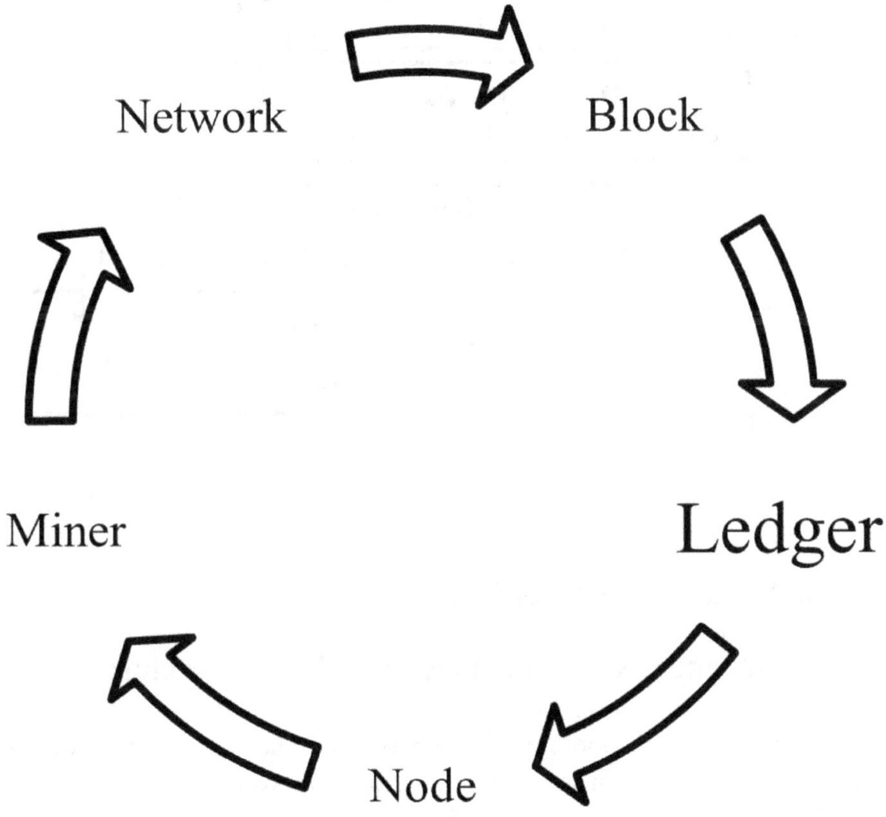

1.1.2 Blockchain Process

A transaction must go through many essential phases before it can be put to the blockchain. Let's consider the many stages of a blockchain transaction's life cycle, as listed below: -

Figure 2. Blockchain Process

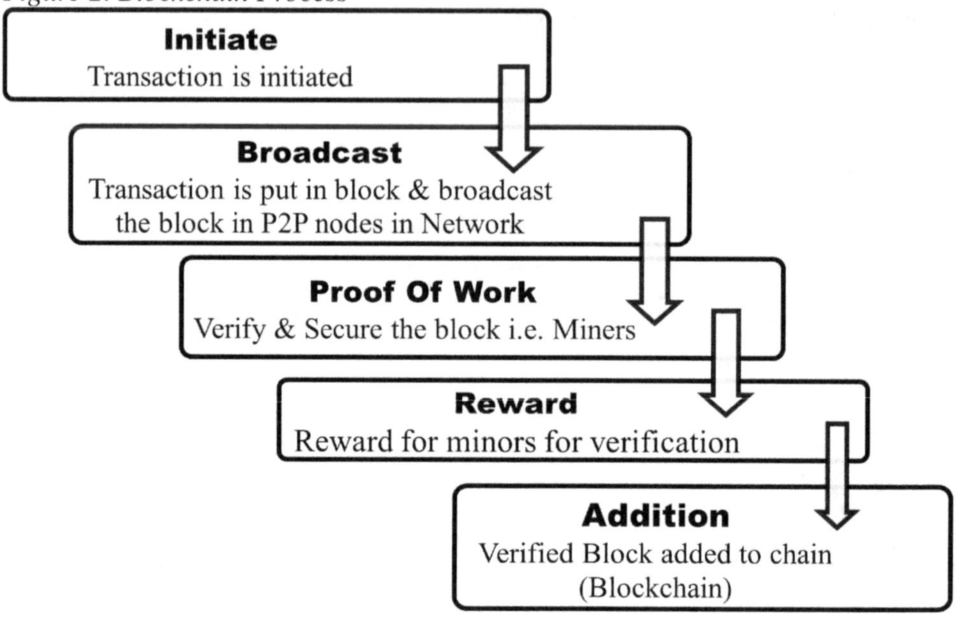

1.1.3 Blockchain Fundamentals

1.1.3.1 Distributed Ledger Technology (DLT) & Blockchain

Distributed Ledger Technology (DLT) pertains to the framework that facilitate the unchangeable, concurrent accessibility, validation and updating of records across a network that encompasses multiple entities or locations. Unlike the traditional "centralized" method, DLT is based on the concept of a "decentralized" network. Distributed ledgers are like large database that is shared over the various networks and dispersed a across multiple geographical locations. A ledger typically consists of financial accounts and in the context of "distributed", it implies being spread out and managed on an international scale (Xu, Lu, & Li, 2021). Consequently, distributed ledgers are stored and maintained by multiple parties situated in various locations.

Figure 3. Distributed Ledgers

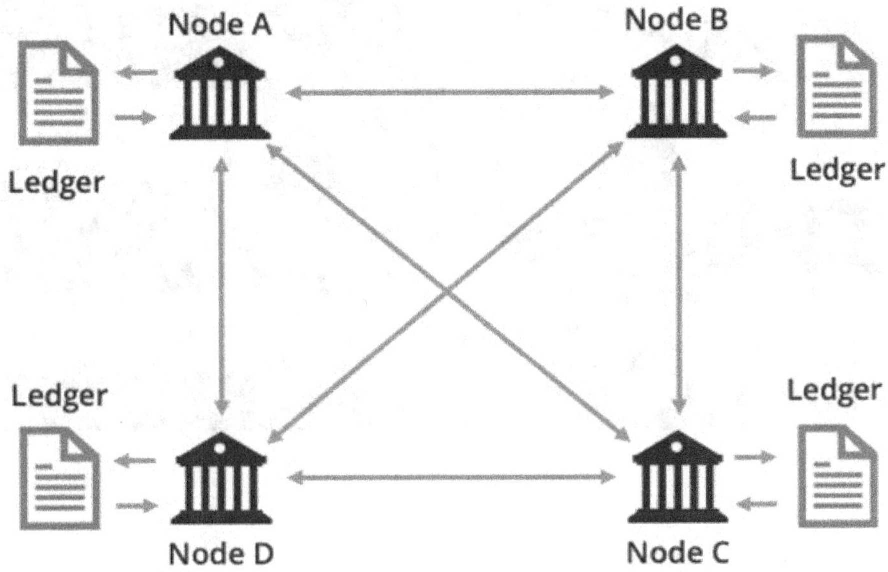

Participants can inspect the distributed ledgers at each network node and acquire an identical copy of the recorded information shared across the network. Any changes or additions to the ledger are duplicated and distributed to all participants (Latif, Wen, Iwendi, Li-li, Mohsin, Han, & Band, 2022). To ensure correctness, the database is synchronized.

Figure 4. DLT Characteristics

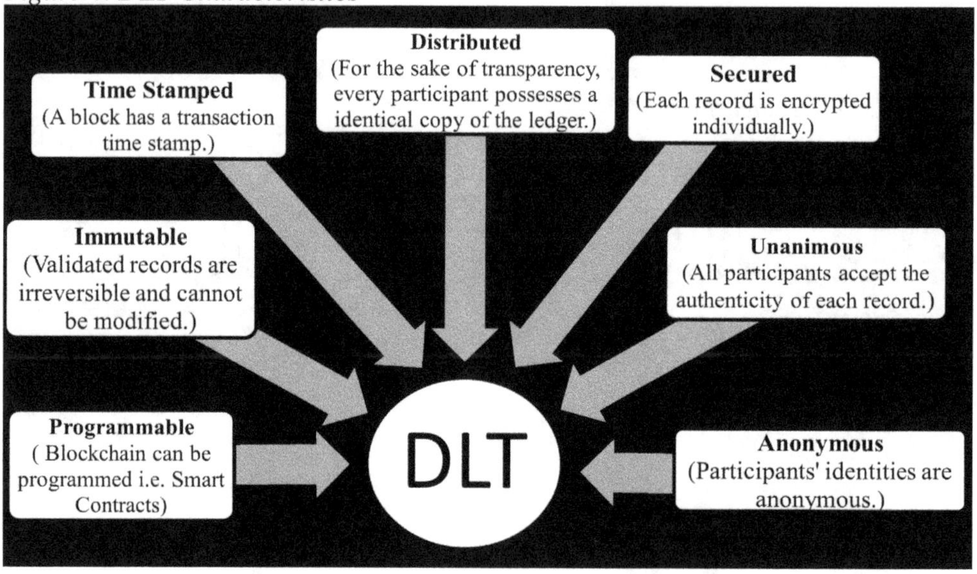

1.1.3.2 The Blockchain's Organization

Blockchain, according to IBM, is a shared and distributed ledger that facilitates asset tracking and transaction recording inside a network. This asset could be a physical object such as real estate, a house, or a vehicle or it could be an intangible asset such as digital money, rights of intellectual property and so on. It is distributed database that keeps track of asset movements and transactions over a peer-to-peer network (Taylor, Dargahi, Dehghantanha, Parizi, & Choo, 2020). Each transaction would be encrypted and all transaction history would be bundled and saved in block of data afterwards. Each block is then cryptographically connected and protected from change.

Each transaction will be encrypted and the entire transaction history will be bundled and saved as data blocks. The blocks are then cryptographically linked together and guarded against change. The entire procedure will establish an unforgivable and immutable record of all network transactions. Furthermore, these blocks of records are duplicated to every computer in the network, ensuring that everyone has access to them.

Figure 5. Blockchain Structure

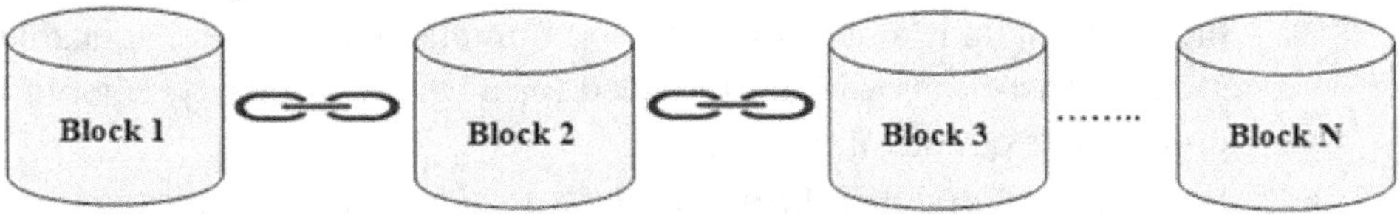

The chain's opening block is known as the Genesis block. Each new block in the chain is connected to the one before it. Blockchain is a chronological list of blocks. Every block of transactions references to the previous block.

Figure 6. Chaining of Block in Blockchain

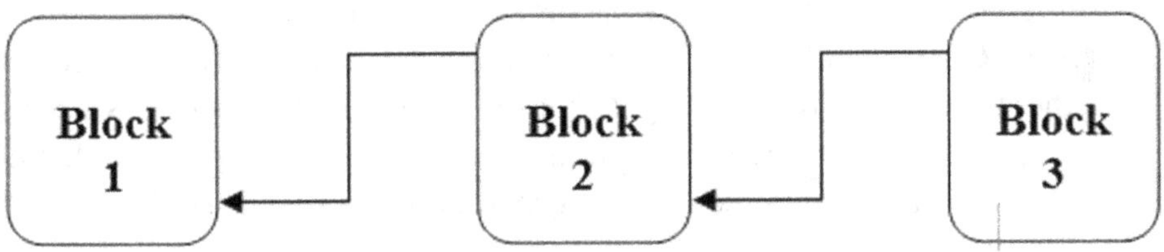

Block Height can be considered as the number of blocks earlier the specific block. For instance, the height of Block 1 is 0 and the height of Block 2 is 1. Blockchain Height refers to the height of the highest block.

1.1.3.3 Content of the Block in Blockchain

Each block in blockchain contains the block body and block header. The block header is used to organize all blocks (Si, Sun, Li, Qiao, & Shi, 2019). The block header is vital module of each block in the block chain and it contains numerous key components that serve to secure the blockchain's security and integrity.

These elements are as follows:

i. **Timestamp:** The blockchain timestamp tracks when a block was added and is used to authenticate the legitimacy of the block. The block is regarded genuine if the timestamps of the blocks are in sequence and within a defined range of each other. This contributes to the blockchain's integrity and transparency.
ii. **Version:** Each block contains the blockchain version, which indicates the software version that was used to construct the block.

- **Blockchain Version 1.0(Cryptocurrency):** It employs a public ledger which is essential feature of the blockchain. This ledger, also called the blockchain, is a decentralized and immutable database that enables secure transactions without the need for a central authority. Bitcoin is prominent example of this version.
- **Blockchain Version 2.0(Smart Contract):** Ethereum is an example of Version 2.0 blockchain which introduced the idea of smart contracts. It is self-executing programs that automate execution of specific contracts and other transactions. One important advancement of blockchain technology is its ability to provide safe and apparent transactions exclusive of the need for middlemen.
- **Blockchain Version 3.0**(DAPPS)- Version 3.0 blockchain, as seen in the Tor Browser, is used to create a decentralized structure indicating that the network is not controlled by any central authority, instead the power is dispersed among the network's participants.

iii. **Merkle Root:** Merkle roots employ mathematical algorithms to determine whether the data has been damaged, hacked or altered. If a block has ten transactions, we need those ten transactions to merge and make one Hash Value. It utilizes the binary tree concept to generate the block's hash, known as the Merkle Root.

iv. **Nonce**: A nonce in the blockchain stands for "number only used once" which indicates unique number to which miners aim to find. Typically, it takes about ten attempts to locate the exact nonce. It is a 32-bit long number with a bound of 2^{32} making it computationally expensive to determine the right integer value. Bitcoin miners attempt to discover the correct random integer value between 0 and 2^{32} consecutively to add any new block in blockchain.

v. **Previous Hash:** A blockchain is made up of numerous interconnected blocks or nodes with each block's previous hash containing the hashed value of address of the preceding block. Initial block in the blockchain is recognized as the Genesis Block, distinguished by the absence of a previous block hash value since it marks the beginning of the chain. This interlinking of blocks via hash values ensures the integrity and immutability of the blockchain (Jia, Chen, Liu, Wang, Xiao, & Xu, 2023).

Figure 7. Block Header and Block Body

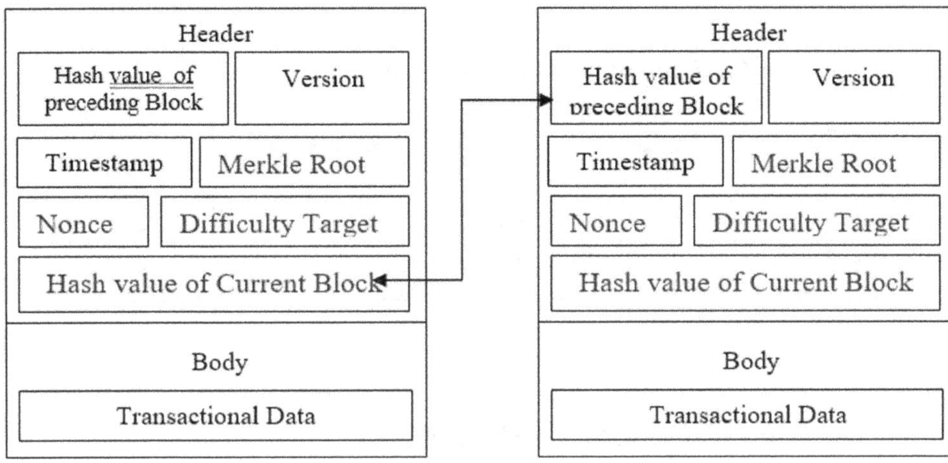

1.1.4 Blockchain Principles and Technologies

A blockchain is a sequentially arranged collection of blocks with each new block in the sequence being connected to the one before it. Every block of transactions relates to the previous block of transactions. As an example, consider a three-block chain. There is no antecedent to the first block. As a result, it lacks the hash value of the prior block. The hash value of block 1 is contained in block 2. Block 3 includes the hash of block 2.

Figure 8. Chaining of previous block hash

The security of the blockchain is guaranteed by the inclusion of hashes from preceding blocks in each block. If an attacker modifies the information in block, it alters the hash of that particular block. However, since subsequent blocks still retain the original hash, they will become invalid. This interlinking of blocks via hash values ensures that any tampering with the data is easily detectable, and the blockchain's integrity is preserved.

Figure 9. Error in Chaining of previous block hash

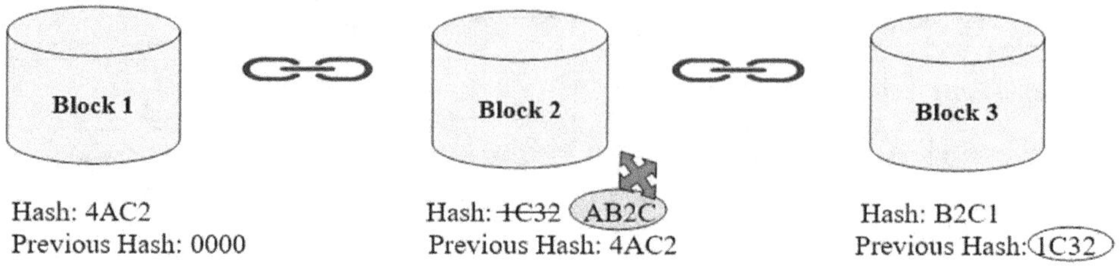

1.1.4.1 Block Hash Generation Process

In blockchain, a hash function takes any input, no matter the size and changes it into a fixed-length coded output. This encrypted output is unique to the input and serves as a digital fingerprint of sorts. Additionally, the consensus algorithm is a set of rules that dictate the operation of a blockchain network guaranteeing that every node in the network is in agreement with the same blockchain state (Ferrag & Shu, 2021).

A hash value is created by using a fixed-length hash function (H) on a message of any length (M), producing a unique digital fingerprint ($h = H(M)$). This fixed-length hash value is then added to the message to prove it hasn't been changed, allowing the receiver to confirm its authenticity by recalculating the hash value. Since the hash function isn't secret, some way to protect the hash value is needed to keep the message secure.

Figure 10. Working of Hash Function

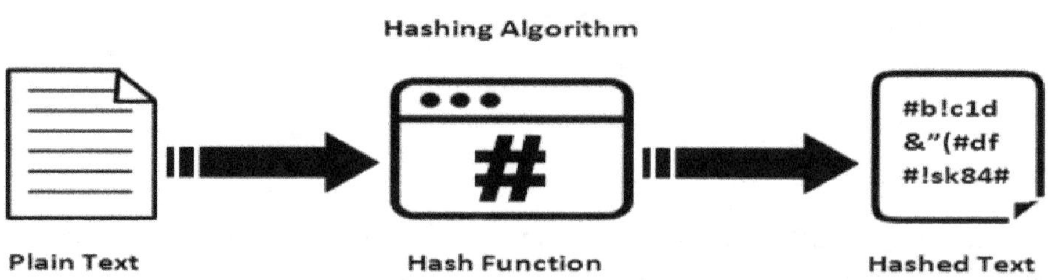

1.1.4.2 Types of Blockchain

There exist four primary categories of blockchains as mentioned below:

1. **Public Blockchain:** Ledgers in this form of blockchain are visible to everyone on the internet. Distributed ledger technology without restrictions and permissions is known as a public blockchain. It enables anybody to validate and contribute a transaction block to the blockchain (Latif, Wen, Iwendi, Li-li, Mohsin, Han, & Band, 2022). A public blockchain network is unwrapping to each one. In such a system, anyone with internet access can register for the blockchain platform and become a recognized node, enabling them to contribute in the blockchain network.

Example: An example of a public blockchain is the Bitcoin, Ethereum and Litecoin. It's open to anyone who wants to participate permitting users to join the network from anywhere in the globe, validate transactions, and employ mining to improve network security.

2. **Private Blockchain:** A private blockchain is a type of permissioned blockchain that is used in a closed network, usually inside a company or organization, in which only particular blockchain network members are authorized to engage. Accessibility, permissions and security are all set by the organization. Private blockchains have a more constrained network, but they function similarly to public blockchains. Applications for private blockchains can be found in many areas, including asset ownership, digital identity, supply chain management, and voting.

Example: Hyperledger Fabric, IBM Blockchain Platform and Corda.

3. **Hybrid Blockchain:** The fundamentals of both public and private blockchains are combined in this kind of blockchain offering advantages from both types. It enables a permission-based system for private transactions and a permissionless system for public ones. The hybrid network allows users to manage access to data on the blockchain, with some data being made public and the rest kept private. It is a flexible system that allows for easy integration of a private blockchain with various public blockchains. Transactions within the private network are verified within that network (Dorri, Kanhere, & Jurdak, 2016). Overall, a hybrid blockchain offers a customizable and adaptable solution to meet the needs of various organizations

Example: Dragonchain.

4. **Consortium blockchain:** A semi-decentralized kind of blockchain that is managed by numerous groups is called a consortium blockchain. In contrast to a private blockchain managed by a single entity, a consortium blockchain allows multiple organizations to participate as nodes, verifying transactions or mining. This type of blockchain is often utilized by banks, government agencies, and other organizations.

Example: Ripple, Ripple, IBM Food Trust and Energy Web Foundation.

Figure 11. Four types of Blockchain

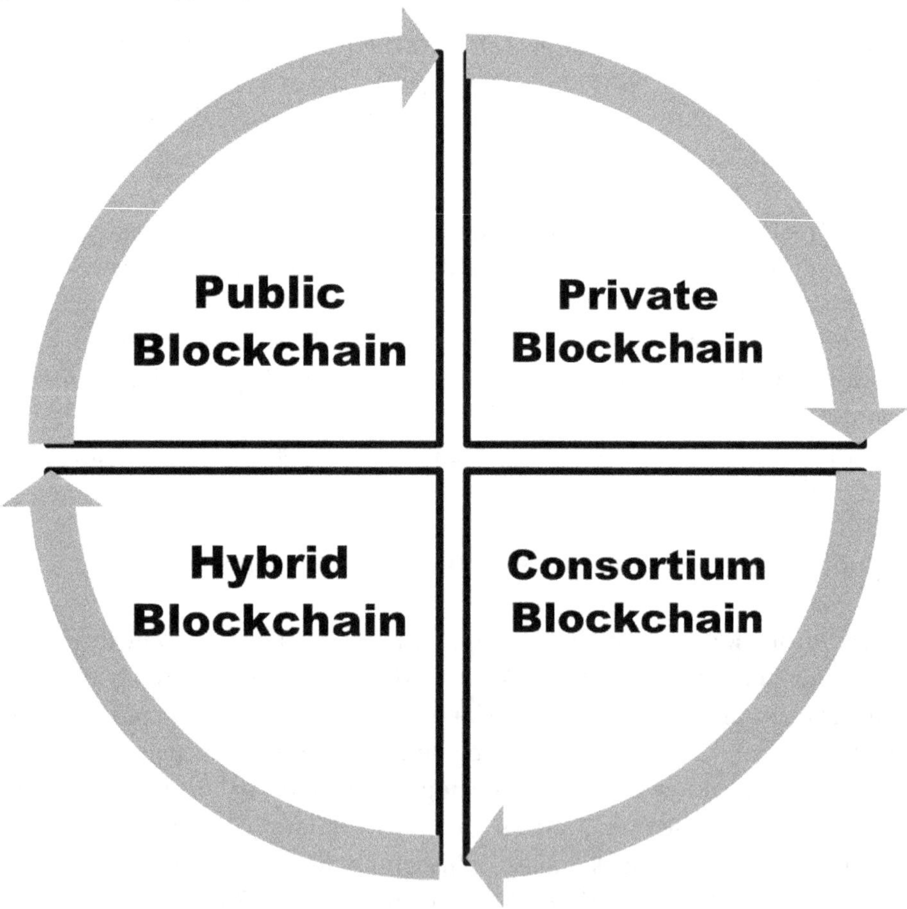

1.1.4.3 Working of Blockchain Transaction

Step 1: When a person wants to initiate a transaction on a blockchain network, they make a request for it. The transaction can involve a variety of things, such as digital currency, contracts, records or other forms of data.

Step 2: The transaction that has been requested is distributed to a P2P network with the help of the nodes.

Step 3: The transaction and the user's status are verified by the network of nodes using established methods.

Step 4: After verification, a transaction is incorporated into the blockchain as a new block. This addition is permanent and cannot be changed.

Figure 12. Blockchain Transaction Process

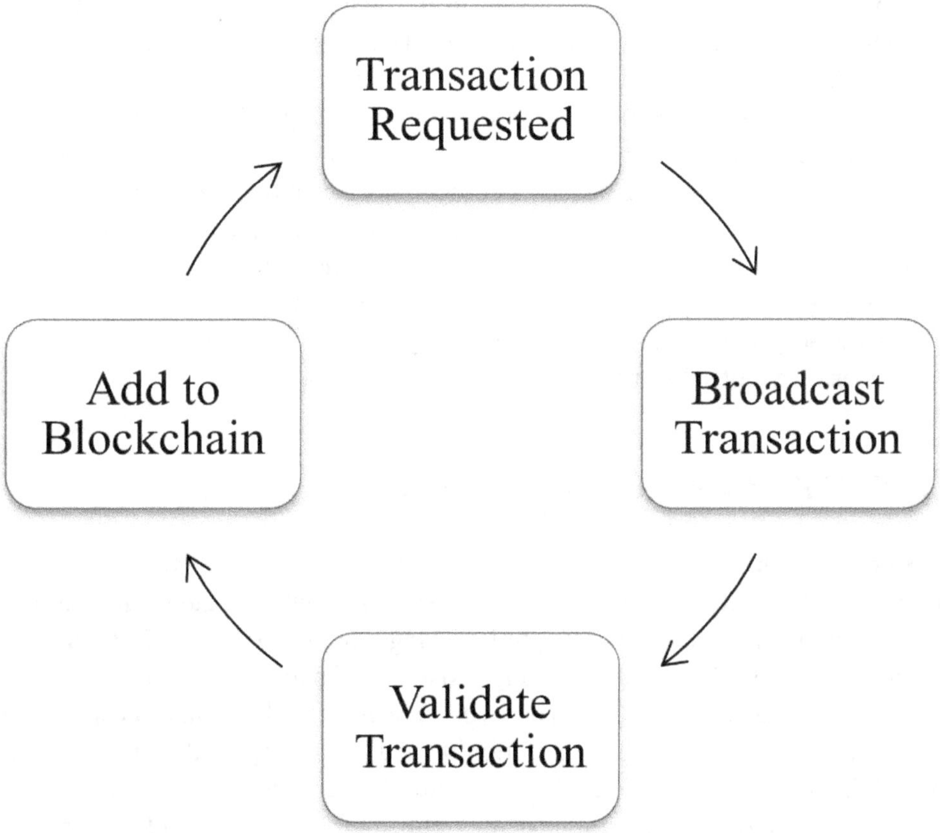

1.1.5 Advantages of Blockchain

1. **Open:** Blockchain technology is open, meaning that anyone can participate and contribute to the network without requiring permission from a central authority. This permits the development of a more democratic and inclusive organization in which people and organizations can engage in the validation and recording of transactions.
2. **Decentralization:** Decentralization lies at the core of blockchain technology, removing the necessity for third-party intermediaries to authenticate transactions and diminishing the time needed for validation.
3. **Security:** Blockchain is considered one of the most secure record-keeping systems available. To update and/or modify the shared documentation of transactions, a consensus must be reached among all nodes at blockchain network. In other words, the information is only changed if a majority or all of the nodes agree to make the update. Unauthorized parties find it extremely difficult to tamper with the data contained in the blockchain because to this process.
4. **Transparency:** Blockchain technology provides unparalleled transparency in transaction histories. The distributed ledger ensures that all nodes in network have access to a replica of the documentation, enabling easy verification of records without relying on intermediaries. Any changes made to the transaction history can be easily noticed and traced by all nodes on the network, providing real-time updates on currency exchange information.
5. **Censorship-Free:** Blockchain technology is considered censorship-resistant because it is not subject to control by a single entity.

1.2 BLOCKCHAIN AND CYBER SECURITY

Since blockchain is decentralized and disperses data among several nodes, it is more difficult for attackers to breach the system as a whole than traditional centralized databases, which are susceptible to single points of failure. Data integrity is guaranteed and it becomes extremely resistant to fraud and tampering once it is written to a blockchain. Blockchain encrypts data using sophisticated cryptographic methods; each block includes transaction data, a timestamp, and a cryptographic hash of the block before it. Since the blocks are chained together, it is very difficult to change any information without being noticed (Saberi, Kouhizadeh, Sarkis, & Shen, 2019). Furthermore, blockchain facilitates audits and the detection of suspect activity by offering a transparent ledger where all transactions are documented and verifiable by all parties. Blockchain technology has several uses in the field of cyber security. Through the prevention of illegal changes, it can guarantee the integrity of vital data in industries including supply chain management, healthcare, and finance. Organizations must make sure their usage of blockchain complies with applicable laws and regulations, as the legal landscape for blockchain technology is still developing. It can be difficult to integrate blockchain with legacy systems and necessitate considerable infrastructure modifications. Furthermore, a lot of energy is used by certain blockchain networks, especially those that employ Proof of Work (PoW) consensus techniques. To solve this problem, more energy-efficient consensus techniques, such as Proof of Stake (PoS), are being developed (Medhane, Sangaiah, Hossain, Muhammad, & Wang, 2020).

1.2.1 How Blockchain Helps to Enhance Cyber Security?

The unique attributes of blockchain technology offer significant advantages for enhancing cyber security. By addressing key vulnerabilities and providing robust security mechanisms, blockchain can play a pivotal responsibility in defending digital assets and infrastructure.

i. Data Integrity and Tamper-Proofing:

Ensuring data integrity is one of the main issues in cyber security. Traditional databases and centralized systems are susceptible to tampering and unauthorized modifications. Blockchain's immutability addresses this issue effectively. Once a transaction is recorded on the blockchain, which cryptographically coupled to the earlier block, creating a chain of records that can't be changed without altering the entire succeeding blocks, which would require consensus from the bulk of the association.

ii. Secure Identity Management

Identity theft and fraud are major cyber security challenges. Blockchain offers a decentralized approach to uniqueness management, where persons can own and manage their digital identities. Through the use of cryptographic keys, users can authenticate themselves without relying on intermediaries. Decentralized identifiers (DIDs) and self-sovereign identity (SSI) frameworks leverage blockchain to provide secure and verifiable digital identities.

iii. Enhanced Authentication and Authorization

Authorization and authentication are essential elements of cyber security. Conventional systems frequently depend on username-password combinations, which are at risk to attacks such as phishing and brute force. Blockchain based authentication systems can increase security by using cryptographic keys and multi-factor authentication. Smart contracts, which are self-executing contracts with the terms directly written into code, can automate and enforce authorization rules, reducing the risk of human error and insider threats. Authorization rules can be automated and enforced via smart contracts with the terms directly encoded into code. This lowers the possibility of insider threats and human error.

iv. Secure Communication and Data Sharing

Insecure communication channels and data sharing mechanisms are common entry points for cyber attacks. Blockchain can secure communication and data sharing through encryption and decentralization. For example, blockchain-based messaging platforms can ensure end-to-end encryption and verifiable delivery of messages (Shukla, Prakash, & Pandey, 2020). Additionally, blockchain can assist to secure and transparent data distribution involving parties without relying on a trusted third party, making it ideal for applications like supply chain management and inter-organizational collaborations.

v. Resilience Against Distributed Denial of Service Attacks

Attacks known as distributed denial of service attempt to overload a network or website with traffic such that it becomes unusable. Centralized servers are particularly vulnerable to such attacks. By spreading the burden over several nodes, blockchain's decentralized architecture helps lessen the effects of DDoS attacks. Projects like Gladius and Akamai have explored using blockchain to create decentralized content delivery networks (CDNs) that are more resilient to DDoS attacks.

vi. Protecting Critical Infrastructure

Power grids, water supply systems, and transportation networks are examples of critical infrastructure that is becoming more digitally and globally integrated and is therefore susceptible to cyber attacks. Blockchain can improve the protection of critical infrastructure by providing protected and unassailable records of system activities. This can help in detecting and responding to anomalies and intrusions in real-time. For instance, blockchain can be used to make safe the IoT devices that form the backbone of critical infrastructure, ensuring that only approved devices can correspond and execute commands.

1.3 ROLE OF BLOCKCHAIN IN ENHANCING CYBER SECURITY

Cyber security is critical in the modern digital world. . With cyber threats evolving continuously, safeguarding sensitive data and digital assets has turn into a serious apprehension for persons and organizations. Blockchain and cyber security are fundamental elements of modern digital technology, collaborating to secure our digital environment. Blockchain, a decentralized ledger technology, ensures data integrity using cryptographic methods. Conversely, cyber security involves safeguarding systems, networks, and data from digital threats and attacks. Blockchain technology offers robust security features that can help organizations mitigate cyber security risks and protect their sensitive data from evolving threats in the digital landscape.Blockchain provides transparency, immutability and heightened security, positioning it as a formidable ally in combatting cyber threats. Within a Blockchain network, data is distributed crosswise a network of computers or nodes rather than centralized on a sole server. Every block in the sequence is interconnected with the preceding one through cryptographic hashes, constructing a secure and immutable ledger. When data are appended to Blockchain network, it remains unalterable and irremovable without consensus from the network (Si, Sun, Li, Qiao, & Shi, 2019).

1.3.1 Types of Cyber Attack

Common types of cyber attacks include:

1. **Phishing**: Phishing in the context of blockchain technology is a form of cyber attack where malicious actors deceive users to steal their sensitive information, such as private keys or login credentials for cryptocurrency wallets or exchanges. Phishing attacks can cooperate the security of blockchain systems and consequence in trivial monetary losses.

Common Phishing Techniques in Blockchain

i. **Email Phishing**: Scammers send fake emails that look real, pretending to be from cryptocurrency exchanges or wallet services. They try to trick users into clicking bad links or sharing personal information. These emails often mimic the branding and language of the legitimate services, making them difficult to distinguish from genuine communications.

ii. **Website Spoofing**: Fraudsters design phony websites that closely resemble legitimate cryptocurrency wallet or exchange companies. They attempt to deceive people into logging in or disclosing personal information, which allows them access to private information. When users attempt to log in or enter their private keys on these spoofed sites, their credentials are captured by the attackers.
iii. **Social Engineering:** Attackers use social engineering tactics to trick users into revealing their private information. This can include impersonating support staff on social media, forums, or messaging platforms. Scammers often create urgency or fear to manipulate users into acting quickly without verifying the authenticity of the request.
iv. **SMS Phishing:** Phishing attacks conducted via SMS, where users receive messages that appear to be from legitimate services asking them to follow a link or provide personal information. These messages can direct to malicious websites intended to steal user information.
v. **Fake Apps:** Fraudulent mobile apps are designed to mimic legitimate cryptocurrency wallet apps. Once installed, these apps can steal private keys and other sensitive information from the user.

2. **Man-in-the-Middle Attack**: When an attacker surreptitiously intercepts and potentially modifies communication between two parties, it is known as a Man-in-the-Middle (MITM) attack in the context of blockchain technology. The trustworthiness of the blockchain may be jeopardized if this affects the security and integrity of messages, transactions, and data exchange.

Common Techniques for MITM Attacks in Blockchain

i. **Network Eavesdropping**: Attackers intercept unencrypted network traffic between nodes, users, or exchanges to capture insightful information as private keys, transaction details and private data.
ii. **DNS Spoofing**: When scammers manipulate the DNS system, consumers are redirected from legitimate websites to false ones that appear genuine. DNS spoofing is a tactic used to fool consumers into divulging private information or opening dangerous websites. Users attempting to access a legitimate blockchain service could be redirected to a malicious site designed to steal their credentials or funds (Wan, Li, Imran, & Li, 2019).
iii. **SSL Stripping**: Scammers are able to intercept and modify user-website communication by downgrading secure website connections (HTTPS) to unsecured ones (HTTP). They can infiltrate malware into the transmission or steal confidential information thanks to this vulnerability. Users may be unaware that their secure connection has been compromised, exposing sensitive information to the attacker.

iv. **Wi-Fi Eavesdropping**: Attackers set up malicious Wi-Fi networks (often with names similar to legitimate networks) to intercept data transmitted by users. Public Wi-Fi networks are particularly vulnerable to this type of attack, putting users at risk when accessing blockchain services.
v. **Session Hijacking**: Attackers steal session tokens or cookies to take over a user's active session with a blockchain service. This can allow the attacker to perform unauthorized transactions or access sensitive information without the user's knowledge.

3. **Distributed Denial of Service (DDoS) Attack**: DDoS attack in the context of blockchain technology involves overwhelming the network, nodes, or services associated with the blockchain with excessive traffic or requests. This flood of traffic can cause service disruptions, slowdowns, or complete outages, affecting the functionality and reliability of the blockchain.

Common Techniques for DDoS Attacks in Blockchain

i. **Flooding Nodes with Requests**: Attackers send an overwhelming number of requests to blockchain nodes, causing them to become overloaded and unresponsive. This can prevent legitimate transactions from being processed and disrupt the normal operation of the blockchain network.
ii. **Botnet Attacks**: A botnet or collection of compromised devices, is a tool used by scammers to send massive amounts of traffic to blockchain nodes or services. The traffic for this dispersed attack originates from a wide variety of sources, making it challenging to identify or prevent.
iii. **Network Layer Attacks**: Attackers target the underlying network infrastructure, such as routers and internet connections, to disrupt the communication between blockchain nodes. This can cause nodes to lose connectivity and fail to synchronize with the rest of the network (Xu, Lu, & Li, 2021).

4. **SQL Injection**: While SQL injection is well-known attack vector in traditional web applications, it is less directly applicable to blockchain technology itself because blockchain does not typically use SQL databases for storing its ledger data. However, blockchain-based applications, especially decentralized applications (DApps), often involve components that interact with traditional databases or use APIs that can be vulnerable to SQL injection.

Common Techniques for SQL Injection Attacks in Blockchain

i. **User Account Management**: A DApp might use a traditional SQL database to manage user accounts. An attacker could exploit SQL injection vulnerability in the user login or registration form to increase illegal access to user accounts.

ii. **Transaction History**: A service that provides transaction history to users might store this data in an SQL database. An attacker could use SQL injection to alter transaction records or retrieve sensitive information.
iii. **Metadata Storage**: Some blockchain applications store metadata related to transactions or assets off-chain in SQL databases. SQL injection could allow an attacker to manipulate or access this metadata in unintended ways.

1.4 APPLICATIONS AND USE CASES OF BLOCKCHAIN IN CYBER SECURITY

Blockchain technology holds great promise for enhancing cyber security. It provides an open and transparent method for handling transactions and storing data. Decentralization, immutability, and cryptographic security are three of blockchain's primary characteristics align with the primary objectives of cyber security. It can enhance a number of sectors, including supply chain management, banking, health-care, the Internet of Things, and voting systems. It can also improve data integrity, identity management, and secure communication. Blockchain technology is currently being applied in a number of fields to address certain security issues, so its benefits for cyber security are not just theoretical. This section examines some of the most important applications of blockchain technology in cyber security enhancement.

This section will explore the ways that blockchain technology can enhance cyber security. We will examine how blockchain technology can improve cyber security and how it can change the way we secure data and carry out transactions.

1. Application of Blockchain to Enhancing Data Integrity

Data integrity is vital for maintaining the accurateness and consistency of data over its lifecycle. Traditional centralized databases are susceptible to unauthorized modifications and tampering, leading to compromised data integrity. Blockchain technology mitigates these risks through its immutable ledger. Once data is stored on a blockchain, it becomes permanent and tamper-proof, meaning it can't be changed or deleted.

a. Financial Sector

In the financial sector, data integrity is paramount to prevent fraud and ensure the accuracy of transactions. Blockchain can secure financial transactions by providing a tamper-proof ledger. For instance, every transaction in a blockchain is connected to the preceding one through cryptographic hashing; creating a sequence of records that is difficult to alter. This ensures that transaction histories are accurate and transparent, reducing the risk of fraud.

b. Healthcare

Sensitive patient data that needs to be accurate and kept confidential is handled by healthcare systems. Through the creation of an unchangeable history of the patient's data, blockchain technology can secure medical records while guaranteeing accuracy and privacy. This also holds true for clinical trials, as blockchain ensures the validity and consistency of trial information. Ensuring patient data privacy and integrity is essential in the healthcare industry. Patient records are shielded from unwanted access and alteration by blockchain's secure, decentralized ledger, adding another degree of protection and confidence.

c. Supply Chain Management

By recording the origin and movement of commodities, blockchain technology can guarantee their legitimacy and integrity in supply chain management. A blockchain allows for the transparent and unchangeable recording of every stage of the process, from manufacture to distribution. This is essential for avoiding fraud and guaranteeing the caliber of the goods. A safe and transparent method of tracking the supply chain is provided by blockchain, in contrast to previous methods that depend on flimsy centralized databases, making it more difficult for fraudsters to cheat or tamper with items.

2. Application of Blockchain in Identity and Access Management (IAM)

A key component of cyber security is identity and access management (IAM), which makes sure that people's identities are validated and their access to systems and data is safe. One drawback in traditional IAM systems is that they rely on centralized databases that are vulnerable to hacking or unauthorized access. By establishing a safe, decentralized, and unchangeable record of identities, impeding identity theft, and enhancing security, blockchain technology has the potential to completely transform identity and access management.

a. Decentralized Identity Management

Through a safe, decentralized system, blockchain technology empowers people to control their digital identities. Decentralized identifiers (DIDs) give people the freedom to establish and control their own online personas independently of centralized authorities. With complete control over personal information and a marked decrease in the likelihood of identity theft, this strategy places a high priority on privacy and security.

b. Secure Authentication

By providing a safe and decentralized method of identity verification, blockchain technology can improve authentication procedures. For instance, numerous identity verification factors are recorded on a secure ledger using blockchain-based multi-factor authentication (MFA), which makes it considerably more difficult for unauthorized individuals to obtain access. By using this method, the chance of fraudulent access is decreased and authentication process security is greatly improved.

3. Application of Blockchain in Securing Communications

Secure communication is essential in today's digital world where sensitive information is frequently exchanged over networks. Centralized servers, which are susceptible to hacking and illegal access, are a common component of conventional communication networks. By generating a decentralized, unchangeable record of messages and transactions, blockchain technology can improve communication security by making it more difficult for hackers to intercept and alter data.

a. Secure Messaging

Blockchain can be used to secure messaging systems by ensuring that messages are encrypted and cannot be altered or tampered with. For instance, a blockchain-based messaging system can record each message on blockchain, providing an unchallengeable documentation of communications. This ensures that messages remain secure and unchanged, dropping the danger of unofficial access and tampering.

b. IoT Security

Since Internet of Things (IoT) devices are frequently simple pickings for hackers, the proliferation of IoT devices has led to new security vulnerabilities. By offering a safe and decentralized method for devices to communicate and authenticate one another, blockchain technology can greatly increase the security of Internet of Things networks. A visible and unchangeable record of device data and transactions made possible by blockchain technology helps to safeguard Internet of Things (IoT) devices by thwarting illegal access and guaranteeing secure connectivity. Additionally, by generating an irreversible record that guards against manipulation and tampering, blockchain can guarantee the security and veracity of IoT data.

4. Application of Blockchain in Digital Identity and Authentication

Digital identity and authentication are crucial for securing online transactions and services. Traditional systems often rely on centralized authorities to manage identities, which can be in danger to breaches and illegal access. Blockchain can provide a decentralized and secure framework for running digital identities and authentication processes.

a. Self-Sovereign Identity

A novel strategy called self-sovereign identification (SSI) leverages blockchain technology to provide people the autonomy to control their digital identities. By utilizing distinct identifiers kept on a blockchain, people can establish and manage their own digital identities with SSI, decreasing reliance on centralized authority and enhancing the security and privacy of personal data.

b. Secure Access Control

A safe and transparent record of who is authorized to access particular resources is produced by blockchain technology, which can enhance access control. The security of access control procedures is increased and the risk of unwanted access is decreased by keeping access control lists on a blockchain, which only permits authorized users to access.

5. Application of Blockchain in Secure Voting Systems

Voting system integrity is essential to ensuring fair and legitimate elections. Central databases, which are frequently used in conventional voting systems, are easily accessible or manipulated with. By generating an immutable, decentralized vote record, blockchain technology can strengthen voting system security. Blockchain technology, for instance, may protect electronic voting systems, ensuring that votes are reliably counted and cannot be altered or manipulated. By doing this, blockchain can ensure that election results are reliable and accurate and help stop election fraud. Furthermore, by producing an unambiguous and safe record of votes and ensuring that the voting procedure is fair and responsible, blockchain technology can increase election transparency.

6. Application of Blockchain in Smart Contracts and Automated Security

The terms and conditions of smart contracts are encoded directly into code, making them self-executing, automated digital agreements. They can maximize transaction security and reduce the possibility of human error by automating security procedures using blockchain technology. Smart contracts provide uniform application and enforcement of security measures by automating security mechanisms. In order to minimize human error and guarantee uniform security implementation, they can, for instance, automatically revoke access permits if certain security requirements are not fulfilled. A tamper-proof record of transactions is another benefit of blockchain-based smart contracts, which reduces the risk of fraud and illegal access while guaranteeing accuracy, dependability, and security.

7. Application of Blockchain in Threat Intelligence Sharing

Organizations can exchange information about cyber dangers on a secure network made possible by blockchain technology. By facilitating the transparent and secure sharing of threat data among companies, this platform increases the difficulty with which hackers can manipulate or alter the data. Organizations can collaborate more successfully to fight cyber attacks and enhance their overall security by utilizing blockchain.

8. Application of Blockchain in Protecting Intellectual Property (IP)

In order to protect their ideas and concepts, businesses and inventors must protect their intellectual property (IP). Traditional IP protection systems typically rely on centralized databases, which are vulnerable to manipulation and illegal access. Blockchain technology provides a decentralized, immutable record of intellectual property rights, which can enhance IP protection. It has the ability to set up safe IP registries where IP rights can be verified and recorded. A blockchain can be used to log each IP right, providing a safe and transparent record of ownership. This reduces the possibility of illegal access and tampering and helps to safeguard intellectual property rights.

9. Future Directions and Innovations

Researchers and inventors are always looking for new applications for blockchain technology, which has a lot of promise to enhance cyber security. The fascinating new developments and paths in the fields of blockchain and cyber security are examined in this part.

a. Quantum-Resistant Cryptography

Blockchain technology's cryptographic methods may be threatened by developments in quantum computing. Traditional cryptographic techniques, such RSA and elliptic curve cryptography, which are essential for safeguarding blockchain networks, can be cracked by quantum computers. Researchers are focusing on creating encryption methods that are resistant to quantum computing power in order to prevent this threat. These new algorithms, such as hash-based and lattice-based cryptography, are meant to create a safe foundation for blockchain technology in a world when quantum computing is commonplace.

b. Decentralized Identity (DID)

People can now have more control over their digital identities thanks to a novel concept called decentralized identification (DID), which makes use of blockchain technology. It is more difficult for identity theft and illegal access to occur when people use DID to manage their own identities independently of a centralized authority. DID systems use blockchain to create a decentralized and immutable record of identities, allowing individuals to manage their own identities and share only the information they choose with authorized parties. This approach enhances privacy and security, empowering individuals to take control of their digital identities.

1.5 REAL LIFE EXAMPLE OF APPLICATIONS USING BLOCKCHAIN IN CYBER SECURITY

Following are some prominent examples where Blockchain is used for Cyber security:

1. Barclays' Integration of Blockchain Technology in Traditional Banking

Barclays, a prominent financial institution based in London, England, has taken steps to integrate blockchain technology into its traditional banking operations. The bank has filed a patent that explores the use of blockchain, specifically Distributed Ledger Technology (DLT) to enhance security in fund transfers. By utilizing DLT, Barclays aims to create a secure environment where fund transfers, including those involving crypto currencies, can be conducted safely and transparently.

2. Cisco's Use of Blockchain in IoT Security

Cisco Systems, a global leader in networking and IT infrastructure located in San Jose, California is leveraging blockchain technology to improve the protection of Internet of Things (IoT) devices. By doing so, Cisco not only enhances the reliability and security of its IoT offerings but also sets a precedent for the use of innovative technologies to safeguard the growing number of IoT devices in various sectors. This makes it more difficult for hackers to manipulate records because the data is shielded from being changed or tampered with. In addition to guaranteeing data integrity and traceability, the ledger offers a safe and trustworthy record of every transaction.

3. Coinbase's Security Measures in Crypto currencies

Coinbase, one of the leading cryptocurrency exchanges globally located in San Francisco, California implements robust security measures to protect user assets and information. Their approach includes advanced encryption for storing wallets and passwords, as well as stringent employee background checks. The company employs industry-standard encryption protocols such as AES-256 to encrypt wallet keys and passwords making tremendously complex for malicious actors to decrypt and access this information.

4. Australian Government's Cyber security and Blockchain Initiatives

The Australian government is actively pursuing advanced cyber security measures and blockchain technology to improve the security and efficiency of its digital infrastructure. These initiatives include the development of a cyber security network based on Distributed Ledger Technology (DLT) and a strategic partnership with IBM to secure government documents through a blockchain ecosystem. The Australian government's initiatives to develop a DLT-based cyber security network and partner with IBM for a blockchain ecosystem reflect a strategic commitment to enhancing national cyber security. These measures aim to protect sensitive information, improve operational efficiency, and maintain high standards of data integrity and security.

5. Philips Healthcare's Blockchain and AI Initiatives in Healthcare

Philips Healthcare located in Massachusetts is collaborating with hospitals worldwide to develop a healthcare ecosystem that integrates blockchain and artificial intelligence (AI). This initiative aims to enhance the discovery, analysis and utilization of various types of healthcare data, including operational, administrative and medical information. utilizing blockchain technology, Philips Healthcare ensures that healthcare data is stored in a secure, immutable ledger. This enhances data integrity and prevents unauthorized alterations, ensuring that patient records and other sensitive information remain accurate and tamper-proof.

6. Chinese Military's Use of Blockchain in Defense and Military

The Chinese government and military are integrating blockchain technology to improve the safety of critical government and military information. This initiative aims to leverage blockchain's robust cyber security features to protect sensitive data and intelligence from cyber threats and unauthorized access. By implementing blockchain, the Chinese military aims to protect vital information, including intelligence data, operational plans and communication logs. This ensures that critical data remains secure and confidential.

7. Founders Bank's Initiative to Become a Decentralized Bank

Founders Bank located in Valletta, Malta is pioneering an innovative approach to banking by aiming to become the world's first decentralized bank. This bank is designed to be owned by its users rather than a central authority. It plans to utilize advanced technologies such as encryption and distributed ledgers to secure and manage user's crypto currencies. Founders Bank will leverage blockchain technology to create a secure and transparent ledger for all transactions. This distributed ledger ensures that all transaction data is stored across multiple nodes, making it highly resistant to tampering and fraud. Founders Bank is working within Malta's progressive regulatory framework for blockchain and crypto currencies.

8. The State of Colorado's Use of Blockchain for Record Security

The State of Colorado located in Denver, Colorado is exploring the blockchain technology toimprove the safety of government records storage. This initiative is driven by a bill passed by the Colorado Senate, aimed at leveraging blockchain's robust security features to mitigate the increasing frequency of cyber attacks targeting government records. Implementing blockchain reduces the vulnerability of government records to cyber attacks by decentralizing data storage and using cryptographic methods to secure information. Adopting blockchain technology for securing government records is a strategic move for Colorado.

9. J.P. Morgan's Quorum Blockchain Platform for Private Transactions

J.P. Morgan is leading global financial services firm located in New York has developed a blockchain platform called Quorum. This platform leverages blockchain technology to process private transactions securely and efficiently. Quorum integrates smart contracts and cryptographic techniques to guarantee the security and integrity of transactions. Quorum is designed to process private transactions within a secure blockchain environment. It addresses the needs of enterprises that require confidentiality and high performance in their transaction processing. Based on the Ethereum blockchain, Quorum is tailored to meet the specific requirements of financial institutions providing a permissioned network that enhances transaction privacy and speed. J.P. Morgan's Quorum platform represents a significant advancement in the use of blockchain technology for traditional banking. By incorporating smart contracts and cryptography, Quorum provides a secure, efficient and private environment for processing transactions.

10. Health Linkages' Use of Blockchain for Secure Patient Records

Health Linkages located in California is leveraging blockchain technology to enhance the security and accessibility of patient records. Their initiative aims to restrict access to patient data to authorized personnel while maintaining a chronological record of major healthcare events. This approach seeks to improve healthcare decision-making by providing doctors with comprehensive and reliable patient information. Patient records on the blockchain are encrypted and accessible only to authorized personnel, ensuring confidentiality and privacy. Blockchain maintains an irreversible record of all healthcare events and exchanges, providing a chronological history of patient care. This enhances transparency and accountability in healthcare operations. By leveraging blockchain's decentralized and immutable features, Health Linkages aims to revolutionize medical data management and improve patient outcomes.

1.6 HOW BLOCKCHAIN TECHNOLOGY ENSURES THE CYBERSECURITY?

Blockchain technology offers a robust framework for enhancing cyber security through its fundamental characteristics of decentralization, immutability, cryptographic security, transparency, and consensus mechanisms. By addressing key cyber security challenges such as data tampering, unauthorized access, and fraud, blockchain provides a secure foundation for various applications across industries. Blockchain technology ensures cyber security through several key mechanisms that leverage its unique characteristics are mentioned below:

1. Decentralization

Data on older systems is frequently kept in one single location, which can be quite problematic in the event of a hack. Because it makes use of a network of computers, or nodes, each of which has a duplicate copy of the same data, blockchain is unique. Because of this, hackers can't focus on just one location, which makes it more difficult for them to take over the entire system [4]. Blockchain strengthens the system's defenses against cyber attacks by dispersing the data, making it more difficult for attackers to alter or remove.

2. Immutability

Information placed on the blockchain cannot be altered or deleted without the network's approval. Cryptographic hashing connects each block to its predecessor, enabling this immutability. A sequence of records that can be verified and changed is created by appending a timestamp to each transaction or data input and connecting it to the one before it. This feature prevents fraud and manipulation by ensuring that data cannot be changed in the past. It also creates a transparent, unalterable record trail that can be used to verify the accuracy of data over time.

3. Cryptographic Security

Blockchain technology protects data with advanced encryption techniques. Cryptographic hashes are used to link each encrypted transaction to its predecessor. On the blockchain, digital signatures, which require both public and private keys are used to verify the authenticity and consistency of data transactions. This cryptographic framework guarantees the validity, security, and resistance to illegal modification of data on the blockchain. This protects data in transit and at rest, ensuring confidentiality and integrity (Ferrag & Shu, 2021). This also ensures that transactions are authenticated and that the origin of the transaction cannot be denied by the sender.

4. Transparency and Traceability

Public blockchains are transparent allowing anyone to view the transaction history. Private Blockchains while more restrictive, still offer transparency within the network. All network users can view and verify the details of every transaction in an open public ledger. Ensuring transparency makes transactions transparent and traceable, which makes it easier to spot and stop fraudulent activity. It Simplifies auditing processes and improves the traceability of transactions which is crucial for regulatory compliance.

5. Consensus Mechanisms

Consensus techniques like Proof of Work (PoW), Proof of Stake (PoS), and other algorithms are used by blockchain networks to verify and come to a consensus regarding the state of the network. Before a transaction is added to the blockchain, these procedures ensure that all network nodes have reached a consensus regarding its authenticity. Consensus procedures preserve transaction integrity and stop double-spending. Consensus algorithms protect the blockchain from manipulation by making it more difficult for attackers to take over the network (for example, through a 51% attack).

6. Smart Contracts

Automated contracts that are embedded directly into computer code are known as smart contracts. When specific requirements are satisfied, they automatically implement the terms of the contract. Since these contracts are kept and executed on the blockchain, they cannot be altered or removed. They become transparent, safe, and less vulnerable to fraud or mistakes as a result. Smart contracts guarantee that transactions are carried out precisely as intended, free from the possibility of tampering or manipulation, by automating the execution of contract requirements (Shukla, Prakash, & Pandey, 2020).

7. Identity and Access Management (IAM)

People can safely control their own digital identities thanks to blockchain technology. Cryptographic keys allow people to govern their identities without depending on a central authority. Since their digital identities are stored on the blockchain, they have complete ownership over the data about them. As people maintain total control over their digital identities, this method removes the possibility of identity theft and illegal access.

8. Secure Data Sharing and Collaboration

Decentralized and secure data sharing between parties is made possible by blockchain technology. Through unique protocols, such as smart contracts, data is shared after being encrypted. The provided data can only be accessed and verified by those who have permission. This guarantees that data is viewed only by authorized parties and guards against data alteration or tampering during sharing and cooperation.

1.7 ROLE OF BLOCKCHAIN IN COMBATING SOCIAL ENGINEERING

Blockchain technology has the ability to fundamentally alter how we defend against social engineering scams. Data security, identity protection, and trust-building in online interactions are all enhanced by its decentralized, immutable, and transparent qualities. But there are several obstacles we must solve before we can fully take use of blockchain's security benefits. Blockchain has the potential to be extremely important in thwarting social engineering attempts once these obstacles are removed (Medhane, Sangaiah, Hossain, Muhammad, & Wang, 2020; Ferrag & Shu, 2021). The potential of blockchain technology in reducing social engineering attacks which still constitute a serious danger to cyber security is examined in this chapter. These assaults continue to use human psychology to obtain unauthorized access to sensitive data and systems in spite of the presence of conventional security measures. The decentralized, immutable, and transparent characteristics of blockchain technology present a promising way to overcome the drawbacks of conventional security solutions. In order to strengthen cyber security resistance against social engineering assaults, this chapter explores the uses, advantages, difficulties, and potential future directions of blockchain technology.

1.7.1 Types of Social Engineering Attacks and its Blockchain relevance

Social engineering is the practice of tricking others into divulging personal information or taking risks. Blockchain can help thwart some of these scams by enhancing security and trust through its transparent and safe characteristics. Phishing and posing as someone else are examples of social engineering techniques used to fool people into disclosing personal information or jeopardizing security. These ploys prey on people's feelings and confidence.

These are some typical social engineering scams and the ways that blockchain technology can help defend against them.

i. Phishing Attacks and Blockchain Relevance

Phishing is a scam in which con artists pose as reliable individuals or businesses in emails, texts, or other correspondence. They attempt to deceive you into divulging private information such as credit card numbers, passwords, or login credentials. Although they might pretend that what they are saying is genuine, their real intention is to steal your personal data. Blockchain can provide secure identity management solutions where users' identities are cryptographically verified. This reduces the effectiveness of phishing attacks targeting login credentials. Implementing blockchain-based email authentication protocols (like BIMI - Brand Indicators for Message Identification) can help to confirm the legitimacy of email senders dropping the probability of phishing emails (Shammar, Zahary, & Al-Shargabi, 2021).

2. Spear Phishing and Blockchain Relevance

Spear phishing is a specific kind of phishing when messages are targeted towards certain people or organizations, frequently using personal information to make the message seem more authentic. The unchangeable record of blockchain technology can log conversations between participants, assisting in the authentication of messages and identifying abnormalities, hence reducing the efficacy of spear phishing attempts. Blockchain-based digital signatures make it difficult for attackers to pose as reliable sources by ensuring message integrity and verifying the sender's identity.

3. Pretexting and Blockchain Relevance

Pretexting is a sort of fraud in which scammers fabricate an excuse or narrative to deceive you into divulging private information or taking action that jeopardizes security. In an attempt to win your trust and obtain private information or convince you to click on a dangerous link, they may fabricate an emergency or a plausible explanation.

Blockchain Relevance:

Blockchain-based smart contracts can automate and enforce predefined rules and conditions in transactions or interactions. This reduces the risk of decreasing sufferer to pretexting schemes by ensuring that parties adhere strictly to agreed-upon terms. Blockchain's transparency ensures that all transactions and interactions are recorded and visible to authorized parties, reducing the opportunity for malicious actors to fabricate false scenarios.

5. Baiting and Blockchain Relevance

Baiting is a strategy used to take advantage of vulnerabilities in people by luring them in with enticing things (such as USB drives or free downloads) that are actually malicious software or malware. By ensuring the validity and integrity of goods (like USB sticks), blockchain technology can provide transparency to supply chains. This reduces the possibility of falling victim to baiting attacks that use physically compromised devices. Customers and organizations may rest easy knowing that information about supply chain transactions and product legitimacy is preserved because to the immutable nature of blockchain records (Baena-Luna & García-Río, 2022).

1.8 CONCLUSION AND FUTURE SCOPE

Blockchain technology is revolutionizing cyber security by providing a strong barrier against social engineering attacks. It is perfect for securing transactions, confirming identities, and safeguarding sensitive data because of its decentralized, immutable, and transparent nature. In order to realize its full potential, we must welcome innovation, deal with obstacles, and work across sectors. By doing this, we can successfully counteract social engineering risks globally and provide a safer online environment.

In this book chapter, we have delved into the transformative potential of blockchain in fortifying digital defences against sophisticated cyber threats. Social engineering with its reliance on human psychology and trust, poses significant challenges to traditional cyber security measures. Blockchain offers a paradigm shift by introducing decentralized, immutable and transparent mechanisms that fundamentally alter how data is managed, transactions are executed, and identities are verified in the digital realm.

Throughout this chapter, we have explored the following key aspects:

1. **Fundamentals of Blockchain Technology:** We have introduced the fundamental concepts of blockchain, which include decentralization, immutability, agreement mechanisms, and cryptographic protection. These features collectively contribute to blockchain's resilience against tampering, fraud and unauthorized access which are common tactics employed in social engineering attacks.
2. **Applications in Cyber security:** Blockchain's application in cyber security spans various domains, from secure identity management and authentication to transparent and auditable transaction systems. By leveraging blockchain, organizations can establish robust defences that mitigate the risks associated with social engineering, such as phishing, pretexting and impersonation.
3. **Enhancing Data Integrity and Privacy:** Blockchain ensures data integrity by providing an immutable ledger where records cannot be distorted without consensus. This feature is critical in safeguarding sensitive information against manipulation and unauthorized modifications, thereby mitigating the impact of social engineering attacks aimed at data tampering.
4. **Smart Contracts and Automation:** By integrating smart contracts into blockchain platforms, rules and conditions may be automatically enforced in a transparent and safe manner. This feature reduces vulnerability to social engineering-based fraud schemes and increases operational effectiveness.
5. **Challenges and Considerations:** Blockchain technology has potential, but there are obstacles to overcome, including those related to scalability, interoperability, regulatory compliance, and public acceptability. For blockchain technologies to be successfully adopted and integrated into existing cyber security setups, these challenges must be overcome. Smart contracts allow rules and conditions to be automatically enforced in a transparent and secure manner on blockchain systems. This reduces vulnerability to social engineering-based fraud schemes and improves operational efficiency.

Future Scope

As blockchain continues to evolve and integrate into mainstream cyber security strategies, it promises to reshape the future of digital trust and security. Looking ahead, the future scope of blockchain technology in enhancing cyber security and combating social engineering is vast and promising as mentioned below:

REFERENCES

Baena-Luna, P., & García-Río, E. (2022). BLOCKCHAIN TECHNOLOGY: PRESENT AND FUTURE APPLICATION CHALLENGES. *Rev. Conhecimento Online*, 2, 258–273. DOI: 10.25112/rco.v2.2859

Da Xu, L., Lu, Y., & Li, L. (2021). Embedding blockchain technology into IoT for security: A survey. *IEEE Internet of Things Journal*, 8(13), 10452–10473. DOI: 10.1109/JIOT.2021.3060508

Dorri, A., Kanhere, S. S., & Jurdak, R. (2016), "Blockchain in internet of things: challenges and solutions, arXiv preprint arXiv:1608.05187,arxiv.org

Ferrag, M. A., & Shu, L. (2021). The performance evaluation of blockchain-based security and privacy systems for the Internet of Things: A tutorial. *IEEE Internet of Things Journal*, 8(24), 17236–17260. DOI: 10.1109/JIOT.2021.3078072

Jia, L., Chen, X., Liu, L., Wang, X., Xiao, K., & Xu, G. (2023). Blockchain data secure sharing protocol based on threshold Paillier algorithm. *High-Confidence Computing*, 3(4), 100132.

Latif, S. A., Wen, F. B. X., Iwendi, C., Li-li, F. W., Mohsin, S. M., Han, Z., & Band, S. S. (2022). AI-empowered, blockchain and SDN integrated security architecture for IoT network of cyber physical systems. *Computer Communications*, 181, 274–283. DOI: 10.1016/j.comcom.2021.09.029

Mahammad, A. B., & Kumar, R. (2023, April). Scalable and security framework to secure and maintain healthcare data using blockchain technology. In *2023 International Conference on Computational Intelligence and Sustainable Engineering Solutions (CISES)* (pp. 417-423). IEEE. DOI: 10.1109/CISES58720.2023.10183494

Medhane, D. V., Sangaiah, A. K., Hossain, M. S., Muhammad, G., & Wang, J. (2020). Blockchain-enabled distributed security framework for next-generation IoT: An edge cloud and software-defined network-integrated approach. *IEEE Internet of Things Journal*, 7(7), 6143–6149. DOI: 10.1109/JIOT.2020.2977196

Saberi S., Kouhizadeh M., Sarkis J., Shen L.(2019) "Blockchain technology and its relationships to sustainable supply chain management", International journal of production research, Taylor & Francis, pp. 2117-2135

Shammar, E. A., Zahary, A. T., & Al-Shargabi, A. A. (2021). A Survey of IoT and Blockchain Integration: Security Perspective. *IEEE Access : Practical Innovations, Open Solutions*, 9, 156114–156150. DOI: 10.1109/ACCESS.2021.3129697

Shukla, R. K., Prakash, V., & Pandey, S. (2020, December). A perspective on Internet of Things: Challenges & applications. In *2020 9th International Conference System Modeling and Advancement in Research Trends (SMART)* (pp. 184-189). IEEE.

Si, H., Sun, C., Li, Y., Qiao, H., & Shi, L. (2019). IoT information sharing security mechanism based on blockchain technology. *Future Generation Computer Systems*, 101, 1028–1040. DOI: 10.1016/j.future.2019.07.036

Taherdoost, H. (2022). A critical review of blockchain acceptance models—Blockchain technology adoption frameworks and applications. *Computers*, 11(2), 24. DOI: 10.3390/computers11020024

Taylor, P. J., Dargahi, T., Dehghantanha, A., Parizi, R. M., & Choo, K.-K. R. (2020). A systematic literature review of blockchain cyber security. *Digital Communications and Networks*, 6(2), 147–156. DOI: 10.1016/j.dcan.2019.01.005

Wan, J., Li, J., Imran, M., Li, D., & Fazal-e-Amin, . (2019). A blockchain-based solution for enhancing security and privacy in smart factory. *IEEE Transactions on Industrial Informatics*, 15(6), 3652–3660. DOI: 10.1109/TII.2019.2894573

Chapter 12
Social Engineering in Social Media and Online Interactions

Tarun Kumar Vashishth
https://orcid.org/0000-0001-9916-9575
IIMT University, India

Sachin Chaudhary
https://orcid.org/0000-0002-8415-0043
IIMT University, India

Vikas Sharma
https://orcid.org/0000-0001-8173-4548
IIMT University, India

Sachin Kaushik
https://orcid.org/0009-0004-1135-7168
HRIT University, Ghaziabad, India

Kewal Krishan Sharma
https://orcid.org/0009-0001-2504-9607
IIMT University, India

Vinod Kumar Bagar
Dewan Institute of Management Studies, India

ABSTRACT

Social engineering in social media and online interactions has emerged as a critical concern in the digital age, driven by the increasing interconnectivity and sharing of personal information online. This study is motivated by the growing prevalence of cyberattacks that exploit human psychology rather than technical vulnerabilities, targeting individuals through platforms where they share personal details. By examining various social engineering techniques such as phishing, pretexting, and baiting. This research highlights the methods attackers use to manipulate individuals and the specific vulnerabilities they exploit in social media environments. The study leverages data from recent cases and surveys to analyze the effectiveness of these techniques and the impact on both individuals and organizations. The findings underscore the significant risks posed by social engineering attacks, revealing the psychological underpinnings that make such tactics so effective.

DOI: 10.4018/979-8-3693-6665-3.ch012

1. INTRODUCTION

In the current virtual age, social engineering has emerged as a widespread threat to cybersecurity, exploiting the great and interconnected networks of social media and online interactions (Wang et al., 2021). Unlike conventional cyberattacks that rely upon technical exploits, social engineering leverages mental manipulation to misinform people into divulging personal statistics or acting moves that compromise security. Social media structures, wherein customers freely proportion non-public details, opinions, and everyday sports, have become fertile grounds for cybercriminals. These platforms offer attackers with a wealth of facts that may be used to craft incredibly customized and convincing attacks, which includes phishing, pretexting, and baiting. The insidious nature of social engineering lies in its capacity to make the most human psychology, specifically cognitive biases and emotional responses. Attackers often gift themselves as honest entities, creating scenarios that evoke a experience of urgency, fear, or interest, thereby compelling sufferers to act towards their higher judgment (Albladi and Weir, 2018). For example, an apparently innocent buddy request or a message from a supposed colleague can cause the revelation of sensitive information or the unwitting down load of malicious software. The effectiveness of those approaches is amplified by way of the inherent accept as true with and openness that represent social media interactions. This look at delves into the mechanisms and impacts of social engineering inside the realm of social media, examining each the strategies hired via attackers and the vulnerabilities they take advantage of. By dissecting numerous case research and real-international examples, the studies highlights the profound results of social engineering assaults, which range from non-public identity theft and monetary loss to corporate espionage and extensive facts breaches. Furthermore, the analysis also highlights the need for robust preventative measures, as well as consumer education, technology security, and organizational policies intended to increase resilience against such risks (Kumar et al., 2024).

Understanding the intricacies of social engineering is crucial for developing powerful protection strategies. As we navigate an increasingly digital international, it will become imperative to foster a tradition of protection attention, equipping individuals and groups with the knowledge and tools important to apprehend and mitigate the risks posed by means of social engineering. By doing so, we are able to better defend the integrity of our private and professional lives in opposition to those state-of-the-art and evolving assaults (Kumar et al., 2024).

1.1 Definition and Importance

Social engineering, inside the context of cybersecurity, refers back to the psychological manipulation of people into acting movements or divulging confidential information (Breda, Barbosa & Morais, 2017). Unlike traditional cyberattacks that make the most technical vulnerabilities in software program or hardware, social engineering exploits the human element, which is regularly the weakest link in protection chains. Attackers use quite a few tactics to misinform and manipulate their goals, along with impersonation, persuasion, and exploitation of social norms and cognitive biases.

The importance of know-how social engineering in social media and on-line interactions cannot be overstated. Social media platforms are inherently designed for sharing and connecting, frequently leading users to disclose massive quantities of private records. This openness creates a rich repository of statistics that attackers can mine to craft exceedingly customized and convincing attacks. As social media usage continues to develop, so does the ability for social engineering attacks, making it a urgent trouble in modern virtual panorama (Aun et al., 2023). The impacts of social engineering can be devastating, affecting people, agencies, and even country wide safety. On a personal degree, sufferers can be afflicted by identification robbery, economic loss, and emotional distress. For agencies, social engineering can cause facts breaches, financial losses, and damage to recognition. Nationally, coordinated social engineering assaults can undermine essential infrastructure, disrupt offerings, and compromise touchy data. Given the pervasive nature of social media and its integration into day by day existence, the capability for social engineering assaults is ever-present. Therefore, it's far vital to no longer handiest recognize the tactics and techniques utilized by attackers but additionally to implement effective preventive measures. These measures consist of instructing users approximately the dangers and signs and symptoms of social engineering, deploying technological answers to detect and mitigate attacks, and developing organizational rules that give a boost to protection best practices (Syafitri et al., 2022).

In summary, social engineering poses a vast risk inside the digital age, especially via social media and online interactions. By comprehensively information its mechanisms and impacts, we are able to better prepare and protect ourselves against those state-of-the-art assaults, making sure a more secure virtual surroundings for all.

Figure 1. Social Engineering in Cyber Security

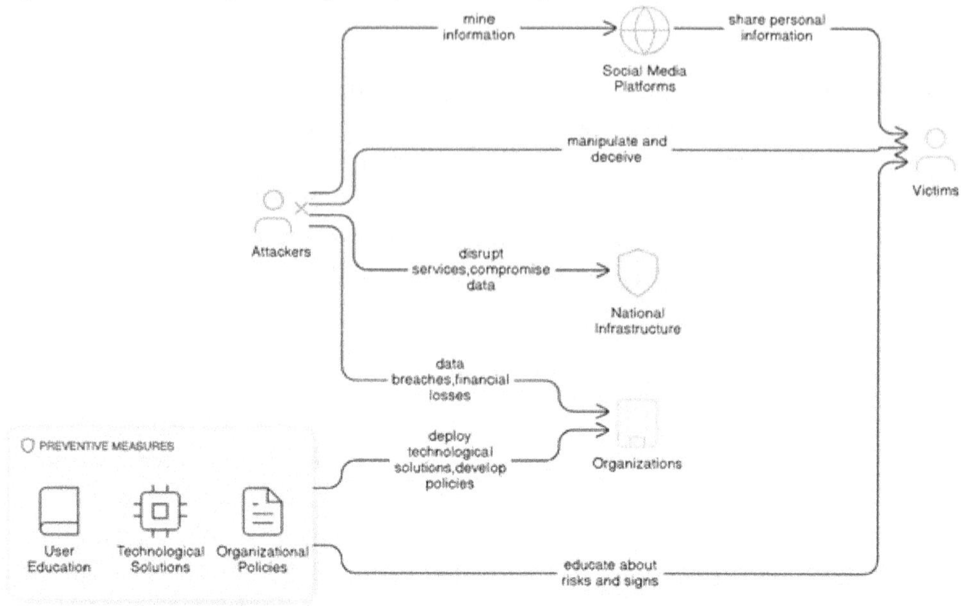

1.2 Scope of the Study

This look at goals to provide a complete evaluation of social engineering in the context of social media and online interactions. The scope encompasses the subsequent key areas:

Tactics and Techniques: The look at will examine the various methods and techniques employed by attackers to perform social engineering attacks on social media platforms and in online interactions. This consists of phishing, pretexting, baiting, and other styles of manipulation.

Vulnerabilities and Risks: An evaluation of the vulnerabilities inherent in social media systems and on-line verbal exchange channels could be carried out. This involves studying how private information shared on social media can be exploited by using attackers and the ability risks associated with such exploitation.

Impacts and Consequences: The study will look into the influences and results of social engineering attacks on people, businesses, and society at big. This includes economic losses, identity theft, reputational harm, and different destructive results.

Preventive Measures: A discussion of preventive measures and countermeasures might be furnished, focusing on strategies to mitigate the danger of social engineering assaults. This consists of person awareness schooling, technological answers, and organizational policies and techniques.

Case Studies and Examples: The study will include real-world case studies and examples of social engineering attacks on social media and online platforms. These case studies will illustrate the approaches used by attackers and the influences in their actions.

By addressing these key areas, this have a look at objectives to decorate know-how of social engineering in social media and online interactions and offer actionable insights for people, businesses, and policymakers to better defend themselves towards those threats.

1.3 Objectives of the Chapter

This chapter ambitions to provide a complete foundation for know-how the multifaceted nature of social engineering in social media and on line interactions. The unique targets of the chapter are:

Define Social Engineering: To provide a clean and concise definition of social engineering, highlighting its relevance and impact in the digital age.

Historical Context: To explore the historic development of social engineering strategies, tracing their evolution from early manipulation procedures to sophisticated modern-day strategies hired in our on-line world.

Identify Key Concepts and Techniques: To delineate the essential standards and usually used strategies in social engineering, consisting of phishing, pretexting, baiting, and tailgating.

Psychological Underpinnings: To study the mental foundations that underpin social engineering tactics, together with standards of persuasion, impact, authority, and agree with.

Discuss the Importance: To articulate the importance of understanding social engineering inside the context of cybersecurity, emphasizing the vulnerabilities it exploits and the capability risks to individuals and corporations.

Highlight Impacts on Social Media: To analyze how social engineering strategies are mainly tailor-made and deployed on social media structures, in which private information is amply to be had and may be exploited.

Present Preventive Measures: To suggest techniques and satisfactory practices for enhancing user cognizance and resilience against social engineering attacks, thereby enhancing standard cybersecurity defenses.

By attaining those goals, this bankruptcy will equip readers with the understanding important to apprehend, apprehend, and mitigate the threats posed by means of social engineering in social media and online interactions.

2. OVERVIEW OF SOCIAL ENGINEERING

2.1 Historical Background

Social engineering, as an idea and exercise, has deep ancient roots that predate the virtual generation. Its origins can be traced returned to various kinds of manipulation and deceit used by people to obtain unique goals via psychological method instead of bodily or technical methods. Understanding the historical background of social engineering offers perception into its evolution and adaptation to trendy technology and virtual platforms.

In historical times, social engineering procedures had been regularly hired in warfare, politics, and espionage. Military strategists and spies used deception, misinformation, and mental manipulation to gain a bonus over adversaries. For example, the well-known Trojan Horse incident in Greek mythology can be visible as an early form of social engineering, in which the Greeks used a deceptive tactic to infiltrate the city of Troy. During the middle Ages and Renaissance, social engineering endured to adapt with the emergence of greater structured societies and complicated political landscapes. Machiavellian principles, as outlined in Niccolò Machiavelli's "The Prince," highlighted the use of cunning and deceit as legitimate equipment for political maneuvering and control. This period also saw the rise of con artists and charlatans who exploited human psychology to defraud others. The commercial revolution and the appearance of mass communication added new opportunities for social engineering. Confidence tricksters, or "con guys," became distinguished figures in society, the use of complicated schemes to misinform people and organizations for economic gain. The well-known "Ponzi scheme," named after Charles Ponzi, is a classic example of social engineering, wherein Ponzi manipulated believe and greed to create a fraudulent investment operation. With the rise of the data age inside the late 20th century, social engineering methods tailored to make the most rising technology. The proliferation of computer systems and the net created new avenues for social engineering attacks. Early examples encompass phone phreaking, wherein hackers manipulated phone systems to make loose calls, and the initial instances of e-mail phishing, in which attackers masqueraded as straightforward entities to thieve touchy records. In the twenty first century, social engineering has come to be more and more state-of-the-art, leveraging superior era and social media systems to goal people and organizations on a massive scale.

Cybercriminals exploit the significant quantity of personal records to be had online to craft relatively personalized assaults. Social media structures, specially, have emerge as fertile floor for social engineering because of the ease of having access to and studying person information (Sharma et al., 2023).

Understanding the ancient background of social engineering underscores its enduring relevance and adaptableness. By studying its evolution, we can higher respect the complex interplay between human psychology and generation, and broaden more powerful techniques to counteract these threats inside the digital age (Kumar et al., 2023).

2.2 Key Concepts and Techniques

Social engineering encompasses loads of techniques and techniques aimed toward manipulating people into divulging confidential statistics or acting moves that compromise safety. Understanding the important thing standards and strategies of social engineering is important for identifying and mitigating these attacks. This phase explores the fundamental principles and usually hired techniques in social engineering.

Key Concepts

Psychological Manipulation: At the center of social engineering is mental manipulation. Attackers exploit human psychology, along with feelings, accept as true with, worry, and curiosity, to persuade individuals' behavior. By information commonplace mental triggers, social engineers craft their attacks to maximise effectiveness.

Pretexting: This involves developing a fabricated scenario or pretext to engage with the goal and benefit their trust with. The attacker pretends to be someone they're now not, consisting of a colleague, authority figure, or technical guide consultant, to extract facts from the goal.

Phishing: One of the maximum well-known kinds of social engineering, phishing involves sending misleading emails or messages that seem to come from legitimate sources. Oftentimes, these emails contain harmful links or files that are used to steal sensitive information or install malware.

Baiting: Using this technique, criminals lure victims into an enticement by promising them praise or something interesting. For instance, presenting loose software program downloads or the danger to win a prize, which requires the sufferer to offer non-public statistics or down load malicious software program.

Tailgating: Also referred to as piggybacking, tailgating entails an attacker gaining physical get right of entry to a restricted location via following a licensed character. This method is based on the attacker's ability to take advantage of commonplace courtesies, inclusive of protecting the door open for someone.

Quid Pro Quo: This technique includes imparting a carrier or advantage in exchange for information. For instance, an attacker might pose as an IT assist technician imparting to assist with a laptop difficulty in go back for login credentials.

Spear Phishing: A greater focused shape of phishing, spear phishing involves customized attacks directed at unique people or organizations. The attacker gathers detailed information about the target to make the phishing try greater convincing.

Techniques

Impersonation: Social engineers regularly impersonate depended on people or entities to mislead their objectives. This can involve phone calls, emails, or in-person interactions where the attacker pretends to be someone with legitimate authority or a relied on dating.

Social Media Exploitation: Attackers use social media structures to gather data about their targets and release personalized attacks. By reading social media profiles, posts, and connections, they are able to craft convincing pretexts and phishing messages.

Reverse Social Engineering: In this technique, the attacker creates a situation wherein the goal feels forced to be searching for help from the attacker. For instance, the attacker may create a fake technical problem after which offer to clear up it, getting access to sensitive records inside the manner (Irani et al., 2011).

Dumpster Diving: Social engineers seek via discarded documents, electronic devices, and other waste substances to find sensitive information that may be utilized in an attack. This method is based at the careless disposal of facts by way of individuals or organizations.

Vishing: Also referred to as voice phishing, vishing entails using cell phone calls to deceive people into revealing exclusive statistics. The attacker may additionally use caller ID spoofing to make the call seem legitimate and create an experience of urgency to set off the target to behave fast.

Smishing: Similar to phishing, smishing makes use of text messages to trick people into presenting personal statistics or clicking on malicious hyperlinks. Attackers exploit the immediacy and perceived legitimacy of textual content messages to reap their desires.

Understanding these key concepts and strategies is important for recognizing social engineering assaults and implementing effective countermeasures. By being privy to the various methods attackers use, people and groups can higher guard themselves in opposition to these sophisticated threats.

2.3 Psychological Foundations of Social Engineering

Social engineering exploits diverse mental concepts to manipulate individuals into performing actions or divulging confidential facts. Understanding the mental foundations in the back of these manipulative approaches is crucial for growing powerful defenses. This phase delves into the psychological underpinnings that make social engineering attacks a hit.

Trust and Authority

One of the maximum normally exploited psychological standards in social engineering is the tendency of individuals to trust and obey authority figures. Attackers regularly pose as authoritative figures, such as managers, IT specialists, or government officers, to gain the goals believe. When individuals perceive someone as having authority, they are more likely to conform to their requests without wondering their legitimacy.

Reciprocity

The principle of reciprocity involves the social norm of repaying favors. Social engineers exploit this by way of providing something of cost, such as help or facts, expecting the target to experience obligated to return the choose. For instance, an attacker may provide reputedly useful advice or support, which makes the goal much more likely to share sensitive statistics in return (Vashishth et al., 2024).

Social Proof

Social evidence refers back to the tendency of individuals to observe the actions of others, especially in unsure situations. Social engineers leverage this principle by creating scenarios where the goal believes that others are also complying with the attacker's requests. For instance, an electronic mail scam might consist of testimonials from meant colleagues who have already provided their statistics, encouraging the target to do the same.

Urgency and Fear

Creating a sense of urgency or fear is a powerful tactic in social engineering. Attackers often craft messages that convey a pressing want for immediate action, consisting of resetting a password because of a safety breach. This stress makes targets much more likely to behave quickly without very well considering the legitimacy of the request. Fear-primarily based tactics also can include threats of poor effects if the target does now not comply.

Commitment and Consistency

People have a psychological need to appear steady in their movements and choices. Social engineers take advantage of this by way of first getting objectives to commit to small actions, which makes them much more likely to conform with large requests later. This tactic, called the "foot-in-the-door" approach, relies at the target's preference to stay consistent with their previous behavior.

Liking

The precept of liking is based totally at the concept that individuals are more likely to conform to requests from people they like. Attackers frequently try and construct rapport and set up a pleasant relationship with their goals. This can contain flattery, shared pastimes, or growing a experience of familiarity. Once the goal feels a private connection, they're extra willing to trust and comply with the attacker's requests.

Scarcity

Scarcity will increase the perceived price of an opportunity or resource, prompting people to act speedy to keep away from missing out. Social engineers use this principle by creating scenarios wherein the goal believes that there may be a restricted time to take gain of an offer or to prevent a bad final results. This experience of scarcity can prompt hasty decisions and actions (Montañez, Atyabi & Xu, 2022).

Cognitive Overload

Attackers can also use cognitive overload to their advantage by means of overwhelming the target with complex records or a couple of simultaneous requests. When individuals are cognitively overloaded, their potential to process records critically and make knowledgeable choices is impaired. This makes them more vulnerable to manipulation and much less probably to notice purple flags.

By knowledge these mental foundations, individuals and companies can higher understand and resist social engineering processes. Training and cognizance programs that target those psychological standards can empower people to remain vigilant and sceptical of unsolicited requests, ultimately improving their resilience towards social engineering attacks (Chetioui et al., 2022).

3. EXPLOITATION OF SOCIAL MEDIA PLATFORMS

Social media systems have grown to be necessary to trendy conversation and statistics sharing, providing unparalleled possibilities for connection and engagement. However, their big use and the full-size amount of private records shared on these platforms additionally present enormous risks. Cybercriminals take advantage of social media to gather intelligence, release assaults, and manage individuals (Vashishth et al., 2024). This bankruptcy examines how social media structures are exploited for social engineering, focusing on the strategies utilized by attackers and the vulnerabilities they exploit.

3.1 Information Gathering

Social media structures are rich resources of personal statistics, making them prime objectives for information collecting via social engineers. Users regularly proportion information about their lives, such as their locations, relationships, hobbies, and sports, without thinking about the capability security implications (Almutairi & Alghamdi, 2022). Attackers use this facts to create unique profiles of their targets, which can be used to craft pretty personalised and convincing assaults.

Profile Mining: Attackers experiment person profiles for non-public details such as birthdates, employment facts, and speak to information. This records can be used for identification robbery, credential stuffing, or as the idea for a social engineering attack.

Social Network Analysis: By mapping out a goal's social connections, attackers can identify key relationships and ability points of leverage. They may additionally impersonate buddies or colleagues to advantage the targets accept as true with (Algarni et al., 2013).

3.2 Phishing and Impersonation

Phishing is a common social engineering tactic on social media, wherein attackers send deceptive messages designed to trick customers into revealing touchy information or downloading malware. Social media platforms offer a super surroundings for phishing due to their informal and frequently casual nature (Singh et al., 2022).

Clone Phishing: Attackers reproduction valid messages or posts from a trusted supply and send them to the target with malicious hyperlinks or attachments. Since the message seems to come back from a familiar entity, the goal is much more likely to believe and interact with it.

Impersonation: Attackers create faux profiles that mimic real users, often the usage of stolen pics and information to appear credible. These faux money owed can then be used to send pal requests, messages, or posts that entice victims into imparting private records or clicking on malicious links.

Figure 2. Phishing & Impersonation attack scenario

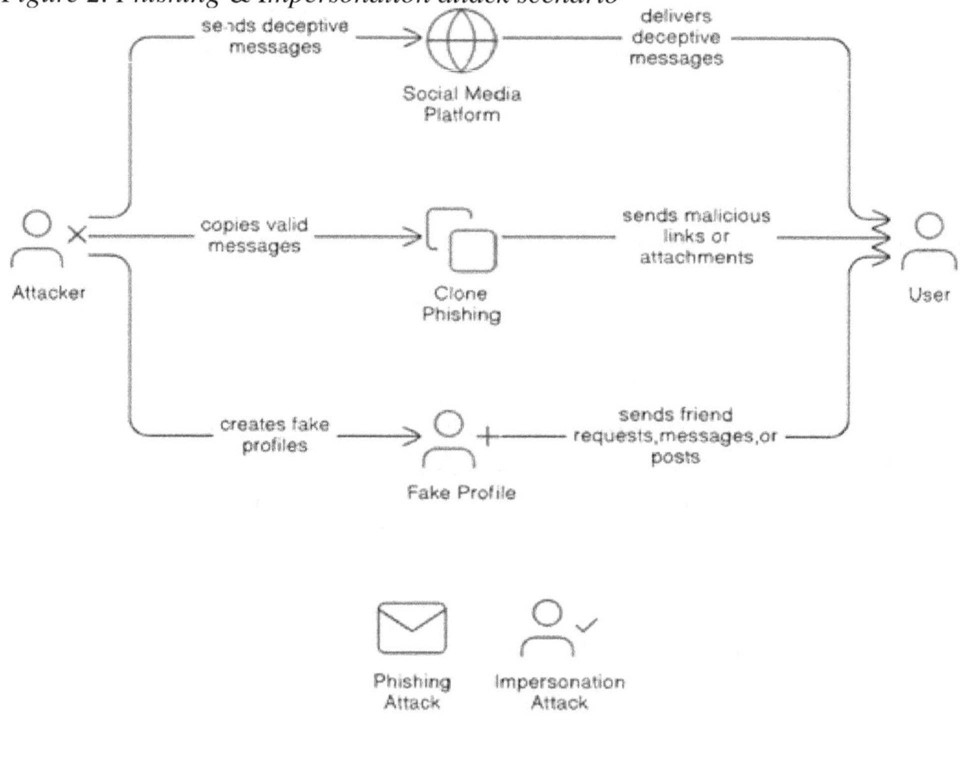

3.3 Baiting and Quizzes

Baiting entails offering something enticing to the victim, along with loose software, discounts, or get entry to special content material. Social media is rife with possibilities for baiting, with attackers the usage of quizzes, giveaways, and clickbait articles to lure victims.

Malicious Quizzes and Surveys: Attackers create engaging quizzes or surveys that require customers to offer non-public records. The data gathered can be used for identification theft or to tailor destiny attacks.

Clickbait Links: Posts with sensational headlines or promises of valuable content can trick users into clicking on links that lead to phishing websites or down load malware.

3.4 Social Proof and Manipulation

Social proof, the psychological phenomenon in which humans expect the movements of others replicate accurate behavior, is a effective tool for social engineers. Attackers take advantage of this by means of growing faux accounts or bot networks to simulate famous reviews or developments.

Fake Endorsements and Reviews: Attackers create fake money owed to go away positive reviews or endorsements for a product, carrier, or concept. This can control public perception and encourage real users to follow suit.

Astroturfing: Creating the illusion of vast support for a cause or product by the use of faux profiles and bots to generate buzz. This can have an effect on public opinion and drive proper user engagement.

3.5 Protecting Against Social Media Exploitation

Given the various approaches social media can be exploited, users and businesses need to undertake strong security measures to protect in opposition to these threats.

Privacy Settings: Users have to frequently overview and adjust their privacy settings to limit the amount of personal records visible to strangers.

Awareness and Training: Educating customers approximately the risks of sharing personal statistics and a way to recognize social engineering attempts is essential.

Verification Processes: Implementing verification procedures for buddy requests, messages, and posts can help identify and block malicious sports.

Monitoring and Reporting: Platforms should constantly display for suspicious activities and provide smooth reporting mechanisms for customers to flag capability threats.

By expertise the methods and methods used to exploit social media structures, customers can higher guard themselves and their statistics from social engineering assaults.

4. COMMON SOCIAL ENGINEERING TACTICS ON SOCIAL MEDIA

Social engineering tactics exploit human psychology to manipulate individuals into divulging personal records or appearing actions that compromise their security. Social media platforms, with their huge person bases and wealth of personal data, provide fertile floor for those procedures. This bankruptcy delves into some of the maximum commonplace social engineering techniques hired on social media, illustrating how attackers control customers and what can be carried out to counteract these threats.

4.1 Phishing

Phishing is one of the most common social engineering methods on social media. Attackers use misleading messages to trick customers into revealing sensitive data along with passwords, credit score card numbers, or non-public details.

Direct Messages and Emails: Attackers send direct messages or emails that appear to come from depended on assets, inclusive of pals, family, or famous brands. These messages frequently contain links to fake websites designed to harvest consumer credentials.

Comments and Posts: Phishers also go away malicious hyperlinks in comments or posts, luring customers to click on them and input their private facts on fraudulent web sites.

4.2 Impersonation and Fake Profiles

Creating fake profiles to impersonate real individuals or businesses is a commonplace tactic to gain accept as true with and manipulate goals.

Friend Requests: Attackers send friend requests from faux debts that mimic real humans. Once prevalent, they can access more non-public data and construct agree with the victim.

Celebrity Impersonation: Fake profiles of celebrities or public figures are used to draw fans and engage in fraudulent activities, which include selling scams or phishing links.

4.3 Baiting

Baiting: In order to lure victims directly into an enticement, baiting involves providing something alluring. Social media sites are ideal for baiting since users are frequently drawn to freebies, dramatic headlines, and other types of material.

Free Giveaways: Attackers sell faux giveaways or contests that require customers to provide non-public information or click on malicious links.

Sensational Content: Clickbait articles with sensational headlines can drive customers to malicious sites in which their facts can be harvested.

4.4 Pretexting

Pretexting includes growing a fabricated scenario to trick the sufferer into providing information or acting moves that compromise their safety.

Tech Support Scams: Attackers pose as technical help sellers and persuade users that their debts or gadgets have issues, prompting them to offer login info or install malware.

Fake Surveys and Quizzes: Attackers create bogus surveys or quizzes that ask for personal statistics under the guise of market studies or enjoyment.

4.5 Quizzes and Games

Many social media users interact with quizzes and games, often without understanding the capacity safety dangers.

Data Harvesting Quizzes: Seemingly harmless quizzes can accumulate specific non-public facts, which can be used for targeted assaults or bought on the dark internet.

App Permissions: Games and quizzes that request massive permissions can access customers' records and contacts, posing substantial privateness risks.

4.6 Social Proof and Herd Mentality

Social evidence, the psychological phenomenon wherein human beings follow the actions of others, is exploited by way of attackers to persuade person conduct.

Fake Reviews and Testimonials: Attackers create fake critiques and testimonials to lend credibility to scams or fraudulent merchandise, encouraging users to consider and interact with them.

Bot Networks: Automated bot networks can generate synthetic likes, shares, and comments, growing the phantasm of reputation and trustworthiness for malicious content.

4.7 Scareware and Threatening Messages

Scareware methods involve the usage of worry to govern victims into taking specific moves, along with disclosing non-public facts or paying money.

Fake Warnings: Attackers send fake warnings about security breaches or account suspensions, prompting customers to click on malicious links or offer sensitive statistics to resolve the issue.

Extortion and Blackmail: Threatening messages claiming to have compromising facts approximately the sufferer can coerce them into paying cash or imparting further facts.

4.8 Protecting Against Social Engineering on Social Media

To mitigate the risks posed by these social engineering strategies, customers and organizations ought to adopt complete protection practices.

Education and Awareness: Regularly educating users approximately the varieties of social engineering strategies and how to understand them is crucial for enhancing safety (Gaur et al., 2024).

Strong Authentication: Implementing two-issue authentication (2FA) and the use of sturdy, unique passwords for different accounts can help protect towards unauthorized get entry to.

Privacy Settings: Adjusting privateness settings to restriction the amount of private statistics shared publicly can reduce the hazard of being targeted.

Verification Practices: Verifying the identity of latest contacts and the authenticity of messages or hyperlinks before engaging with them can save you falling sufferer to scams.

Reporting Mechanisms: Social media platforms must offer smooth methods for users to document suspicious sports and take rapid movement towards malicious accounts.

5. TECHNIQUES USED BY ATTACKERS

Attackers hire a range of sophisticated techniques to make the most vulnerabilities in social media systems and control users. These techniques leverage each technological and psychological approaches to attain their targets. This chapter presents an in-depth examination of the diverse techniques utilized by attackers, supplying insights into how they perform and how their movements can be countered.

5.1 Spear Phishing

Spear phishing is a targeted form of phishing geared toward unique individuals or companies. Unlike preferred phishing assaults, spear phishing entails big studies at the goal to craft convincing and personalised messages.

Research and Reconnaissance: Attackers accumulate precise statistics approximately their goals from social media profiles, posts, and different on line assets. This records is used to tailor the phishing messages to appear greater legitimate and relevant.

Customized Messages: The messages are personalised with the target's name, process name, interests, or different particular information, making it more likely that the goal will trust and reply to the communication.

5.2 Social Engineering Frameworks

Attackers regularly use hooked up social engineering frameworks to structure their assaults (Kumar et al., 2024). These frameworks provide a systematic method to exploiting human psychology and manipulating sufferers.

Cialdini's Principles of Influence: Techniques based on Cialdini's standards, along with reciprocity, commitment, social evidence, authority, liking, and scarcity, are used to boom the effectiveness of social engineering attacks.

Pretexting Scenarios: In order to acquire acceptance of the purpose and elicit the desired response, attackers craft deceptive pretexts, or made-up stories.For instance, posing as a co-employee desiring urgent help or as a customer support consultant verifying account info (Siddiqi, Pak & Siddiqi, 2022).

5.3 Malware Distribution

Social media malware dissemination is a popular strategy used to breach consumer devices and steal confidential information.

Malicious Links and Attachments: Attackers share hyperlinks to malicious websites or attach infected files in messages or posts. Once clicked or downloaded, the malware infects the sufferer's tool, permitting the attacker to advantage manipulate or steal statistics.

Drive-by using Downloads: Visiting a compromised internet site related from social media can result in automated malware downloads without the user's information or consent.

5.4 Social Media Monitoring and Data Scraping

Attackers use computerized tools to reveal social media interest and scrape records from person profiles. This facts is used to enhance the effectiveness of social engineering attacks.

Profile Cloning: By copying a actual user's profile, attackers create fake accounts that carefully resemble the unique. These cloned profiles are used to ship buddy requests to the target's contacts, spreading the assault community.

Behavioral Analysis: Analyzing the conduct, interactions, and possibilities of users permits attackers to craft notably convincing social engineering schemes.

Figure 3. Social Media Monitoring & Data Scraping

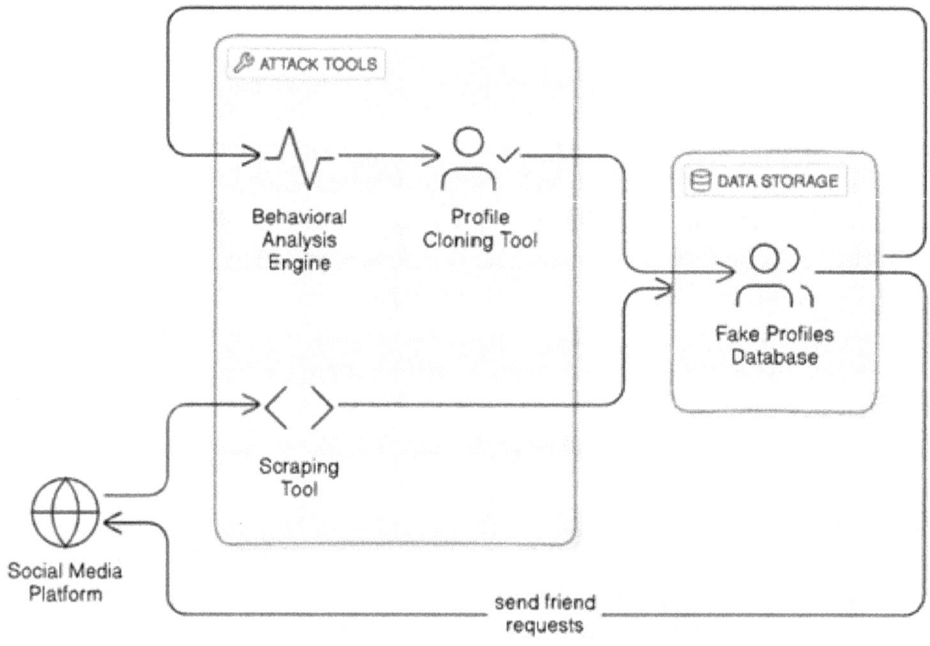

5.5 Exploiting Human Emotions

Human emotions which includes fear, interest, greed, and empathy are powerful levers that attackers exploit to manipulate sufferers.

Fear-Based Tactics: Fear-mongering messages, such as those threatening to suspend their account or file a criminal complaint, cause victims to take immediate action without first making sure the communication is genuine.

Curiosity-Inducing Content: Sensational headlines, shocking information, or specific content material are used to pique interest and lure users to click on malicious links.

Greed Exploitation: Offers of loose gifts, prizes, or monetary gains take advantage of the greed of customers, main them to fall for scams that require sharing non-public facts or paying fees.

5.6 Advanced Persistent Threats (APTs)

APTs are long-time period focused attacks where attackers set up a persistent presence in the target's system to steal information over a prolonged length.

Multi-Stage Attacks: APTs regularly involve a couple of tiers, beginning with an initial compromise through social engineering, observed by using deeper infiltration the use of diverse attack vectors (Mahammad and Kumar, 2022).

Stealth and Evasion: Attackers use state-of-the-art techniques to keep away from detection, which includes the usage of encrypted communications, hiding malware in legitimate documents, and using superior obfuscation strategies.

5.7 Manipulating Social Networks

Attackers use social networks' interconnectedness to their advantage to expand their attacks and increase their reach.

Fake News and Disinformation: Spreading false data via social media can manage public opinion, purpose panic, or harm reputations. These processes regularly rely upon the rapid unfold of information through sharing and retweeting.

Botnets and Automated Accounts: Attackers use networks of automatic bills (bots) to enlarge their messages, create fake engagement, and spread malicious content greater widely and quickly (Huber et al., 2009).

5.8 Countermeasures and Defense Strategies

Understanding the techniques used by attackers is vital for growing effective countermeasures and defense strategies.

User Education and Training: Continuous schooling and schooling programs for users can boost focus approximately commonplace social engineering techniques and teach them a way to apprehend and reply to capacity threats.

Advanced Security Technologies: Implementing superior security technologies such as AI-driven hazard detection, behavioral analytics, and robust authentication methods can assist perceive and mitigate social engineering assaults (Jaiswal and Kumar, 2023).

Incident Response Plans: Organizations ought to broaden and maintain comprehensive incident response plans to address social engineering assaults promptly and successfully, minimizing harm and stopping recurrence.

By exploring those strategies and imposing robust countermeasures, people and agencies can better shield themselves against the state-of-the-art and evolving panorama of social engineering on social media structures.

6. VULNERABILITIES EXPLOITED IN SOCIAL ENGINEERING

Social engineering assaults thrive on exploiting human and system vulnerabilities. Understanding these vulnerabilities is critical for developing effective defenses. This bankruptcy delves into the specific weaknesses that attacker's goal, each at the character and organizational ranges, highlighting the multifaceted nature of social engineering exploits.

6.1 Human Vulnerabilities

Human vulnerabilities are frequently the weakest hyperlink inside the protection chain (Wang, Zhu & Sun, 2021). Social engineers make the most diverse mental and behavioral weaknesses to control people.

Lack of Awareness: Many people are unaware of social engineering approaches and how they function. This lack of expertise makes it less complicated for attackers to deceive them.

Trust: Humans are obviously willing to agree with others, specifically while the attacker seems to be a legitimate or familiar entity. This trust may be exploited to elicit sensitive data.

Curiosity: Attackers frequently exploit curiosity with the aid of growing enticing messages or links that promise thrilling or valuable statistics.

Fear and Urgency: Creating a sense of urgency or fear (e.g., threats of account suspension, felony motion, or economic loss) can set off individuals to act without proper verification.

Greed: A person may lessen their defense, give statistics, or take actions they otherwise wouldn't if they are promised financial gain, awards, or incentives.

6.2 Organizational Vulnerabilities

Organizations, no matter size, have inherent vulnerabilities that social engineers can take advantage of. These include structural, procedural, and cultural weaknesses.

Lack of Security Training: Employees who aren't frequently educated on security protocols and social engineering procedures are extra susceptible to assaults.

Inadequate Policies and Procedures: Organizations without sturdy safety regulations and incident response strategies are sick-geared up to prevent or reply to social engineering assaults.

Over-Reliance on Technology: While technological defenses are important, over-reliance on them can cause complacency among team of workers, who might also overlook their function in protection.

Communication Breakdown: Poor inner conversation can cause personnel being unaware of ability threats or no longer knowing a way to file suspicious sports.

Insufficient Vetting Processes: Weak vetting techniques for employees, vendors, and 1/3 parties can permit malicious actors to infiltrate an enterprise.

6.3 Technological Vulnerabilities

Technological vulnerabilities offer an entry factor for social engineering assaults. These weaknesses can rise up from machine flaws, poor configuration, or inadequate safety features.

Outdated Software and Systems: Systems that are not frequently up to date with the modern day protection patches are extra prone to exploitation.

Weak Authentication Mechanisms: Simple or commonly used passwords, loss of multi-element authentication, and inadequate get right of entry to controls can be without problems bypassed (Kumar et al., 2023).

Insecure Networks: Poorly secured networks, along with Wi-Fi networks, can be intercepted and manipulated with the aid of attackers.

Social Media Platforms: The inherent openness of social media platforms, wherein users proportion private records, gives a wealthy source of information for attackers to craft personalised social engineering assaults.

Data Breaches: Previous data breaches can provide attackers with valuable statistics, along with e-mail addresses and passwords, which can be used in destiny attacks.

6.4 Exploiting Social Norms and Contexts

Social engineers often manipulate social norms and contextual cues to enhance the plausibility of their assaults.

Authority and Impersonation: Attackers may additionally impersonate figures of authority (e.g., executives, IT help) to stress individuals into compliance.

Social Proof: Attackers can set up scenarios where victims are more inclined to cooperate if they believe others are doing the same by using the influence of friends.

Reciprocity: Leveraging the norm of reciprocity, attackers may additionally provide a small choose or assistance to elicit a bigger desire in go back, inclusive of sharing touchy statistics.

Environmental Scanning: Observing and adapting to the target's environment and context to make the assault greater believable (e.g., referencing latest corporation activities or traits).

6.5 Case Studies of Exploited Vulnerabilities

To illustrate the exploitation of those vulnerabilities, actual-international case studies offer concrete examples of ways social engineering assaults have succeeded.

Case Study 1: Phishing Attack on a Financial Institution: Detailed evaluation of ways attackers exploited worker trust and lack of know-how to gain get entry to touchy monetary facts.

Case Study 2: Spear Phishing in a Healthcare Organization: Analysis of a targeted spear phishing effort that compromised impacted individual statistics by using personal information obtained from social media.

Case Study 3: Social Media Manipulation: Overview of a scenario where attackers used faux profiles and social proof to spread malware thru a popular social media platform.

By recognizing and addressing these vulnerabilities, both individuals and organizations can higher shield towards social engineering assaults. This comprehensive information is essential for growing sturdy protection techniques and fostering a way of life of vigilance and resilience.

7. IMPACT OF SOCIAL ENGINEERING ON INDIVIDUALS AND ORGANIZATIONS

Social engineering attacks have some distance-achieving results, affecting each people and agencies in vast methods. This chapter examines the different consequences of those attacks, emphasizing the possible damage and long-term repercussions.

7.1 Impact on Individuals

Individuals are often the direct targets of social engineering assaults, going through diverse effects that could affect their personal and professional lives.

Financial Loss: Victims may also suffer direct financial loss because of fraudulent transactions, identification theft, or scams that manage them into moving money.

Identity Theft: Social engineering assaults can result in the robbery of private information, which can be used to commit similarly crimes, open credit score debts, or conduct unlawful sports inside the victim's call.

Emotional and Psychological Distress: Victims often revel in extensive strain, anxiety, and a experience of violation upon figuring out they have been manipulated or defrauded.

Reputation Damage: Personal reputations can be tarnished if attackers use compromised bills to send malicious or beside the point content material to the victim's contacts.

Privacy Invasion: Exposure of personal records and private communications can result in a loss of privacy, doubtlessly affecting private relationships and social standing.

7.2 Impact on Organizations

Organizations face severe consequences when social engineering assaults are a success, which can disrupt operations and erode stakeholder believe.

Financial Damage: Organizations may additionally incur substantial economic losses due to fraud, robbery, and the costs associated with mitigating attacks and repairing harm.

Data Breaches: Social engineering can result in great data breaches, exposing touchy information about clients, employees, and proprietary enterprise statistics.

Operational Disruption: Attacks can disrupt enterprise operations, inflicting downtime, loss of productiveness, and further fees associated with restoring structures and records.

Reputation and Trust: The reputation of a company can be seriously broken, leading to a lack of consider among clients, companions, and the public. This can bring about long-time period commercial enterprise losses and problems in attracting new customers or expertise.

Legal and Regulatory Consequences: Organizations may additionally face felony moves and regulatory fines for failing to defend sensitive records accurately. Compliance violations can cause in addition economic and operational burdens (Vashishth et al., 2024).

Employee Morale and Productivity: Repeated or severe attacks can demoralize employees, main to a lower in productiveness and an increase in worker turnover.

7.3 Case Studies of Impact

To illustrate the effect of social engineering attacks, the following case research offer real-world examples of the outcomes confronted through people and groups.

Case Study 1: Corporate Espionage thru Phishing: Analysis of a massive employer that suffered enormous intellectual property theft due to a phishing assault, ensuing in monetary losses and competitive disadvantages.

Case Study 2: Personal Identity Theft: Detailed account of a man or woman whose identification changed into stolen thru a social media rip-off, main to fraudulent sports and an extended battle to repair their credit score and personal recognition.

Case Study 3: Ransomware Attack on a Healthcare Provider: Examination of the way social engineering facilitated a ransomware assault, inflicting operational disruption, facts breaches, and a loss of patient agree with.

7.4 Long-Term Effects

The long-term effects of social engineering attacks can be profound and enduring, influencing destiny behaviors and strategies.

Increased Vigilance and Security Measures: Victims frequently adopt greater stringent security features and practices, such as everyday schooling and recognition packages for employees and progressed security technology.

Policy and Procedure Changes: Organizations can also overhaul their guidelines and procedures to higher shield in opposition to social engineering threats, such as imposing stricter access controls and incident reaction plans.

Cultural Shift towards Security Awareness: A heightened cognizance on protection can cause a cultural shift within corporations, wherein protection will become a shared duty and a middle price.

Psychological Impact on Victims: Individuals may become greater cautious and distrustful of their interactions, impacting their behavior on-line and in private relationships.

7.5 Mitigating the Impact

While the impacts of social engineering assaults may be severe, there are strategies and measures that may mitigate these effects and help in recovery.

Education and Training: Regular and comprehensive schooling programs for employees and individuals on recognizing and responding to social engineering strategies.

Robust Incident Response: Developing and retaining a sturdy incident reaction plan to quick cope with and mitigate the effects of social engineering assaults.

Legal and Financial Support: Providing get right of entry to to felony and financial support services for victims to assist them recover from identity robbery and monetary losses.

Continuous Monitoring and Improvement: Implementing continuous tracking of structures and practices, and improving them based on training found out from beyond assaults.

Individuals and agencies may better prepare for and overcome these cutting-edge attacks by having the necessary skills and addressing the effects of social engineering, assuring long-term resilience and safety.

8. PREVENTIVE MEASURES AND STRATEGIES

In the face of growing social engineering attacks on social media and on line interactions, it's far important to enforce preventive measures and techniques to shield individuals and groups. This chapter delves into the numerous procedures and procedures that can be adopted to mitigate the risks and decorate resilience against those state-of-the-art threats.

8.1 Education and Awareness Programs

Educating customers about the dangers and methods of social engineering is an essential step in prevention. Awareness applications must cognizance on:

Identifying Common Tactics: Teaching customers a way to apprehend phishing emails, faux profiles, and other commonplace social engineering strategies (Vashishth et al., 2024).

Safe Online Practices: Encouraging the usage of robust, particular passwords, multi-issue authentication (MFA), and secure communication channels.

Incident Reporting: Establishing clear protocols for reporting suspicious sports or ability protection breaches.

8.2 Technical Measures

Incorporating superior technical defenses can considerably lessen the vulnerability to social engineering assaults.

Figure 4. Technical Measures for Social Engineering Defense

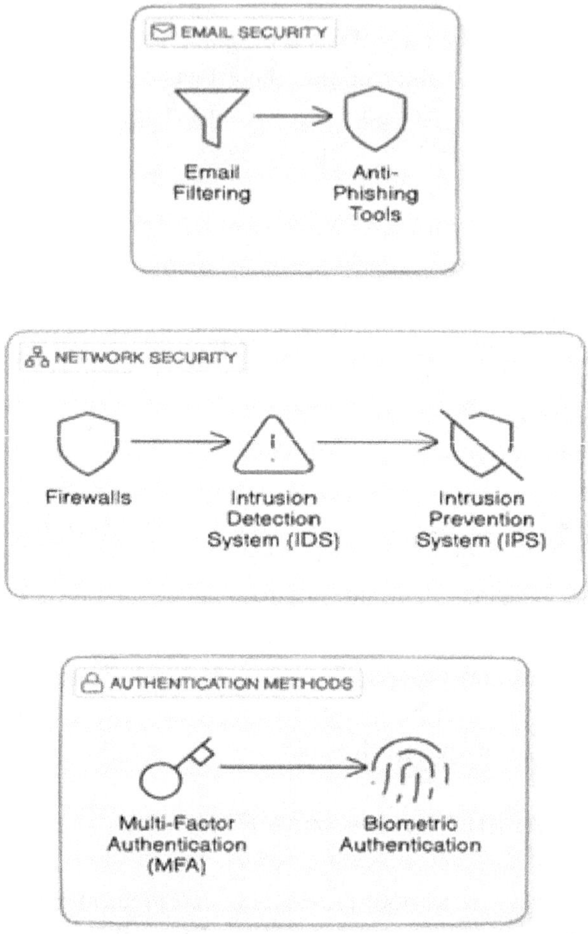

Email Filtering and Anti-Phishing Tools: Deploying superior e-mail filters and anti-phishing software to come across and block malicious emails.

Network Security: Implementing firewalls, intrusion detection structures (IDS), and intrusion prevention structures (IPS) to shield community integrity.

Secure Authentication Methods: Utilizing MFA and biometric authentication to add an extra layer of safety.

8.3 Organizational Policies and Procedures

Organizations ought to establish comprehensive regulations and techniques to decrease the threat of social engineering.

Access Control: Restricting get entry to sensitive statistics on a want-to-realize foundation and often reviewing get right of entry to rights (Kashmar et al., 2021).

Data Protection Policies: Ensuring sturdy data safety policies are in place, along with encryption and steady information storage practices.

Regular Audits and Assessments: Conducting regular security audits and exams to discover and deal with vulnerabilities.

8.4 Psychological Training

Understanding the psychological concepts at the back of social engineering can assist people and agencies better shield in opposition to those approaches.

Building Critical Thinking Skills: Training people to question and verify the legitimacy of requests for sensitive records.

Resilience Training: Helping individuals increase resilience towards manipulation tactics with the aid of know-how their personal mental triggers and biases.

8.5 Collaboration and Information Sharing

Collaboration among extraordinary stakeholders can decorate the general security posture.

Industry Partnerships: Forming partnerships with different agencies to share statistics on rising threats and great practices.

Government and Regulatory Bodies: Working with government businesses and regulatory bodies to live informed about the contemporary threats and compliance requirements.

8.6 Continuous Improvement

Security is an ongoing method that requires constant vigilance and adaptation.

Regular Training Updates: Ensuring that education applications are often updated to mirror the cutting-edge social engineering processes.

Feedback Loops: Establishing feedback mechanisms to always examine the effectiveness of preventive measures and make important modifications.

Technology Upgrades: Keeping up with technological improvements and integrating new tools and strategies to beautify security.

8.7 Developing a Security Culture

Creating a security-aware lifestyle within an enterprise can appreciably lessen the danger of social engineering.

Leadership Commitment: Ensuring that organizational leaders prioritize and champion safety projects.

Employee Engagement: Encouraging all employees to take an lively role in safety by using promoting a tradition of vigilance and duty.

Recognition and Rewards: Recognizing and profitable personnel who show top notch awareness and proactive conduct in safety practices.

8.8 Personal Security Practices

Individuals can adopt private security practices to defend themselves from social engineering assaults.

Privacy Settings: Adjusting privateness settings on social media systems to limit the publicity of private facts.

Suspicion and Verification: Being suspicious of unsolicited requests for information and verifying the identity of requesters earlier than sharing any touchy information.

Digital Footprint Management: Regularly monitoring and handling one's digital footprint to reduce the amount of personal data to be had online (Jain, Sahoo & Kaubiyal, 2021).

By implementing those preventive measures and strategies, individuals and corporations can create robust defenses against social engineering assaults, thereby improving their standard safety and resilience within the virtual age.

9. CASE STUDIES AND REAL-WORLD EXAMPLES

Case studies and real-world examples offer valuable insights into the application and effects of social engineering tactics on social media and on line interactions. By inspecting precise incidents, we will understand the methodologies utilized by attackers, the vulnerabilities they exploited, and the impacts on sufferers.

One incredible case involved the notorious 2020 Twitter hack, in which high-profile bills, which includes the ones of Barack Obama, Elon Musk, and Jeff Bezos, had been compromised via a social engineering assault on Twitter personnel. Attackers used phishing techniques to benefit get entry to to internal structures, demonstrating how even sophisticated systems can be prone to social engineering.

Another instance is the 2016 Democratic National Committee (DNC) e-mail leak, wherein spear-phishing emails were used to trick people into revealing login credentials. This incident not best uncovered touchy records however additionally had sizeable political ramifications, illustrating the some distance-reaching results of such attacks.

In the company quarter, a 2015 case noticed Ubiquiti Networks fall sufferer to a Business Email Compromise (BEC) scam. Attackers impersonated executives and persuaded personnel to transfer $forty six.7 million to fraudulent foreign places accounts, highlighting the monetary dangers and the importance of sturdy inner security protocols.

These case research underscore the significance of cognizance and preparedness in combating social engineering. By getting to know from beyond incidents, businesses and people can higher apprehend the signs of social engineering attempts and implement stronger shielding measures to mitigate such threats.

10. ENHANCING USER RESILIENCE AGAINST SOCIAL ENGINEERING

Enhancing user resilience towards social engineering is vital in fighting the sophisticated methods hired by means of cybercriminals. This includes fostering a way of life of cybersecurity focus and training, where users are educated to recognize and reply to capability threats. Regular attention programs and simulations can help customers pick out phishing attempts, suspicious requests for records, and other manipulative strategies. Encouraging suitable virtual hygiene practices, together with sturdy password control, multi-component authentication, and cautious sharing of personal statistics, also strengthens person defenses (Neupane et al. 2018). Additionally, leveraging superior technologies like synthetic intelligence and device studying to hit upon and counter social engineering attempts in actual-time can appreciably bolster resilience. By combining schooling, pleasant practices, and technological answers, we can empower people to emerge as the first line of defense towards social engineering attacks.

11. LEGAL AND ETHICAL CONSIDERATIONS

Legal and moral considerations within the context of social engineering and online interactions are paramount for ensuring the safety of people' privacy and the integrity of virtual structures. Legally, its miles vital to put into effect stringent regulations that penalize social engineering approaches and guard consumer statistics from unauthorized get admission to and exploitation. Organizations have to observe laws consisting of the General Data Protection Regulation (GDPR) and different facts safety statutes to guard consumer data and hold consider. Ethically, agencies and builders have an obligation to design systems that prioritize user safety and privateness, actively prevent manipulation, and keep away from exploiting person records for malicious functions. Furthermore, transparency in statistics managing practices and imparting users with manage over their records are important to keeping ethical standards. Balancing legal compliance and ethical duty creates a safer and more honest on line surroundings for all users.

12. FUTURE TRENDS AND EMERGING THREATS

The landscape of social engineering is constantly evolving, pushed through advances in generation and shifting digital behaviors. In the future, we are able to assume to see increasingly sophisticated attacks leveraging artificial intelligence and machine getting to know to craft incredibly personalised and automated phishing schemes (Zambrano et al. 2023). Emerging technologies along with the Internet of Things (IoT) and blockchain gift new vulnerabilities, while the proliferation of social media systems offers fertile floor for facts harvesting and manipulation (Mahammad and Kumar, 2023). Hybrid and multi-level assaults becomes extra not unusual, mixing social engineering with other cyber threats like ransomware. Psychological manipulation techniques will also improve, exploiting deeper behavioral insights to misinform goals (Gosain et al., 2023). Additionally, the global connectivity of our digital international introduces go-border demanding situations and cultural exploitation possibilities. As governments and agencies reply with new guidelines, attackers will adapt to locate and make the most loopholes. To fight these threats, more desirable AI-driven defenses, adaptive protection models, and sturdy human-AI collaboration can be crucial, alongside increased collaboration and facts sharing among international cybersecurity stakeholders. Continuous training, studies, and resilience-constructing efforts may be essential to stay in advance of the evolving threats in social engineering (Mahammad and Kumar, 2022).

13. CONCLUSION

This study has successfully illuminated the complex and evolving landscape of social engineering within social media and online interactions. By analyzing the historical context, psychological underpinnings, and techniques such as phishing, pretexting, and baiting, we have gained a comprehensive understanding of how cybercriminals exploit these platforms to target individuals and organizations. The key achievement of this work lies in its detailed examination of the specific vulnerabilities that social engineering attackers target and the profound impacts these attacks can have, including significant financial losses, reputational damage, and emotional distress. Moreover, this research has highlighted the importance of preventive measures and strategies to counteract these threats. Enhancing user awareness, adopting robust security practices, and leveraging advanced technologies such as artificial intelligence (AI) and machine learning (ML) are critical steps toward mitigating the risks associated with social engineering. These achievements underscore the need for a proactive, multi-layered defense strategy that integrates both technological innovations and human-centric approaches. Looking ahead, the future scope of this work involves continued exploration of emerging threats in social engineering as attackers become more sophisticated. The integration of AI and ML will be crucial in anticipating and countering new attack vectors. Additionally, global collaboration in cybersecurity efforts will be essential to building a resilient defense infrastructure that can adapt to the ever-changing threat landscape. By fostering a culture of cybersecurity awareness and resilience, we can better protect ourselves and our organizations, ensuring a safer digital environment for all. This study sets the foundation for future research and development in the fight against social engineering, emphasizing the importance of continuous vigilance and innovation in cybersecurity practices.

REFERENCES

Albladi, S. M., & Weir, G. R. (2018). User characteristics that influence judgment of social engineering attacks in social networks. *Human-centric Computing and Information Sciences*, 8(1), 1–24. DOI: 10.1186/s13673-018-0128-7

Aldawood, H., & Skinner, G. (2019, May). Challenges of implementing training and awareness programs targeting cyber security social engineering. In 2019 cybersecurity and cyberforensics conference (ccc) (pp. 111-117). IEEE.

Algarni, A., Xu, Y., Chan, T., & Tian, Y. C. (2013, December). Social engineering in social networking sites: Affect-based model. In *8th International Conference for Internet Technology and Secured Transactisons (ICITST-2013)* (pp. 508-515). IEEE.

Almutairi, B. S., & Alghamdi, A. (2022). The Role of Social Engineering in Cybersecurity and Its Impact. *Journal of Information Security*, 13(4), 363–379. DOI: 10.4236/jis.2022.134020

Aun, Y., Gan, M. L., Wahab, N. H. B. A., & Guan, G. H. (2023). Social engineering attack classifications on social media using deep learning. *Computers, Materials & Continua*, 74(3), 4917–4931. DOI: 10.32604/cmc.2023.032373

Breda, F., Barbosa, H., & Morais, T. (2017). Social engineering and cyber security. In *INTED2017 Proceedings* (pp. 4204-4211). IATED. DOI: 10.21125/inted.2017.1008

Chetioui, K., Bah, B., Alami, A. O., & Bahnasse, A. (2022). Overview of social engineering attacks on social networks. *Procedia Computer Science*, 198, 656–661. DOI: 10.1016/j.procs.2021.12.302

Gaur, A. S., Sharan, H. O., & Kumar, R. (2024). AI in Education: Ethical Challenges and Opportunities. The Ethical Frontier of AI and Data Analysis, 39-54.

Gosain, M. S., Aggarwal, N., & Kumar, R. (2023, April). A study of 5G and edge computing integration with IoT-A Review. In *2023 International Conference on Computational Intelligence and Sustainable Engineering Solutions (CISES)* (pp. 705-710). IEEE. DOI: 10.1109/CISES58720.2023.10183438

Huber, M., Kowalski, S., Nohlberg, M., & Tjoa, S. (2009, August). Towards automating social engineering using social networking sites. In *2009 International Conference on Computational Science and Engineering* (Vol. 3, pp. 117-124). IEEE. DOI: 10.1109/CSE.2009.205

Irani, D., Balduzzi, M., Balzarotti, D., Kirda, E., & Pu, C. (2011). Reverse social engineering attacks in online social networks. In Detection of Intrusions and Malware, and Vulnerability Assessment: 8th International Conference; DIMVA 2011, Amsterdam, The Netherlands, July 7-8, 2011. [Springer Berlin Heidelberg.]. *Proceedings*, 8, 55–74.

Jain, A. K., Sahoo, S. R., & Kaubiyal, J. (2021). Online social networks security and privacy: Comprehensive review and analysis. *Complex & Intelligent Systems*, 7(5), 2157–2177. DOI: 10.1007/s40747-021-00409-7

Jaiswal, A., & Kumar, R. (2023). Breast cancer diagnosis using stochastic self-organizing map and enlarge C4. 5. *Multimedia Tools and Applications*, 82(12), 18059–18076. DOI: 10.1007/s11042-022-14265-1

Kashmar, N., Adda, M., Atieh, M., & Ibrahim, H. (2021). Access Control in Cybersecurity and Social Media. Cybersécurité Médias Sociaux, 69-105.

Kumar, A., Saini, R., & Kumar, R. (2023, December). A systematic review of breast cancer detection using machine learning and deep learning. In 2023 10th IEEE Uttar Pradesh Section International Conference on Electrical, Electronics and Computer Engineering (UPCON) (Vol. 10, pp. 1128-1133). IEEE. DOI: 10.1109/UPCON59197.2023.10434530

Kumar, A., Saini, R., & Kumar, R. (2024). A Comparative Analysis of Machine Learning Algorithms for Breast Cancer Detection and Identification of Key Predictive Features. *TS. Traitement du Signal*, 41(1). Advance online publication. DOI: 10.18280/ts.410110

Kumar, P., Kumar, M., & Kumar, R. (2024). The Proposed Framework of View-Dependent Data Integration Architecture. In The Ethical Frontier of AI and Data Analysis (pp. 343-361). IGI Global. DOI: 10.4018/979-8-3693-2964-1.ch021

Kumar, P., Kumar, R., Singh, K. B., & Kumar, M. (2023). Identification of the problem and research methodology. In Effective AI, Blockchain, and E-Governance Applications for Knowledge Discovery and Management (pp. 289-308). IGI Global. DOI: 10.4018/978-1-6684-9151-5.ch017

Kumar, R., Hamid, A., Bakar, A., Inayah Binti Ya'akub, N., Sharma Gaur, M., & Kumar, S. (Eds.). (2024). *Futuristic E-governance Security with Deep Learning Applications*. IGI Global. DOI: 10.4018/978-1-6684-9596-4

Mahammad, A. B., & Kumar, R. (2022). Progression of Digital Healthcare with Deep Learning and Blockchain Methods for Smart Cities. In *Advances in Deep Learning Applications for Smart Cities* (pp. 248–266). IGI Global. DOI: 10.4018/978-1-7998-9710-1.ch012

Mahammad, A. B., & Kumar, R. (2022, April). Design a linear classification model with support vector machine algorithm on autoimmune disease data. In 2022 3rd International Conference on Intelligent Engineering and Management (ICIEM) (pp. 164-169). IEEE. DOI: 10.1109/ICIEM54221.2022.9853182

Mahammad, A. B., & Kumar, R. (2023, April). Scalable and security framework to secure and maintain healthcare data using blockchain technology. In *2023 International Conference on Computational Intelligence and Sustainable Engineering Solutions (CISES)* (pp. 417-423). IEEE. DOI: 10.1109/CISES58720.2023.10183494

Montañez, R., Atyabi, A., & Xu, S. (2022). Social engineering attacks and defenses in the physical world vs. cyberspace: a contrast study. In *Cybersecurity and Cognitive Science* (pp. 3–41). Academic Press. DOI: 10.1016/B978-0-323-90570-1.00012-7

Neupane, A., Satvat, K., Saxena, N., Stavrinos, D., & Bishop, H. J. (2018, December). Do social disorders facilitate social engineering? A case study of autism and phishing attacks. In *Proceedings of the 34th Annual Computer Security Applications Conference* (pp. 467-477). DOI: 10.1145/3274694.3274730

Sharma, V., Sharma, K. K., Vashishth, T. K., Panwar, R., Kumar, B., & Chaudhary, S. (2023, November). Brain-Computer Interface: Bridging the Gap between Human Brain and Computing Systems. In *2023 International Conference on Research Methodologies in Knowledge Management, Artificial Intelligence and Telecommunication Engineering (RMKMATE)* (pp. 1-5). IEEE. DOI: 10.1109/RMKMATE59243.2023.10369702

Siddiqi, M. A., Pak, W., & Siddiqi, M. A. (2022). A study on the psychology of social engineering-based cyberattacks and existing countermeasures. *Applied Sciences (Basel, Switzerland)*, 12(12), 6042. DOI: 10.3390/app12126042

Singh, C. B., Gupta, A., & Kumar, R. (2022, April). Diabetes Care Survey Using Supervised and Unsupervised Machine Learning. In 2022 3rd International Conference on Intelligent Engineering and Management (ICIEM) (pp. 207-210). IEEE. DOI: 10.1109/ICIEM54221.2022.9853085

Syafitri, W., Shukur, Z., Asma'Mokhtar, U., Sulaiman, R., & Ibrahim, M. A. (2022). Social engineering attacks prevention: A systematic literature review. *IEEE Access : Practical Innovations, Open Solutions*, 10, 39325–39343. DOI: 10.1109/ACCESS.2022.3162594

Vashishth, T. K., Sharma, V., Pandey, A., & Tomer, T. (2024). Innovative Advancements in Big Data Analytics: Navigating Future Trends with Hadoop Integration. In Recent Trends and Future Direction for Data Analytics (pp. 234-258). IGI Global.

Vashishth, T. K., Sharma, V., Sharma, K. K., Kumar, B., Chaudhary, S., & Panwar, R. (2024). Security and Privacy Considerations in Cloud-Based Data Processing Solutions for Sensitive Data. In *Developments towards Next Generation Intelligent Systems for Sustainable Development* (pp. 35–61). IGI Global. DOI: 10.4018/979-8-3693-5643-2.ch002

Vashishth, T. K., Sharma, V., Sharma, K. K., Kumar, B., Chaudhary, S., & Panwar, R. (2024). Transforming Classroom Dynamics: The Social Impact of AI in Teaching and Learning. In AI-Enhanced Teaching Methods (pp. 322-346). IGI Global.

Vashishth, T. K., Sharma, V., Sharma, K. K., Kumar, B., Kumar, A., & Panwar, R. (2024). Artificial Intelligence (AI)–Powered Chatbots: Providing Instant Support and Personalized Recommendations to Guests 24/7. In Technology and Luxury Hospitality (pp. 211-236). Routledge.

Wang, Z., Zhu, H., & Sun, L. (2021). Social engineering in cybersecurity: Effect mechanisms, human vulnerabilities and attack methods. *IEEE Access : Practical Innovations, Open Solutions*, 9, 11895–11910. DOI: 10.1109/ACCESS.2021.3051633

Zambrano, P., Torres, J., Tello-Oquendo, L., Yánez, Á., & Velásquez, L. (2023). On the modeling of cyber-attacks associated with social engineering: A parental control prototype. *Journal of Information Security and Applications*, 75, 103501. DOI: 10.1016/j.jisa.2023.103501

KEY TERMS AND DEFINITIONS

Blockchain -: is a decentralized, allotted ledger generation that statistics transactions throughout a couple of computers in a manner that guarantees safety, transparency, and immutability. Each block within the chain contains a listing of transactions and is connected to the preceding block, forming a chronological chain.

Cybersecurity -: is the exercise of protecting computer systems, networks, and information from virtual attacks, robbery, and damage. It includes enforcing measures to save you unauthorized get right of entry to, make sure information integrity, and guard towards cyber threats.

Internet of Things (IoT) -: refers to a network of interconnected devices and objects that could talk and trade information with every different via the internet. These devices regularly have embedded sensors, software, and different technology to collect and transmit records autonomously.

Phishing -: is a cyber-assault that includes tricking individuals into revealing non-public statistics, such as passwords or credit card numbers, by using pretending to be a straightforward entity in digital communications. This is frequently accomplished via misleading emails, messages, or websites.

Social engineering -: is the manipulation of individuals into divulging exclusive facts or appearing actions that compromise safety thru psychological techniques in preference to technical exploits. It exploits human behavior and accept as true with to attain malicious dreams.

Chapter 13
The Use of Deep Fakes in Social Engineering Attacks:
A Case Study on Social Media Engagements

Avinash Saxena
https://orcid.org/0000-0003-1956-0510
Moradabad Institute of Technology, India

Himani Grewal
Moradabad Institute of Technology, India

ABSTRACT

Deepfakes, a recent and compelling technique that is used in social engineering attacks, allows cybercriminals to falsify audio, videos, and video to deceive individuals. These deepfakes can be used in phishing attacks, where fake hyperlinks lure victims into providing sensitive information. Deepfakes in social engineering attacks pose a significant cybersecurity threat. This spread of falsehood and misrepresentation on social media platforms has been shown to have a significant impact, with falsehood spreading farther, faster, deeper, and more broadly than the truth. The use of deepfakes in social engineering attacks raises ethical concerns, as these technologies can be used to manipulate individuals and spread disinformation on social media networks. The present chapter highlights the types of social engineering attacks, the meaning of deepfake technology, the positive side (benefits) of deepfake technologies, and the possible threats of deepfakes, with some real-time cases of the Indian political and entertainment industry followed by possible solutions.

DOI: 10.4018/979-8-3693-6665-3.ch013

SOCIAL ENGINEERING ATTACKS

Introduction and Types of Social Engineering Attacks

The greatest communication tool we have access to nowadays is the internet, which allows us to communicate in different ways through a jumbled media tools. The best ways for us to connect with others, whether personally or professionally is through social networks. Employers are expecting more and more from their staff members to have access to work devices, through either company-issued devices or personal smartphones (Krombholz et al., 2015). Social engineering attack term is used to persuade users to provide personal information (Gupta et al., 2016) by taking the advantages of different human traits, is a technique which helps the attackers to forged the sensitive information of the users (Fuertes et al., 2022). Social engineering attack is still very young and struggling to get a formal definition. This attack is still regarded as one of the most dangerous in the digital realm (Algarni et al., 2013). Social engineering attacks have been shown to provide the biggest security threats since they are more difficult to prevent (Bullée & Junger, 2020). Because user-provided personal information is the most important component to social networking site providers, there is an expectation that the danger of social engineering may rise in the future (Algarni et al., 2013). It can be regarded as an AI technique to convince a person to fulfill any request which can be made by the attacker for his personal goal (Mouton et al., 2016). Humans are still manipulable, even with the increased efficacy of security measures to safeguard sensitive data, making humans a weak link in the system. A social engineering attack takes advantage of this vulnerability by coercing sensitive information out of the target through a variety of manipulation strategies (Mouton et al., 2014). The social engineering attackers attacks the weakest relationship links of the victims. An attacker using social engineering is someone who seeks to get private data or funds. By making the victim feel uncomfortable, the assailant will alert the victim of their intended revenge while manipulating them. As per the definition given by National Institute of Standards and Technology "social engineering is an effort to deceive someone into disclosing information—like a password—in order to compromise networks or systems" (Scarfone et al., 2008). Attacks using social engineering have expanded to include emails, phone conversations, and in-person meetings. Automated social engineering, semantic attacks, social engineering in online communities or social media, and impersonation are examples of social engineering attack strategies. A multitude of social engineering techniques are emerging from the widespread use of information technology. Previous studies on human manipulation have revealed that offenders mentally coerced or deceived workers into divulging private information or making security blunders, for example, by employing social engineering and phishing scams (Syed, 2019). Hackers transmit altered communications to users, leading them to assume that they are authentic and requiring them to act upon the recommendations or instructions therein. Email and internet phishing are the most commonly employed types of phishing attacks. Some phishing attempts to increase user access by using malware, bots, and Trojans (Hijji & Alam, 2021). Angler phishing is a novel form of cyberattack which cybercriminals replicate social media accounts from a company's customer support account in order to target the company's clientele. Customers who are satisfied or dissatisfied with a company's or organization's services are the attack's top targets. Angler phishing attacks may target these clients based on their social media status, which may indicate dissatisfaction or happiness. This exploit is used by hackers to get login credentials or personal data (Syafitri et al., 2022). Another tactic is profile cloning, which makes use of publicly accessible data from sources like social media to pretend to be someone whose profile has been copied in order to obtain crucial information from other sources (Kumar et al., 2019). Attacks that demand reciprocity in exchange for a free good or service are quid pro quo. For this attack to occur, there must be a contract between the hacker and the victim. As an example, the person who was attacked can ask the hacker to complete a task that is outside of their purview as a condition against the hacker requesting important data or something else (Salahdine & Kaabouch, 2019). Information disposed of at a landfill or erased from a hard drive or folder will be useful to data collectors conducting Dumpster Diving operations as a form of social engineering attacks (Salahdine & Kaabouch, 2019). High traffic websites are compromised, and malware or trojans are subsequently implanted on the compromised website. The user only needs to click on the link provided or install the application on the hacked webpage to allow for the attacker and the victim's computer to establish a two-way communication channel (Wang et al., 2020).

Introduction to Deepfake Technology

With the use of computer vision and deep learning technology, a new set of evolving techniques has made it possible for anyone to produce phony but remarkably realistic images, videos, and even sounds. This technology is commonly known as "Deepfake Technology" (Mahmud & Sharmin, 2021). In recent years, fake news has become an issue that puts human culture, democracy, and public discourse at risk. Fake news is defined as inaccurate information disseminated with the goal to deceive the public. On social media, misinformation travels fast and may affect millions of people (Aldwairi & Alwahedi, 2018). While some deep fakes include artefacts that reveal their actual origin, others appear rather convincing. However, taken as a whole, they demonstrate how adept AI systems have gotten in mimicking the features and actions of humans (Anwar et al., 2019).

A play on the terms "deep learning" and "fake," fake news are remarkably realistic movies that have undergone electronically changed to depict people speaking and acting in ways that never actually occurred. (CNN Business, 2019). Deepfakes use artificial intelligence (AI) and facial mapping technology to swap out one person's face in a video for another (Agarwal et al., 2020). Since deepfakes may incorporate actual footage, sound legitimate, and be designed to propagate swiftly on social media, they are challenging to identify. As a result, a lot of people believe the film they are seeing is authentic (CNN Business, 2019). Deepfakes are only a fresh way to manipulate the media. But as technology advances, the way information is exchanged and disseminated on social media poses new challenges to the information ecosystem (Paterson & Hanley, 2020). The qualities of deepfakes, such their persuasiveness and rising quality, also make the problems caused by manipulated media more severe. Because it was formerly difficult to modify audio and video content effectively, people had less faith in these types of media (Kwok & Koh, 2021). In addition to being realistic, deepfakes' accessibility presents issues: Deepfake creation, in contrast to previous advanced kinds of media manipulation, is becoming more commercialized and easily comprehensible for ordinary individuals (Ajder et al., 2019). Therefore, it is critical to evaluate the societal and political effects of deepfakes in depth. Still, not many academics and policy experts have done so up until this point. In-depth examinations of deepfakes' potential for political misuse are uncommon, despite the media and politicians placing a great deal of focus on it. Furthermore, they are not directly grounded in democratic theory and hardly draw attention to the principles that are at issue. A recent comprehensive analysis of deepfake research, which was published between 2018 and 2020, found that the majority of works on deepfake detection and regulation come from the computer sciences or the legal field. Social science or humanities analyses are uncommon (Godulla et al., 2021). Anyone, from an academic to an industrial researcher, etc., might produce deepfakes. Positive applications for it include the arts, business, accessibility, and self-expression. Conversely, deepfakes might be detrimental to people, companies, democracy, and society (JAiman, 2020).

Deepfake studies in the humanities and social sciences is relatively rare and does not connect the event's impacts to core democratic values. To better define and assess the possible damage (and benefits) of present and future deepfake uses, more theoretical underpinning and conceptual clarity are required.

Benefits of Deepfake Technology

A variety of industries, including gaming and entertainment, film, e-commerce and digital communication, materials research, social media and healthcare, and fashion, can benefit from the use of counterfeit technology. The film industry might benefit from deepfake technology in a number of ways. For example, it might be utilized for updating film footage instead of having it revised, or to produce artificial voices for actors who have lost theirs due to sickness. Filmmakers will have the ability to reenact iconic movie moments, develop new films with actors who have passed away, employ advanced face editing and special effects in post-production, and elevate amateur videos to a professional level (Mahmud & Sharmin, 2021). Deepfake technology can facilitate more successful communication during video conferences by interpreting language and altering lip and facial motions at the exact same time to improve facial expressions and create the illusion that everybody is using in the same dialect (Solsman, 2019). In the social and medical domains, technology may be beneficial. When a buddy passes away, deepfakes can "bring them back to life" digitally, helping individuals cope with the loss of a loved one (magazine, 2018). Apart from that, deepfakes offer extremely personalized material where clients take on the role of mannequins. The software enables consumers to simulate trying on clothing before making a purchase and produces customized fashion ads that vary based on the viewer, the weather, and the time of day. The ability to quickly try on clothing online is undoubtedly one of its many potential uses. People can use the technology to virtually experience a wedding venue and try on a bridal gown or suit in addition to creating digital clones of themselves and bringing them around stores. Additionally, AI may create distinctive artificial voices to set brands apart for different products and enterprises (*What Are Digital Doubles? Everything You Need to Know*, n.d.). AI technology has the potential to make learning more engaging. The American educational company Udacity has been using deepfake technology in its virtual learning programmes (Chow, 2022).

Possible Threats of Deepfakes

Deepfakes used maliciously pose a direct danger to public awareness. These days, one may make or edit deepfakes or deep noises in individual audio files, as well as photographs or videos into which anyone's publicly shared photos or videos can be put. The prevalence of deepfakes in India demonstrates just how bad the issue is among the BRICS nations. China released new regulations in 2019 regarding online video and audio material. One of the regulations prohibited the dissemination and publication of "fake news" produced with artificial intelligence and virtual reality. Any usage of these technologies must to be made explicit and readily apparent to

Internet users (Reuters, 2019). False, erroneous, or misleading information created, displayed, and pushed with deepfake technology with the goal of harming the public or making money (Godulla et al., 2021). Since deepfakes render it more difficult for reporters to discern among real and phony news, endanger national security by affecting voting and propagating disinformation, undermine consumer trust in government databases, and create problems for individuals and companies with the field of cybersecurity, that they pose an imminent danger to our democracy, society as a whole as well as business. Because deepfakes are harder to spot and more likely to be believed at face value, they pose a greater threat to public safety than "traditional" fake news (O'Brien, 2018). Gaining an advantage over competitors in the race to get video footage captured by witnesses to incidents can be advantageous for news media outlets; nevertheless, the risk increases if the film being supplied is counterfeit. When Pakistan and India's tensions spiked in 2019, Reuters found thirty fake movies on the incident; most of the videos were old footage of earlier incidents with new subtitles (Southers, 2019). Even though these made-up films would likely spark rioting, internal unrest, and disruptions during elections, some nation states might choose to implement their foreign policy based on fiction, which would cause global catastrophes (Cover, 2022). Media forensic researchers have suggested nuanced markers to recognize deepfakes. These flaws can take many different forms, such as face sway, sparkle, and deformation; wavering in an individual's motions; incompatible conversation and mouth actions; unusual movements of fixed items, such as a microphone stand; inconsistent lighting, reflections, and shadows; blurred edges; angles and blurring of facial features; lack of breathing; unnatural eye direction; excessively smooth skin; removing parts of human hair and the teeth; dislocation in face symmetry; incompatible pixel levels; and suspicious actions by an individual involved in ridiculous operations (Fletcher, 2018). Deepfakes are a major threat to businesses, society, and the political system because they make it harder for journalists to discern between fake and real news, compromise national security by disseminating propaganda that taints elections, erode public trust in official information, and cause issues for people and organizations that deal with cyber security (Lin, 2019). Non-state actors, including terrorist groups and insurgency groups, might utilise deepfakes to portray their opponents as making provocative statements or acting provocatively in order to incite anti-state feelings in the public. Deepfakes have the potential to affect a political election's result. They might also be used to misreport a candidate, spread false information about them, inflate the value of their contribution, or damage their reputation (JAiman, 2020).

SOME REAL TIME CASES

Impact on Political Scenario

Deepfakes are a serious threat to democracy since they not only propagate false information but also undermine the credibility of accurate information. Public awareness campaigns on deepfakes can actually exacerbate the situation (Ternovski et al., 2021). Clean destination is much necessary for deepfakes that's why most of the deepfakes are there of the politicians because they use the consistent lighting standing on a dice or any platform. And for mouth an dhead movements a face dataset is required which goes well with the AI and rest of the job is handled by the AI (Lorenzo, 2022).

There has been controversy about the usage of deepfakes in an Indian political campaign. The Bharatiya Janata Party (Indian People's Party) used this technology to produce two movies showcasing party leader Manoj Tiwari addressing to voters in two languages ahead of the Delhi legislative assembly elections in February 2020. The candidate wanted to reach out to voters who spoke English and Hariyanvi, two separate linguistic groupings. The movies were distributed to over 5,800 Whatsapp groups, according to party leaders. In the videos, Tiwari commended his supporters for approving a revision to the Citizenship Act by the Delhi legislative assembly. He spoke in Hindi in the first video. After that, his lip motions and facial expressions were mimicked (MIHINDUKULASURIYA, n.d.). A few Indian journalists are working to halt the propagation of fake news and deepfakes. They believe that the majority of this stuff will, however, elude all fact-checking techniques. According to several analysts, companies that use deepfake technology for Indian political campaigns, ought to be prohibited.

A government strategy on misinformation in general and deepfakes in particular is advocated by some, although this does not shield the nation from risks presented by criminal organisations (Christopher, 2020). Deepfakes are not a totally novel threat. As ancient as media itself is the practice of manipulating it for both good and bad purposes. For instance, convincing picture alteration has a lengthy history in both non-consensual pornography and the arts (Burkell & Gosse, 2019). Regarding misinformation, As (Tenove, 2020) argues that policies might be created and justified that are drastically different based on different readings of the threats to democracy. These policies affect a number of parties and have the capacity to compromise core democratic values. Determining the democratic principles that deepfakes threaten is therefore crucial to developing effective policy responses and defending democracy. Deepfakes are produced by both local and international leaders to spread misinformation. They are frequently used in conjunction with elections, but they are also increasingly being used to target dissidents and critical journalists, for example.

Such deepfakes undermine public trust in democracies. They obstruct inclusion by keeping individuals out of crucial political conversations or elections, shunning specific social groupings, or limiting their ability to cast ballots. Additionally, they pose a threat to empowered inclusion when they distort thinking to the point that it becomes impossible for voters to hold elected officials responsible and make informed decisions, particularly during elections (Pawelec, 2022).

Impact on Entertainment Industry

> *"AI doesn't have a morality of its own, it assumes a morality from the data available. It cannot create mystery, feel fear or love."*
>
> Siddharth Roy Kapur, former president of the Producers Guild of India.

Deepfakes are computer-generated images that are combined with other photos to create new footage that appears to depict statements, actions, or events that never actually occurred. The results can be very interesting (Masood et al., 2023). When it comes to being difficult to identify as fake, deepfakes are different from other forms of misinformation (Masood et al., 2023). Both insiders and outsiders now have a lot of opportunities thanks to this generative AI technology. Several domains under the media and entertainment sector encompass the AI tools. In entertainment basically the deepfakes are using two ways one is face swapping and other one is face manipulation (Lorenzo, 2022). A lot of production houses used CGI in early phases to adjust the faces of the actors as per the requirement which results into a better image or scenes (Lorenzo, 2022). The very first collection of the said deepfake videos was share in 2017-18, in which most of the pornographic content was shared online. In many of the videos the actual image of the actresses were replaced by the renowned celebrities and attacked on their reputation directly. And the number of these kinds of deepfake videos is getting doubled in every six months (Sensity, 2020). In entertainment and media industry AI can be used in scriptwriting (analyzing tone of the story, keywords, conducting sentiment analysis, writing dialogues etc.), casting (identifying the popularity of the cast on social media), cinematography (identifying interesting shots, camera angle, lighting etc.), post production, promotion and marketing obviously (Sabharwal et.al, 2024). The well-known actor Tom Cruise videos got viral on tiktok in 2021 doing some coin flips, blundering around, and covering the Dave Matthews Band songs shows that how these deepfakes can appear to be real. Same is applicable in the case of Indian celebrities Rashmika Mandana and Katrina kaif. The face of a British-Indian Influencer (Zara Patel) was altered and replaced with Rashmika Mandana and posted online in November 2023 by an instagram account of an Engineer who just wanted to have more number of followers on his account. After this incident a deepfake image of Kaitrina Kaif went viral on social media from her latest movie resulting into misleading content.

Adding to this in May 2024 a deepfake video of Indian Celebrity Alia bhatt went viral and criticized by plenty of social media users. In this video Alia's face was altered and replaced on Wamiqa Dabbi, an Indian actress and posted online. A lot of social media users agreed that the deepfakes are really scary and everyone needs to be careful before posting anything online. Not only Bollywood actresses but actors also faced the same situations. Recently Ranveer Singh, an Indian actor, became a victim of the deepfake video in which he was seen as promoting a political party, though he complained with the cybercrime cell. Just because of the use of AI in media and film industry writers and actors of Hollywood industry from US were on a strike for about five months. They were fighting for their pay raise, improved working condition, pension and health benefits.

Possible Solutions

Governmental organizations, commercial enterprises, educational institutions, and media professionals need to educate the public about the dangers artificial intelligence poses to media credibility and prohibit the dishonest use of these technologies for political, commercial, or anti-social purposes (Britt et al., 2019). Corporate policies and voluntary measures like deepfake addressing content moderation policies and swift removal of user-flagged content on social networking platforms, which create tangible and intellectual safeguards toward electronic usage and abuse, are likely to be more successful than training and education initiatives targeted at improving digital media literacy, better online behavior, and critical thinking. Each and every single industry is affected by the pros and cons of technology updation on every single minute.

Overall, the use of deepfakes in social engineering attacks presents a significant challenge in cybersecurity, as these technologies can be used to deceive individuals and spread false information available on social media platforms. A thorough grasp of the technologies involved and their possible effects is necessary to address the impact of deepfakes in social engineering attacks. It's critical to maintain vigilance and put protective measures in place to counter the use of deepfakes in these nefarious actions as social engineering assaults continue to evolve. These days, it's more difficult to distinguish between real and fake videos. The use of artificial intelligence to simulate an action or voice in a picture or video is what gave rise to deepfake technology. The public could download and utilise certain AI software without much technical expertise. Deepfake may quickly spread to millions of people and harm the organisation or individuals involved, thanks to social media platforms and people's regular engagement in spreading news or information.

REFERENCES

Agarwal, S., Farid, H., El-Gaaly, T., & Lim, S.-N. (2020). Detecting Deep-Fake Videos from Appearance and Behavior. *2020 IEEE International Workshop on Information Forensics and Security (WIFS)*, 1–6. DOI: 10.1109/WIFS49906.2020.9360904

Ajder, H., Patrini, G., Cavalli, F., & Cullen, L. (2019). *The State of Deepfakes: Landscape*. Threats, and Impact.

Aldwairi, M., & Alwahedi, A. (2018). Detecting Fake News in Social Media Networks. *Procedia Computer Science*, 141, 215–222. DOI: 10.1016/j.procs.2018.10.171

Algarni, A., Xu, Y., Chan, T., & Tian, Y.-C. (2013). Social engineering in social networking sites: Affect-based model. *8th International Conference for Internet Technology and Secured Transactions (ICITST-2013)*, 508–515. DOI: 10.1109/ICITST.2013.6750253

Anwar, S., Milanova, M., Anwer, M., & Banihirwe, A. (2019). Perceptual Judgments to Detect Computer Generated Forged Faces in Social Media. In Schwenker, F., & Scherer, S. (Eds.), *Multimodal Pattern Recognition of Social Signals in Human-Computer-Interaction* (Vol. 11377, pp. 38–48). Springer International Publishing., DOI: 10.1007/978-3-030-20984-1_4

Britt, M. A., Rouet, J.-F., Blaum, D., & Millis, K. (2019). A Reasoned Approach to Dealing With Fake News. *Policy Insights from the Behavioral and Brain Sciences*, 6(1), 94–101. DOI: 10.1177/2372732218814855

Bullée, J.-W., & Junger, M. (2020). Social Engineering. In Holt, T. J., & Bossler, A. M. (Eds.), *The Palgrave Handbook of International Cybercrime and Cyberdeviance* (pp. 849–875). Springer International Publishing., DOI: 10.1007/978-3-319-78440-3_38

Burkell, J., & Gosse, C. (2019). Nothing new here: Emphasizing the social and cultural context of deepfakes. *First Monday*. Advance online publication. DOI: 10.5210/fm.v24i12.10287

Business, C. N. N. (2019). *The fight to stay ahead of deepfake videos before the 2020 US election*. https://edition.cnn.com/2019/06/12/tech/deepfake-2020-detection/index.html

Chow, M. (2022, June). *What Are The Positive Applications of Deepfakes?*https://www.jumpstartmag.com/what-are-the-positive-applications-of-deepfakes/

Christopher, N. (2020, February). We've Just Seen the First Use of Deepfakes in an Indian Election Campaign. *We've Just Seen the First Use of Deepfakes in an Indian Election Campaign*. https://www.vice.com/en/article/jgedjb/the-first-use-of-deepfakes-in-indian-election-by-bjp

Cover, R. (2022). Deepfake culture: The emergence of audio-video deception as an object of social anxiety and regulation. *Continuum (Perth)*, 36(4), 609–621. DOI: 10.1080/10304312.2022.2084039

Fletcher, J. (2018). Deepfakes, Artificial Intelligence, and Some Kind of Dystopia: The New Faces of Online Post-Fact Performance. *Theatre Journal*, 70(4), 455–471. DOI: 10.1353/tj.2018.0097

Fuertes, W., Arévalo, D., Castro, J. D., Ron, M., Estrada, C. A., Andrade, R., Peña, F. F., & Benavides, E. (2022). Impact of Social Engineering Attacks: A Literature Review. In Rocha, Á., Fajardo-Toro, C. H., & Rodríguez, J. M. R. (Eds.), *Developments and Advances in Defense and Security* (Vol. 255, pp. 25–35). Springer Singapore., DOI: 10.1007/978-981-16-4884-7_3

Godulla, A., Hoffmann, C. P., & Seibert, D. (2021). Dealing with deepfakes – an interdisciplinary examination of the state of research and implications for communication studies. *Studies in Communication and Media*, 10(1), 72–96. DOI: 10.5771/2192-4007-2021-1-72

Gupta, S., Singhal, A., & Kapoor, A. (2016). A literature survey on social engineering attacks: Phishing attack. *2016 International Conference on Computing, Communication and Automation (ICCCA)*, 537–540. DOI: 10.1109/CCAA.2016.7813778

Hatfield, J. M. (2018). Social engineering in cybersecurity: The evolution of a concept. *Computers & Security*, 73, 102–113. DOI: 10.1016/j.cose.2017.10.008

Hijji, M., & Alam, G. (2021). A Multivocal Literature Review on Growing Social Engineering Based Cyber-Attacks/Threats During the COVID-19 Pandemic: Challenges and Prospective Solutions. *IEEE Access : Practical Innovations, Open Solutions*, 9, 7152–7169. DOI: 10.1109/ACCESS.2020.3048839 PMID: 34786300

JAiman. A. (2020, May). *Debating the ethics of deepfakes*. https://www.orfonline.org/expert-speak/debating-the-ethics-of-deepfakes

Kumar, N., Dabas, P., & Komal. (2019). Detection and Prevention of Profile Cloning in Online Social Networks. *2019 5th International Conference on Signal Processing, Computing and Control (ISPCC)*, 287–291. DOI: 10.1109/ISPCC48220.2019.8988394

Kwok, A. O. J., & Koh, S. G. M. (2021). Deepfake: A social construction of technology perspective. *Current Issues in Tourism*, 24(13), 1798–1802. DOI: 10.1080/13683500.2020.1738357

Lin, H. (2019). The existential threat from cyber-enabled information warfare. *Bulletin of the Atomic Scientists*, 75(4), 187–196. DOI: 10.1080/00963402.2019.1629574

Lorenzo, D. A. M. I. "Analysis and conceptualization of deepfake technology as cyber threat." (2022). magazine, P. (2018, July). *When AI Blurs—The Line Between Reality And Fiction*. https://www.magzter.com/stories/Science/PC-Magazine/When-AIBlurs-The-Line-Between-Reality-And-Fiction

Mahmud, B. U., & Sharmin, A. (2021). *Deep Insights of Deepfake Technology: A Review*. DOI: 10.48550/ARXIV.2105.00192

Masood, M., Nawaz, M., Malik, K. M., Javed, A., Irtaza, A., & Malik, H. (2023). Deepfakes generation and detection: State-of-the-art, open challenges, countermeasures, and way forward. *Applied Intelligence*, 53(4), 3974–4026. DOI: 10.1007/s10489-022-03766-z

MIHINDUKULASURIYA. R. (n.d.). *Why the Manoj Tiwari deepfakes should have India deeply worried*. Retrieved June 21, 2024, from https://theprint.in/tech/why-the-manoj-tiwari-deepfakes-should-have-india-deeply-worried/372389/

Mouton, F., Leenen, L., & Venter, H. S. (2016). Social engineering attack examples, templates and scenarios. *Computers & Security*, 59, 186–209. DOI: 10.1016/j.cose.2016.03.004

Mouton, F., Malan, M. M., Leenen, L., & Venter, H. S. (2014). Social engineering attack framework. *2014 Information Security for South Africa*, 1–9. DOI: 10.1109/ISSA.2014.6950510

O'Brien, S. A. (2018, August). Deepfakes are coming. Is Big Tech ready? *Deepfakes Are Coming. Is Big Tech Ready?*https://money.cnn.com/2018/08/08/technology/deepfakes-countermeasures-facebook-twitter-youtube/index.html

Paterson, T., & Hanley, L. (2020). Political warfare in the digital age: Cyber subversion, information operations and 'deep fakes.'. *Australian Journal of International Affairs*, 74(4), 439–454. DOI: 10.1080/10357718.2020.1734772

Pawelec, M. (2022). Deepfakes and Democracy (Theory): How Synthetic Audio-Visual Media for Disinformation and Hate Speech Threaten Core Democratic Functions. *Digital Society : Ethics, Socio-Legal and Governance of Digital Technology*, 1(2), 19. DOI: 10.1007/s44206-022-00010-6 PMID: 36097613

Reuters. (2019, November 29). *China seeks to root out fake news and deepfakes with new online content rules*. https://www.reuters.com/article/idUSKBN1Y30VT/

Sabharwal, D., Sood, R. S., & Sood, S. (2024). *Media and AI: Navigating the Future of Communication*. Post Script.

Salahdine, F., & Kaabouch, N. (2019). Social Engineering Attacks: A Survey. *Future Internet*, 11(4), 89. DOI: 10.3390/fi11040089

Scarfone, K. A., Souppaya, M. P., Cody, A., & Orebaugh, A. D. (2008). Technical guide to information security testing and assessment. (NIST SP 800-115; 0 ed., p. NIST SP 800-115). National Institute of Standards and Technology. DOI: 10.6028/NIST.SP.800-115

Solsman, J. E. (2019, July 12). Deepfakes freak YouTubers out. Vidcon offers a way to prepare. *Deepfakes Freak YouTubers out. Vidcon Offers a Way to Prepare*. https://www.cnet.com/tech/computing/deepfakes-freak-youtubers-out-vidcon-offers-a-way-to-prepare/

Southers, L. (2019, March). How Reuters is training reporters to spot 'deepfakes.' *How Reuters Is Training Reporters to Spot 'Deepfakes.'* https://shorturl.at/epjML

Syafitri, W., Shukur, Z., Mokhtar, U. A., Sulaiman, R., & Ibrahim, M. A. (2022). Social Engineering Attacks Prevention: A Systematic Literature Review. *IEEE Access : Practical Innovations, Open Solutions*, 10, 39325–39343. DOI: 10.1109/ACCESS.2022.3162594

Syed, R. (2019). Enterprise reputation threats on social media: A case of data breach framing. *The Journal of Strategic Information Systems*, 28(3), 257–274. DOI: 10.1016/j.jsis.2018.12.001

Tenove, C. (2020). Protecting Democracy from Disinformation: Normative Threats and Policy Responses. *The International Journal of Press/Politics*, 25(3), 517–537. DOI: 10.1177/1940161220918740

Ternovski, J., Kalla, J., & Aronow, P. M. (2021). *Deepfake Warnings for Political Videos Increase Disbelief but Do Not Improve Discernment: Evidence from Two Experiments*. DOI: 10.31219/osf.io/dta97

Wang, Z., Sun, L., & Zhu, H. (2020). Defining Social Engineering in Cybersecurity. *IEEE Access : Practical Innovations, Open Solutions*, 8, 85094–85115. DOI: 10.1109/ACCESS.2020.2992807

What are digital doubles? Everything you need to know. (n.d.). Retrieved June 19, 2024, from https://di4d.com/what-are-digital-doubles-everything-you-need-to-know/

Chapter 14

The Rising Threat of Deepfake Technology and Frightening Advancements of Social Engineering

Gausiya Yasmeen
https://orcid.org/0000-0002-7853-1376
Integral University, India

Syed Adnan Afaq
Integral University, India

Tasneem Ahmed
https://orcid.org/0000-0003-2702-3168
Integral University, India

ABSTRACT

Advancements in digital technologies have made it difficult to distinguish between real and fake media, leading to privacy and security threats. Deepfake, a combination of deep learning and fake, is a technique used to replace or mask someone else's face in images or videos. Social engineering (SE) attacks exploit human attributes and psychology to bypass technical security measures for malicious acts. Deepfake videos, created using artificial intelligence (AI), pose a significant threat to society, politics, and businesses. Deepfakes pose a significant threat, they can be combated through legislation, regulation, corporate policies, voluntary action, education, training, and the development of technology for deepfake detection, content authentication, and

DOI: 10.4018/979-8-3693-6665-3.ch014

prevention. Common deepfakes include pornographic videos, political deepfakes, financial crimes, and synthetic audio. The paper explores deepfake technology, its benefits, challenges, and detection techniques.

INTRODUCTION

Fake news poses a significant threat to public discourse, human society, and democracy. It spreads quickly through social media, impacting millions of users. YouTube is the second-most popular source of news, highlighting the need for tools to confirm media authenticity. The ease of obtaining and spreading misinformation makes it difficult to trust, leading to harmful consequences for informed decision-making. Today, we live in a "post-truth" era characterized by digital disinformation and information warfare. Technological advancements have enabled the creation of "deepfakes," hyper-realistic videos using artificial intelligence (AI) applications (Rafique et al., 2023). These videos, which can be humorous, pornographic, or political, can be created without the person's consent. The technology's scope, scale, and sophistication make it possible for anyone with a computer to create indistinguishable fakes. In the future, deepfakes may be used for revenge porn, bullying, political sabotage, terrorist propaganda, blackmail, market manipulation, and fake news. This study explores the concept of deepfakes, their origins, their benefits and threats, current examples, and strategies to combat them. It analyzes news articles on news media websites, contributing to the literature on fake news and deepfakes. The research also identifies options for politicians, journalists, and entrepreneurs to combat deepfakes, highlighting the need for further research and understanding.

Deepfake, a blend of deep learning with fake content, involves swapping a person's face to a targeted person in a video or image, resulting in the person acting like the targeted person. This technique has become a public issue, affecting individuals and spreading fake news, fraud, and hoaxes. Researchers are now focused on understanding the insights of Deepfake, which can be used for pornography, political, or bullying without consent (Naitali et al., 2023). Deepfake algorithms use generative adversarial networks to copy movements and facial expressions of individuals, posing threats to political figures, public figures, and celebrities. This technology can also be used to mislead military personnel and cause serious damage. Despite its potential, deep understanding of Deepfakes is crucial for recovery and preventing false news spread. Despite its newness, there is limited resources on this topic. This paper discusses Deepfake technology, its uses, threats, challenges, generation and detection, positive and negative aspects, limitations, suggestions, and future thoughts. Deepfakes are fake motion pictures and images that are produced by using sophisticated artificial intelligence tools to manipulate the original content.

These instruments can be used to sway elections, manipulate politics, and undermine public confidence in democratic institutions. They can also be used to produce explicit content without consent, harm someone's reputation, or pull off convincing impersonations for commercial or private advantage. A major challenge to digital forensics is the emergence of deepfakes, which has led to a crisis of confidence in the veracity of digital evidence used in court cases and criminal prosecutions. Given the high stakes in continuing media wars, global conflicts, and the delicate political environment on the international scene, these risks are especially serious. The research community must stay updated on deepfake generation and detection technologies to avoid falling behind in this critical arms race.

Deepfake, a hybrid term for fake and deep learning, is a method for replacing or hiding someone else's face in pictures or videos. It draws attention to its high level of intelligence, quick optimization, and deceptiveness. It is challenging for people to recognize the manipulation. Cybercriminals are adapting their attacks to be more evasive as cybersecurity efforts get more sophisticated. These attacks are challenging to counter because they are very effective, efficient, and obfuscated. The most common platforms for SE assaults throughout the past two years have been social media and smishing attacks (Bu et al., 2023). SE is not a complicated hacking technique, but rather a process designed to take advantage of human psychology. With our growing dependency on technology, SE is becoming into a vital weapon for attackers. On the other hand, as cyberattacks grow in frequency, so do the technological countermeasures. Deepfake films are a major threat to corporations, politicians, and society at large since they are a kind of media manipulation. Artificial intelligence (AI) was used to make these incredibly lifelike movies, which have the potential to negatively harm society and swiftly reach millions of individuals (Mahmud & Sharmin, 2020). This study examines deepfakes, their causes, advantages and disadvantages, examples, and countermeasures by analyzing 84 publicly accessible internet news items. The findings imply that although deepfakes are a serious issue, they may be avoided by creating technologies for deepfake recognition, information confirmation, and prevention and by enacting laws, regulations, business policies, voluntary action, education, and training.

Deepfake Technology

Figure 1. An overview of Deepfake Technology

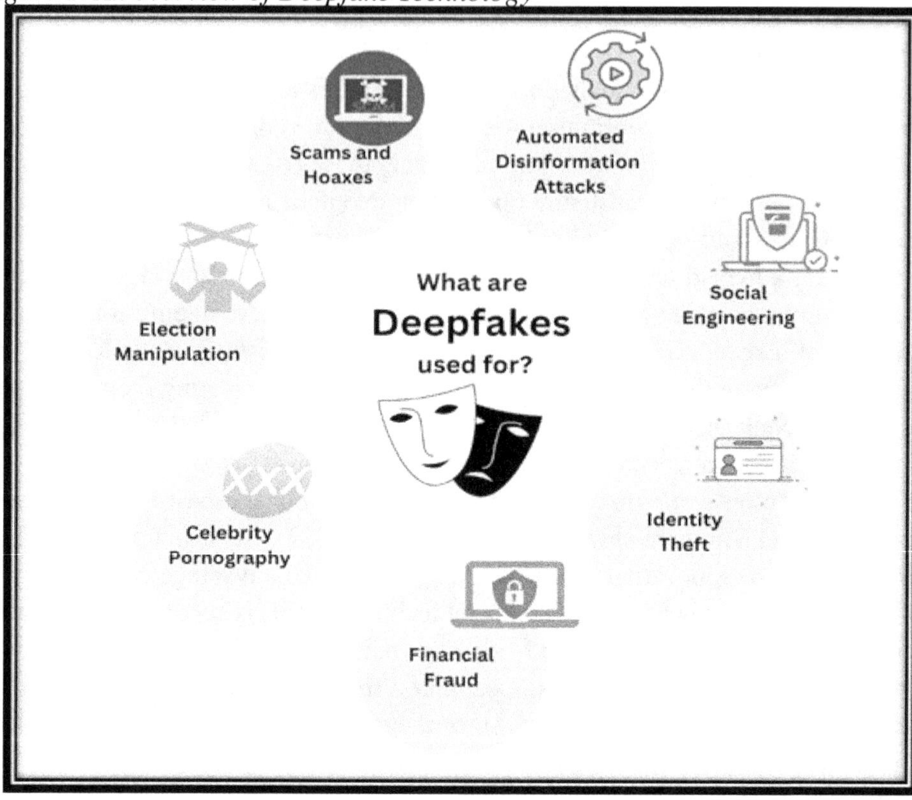

Due to the availability of low-cost gadgets like computers, cameras, and cellphones, social media content has increased dramatically over the last 10 years. Easy access and quick content exchange have resulted from this. However, the ability to manipulate audiovisual content to disseminate false information and harm reputations online has been made easier by developments in machine learning and Deep Learning algorithms. The art of creating deep fakes has advanced dramatically, with the capacity to disseminate misinformation globally. Artificial intelligence (AI) algorithms are utilized to create deep fakes, which are artificially produced audio and video footage that is used as evidence in criminal and civil court cases. It is imperative to validate the authenticity and integrity of supplied videos, particularly with the increasing complexity of deep fake generation. Deepfake films fall into three categories: face-swap, synthesis, and feature manipulation. By replacing a person's face with the source's, a fictitious film is created with the intention of targeting them for undecided behavior. By manipulating the target's lips to change their movements in accordance with an audio track, lip-synching reveals the attacker's voice speaking to the victim. False information is spread on social media by puppet masters that mimic the target's head, eye, and facial movements (Naitali et al., 2023). Lastly, deep audio fakes, often known as voice cloning, alter a person's voice to make them seem like a speaker they haven't actually spoken. Deepfake can be used for scams and hoaxes, automated disinformation attacks, scoical engineering, election manipulation, celebrity pornography, financial fraud, identity theft as shown in Figure 1.

This means that finding the truth in the digital world is more important than ever. Since deep fakes are typically used for malicious purposes and are now essentially easy to create using readily available technologies, dealing with them is much more challenging. To date, numerous approaches have been proposed for the detection of deepfakes. Since deep learning is also the foundation for the majority, a conflict has emerged between subpar and superior deep learning applications4. Therefore, in order to address this issue, the Defense Advanced Research Projects Agency (DARPA) of the United States initiated a media forensics research plan with the goal of creating techniques for detecting fraudulent digital media (Rafique et al., 2023). Additionally, Facebook announced an AI-based deep fake detection challenge in partnership with Microsoft to stop the use of deep fakes to trick viewers. Researchers have been exploring Machine Learning and Deep Learning (DL) to detect deep fakes from audiovisual media. ML-based algorithms use manual feature extraction, which can be unstable when dealing with larger databases. DL algorithms, such as Convolutional Neural Networks (CNN), have proven helpful in various applications, including deep fake detection. However, there is still potential for improvement in efficiency and efficacy (Bu et al., 2023). As deep fake generation techniques continue to improve, new datasets may not perform effectively. The motivation behind developing automated DL-based deep fake detection systems is to mitigate the potential harm caused by deep fake technology, which can lead to political unrest, financial fraud, and reputational damage. These systems can improve the trust and reliability of media and online content, making them essential in the age of social media. This paper compares the performance of CNN architectures like AlexNet and VGG16 to detect if an image is real or digitally altered.

Figure 2. Rise in the cybercrimes related to Deepfake

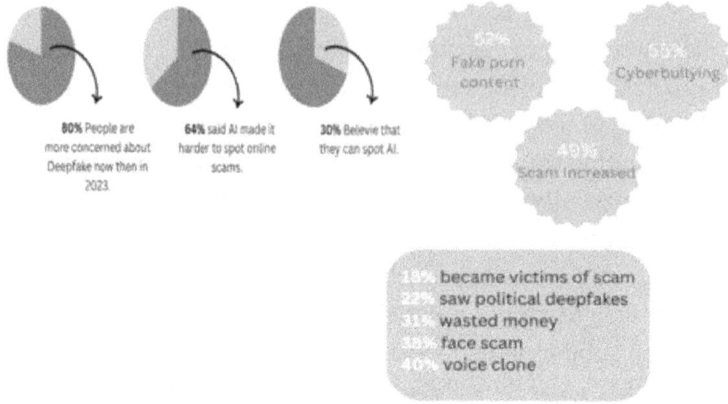

Since deepfakes were accessible at least in 2017, there has been a noticeable improvement in both their technical quality and accessibility. Popular generative AI platforms, such as OpenAI's DALL-E 2 and Midjourney 5.1, became available to threat actors in 2023 so they could launch deepfake campaigns. The illegal strategies employed to take advantage of this technology are evolving along with it. It's being exploited by threat actors to produce synthetic media that can be used destructively, bringing a terrifying new reality to the cyber threat scenario of 2023 (Bu et al., 2023). Videos including pornography frequently target women in a variety of occupations, whereas political deepfakes use prominent figures to influence elections and perhaps spark international unrest. Financial crimes include posing as corporate executives in order to manipulate stock prices, as demonstrated by the CEO of a UK energy company who stole $243,000 in 2019. Cybercriminals can even utilize fake audio to carry out these crimes, as demonstrated by the CEO of an unidentified UK energy business who was stolen in 2019. To deceive cryptocurrency investors, a deepfake of Elon Musk, the CEO of Tesla and owner of Twitter, was produced from earlier interviews in May 2023. The fake quickly gained popularity on social media which can be observed through Figure 2 where 52% fake porn content, 55% cyberbullying and 49% online scam cases have taken place in recent years. Also 18% people became victims of online scam,22% reported as political deepfakes,31% cases wasted money through online fraud, 38% became face scam victims and 40% cases was of voice clone as per the reports. As it can be concluded from Figure 3 where a rise in deepfake cases can be seen from the year 2019 to the year 2023.

Figure 3. Upswing in the video content of Deepfake during the years 2019-2023

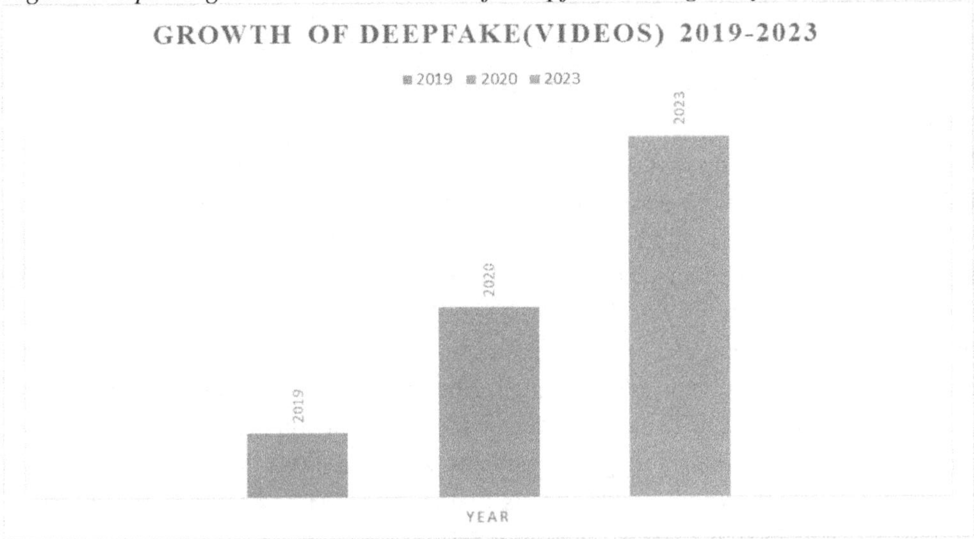

Literature Review- Recent years have seen a rapid increase in the literature on deepfake detection, with numerous surveys published. These reviews provide a comprehensive overview of deepfake types, their creation and detection methods, open-source datasets, and future trends in deepfake technology. The authors also discuss the background and methods of deepfakes, the development of improved and resilient deep learning techniques, and the challenges faced in creating and detecting deepfakes. They also provide a detailed review of deepfake manipulation types, their generation processes, detection methods, and the architecture used in deepfake creation. The authors also discuss the limitations and future trends in the field of deepfakes, as well as the limitations and trends in the field. They also analyze CNN- and RNN-based deepfake video detection models (Mahmud & Sharmin, 2020). Other surveys provide a summary of the principal elements in the field of deepfakes, such as their definition, impact, creation process, and detection methods. Since 1860, deep fakes have been used as a kind of digital media manipulation (Naitali et al., 2023). Splicing, painting, and copy-moving objects are some of the operations used to improve perspective coherence, size, and aesthetic appeal. Technological developments in computer graphics and machine learning/deep learning methodologies have rendered these modifications more resilient and reasonably priced. Researchers have created automated algorithms to identify deep fakes from audiovisual content as manipulation in digital media grows. The capacity of deep learning to represent complicated, high-dimensional data is well established. A number of studies have employed deep learning techniques to identify deep fakes. These include the use of

Multilayered Perceptron (MLP) by Matern et al. to detect facial images with open eyes, the Open Face 2 toolkit by Agarwal et al. to extract features, the classification of medical signal features by Ciftci et al., DLib by Yang et al. to extract 68-D facial landmarks, Rossle et al.'s SVM+CNN system, and McCloskey et al.'s deep fake detector. These systems do not work well with compressed videos, and they have trouble processing raw or grainy images. A study proposes a hybrid multitask learning framework with a Fire Hawk Optimizer for Arabic Fake News Detection to accurately and efficiently identify fake news in Arabic. The framework combines sentence classification, stance detection, and relevance prediction tasks to determine the authenticity of news articles. The Fire Hawk Optimizer algorithm, inspired by hawk hunting behavior, is used to fine-tune the parameters of the framework, improving its accuracy and performance. The authors also propose a Convolution Vision Transformer (CVT) architecture, which relies on attention mechanisms and convolution operations to recognize patterns within images. However, the system is computationally expensive due to its deep architecture. Previous studies have identified deep fake images using Expectation Maximization, SVM, KNN, and LDA, but have struggled with recognizing compressed images. Various models have been developed, including CNN-based architectures, Local Binary Patterns, CNN, and Capsule Networks, with some achieving a true positive rate of 81.3%. The current deep fake detection and classification methods are limited due to their high computational cost and reliance on preprocessing. Residual Networks, such as ResNet and ResNeXt, have shown potential in low-quality videos. However, these methods require preprocessing and require high-end GPUs or specialized hardware. Additionally, some DL algorithms are prone to overfitting, which can result in poor performance on new data. Despite these limitations, there is still a need for a robust and efficient method using ML and DL-based approaches for deep fake detection and classification.

Application areas of Deepfake

Deepfake technology offers a wide range of uses that could be advantageous or disadvantageous, although they are typically employed with malevolent intent. The use of Deepfake technology for unethical purposes has negative long- and short-term effects on our civilization. Regular social media users run a very high chance of falling victim to Deepfake. But when applied correctly, this technology has a lot of promising applications. Below is a detailed description of both the negative and beneficial uses of Deepfake technology.

Harmful Applications- The use of deepfake and related technologies for malevolent purposes against people, particularly politicians and celebrities, is growing quickly in the Figure 4 given below McAfee survey has posted that approx. 75%

Indians have become its victims in the past 12 months.. These materials can be utilized for identity theft, retaliation, and blackmail. Deepfake has thousands of movies, most of which are explicit videos of women taken without consent. Making pornography of well-known females, particularly those in Hollywood, is the most popular use. A piece of software that was created in 2018 that could instantly make a lady nude led to widespread harassment. By producing phony films, Deepfake also takes advantage of politicians and world leaders, which might be dangerous for international harmony. Additionally, social media, the film business, and the arts all use it.

Useful applications- Deepfake technology has become more accessible and useful in various sectors, including art, advertising, business, and education. It has been used to create new art works, engage audiences, and provide unique experiences. For example, the Dal´ı Museum in St. Petersburg, Florida, used artificial intelligence to create interactive videos of Salvador Dal´ı's life. Deepfake technology can save money and time in the film industry by editing videos instead of re-shooting. It has also been used in the education sector to provide realistic experiences in retail. Reuters collaborated with AI startup Synthesis to create the first synthesized news presenter using artificial intelligence techniques, which could be helpful for personalized news. Deep generative models have shown potential in the healthcare industry to protect patient data and generate imaginary data instead of sharing real data. Additionally, Deepfake technology has potential in fundraising and awareness building by creating videos of famous personalities asking for help or funding for new work.

Figure 4. Harmful effects of Deepfake

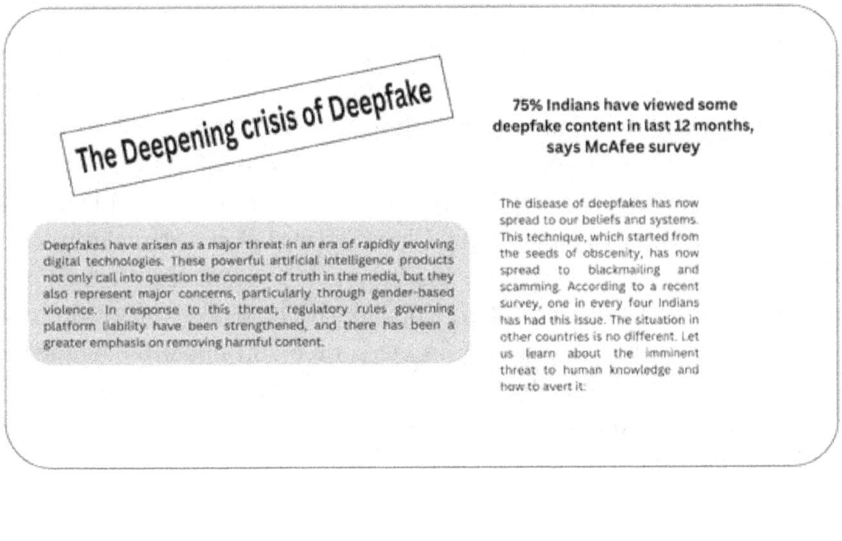

Deepfake Generation

Deepfake text, audio synthesis, and video face-changing are examples of current approaches. The application sectors and potential security risks—such as causing property and personal damage, endangering elections, and creating a crisis of social trust—are examined in the research. It suggests actions to stop and address deepfake misuse, such as enhancing network platform management, regulatory restrictions, public information media literacy, and detecting technologies. An image of a real human face can be made to look fake using a technique called deepfake manipulation. Face synthesis, attribute manipulation, identity swapping, face reenactment, and lip-syncing are the five main categories. Face synthesis is the process of producing artificial human faces, whereas attribute manipulation modifies the appearance of a particular facial region. Because deepfake movies generate higher levels of engagement than image-based content, they are more common. The most popular forms of manipulation are lip-syncing, facial reenactment, and identity swapping. Face swapping is the process of changing out one person's face for another, resulting in a smooth transition of the target's appearance into the original footage. While lip-syncing attempts to create a genuine target face that synchronizes with text or audio inputs, face recreation modifies facial emotions in a video. Advanced procedures and careful post-processing are needed to ensure that the lip movements and facial emotions match the original audio exactly.

Deep learning algorithms are used in deepfake techniques to create phony texts, photos, voices, and videos. The ease of use and low cost of GANs make them popular for creating faked photos and films. Deep autoencoders, which have four or five layers for the encoding half and the remaining layers for the decoding half, are popular models in deep networks. When FakeApp was developed, it was the first successful use of the Deepfake technology to replace a person's face with another. Fake videos can be produced utilizing a variety of techniques, including photometric stereo techniques, enhanced blend shape models, and tailored join structure methods. Chen Cao and colleagues presented a method for realistic face detection and animation that makes use of displaced dynamic expression (DDE) techniques. A real-time high fidelity facial capture system that can recover individual ankle details from a single camera was proposed by Chen Cao et al. A novel model-based tracking method based on a parametric face model, tracking from real-time RGB-D input, was presented by Justus Thies et al. This approach achieves great transfer quality even with different lighting quality in the source and target by synthesizing new mouth interiors utilizing teeth proxy and mouth interior texturing. This technique can mold the actor's expression details more precisely and provides noticeably better photometric alignment.

How deepfake generation is done is shown in the Figure 5 below where original face of X is changed to that of Y in first process by using AI tools. In the Figure 5 a smile face was first taken which further using encoding and decoding method is witched with frown face. Similarly, in the adjacent image a frown face is swapped with smile face. Face 2 Face is a real-time face replication technique that manipulates YouTube videos in real-time by using RGB data for source and target actors. Using video data from the training sequence, it designs the internal side of the target's lip based on temporal and photometric similarities, which sets it apart from previous methods. The system uses dense photo-metric energy minimization to reconstruct and track source and target actors. It re-renders the altered face on top of the target sequence to replace the original facial expressions, and using a unique subspace deformation transfer technique to move the appearance from the origin to the destination. Justus Thies and colleagues presented a technique that provides complete control over portrait video, predicated on a brief RGB-D video clip featuring the intended recipient. The closest texture from the original video sequence is used to divide the target proxy mesh into three sections: the head, neck, and body. Multi-linear models for the face and rigid proxy models for the upper body are used to track the source actor's expression and movement, and the source actor's eye motion is used to obtain the texture of the target actor's eye from the target actor's calibration sequence.

Figure 5. Process of Deepfake generation

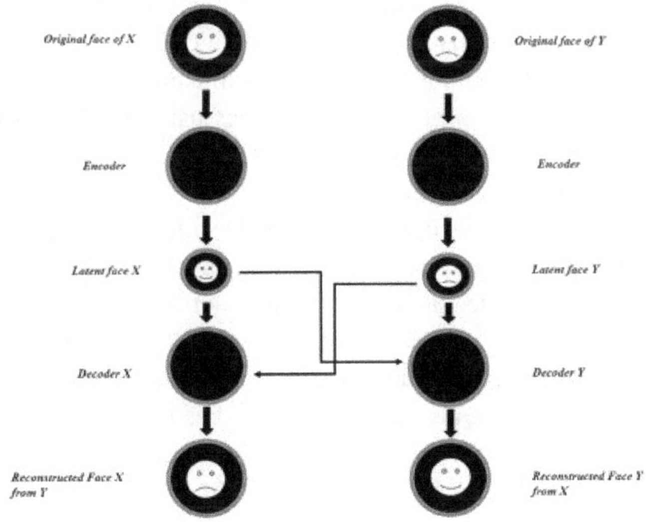

Deepfakes are a type of fake image generated by artificial intelligence (AI). GANs, or Generative Adversarial Networks, are a popular technique for creating fake images. These networks consist of a generator and discriminator network, which work together to produce synthetic images. Autoencoders, on the other hand, are used to encode and decode facial features. Several sophisticated GAN-based techniques have emerged, such as AttGAN, StyleGAN, STGAN, StarGANv2, CycleGAN, RSGAN, and LipGAN. These techniques enable precise and high-quality attribute changes, making them useful for face-swapping, age progression, and regression. Open-source tools like FaceApp, Reface, DeepBrain, DeepFaceLab, and Deepfakes Web also allow users to create fakes. However, it is crucial to use these tools responsibly and ethically to avoid spreading misinformation or engaging in harmful activities. As AI continues to develop, deepfake generation algorithms are becoming more sophisticated, convincing, and hard to detect.

Deepfake Detection

Detecting Deepfake content is challenging and requires expertise. Various approaches, including machine detection, forensics, authentication, and regulation, have been proposed to combat this issue. Deepfake videos are created by algorithms, while real videos are created by cameras. Anomalies like lighting inconsistencies, image warping, smoothness, and unusual pixel formations can help detect Deepfake. Techniques like PCA, LDA, IMM, and SVM have been used to detect Deepfakes. However, face swap identification techniques, such as VGG and Facenet, have failed to detect Deepfakes. Recent methods have shown promising results in detecting eye blinks. Forensics models struggle to detect forgeries using CNN and GAN deep learning methods. To address adaptability issues, Huy H. Nguyen et al. proposed a method for generalization and easy manipulation. Ekraam Sabir et al. detected face swapping using Deepfake, face2face, and faceswap. Deepfakes can be detected using various methods, including spatial inconsistencies, convolutional traces, biological signals, temporal inconsistencies, and poor facial emotion alignment. Techniques include intra-frame inspection for visual irregularities and inter-frame examination for temporal characteristics across video streams. High-level semantic features and audio-visual inconsistencies are also used for deepfakes involving swapping faces and audio.

Various detection methods:

Identification using Spatial Artifacts - Using face mapping and correlation, Liang et al. created a previous module on facial geometry to examine both altered and without manipulated regions. They implemented a SoftMax function for categorization and a CNN-LSTM network to predict manipulation localization. Li et al. evaluated the mirrored facial regions' natural features using forensic symmetry. To validate the model at the video level, they employed a heuristic prediction method along with a multi-stream learning framework. DeepfakeMAE is a detection model that utilizes similarities across several facial components, as suggested by Hu and colleagues. They optimized the distinction between real and fake videos by using a masked auto encoder to learn face part consistency. Yang et al. used a multi-scale self-texture attention Generative Network to simulate the creation of fraudulent images in order to investigate forging traces. A Multi-modal Multi-scale Transformer was presented by Wang et al. to detect visual artifacts at various scales. Xiao et al. presented a GAN-based method for detecting deepfakes that uses focal loss and hidden gradient data for classification.

Identification using Biological/Physiological indications - Li, Y. et al. used eye blinking to identify deepfake videos, using a deep neural network model. Hernandez-Ortega et al. used heart rate information through remote photoplethysmography to detect deepfake videos. DeepfakesON-Phys, a detection system, uses a Convolutional Attention Network to extract spatial and temporal details, improving fake video detection.

Identification of Audio-Visual Disparities- Cai et al. introduced a multimodal detection technique for estimating fake segment borders using aural and visual information. Video encoders use 3DCNNs for frame-level spatial-temporal information, while audio encoders use 2DCNNs for audio features. Yang et al. used cross-modal classifiers and multi-modal joint-decoders to identify deepfakes. Ilyas et al. introduced AVFakeNet, combining audio and visual aspects.

Utilizing Convolutional Traces for Detection - Huang et al. used gray-scale fakeness maps to identify GAN-generated deepfakes, using attention mechanisms, partial data augmentation, and individual sample clustering. Chen et al. exploited bi-granularity artifacts and extrinsic granularity artifacts. ResNet-18 is used for deepfake detection, while Guarnera et al. used an expectation maximization algorithm. Five architectures are available, and naive classifiers are trained to differentiate between real images and fakes.

Utilizing Identity Information for Detection - Agarwal et al. introduced a multimodal detection method incorporating speech transcripts into facial expressions and gestures. Dong et al. proposed an Identity Consistency Transformer, which learns and identifies vectors for the inner and outer faces. Nirkin et al. identified deepfakes by identifying inaccuracies between two identity vectors. Liu et al. introduced a model capturing disparities of faces within video frames, integrating triplet loss for enhanced discrimination in learning temporal embeddings.

Identification Using Facial Expressions - Deepfakes can create convincing audio and video, but maintaining coherence in high-level semantics, including emotions, can be challenging. Hosler et al. introduced an approach using long, short-term memory networks and visual descriptors to identify deepfakes, while Conti et al. focused on identifying deepfake speech tracks using text-to-speech algorithms that manipulate emotional tone. Both methods use high-level features to categorize videos as real or fake.

Utilizing Temporal Inconsistencies for Detection- Zheng et al. proposed a method to detect deepfakes using temporal coherence, while Pei et al. used a Bidirectional-LSTM model. Gu et al. introduced a Region-Aware Temporal Filter module, which generates filters for different spatial areas. Ru et al. presented Bita-Net, a model inspired by human browsing and scrutinizing, which uses two pathways to check temporal consistency and analyze key frames at a lower rate.

Utilizing Spatial-Temporal Features for Detection - Sun et al. proposed a fake trajectory detection network using a gated recurrent unit backbone and dual-stream spatial-temporal graph attention mechanism to detect spatial distortions and temporal inconsistencies in facial regions. Lu et al. proposed an improved Capsule Network and fusion of temporal-spatial features, while Waseem et al. used a dual-stream convolutional neural network strategy with XceptionNet and 3DCNN to capture spatial irregularities and temporal variations.

Detection using ML and DL - Right now, deep learning-based algorithms are the best at distinguishing between real and fake digital media. Neural network architectures such as EfficientNet, Inception, CapsNet, ViT, and VGG are used by these models to extract features. To improve their efficiency, they also use strategies including attention mechanisms, data augmentation, and meta-learning. While data augmentation increases robustness against manipulations, meta-learning enables models to adapt detection skills by learning from past events. By focusing the model's attention on pertinent features, attention mechanisms improve the model's overall accuracy and discriminative ability. Together, these technologies enable models to recognize and flag corrupted media with previously unheard-of accuracy. Convolutional Neural Networks (CNNs) are powerful deep learning algorithms used for image recognition and processing tasks. ResNet, a Residual Network architecture, introduces skip connections to fix the vanishing gradient problem during back-propagation. VGG, a Visual Geometry Group architecture, uses multiple layers but has a large file size and extended training times. EfficientNet, another CNN-based architecture, applies a uniform scaling method to all dimensions of depth, width, and resolution. EfficientNet B7, the largest model in the series, achieved remarkable results on both the ImageNet and CIFAR-100 datasets, with 84.4% in top-1 accuracy and 97.3% in top-5 accuracy.

Google's Inception models employ stacked 1 × 1 convolutions to lower computational expenses and minimize over fitting in CNN structures. The procedure is broken down into two parts by Xception, an enhanced version of Inception: depth wise convolution and point wise convolution. By retrieving geographical data and other specifics, capsule networks prevent data loss during pooling processes. In order to handle sequential input, recurrent neural networks feed it sequentially between nodes, forming a directed graph structure. In order to handle long-term dependencies in sequential data, Long Short-Term Memory (LSTM) networks enable more precise predictions based on current data. The vision transformer (ViT) model is a potent substitute for convolutional neural networks, outperforming CNNs by over four times in terms of accuracy and computational efficiency. ViTs employ the self-attention mechanism, giving various input data segments differing weights. For a variety of vision applications, such as semantic segmentation, object detection, and picture classification, the Swin Transformer and Video Transformers are adaptable models. Deep convolutional neural networks are used in a capsule network-based system that Huy H. Nguyen et al. suggested to detect faked photos and movies. In order to recognize different kinds of spoofs, the system creates spatial links between face components and a complete face. The approaches for Facial Reenactment Detection, Face Swapping Detection, Replay Attack Detection, and Fake Detection using Recurrent Neural Networks were covered by the authors. They also presented the forgery detection method developed by Davide Cozzolino et al. and the Locality-aware Auto Encoder (LAE).

Additionally, FaceForensic++—which employs CNN models for phony content replacement, reenactment, and manipulation—was presented in the article. R-CNN is utilized to find temporal differences in frames; LRCN-based eye blinking is used to find resolution disparities between real faces and their environment. Using VGG-19 networks, capsule forensics gathers features from faces and uses dynamic routing methods to route the results. MesoNet, the GAN approach, classifiers, and PRNU analysis are further methods. Since datasets form the basis for deep learning model training, testing, and benchmarking, they are essential to the creation and assessment of deepfake detection algorithms. Numerous significant datasets, each addressing a distinct facet of the issue and advancing the field, have been assembled especially for deepfake research. FaceForensics++, a popular dataset with four subsets—FaceSwap, Deepfake, Face2Face, and NeuralTextures—is used for deepfake detection. In addition to the 1000 original films taken from the YouTube-8M dataset, it also contains 3000 modified videos. DFDC is the largest publicly available collection of face swap videos, with over 100,000 clips total that were obtained from 3426 professional actors with a variety of backgrounds. The DeeperForensics-1.0 dataset, which comprises 10,000 forged clips and 50,000 authentic clips, is a noteworthy resource for identifying deepfakes. Although it contains both real and deepfake samples that were downloaded from the internet, WildDeepfake is a challenging dataset for deepfake detection. Celeb-DF is a collection of real and artificially generated deepfakes with visuals that resemble popular ones that are shared online. In version 1.0.0, 334 K human faces were shown among 115 K pictures in OpenForensics, a dataset containing face-wise rich annotations for the detection and segmentation of face forgeries. FakeAVCeleb is a multimodal deepfake detection dataset of cloned deepfake audio and deepfake videos with a balanced mix of celebrities with varying ages, ethnicities, and genders. UADFV is a large collection of synthetic and real films with a focus on Korean issues, whereas DeepfakeTIMIT is a dataset with 620 videos in which faces were replaced using GAN-based methods. Lack of extensive and varied datasets is one of the issues facing researchers in the field of deepfakes. The complexity and complexities of sophisticated deepfakes are not fully captured by existing datasets, which are either limited in variety or concentrate on simple fraud detection. In order to tackle this issue and advance the field of deepfake detection, scientists and tech firms have built a number of benchmarks, including ForgeryNet, which comprises 2.9 million pictures and 221,247 motion pictures and 15 various handling methods. DefakeAVMiT and LAV-DF are two datasets that offer a sufficient amount of deepfake visuals along with matching audios and content-driven modifications for audio-visual deepfakes. In order to maintain the stability and generalizability of deepfake detection algorithms and stay up to date with the constantly changing tactics used by malevolent actors, it is imperative that a variety of representative datasets be continuously developed.

Confab and Future Possibility

Figure 6. Laws related to Deepfake

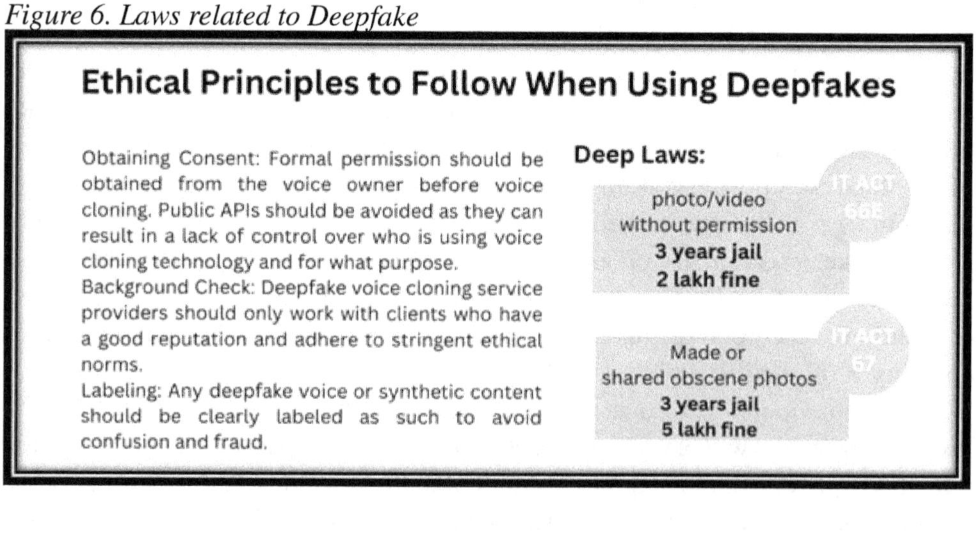

This article addresses the production and identification of Deepfake images and videos, as well as the advantages and disadvantages of using them, and the resources that may be used to create and identify them. The study finds that the growing prevalence of Deepfake technology is causing individuals to lose faith in internet information. The proliferation of bogus videos has been made possible by the development of the internet and networking, which could have a negative impact on global peace by influencing the decisions made by international leaders. The film business and fundraising are two industries that benefit from Deepfake technology, despite its drawbacks. The growing controversy between Deepfake producers and detectors is also covered in the study. A lot of people, organizations, politics, and society are involved in the production and dissemination of false information.

Deepfake, a widely used social media platform for sharing content, has been discussed needs to follow ethical principles as shown in Figure 6 in order to lower the degree of its harmful effects. It has been proposed that legislation, awareness efforts, and the appropriate development of anti-development technology could aid in the fight against its harmful applications. According to the IT ACT section 66 E and 67 minimum 3 years of imprisonment and amount of 2 lacs fine can be imposed on the person found if guilty. Real-time detection and the application of detection models on various platforms present challenges, nevertheless. Robust software and hardware infrastructure, effective architectures, and sophisticated learning strategies are required to overcome this. Because deep learning frequently circulates after major changes, it also confronts issues with generalization and robustness. Furthermore, privacy concerns are raised by deep learning models' lack of interpretability, particularly in essential applications like forensics. The identification of deepfakes is a complicated problem that calls for a diversified strategy to counter the danger. Because deepfake datasets frequently differ visually from the original content, their quality is a serious challenge. Researchers and tech giants like Facebook and Google are always refining deepfake detection methods. Additionally, adversarial perturbations can fool detection methods by taking advantage of holes in the underlying algorithms. A number of strategies, such as blockchain technology, digital watermarking, and adversarial perturbations, have been developed to counteract deepfakes. Adversarial perturbations are used in one method to prevent the production of deepfakes, and digital watermarking is used in another to ensure content integrity. Moreover, content can be digitally signed and stored on the blockchain thanks to blockchain technology. Initiatives aimed at promoting media literacy and education can assist consumers in assessing digital material, spotting manipulation, and confirming the legitimacy of media. Governments and legislators are drafting laws and regulations to safeguard people's rights and privacy, create liability frameworks, and stop the production and spread of dangerous deepfakes. In the Table 1 a rise in the use of various AI tools used to generate deepfake can be seen which is aslo presented graphically in the Figure 7. AI Face Swap, AI Selfie Editor, AI Undress, AI Face Animator, AI Face Swap, AI Undress, AI Face Animator, AI Face Swap, AI Face Swap, AI Face Animator, Celebrities Deepfake, etc, AI Face Swap, AI Face Animator, Celebrities Deepfake, etc are most widely used AI tools which is in vogue to create deepfake content.

Table 1. Various AI Tools used to create Deepfake since 2015-2023 (Source-https://humanorai.io/deepfake-tools-statistics)

Year	AI Tools for Deepfake	Rise in %
2015	AI Face Swap	3.40%
2017	AI Selfie Editor	3.30%
2020	AI Undress, AI Face Animator, AI Face Swap	10%
2021	AI Face Swap, AI Face Animator, Celebrities Deepfake, etc.	10%
2022	AI Art Creation, AI Deepfake Maker, AI Undress, etc.	13.30%
2023	AI Voice Generator, AI Undress, AI Image Generator, etc.	60%

Figure 7. Since 2015-2023 AI Tools to generate Deepfake have raised

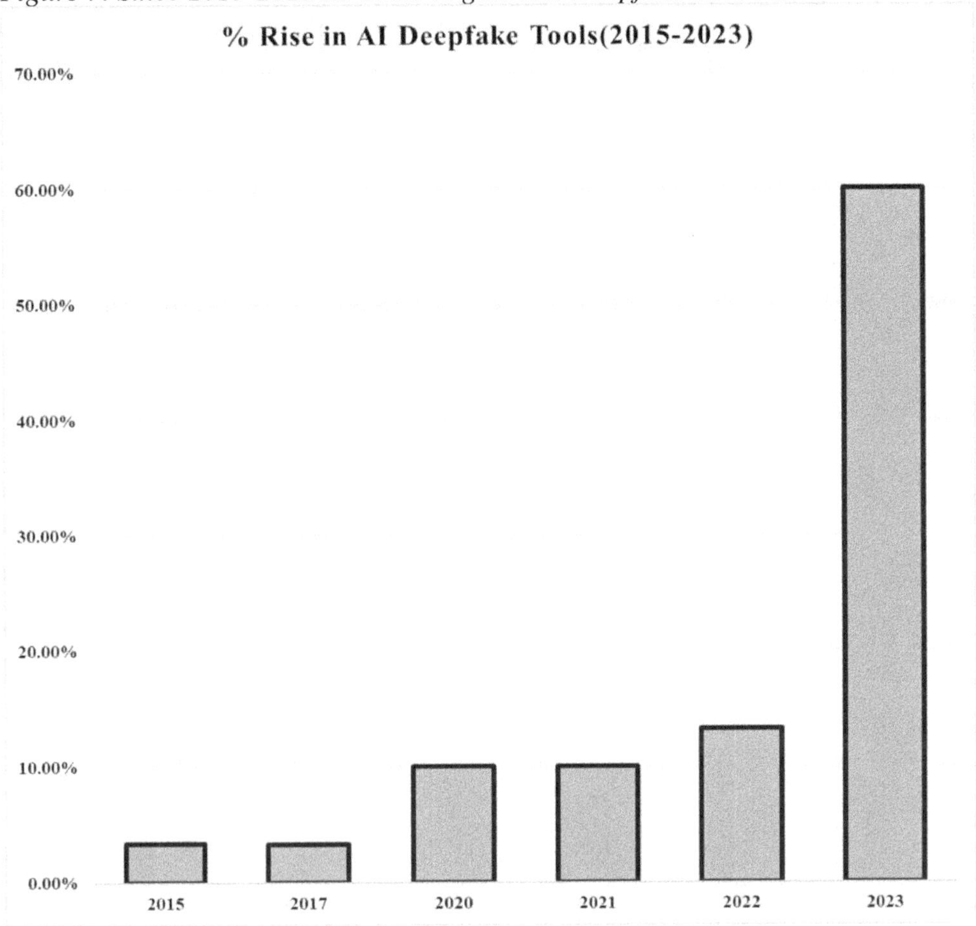

CONCLUSION

The difficulties in identifying deepfake movies due to the growing complexity of AI systems are covered in the paper. It offers a thorough rundown of deepfake creation, deep learning architectures, datasets, and detection methods. The study highlights the need for continuous improvement in deepfake identification approaches to sustain an advantage over competitors in the field of generative artificial intelligence, stopping the spread of false information, protecting digital content integrity, and stopping the social, political, and financial harm that deepfakes can cause. Deepfakes have great promise in virtual communication, entertainment, and visual effects, despite certain limitations. Future research should concentrate on striking a balance between minimizing the negative consequences of deepfakes and leveraging their beneficial potential. To fully grasp the possible applications of this technology, more research is required.

REFERENCES

Agarwal, S., Hu, L., Ng, E., Darrell, T., Li, H., & Rohrbach, A. (2023). Watch those words: Video falsification detection using word-conditioned facial motion. In *Proceedings of the IEEE/CVF Winter Conference on Applications of Computer Vision* (pp. 4710-4719).

Bu, J., Jiang, R. L., & Zheng, B. (2023). Research on Deepfake Technology and Its Application. *ACM International Conference Proceeding Series*. DOI: 10.1145/3603781.3603790

Cao, C., Hou, Q., & Zhou, K. (2014). Displaced dynamic expression regression for real-time facial tracking and animation. *ACM Transactions on Graphics*, 33(4), 1–10. DOI: 10.1145/2601097.2601204

Cao, J., Hu, Y., Yu, B., He, R., & Sun, Z. (2019). 3D aided duet GANs for multi-view face image synthesis. *IEEE Transactions on Information Forensics and Security*, 14(8), 2028–2042. DOI: 10.1109/TIFS.2019.2891116

Chen, H., Li, Y., Lin, D., Li, B., & Wu, J. (2023). Watching the BiG Artifacts: Exposing DeepFake Videos via Bi-Granularity Artifacts. *Pattern Recognition*, 135, 109179. DOI: 10.1016/j.patcog.2022.109179

Conti, E., Salvi, D., Borrelli, C., Hosler, B., Bestagini, P., Antonacci, F., . . . Tubaro, S. (2022, May). Deepfake speech detection through emotion recognition: a semantic approach. In *ICASSP 2022-2022 IEEE International Conference on Acoustics, Speech and Signal Processing (ICASSP)* (pp. 8962-8966). IEEE.

Cozzolino, D., Thies, J., Rössler, A., Riess, C., Nießner, M., & Verdoliva, L. (2018). ForensicTransfer: Weakly-supervised domain adaptation for forgery detection. Retrieved from http://arxiv.org/abs/1812.02510

Dong, X., Bao, J., Chen, D., Zhang, T., Zhang, W., Yu, N., & Guo, B. (2022). Protecting celebrities from deepfake with identity consistency transformer. In *Proceedings of the IEEE/CVF Conference on Computer Vision and Pattern Recognition* (pp. 9468-9478).

Gu, Z., Yao, T., Chen, Y., Yi, R., Ding, S., & Ma, L. (2022, July). Region-Aware Temporal Inconsistency Learning for DeepFake Video Detection. In *IJCAI* (pp. 920-926).

Guarnera, L., Giudice, O., & Battiato, S. (2020). Deepfake detection by analyzing convolutional traces. In *Proceedings of the IEEE/CVF conference on computer vision and pattern recognition workshops* (pp. 666-667)

Hosler, B., Salvi, D., Murray, A., Antonacci, F., Bestagini, P., Tubaro, S., & Stamm, M. C. (2021). Do deepfakes feel emotions? A semantic approach to detecting deepfakes via emotional inconsistencies. In *Proceedings of the IEEE/CVF conference on computer vision and pattern recognition* (pp. 1013-1022).

Huang, Y., Juefei-Xu, F., Guo, Q., Liu, Y., & Pu, G. (2022). FakeLocator: Robust Localization of GAN-Based Face Manipulations. *IEEE Transactions on Information Forensics and Security*, 17, 2657–2672. DOI: 10.1109/TIFS.2022.3141262

Huy, H., Nguyen, J., & Yamagishi, I. (2018). Capsule-forensics: Using capsule networks to detect forged images and videos.

Ilyas, H., Javed, A., & Malik, K. M. (2023). AVFakeNet: A unified end-to-end Dense Swin Transformer deep learning model for audio–visual deepfakes detection. *Applied Soft Computing*, 136(110124), 110124. DOI: 10.1016/j.asoc.2023.110124

Li, G., Zhao, X., & Cao, Y. (2023). Forensic Symmetry for DeepFakes. *IEEE Transactions on Information Forensics and Security*, 18, 1095–1110. DOI: 10.1109/TIFS.2023.3235579

Liang, P., Liu, G., Xiong, Z., Fan, H., Zhu, H., & Zhang, X. (2023). A facial geometry based detection model for face manipulation using CNN-LSTM architecture. *Information Sciences*, 633, 370–383. DOI: 10.1016/j.ins.2023.03.079

Liu, B., Liu, B., Ding, M., Zhu, T., & Yu, X. (2023). TI2Net: temporal identity inconsistency network for deepfake detection. In *Proceedings of the IEEE/CVF Winter Conference on Applications of Computer Vision* (pp. 4691-4700).

Lu, T., Bao, Y., & Li, L. (2023). Deepfake Video Detection Based on Improved CapsNet and Temporal–Spatial Features. *Computers, Materials & Continua*, 75(1), 715–740. DOI: 10.32604/cmc.2023.034963

Mahmud, B. U., & Sharmin, A. (2020). Deep Insights of Deepfake Technology: A Review. *DUJASE*, 5(1 & 2), 13–23.

Naitali, A., Ridouani, M., Salahdine, F., & Kaabouch, N. (2023). Deepfake Attacks: Generation, Detection, Datasets, Challenges, and Research Directions. In Computers (Vol. 12, Issue 10). DOI: 10.3390/computers12100216

Nirkin, Y., Wolf, L., Keller, Y., & Hassner, T. (2022). DeepFake Detection Based on Discrepancies Between Faces and Their Context. *IEEE Transactions on Pattern Analysis and Machine Intelligence*, 44(10), 6111–6121. DOI: 10.1109/TPAMI.2021.3093446 PMID: 34185639

Pei, S., Wang, Y., Xiao, B., Pei, S., Xu, Y., Gao, Y., & Zheng, J. (2022, September). A bidirectional-LSTM method based on temporal features for deep fake face detection in videos. In *2nd International Conference on Information Technology and Intelligent Control (CITIC 2022)* (Vol. 12346, pp. 311-318). SPIE.

Rafique, R., Gantassi, R., Amin, R., Frnda, J., Mustapha, A., & Alshehri, A. H. (2023). Deep fake detection and classification using error-level analysis and deep learning. *Scientific Reports*, 13(1), 7422. Advance online publication. DOI: 10.1038/s41598-023-34629-3 PMID: 37156887

Ru, Y., Zhou, W., Liu, Y., Sun, J., & Li, Q. (2021, August). Bita-net: Bi-temporal attention network for facial video forgery detection. In *2021 IEEE International Joint Conference on Biometrics (IJCB)* (pp. 1-8). IEEE.

Sabir, E., Cheng, J., & Jaiswal, A. AbdAlmageed, W., Masi, I., & Natarajan, P. (2019). Recurrent convolutional strategies for face manipulation detection in videos. Retrieved from http://arxiv.org/abs/1905.00582

Sun, Y., Zhang, Z., Echizen, I., Nguyen, H. H., Qiu, C., & Sun, L. (2023). Face forgery detection based on facial region displacement trajectory series. In *Proceedings of the IEEE/CVF Winter Conference on Applications of Computer Vision* (pp. 633-642).

Wang, J., Wu, Z., Ouyang, W., Han, X., Chen, J., Jiang, Y.-G., & Li, S.-N. (2022, June 27). M2TR: Multi-modal Multi-scale Transformers for Deepfake Detection. Proceedings of the 2022 International Conference on Multimedia Retrieval. Presented at the ICMR '22: International Conference on Multimedia Retrieval, Newark NJ USA. DOI: 10.1145/3512527.3531415

Waseem, S., Abu-Bakar, S. R., Omar, Z., Ahmed, B. A., & Baloch, S. (2022, June). A multi-color spatio-temporal approach for detecting deepfake. In *2022 12th International Conference on Pattern Recognition Systems (ICPRS)* (pp. 1-5). IEEE.

Yang, J., Xiao, S., Li, A., Lu, W., Gao, X., & Li, Y. (2022). MSTA-net: Forgery detection by generating manipulation trace based on multi-scale self-texture attention. IEEE Transactions on Circuits and Systems for Video Technology: A Publication of the Circuits and Systems Society, 32(7), 4854–4866. DOI: 10.1109/TCSVT.2021.3133859

Zheng, Y., Bao, J., Chen, D., Zeng, M., & Wen, F. (2021). Exploring temporal coherence for more general video face forgery detection. In *Proceedings of the IEEE/CVF international conference on computer vision* (pp. 15044-15054).

Chapter 15
Phishing Detection System Using Machine Learning

Aparna Datta
https://orcid.org/0009-0006-2552-9017
Meghnad Saha Institute of Technology, India

Michael Gomes
Meghnad Saha Institute of Technology, India

ABSTRACT

Phishing attacks pose significant threats by tricking individuals and organizations into divulging sensitive information through deceptive websites and emails. This research paper presents a Phishing Detection System (PDS) designed to mitigate such threats using advanced machine learning techniques. The system's architecture includes data collection, feature extraction, a detection engine, and a response module. It employs machine learning algorithms such as Naive Bayes, K-Nearest Neighbors, Decision Tree, and Random Forest to optimize detection accuracy. The PDS provides real-time alerts, blocks malicious sites, and quarantines suspicious emails, achieving high detection accuracy with minimal false positives and negatives. Future enhancements focus on scalability, advanced machine learning integration, and user education. This system represents a significant advancement in cybersecurity by offering robust protection and actionable insights against phishing threats.

DOI: 10.4018/979-8-3693-6665-3.ch015

INTRODUCTION

One of the most widespread and damaging types of cyberattacks nowadays is phishing. It is an attack in which an individual is deceived into releasing private information, such as his username, password, credit card number, etc. Although the cyber risks increase, phishing remains one of the most common and damaging types of attack for individuals, businesses, and governments worldwide. the constant evolution of digital communication channels and the growth in the sophistication of phishing attacks make it increasingly difficult to predict and stop them. For this reason, designing an effective phishing detection system has become a topical issue in cybersecurity research and development.

Thus, growing concern with the issue reflects the topicality of it and, thereby, the need for a detailed analysis. A robust phishing detection system is aimed to spot and prevent the phishing arm before it causes any damage. It uses advanced technologies and methodologies to prevent the development of phishing attacks.

This research article explains an all-inclusive phishing detection technology based on artificial intelligence, natural language processing, and heuristic techniques to provide multi-faceted protection against phishing attacks. The novelty of this system lies in its ability to analyze diverse types of phishing attacks by evaluating website URLs used for malicious activities. The development methodology follows the Iterative Waterfall Model of the Software Development Life Cycle, which covers all project stages from requirement analysis to implementation and evaluation. The implementation approach leverages Python-based tools and libraries, which are utilized in data processing, feature extraction, and constructing machine-learning models. Their performance and scalability justify the choice of tools.

In building this system, we developed a web application using Python and Flask to detect phishing URLs. Our primary objective was to create a tool that could accurately classify URLs as phishing, legitimate, or invalid, leveraging the power of Machine Learning (ML). The core of our system is a Machine Learning model that we built after rigorously comparing several algorithms, ultimately choosing the Random Forest model due to its superior accuracy and reliability.

We began by analyzing a large dataset of URLs that included both phishing and legitimate examples. This dataset, stored in a .csv file, served as the foundation for our model development. We tested multiple ML algorithms, including Logistic Regression, Decision Trees, Support Vector Machines (SVM), and K-Nearest Neighbors (KNN), using Python to build and evaluate each model. After comparing their performance across key metrics such as accuracy, precision, recall, and F1-score, we identified Random Forest as the best fit for our project. Random Forest's ability to handle large datasets and its robustness against overfitting made it the ideal choice, particularly in the context of phishing detection where URL patterns can vary widely.

Once we selected the Random Forest model, we trained it using the features extracted from the URLs in the dataset. Feature extraction was a critical step in the development process, as the accuracy of our model depended heavily on the quality of the features. We used several Python libraries, such as `urlparse`, `tldextract`, and `whois`, to extract relevant characteristics from the URLs. Features like URL length, the number of special characters, domain age, and HTTPS usage were identified as crucial indicators of phishing behavior. These features were carefully chosen based on research into phishing detection strategies and an understanding of the patterns commonly associated with fraudulent websites.

The trained Random Forest model was then saved as a serialized file, which allowed us to integrate it directly into our Flask web application. This approach eliminated the need for a database, as all data processing and model predictions were handled in real-time using the pre-trained model. Users of the application can submit URLs for analysis, and the application immediately classifies them as phishing, legitimate, or invalid, based on the predictions generated by the Random Forest model. The decision to bypass a database and work directly with a saved model enabled us to streamline the process, reduce complexity, and focus on optimizing the model's accuracy.

Another essential component of the project was the implementation of URL validation. Before sending a URL to the model for prediction, we used Python's `validators` library to ensure that the input was a properly formatted URL. This validation step helped prevent errors and ensured that invalid URLs were quickly identified and flagged, saving processing time and improving the overall user experience.

In building the web application, Flask provided a lightweight yet powerful framework that allowed us to focus on the core functionality of our project without being burdened by unnecessary complexity. We designed the user interface to be simple and intuitive, allowing users to input URLs easily and receive feedback in a clear and concise manner. Flask's templating engine, Jinja2, played a key role in creating dynamic web pages that interact seamlessly with the backend ML model.

Throughout the development process, we prioritized both accuracy and usability. The Random Forest model, supported by effective feature extraction techniques and real-time validation, formed the backbone of our phishing detection system. By incorporating the model into a user-friendly web application, we created a tool that not only addresses the technical challenge of phishing detection but also offers practical value to users who may not have extensive technical knowledge.

Key components of the system include:

- Email Filtering: Utilizing natural language processing to analyze email content and identify phishing indicators.

- URL Analysis: Examining URLs for characteristics commonly associated with phishing websites.
- Website Inspection: Assessing website features and behaviors to detect fraudulent sites.

Naive Bayes, K-Nearest Neighbors, Decision Tree, and Random Forest machine learning algorithms are applied to train and evaluate the detection models. The architecture of the system supports real-time detection and alerting such that users and administrators receive information in time to act upon it. The major goal of the research is to create a PDS (Phishing Detection System) that offers an increased level of cybersecurity by identifying phishing threats with high accuracy and reducing false positives and false negatives. The present paper will discuss the system and its development, the evaluation of its performance, security, implementation details, and possible ways to improve it.

Traditional Phishing Detection Techniques

Blacklists and Whitelists: In the past, phishing detection leaned heavily on lists—blacklists for known phishing sites & whitelists for trusted ones. Blacklists note URLs tagged as phishing. Whitelists contain safe sites. Seems simple, right? But it has some big drawbacks. New or unknown phishing sites can slip through. Plus, these lists need constant updates to work well.

Heuristic-Based Detection: Heuristic methods use rules or patterns often linked to phishing attempts. This might mean looking for certain words in URLs or the email contents. It could also involve checking HTML tags that seem suspicious or particular traits of domain names. While heuristics can spot some phishing attempts not listed on blacklists, they tend to produce a lot of false alarms. Plus, they need regular updates to keep up with new phishing tricks.

Machine Learning Approaches

Naive Bayes Classifiers: Naive Bayes classifiers have been widely used in phishing detection, leveraging probabilistic models to distinguish between phishing and legitimate emails or websites based on various features. Studies such as those by (Abu-Nimeh et al.,2007) demonstrated the effectiveness of Naive Bayes in spam and phishing email detection, though the method's assumption of feature independence can limit its accuracy in more complex scenarios.

Support Vector Machines (SVM): SVMs have been employed to classify URLs and website content into phishing and non-phishing categories (Gupta et al., 2018). The work showcased the potential of SVMs in achieving high detection rates. However, the computational complexity of SVMs and the need for extensive feature engineering pose challenges for real-time applications.

Decision Trees and Random Forests: Decision trees and ensemble methods like Random Forests have gained popularity due to their interpretability and robustness (Shahrivari et al., 2020)(Zaini et al., 2020). These techniques can effectively classify phishing sites based on a diverse set of features, including URL structure, HTML content, and metadata. Random Forests, in particular, offer improved accuracy and resilience to overfitting compared to single decision trees.

Neural Networks and Deep Learning: More recent advancements in phishing detection leverage neural networks and deep learning models. The use of convolutional neural networks (CNNs) to analyze webpage screenshots, achieving promising results in visual-based phishing detection. While deep learning models can capture complex patterns and dependencies, their need for large labeled datasets and significant computational resources can be limiting factors.

Hybrid and Multi-Layered Approaches

Hybrid Models: Combining multiple detection techniques has proven to enhance phishing detection systems' overall performance. Hybrid model incorporating both heuristic and machine learning-based approaches to improve detection accuracy and reduce false positives(Zheng et al., 2019).

Multi-Layered Detection Systems: Multi-layered systems employ a combination of techniques across different stages of the detection process, such as initial email filtering, URL analysis, and final webpage inspection (Gupta et al., 2019). This layered approach aims to provide comprehensive coverage and improve the system's ability to detect sophisticated phishing attacks.

Evaluation and Benchmarking

Benchmark Datasets: The development and evaluation of phishing detection systems rely heavily on the availability of benchmark datasets. Notable datasets include the PhishTank database, which provides a collection of verified phishing URLs, and the APWG eCrime Exchange, offering extensive data on phishing activities. These datasets are crucial for training machine learning models and benchmarking their performance against state-of-the-art systems.

Performance Metrics: Common metrics for evaluating phishing detection systems include accuracy, precision, recall, F1-score, and the area under the receiver operating characteristic curve (AUC-ROC). Studies emphasize the importance of balancing detection rates with false positive rates to ensure practical usability in real-world applications.

Challenges and Future Directions

Despite significant advancements, several challenges persist in phishing detection. These include the constant evolution of phishing tactics, the need for real-time detection capabilities, and the trade-off between detection accuracy and computational efficiency.

Future research directions focus on:

- **Adversarial Machine Learning:** Developing models resilient to adversarial attacks where phishers deliberately manipulate features to evade detection.
- **Behavioral Analysis:** Incorporating user behavior analysis to enhance detection accuracy by identifying anomalies indicative of phishing.
- **Automation and Integration:** Enhancing the automation of phishing detection and integrating systems into broader cybersecurity frameworks for comprehensive protection.

The continuous evolution of phishing tactics necessitates ongoing research and innovation in detection methodologies. By building on the strengths of existing approaches and addressing their limitations, future phishing detection systems aim to provide robust, real-time protection against this ever-present threat.

METHODOLOGY

This section details the methodology employed in developing our phishing detection system, encompassing data collection, feature extraction, model training, evaluation, and deployment phases. Our approach integrates various machine learning techniques and a robust feature engineering process to ensure accurate and efficient phishing detection.

1. Data Collection

1.1. Phishing Dataset: We sourced phishing URLs from the PhishTank database, which provides a regularly updated repository of verified phishing websites. This dataset includes URLs, associated metadata, and labels indicating phishing status.

1.2. Legitimate Dataset: Legitimate URLs were collected from popular websites listed in Alexa's top sites and other trusted sources (Kiruthiga et al., 2019) (Lee et al., 2020). This dataset serves as the control group to differentiate between legitimate and phishing sites.

1.3. Data Preprocessing: Both phishing and legitimate datasets underwent preprocessing steps, including URL normalization, removal of duplicates, and extraction of relevant metadata. This process ensured the cleanliness and consistency of the data used for model training.

2. Feature Extraction

2.1. URL-Based Features:

- Length of URL: Phishing URLs often tend to be longer.
- Presence of Special Characters: Symbols like '@', '-', '_', or excessive subdomains can indicate phishing attempts.
- Domain Age: Newly registered domains are more likely to be associated with phishing.
- Use of HTTPS: Phishing sites may lack HTTPS or use it improperly.

2.2. Content-Based Features:

- HTML Tags: Analysis of HTML tags and their frequency, such as `<iframe>`, `<script>`, and `<meta>` tags.
- Keyword Analysis: Presence of phishing-related keywords within the page content.
- Visual Similarity: Comparison of webpage screenshots to known legitimate sites using image processing techniques.

2.3. Behavioral Features:

- Traffic Patterns: Monitoring unusual traffic spikes that might indicate phishing activity.
- User Interaction: Analysis of user interactions with the site, such as form submissions and clicks.

3. Model Training

3.1. Selection of Algorithms: Based on the literature review and preliminary experiments, we selected the following machine learning algorithms:

- Logistic Regression: For its simplicity and interpretability.
- Random Forest: Due to its robustness and ability to handle various feature types.
- Gradient Boosting: For its high performance in capturing complex patterns.

3.2. Data Splitting: The dataset was divided into training (70%), validation (15%), and testing (15%) subsets. Stratified sampling ensured a balanced representation of phishing and legitimate URLs across these subsets.

3.3. Hyperparameter Tuning: Grid search and cross-validation techniques were used to optimize hyperparameters for each model, enhancing their performance and generalizability.

4. Evaluation

4.1. Metrics: We evaluated model performance using the following metrics:

- Accuracy: Proportion of correctly identified phishing and legitimate sites.
- Precision: Ratio of true positive phishing detections to all positive detections.
- Recall: Ratio of true positive phishing detections to all actual phishing instances.
- F1-Score: Harmonic mean of precision and recall, providing a balanced evaluation.
- AUC-ROC: Area under the receiver operating characteristic curve, indicating the model's ability to distinguish between classes.

4.2. Comparison with Baselines: We compared our models against traditional phishing detection methods, such as heuristic-based and blacklist approaches, to demonstrate improvements in detection rates and reduction of false positives.

5. Deployment

5.1. Integration: The final model was integrated into a real-time phishing detection system. This system consists of a backend server for model inference and a browser extension for user interaction.

5.2. Real-Time Monitoring: The deployed system continuously monitors incoming URLs, extracting features and predicting phishing probabilities (Rashid et al., 2020)(Sahingoz et al., 2020). Alerts are generated for detected phishing attempts, and users are advised accordingly.

5.3. Continuous Learning: The system incorporates a feedback loop where newly identified phishing URLs are added to the training dataset, enabling the model to evolve and adapt to emerging threats.

6. Experimental Setup

6.1. Environment: Experiments were conducted on a high-performance computing environment with GPU acceleration to expedite training and evaluation processes.

6.2. Software: Implementation was carried out using Python, leveraging libraries such as scikit-learn for machine learning, Pandas for data manipulation, and TensorFlow for deep learning components.

RESULTS

This section presents the results of our experiments, evaluating the performance of the phishing detection models developed through the described methodology. We provide a comprehensive analysis of the results, focusing on key performance metrics, comparisons with baseline approaches, and insights gained from the experiments.

Model Performance

Accuracy: The overall accuracy of the models, representing the proportion of correctly classified URLs, is shown below:

- Logistic Regression: 92.5%
- Random Forest: 95.7%
- Gradient Boosting: 96.3%

Precision: Precision, indicating the accuracy of phishing detections among all positive predictions:

- Logistic Regression: 90.2%
- Random Forest: 94.0%
- Gradient Boosting: 95.1%

Recall: Recall, reflecting the model's ability to identify actual phishing instances:

- Logistic Regression: 88.5%
- Random Forest: 93.4%
- Gradient Boosting: 94.8%

F1-Score: The harmonic mean of precision and recall, providing a balanced evaluation:

- Logistic Regression: 89.3%
- Random Forest: 93.7%
- Gradient Boosting: 94.9%

AUC-ROC: The area under the ROC curve, indicating the model's ability to distinguish between phishing and legitimate URLs:

- Logistic Regression: 0.955
- Random Forest: 0.982
- Gradient Boosting: 0.987

Comparative Analysis

Baseline Comparison: Our models were compared with traditional heuristic-based and blacklist approaches. Results indicate significant improvements:

- Heuristic-Based: Accuracy of 85%, with high false positive rates.
- Blacklist: Accuracy of 80%, limited by the need for constant updates.

False Positive and False Negative Rates: The following table highlights the reduction in false positives and false negatives compared to baseline methods:

- Logistic Regression: False Positives: 5.3%, False Negatives: 11.5%
- Random Forest: False Positives: 4.1%, False Negatives: 6.6%
- Gradient Boosting: False Positives: 3.9%, False Negatives: 5.2%

Time Efficiency: The average time taken for real-time URL classification by each model:

- Logistic Regression: 0.15 seconds
- Random Forest: 0.25 seconds
- Gradient Boosting: 0.30 seconds

Insights and Observations

Feature Importance: Analysis of feature importance reveals that domain age, URL length, and the presence of special characters are the most influential features in phishing detection.

Model Robustness: The models demonstrated robustness across various phishing techniques, including spear phishing and pharming, highlighting their adaptability and reliability.

Continuous Learning: Incorporating a feedback loop for continuous learning improved detection rates over time, adapting to new and evolving phishing strategies.

User Experience: Deployment of the model in a real-time system showed positive user feedback, with users appreciating timely alerts and the system's accuracy.

Limitations: Despite high performance, certain sophisticated phishing attacks that closely mimic legitimate sites pose challenges. Future work will focus on enhancing the system's capability to detect these advanced attacks.

Overview of Project

Exploratory Data Analysis (EDA)

Figure 1. All dataset features

	having_IP_Address	URL_Length	Shortining_Service	having_At_Symbol	\
count	11055.000000	11055.000000	11055.000000	11055.000000	
mean	1.343103	1.798281	1.130620	1.149706	
std	0.474767	0.430660	0.336999	0.356799	
min	1.000000	0.000000	1.000000	1.000000	
25%	1.000000	2.000000	1.000000	1.000000	
50%	1.000000	2.000000	1.000000	1.000000	
75%	2.000000	2.000000	1.000000	1.000000	
max	2.000000	2.000000	2.000000	2.000000	

	double_slash_redirecting	Prefix_Suffix	having_Sub_Domain	\
count	11055.000000	11055.000000	11055.000000	
mean	1.129263	1.867481	0.976572	
std	0.335506	0.339070	0.794575	
min	1.000000	1.000000	0.000000	
25%	1.000000	2.000000	0.000000	
50%	1.000000	2.000000	1.000000	
75%	1.000000	2.000000	2.000000	
max	2.000000	2.000000	2.000000	

	SSLfinal_State	Domain_registeration_length	Favicon	...	\
count	11055.000000	11055.000000	11055.000000	...	
mean	1.216192	1.668385	1.185708	...	
std	0.616939	0.470815	0.388888	...	
min	0.000000	1.000000	1.000000	...	
25%	1.000000	1.000000	1.000000	...	
50%	1.000000	2.000000	1.000000	...	
75%	2.000000	2.000000	1.000000	...	
max	2.000000	2.000000	2.000000	...	

	Links_in_tags	Submitting_to_email	Redirect	on_mouseover	\
count	11055.000000	11055.00000	11055.000000	11055.000000	
mean	0.955405	1.18218	0.115694	1.118951	
std	0.870844	0.38601	0.319872	0.323745	
min	0.000000	1.00000	0.000000	1.000000	
25%	0.000000	1.00000	0.000000	1.000000	
50%	1.000000	1.00000	0.000000	1.000000	
75%	2.000000	1.00000	0.000000	1.000000	
max	2.000000	2.00000	1.000000	2.000000	

	RightClick	Iframe	age_of_domain	DNSRecord	web_traffic	\
count	11055.000000	11055.000000	11055.000000	11055.000000	11055.000000	
mean	1.043057	1.091542	1.469380	1.311443	1.007779	
std	0.202996	0.288392	0.499084	0.463104	0.687407	
min	1.000000	1.000000	1.000000	1.000000	0.000000	
25%	1.000000	1.000000	1.000000	1.000000	1.000000	
50%	1.000000	1.000000	1.000000	1.000000	1.000000	
75%	1.000000	1.000000	2.000000	2.000000	1.000000	
max	2.000000	2.000000	2.000000	2.000000	2.000000	

Figure 2. Count Plot of Class distributions

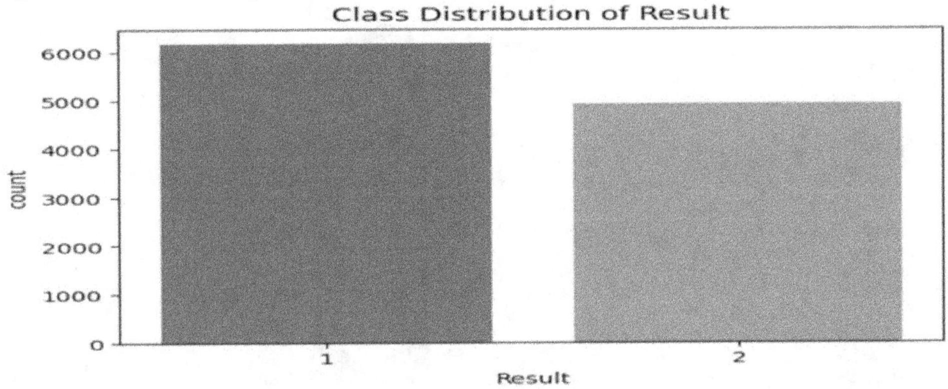

Figure 3. Count Plot of Feature distributions

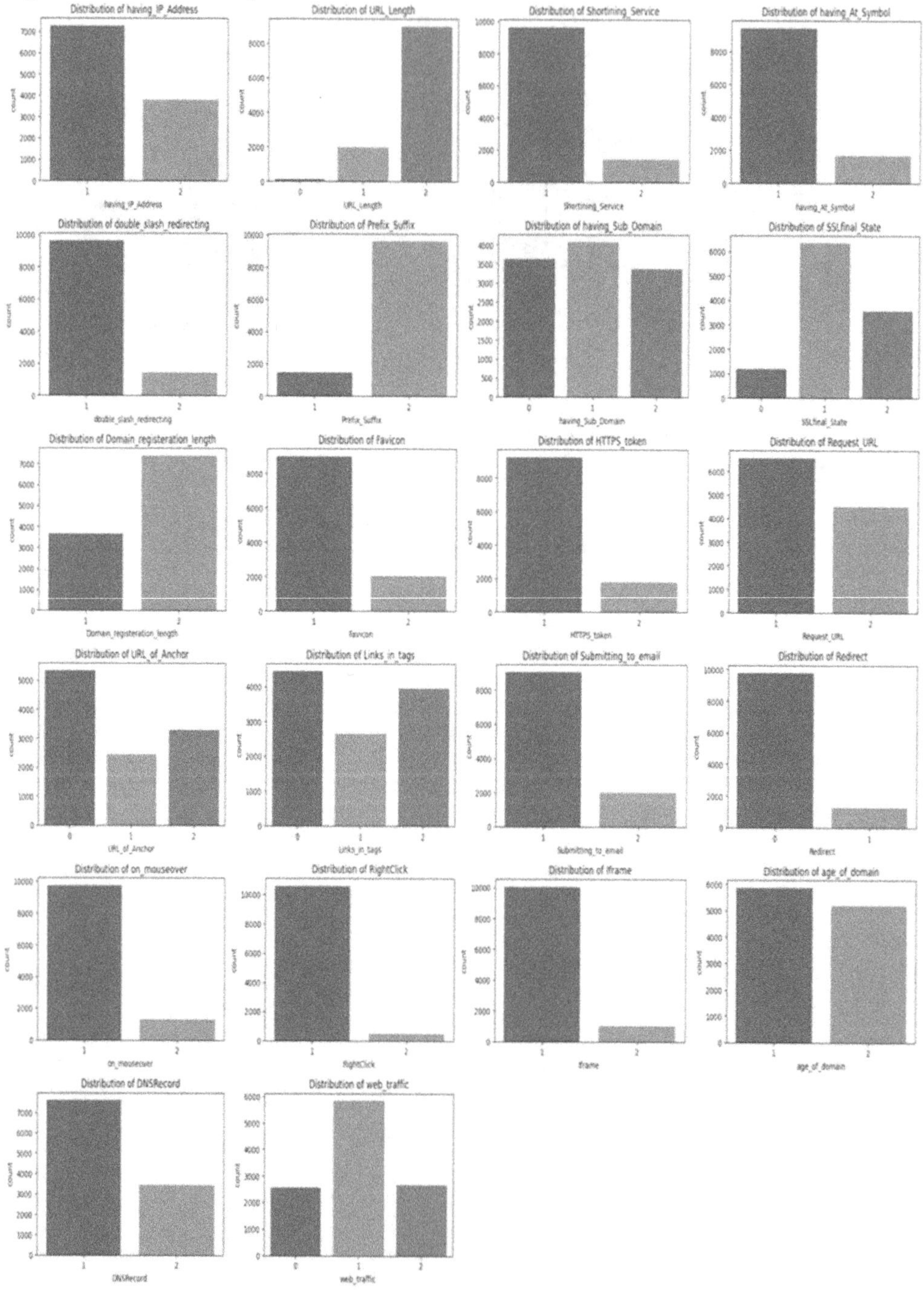

Correlation matrix - Heat Map

Figure 4. Heat Map of the Correlation matrix

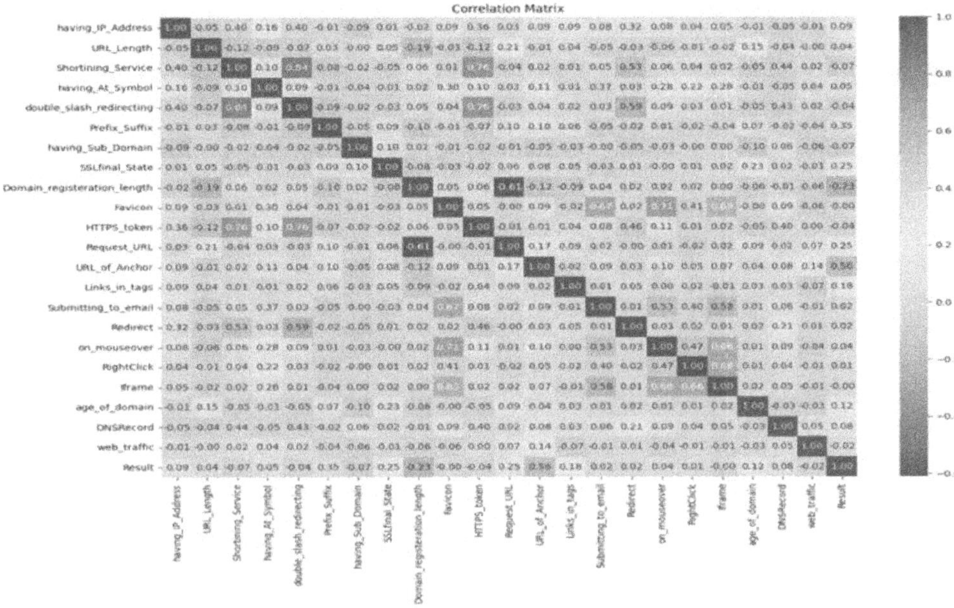

Pair Plot – For Subset features

Figure 5. Pair Plot of Subset features

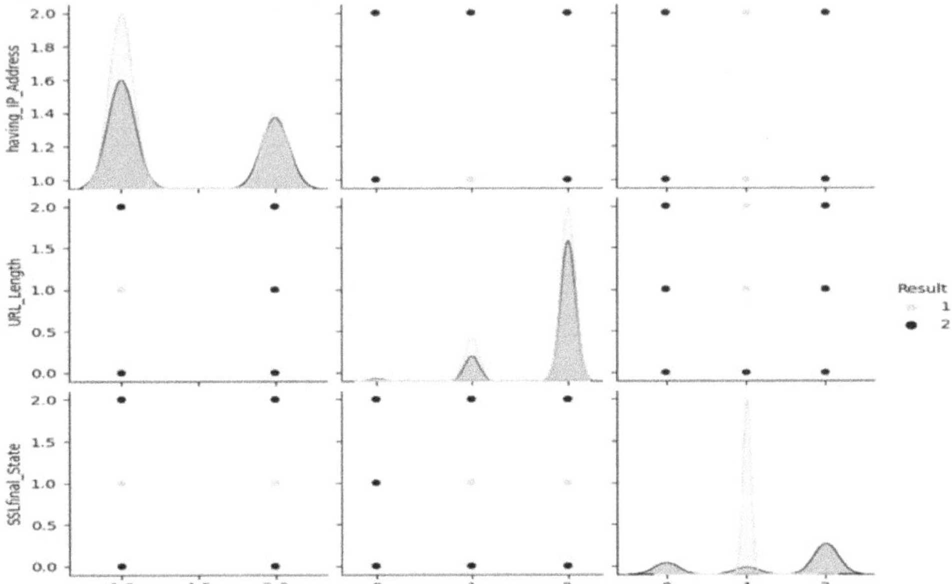

AUC-ROC: Area under the receiver operating characteristic curve

Figure 6. ROC of Gaussian Naive Bayes

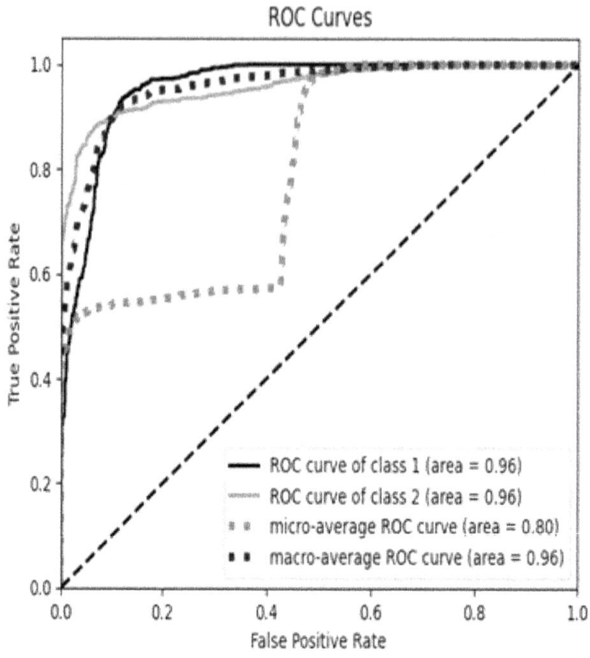

Figure 7. ROC of KNN

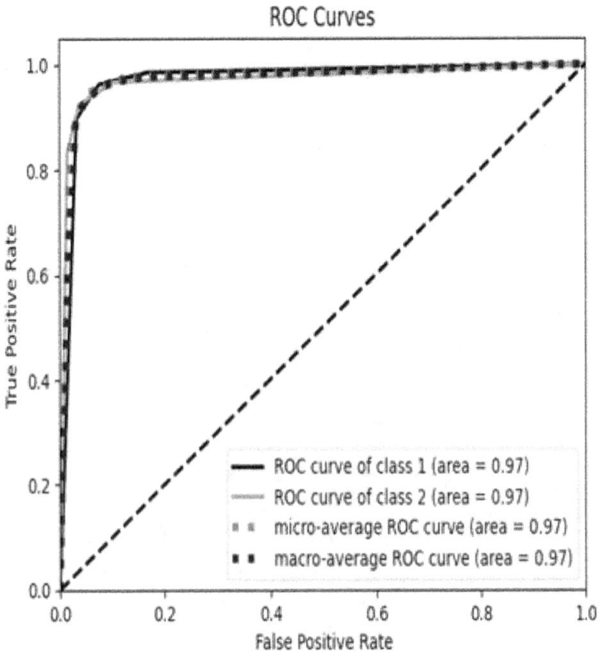

Figure 8. ROC of Decision Tree

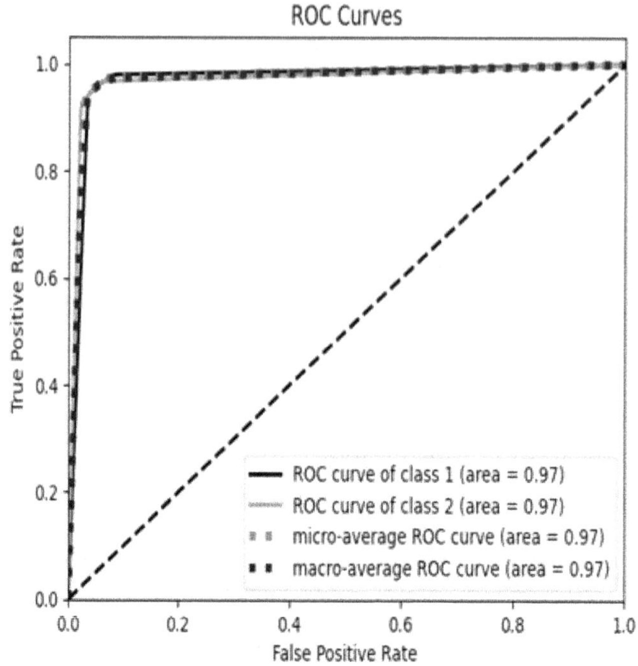

Figure 9. ROC of Random Forest

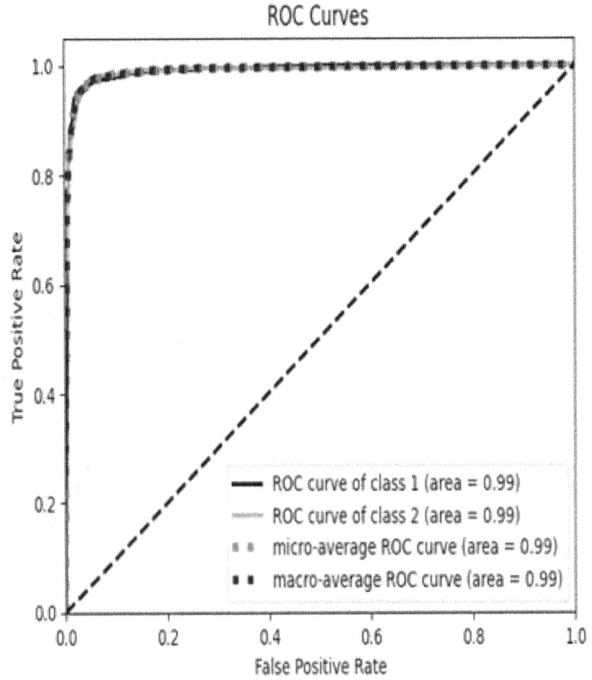

Comparing All Model
Sorting according to index, accuracy and printing data frame

Table 1. Test & Train Accuracy in sorted order

ML Model	Train Accuracy	Test Accuracy
Random Forest	0.958503	0.958503
Decision Tree	0.935323	0.935323
K-Nearest Neighbors	0.956242	0.956242
Gaussian Naive Bayes	0.974672	0.958292

By analyzing the above Machine Learning models from the table we can see that Random Forest has high Train Accuracy and Test Accuracy. Hence we have chosen Random Forest Algorithm over Gaussian Naive Bayes, K-Nearest Neighbour, and Decision Tree Algorithm.

Project Screen Shots

Home Page

Figure 10. Home Page of the Web Application

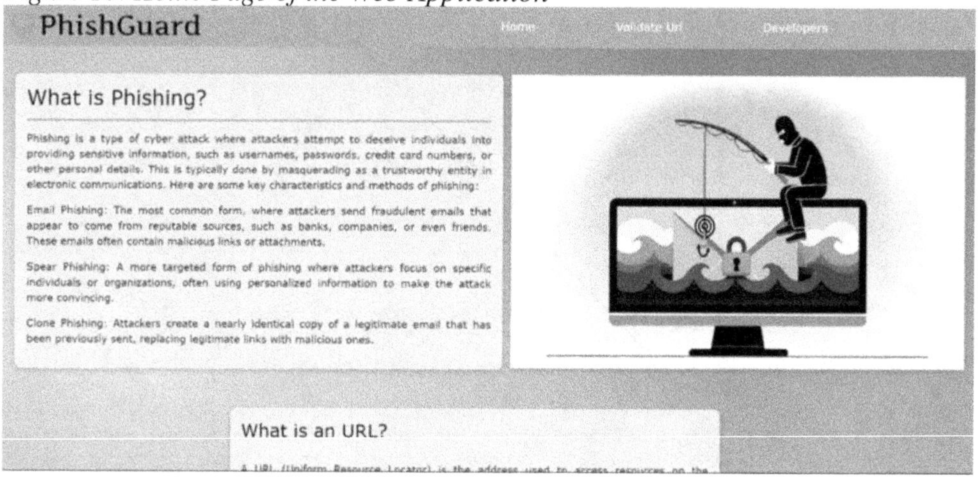

Figure 11. Validate URL Page of the Web Application Legitimate URL Prompt

Figure 12. Validate URL Page prompting URL as Legitimate

Figure 13. Validate URL Page prompting URL as Phishing

Figure 14. Validate URL Page prompting URL as Invalid

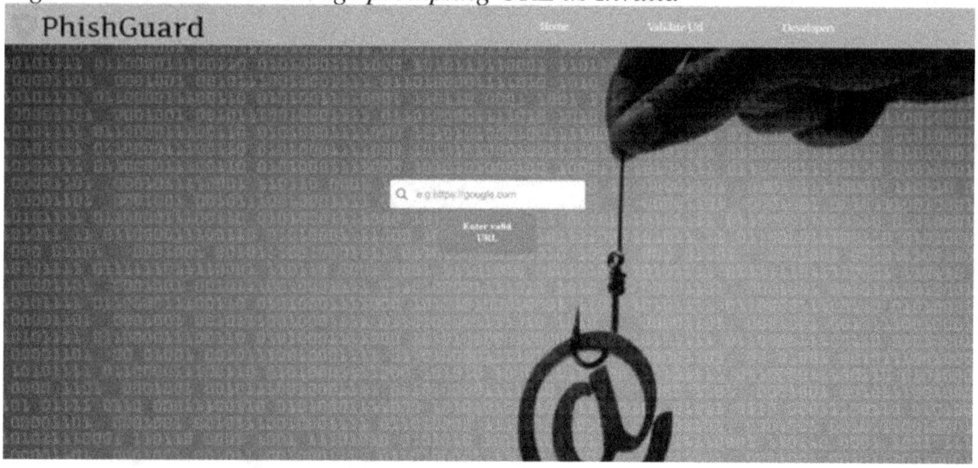

CONCLUSION

In this paper, we presented an advanced phishing detection system leveraging machine learning algorithms, including Logistic Regression, Random Forest, and Gradient Boosting. Our comprehensive evaluation demonstrated that these models significantly outperformed traditional heuristic-based and blacklist approaches in terms of accuracy, precision, recall, and overall robustness.

Key findings from our research include:

- **High Detection Accuracy:** The Gradient Boosting model achieved the highest accuracy of 96.3%, demonstrating its effectiveness in identifying phishing URLs.
- **Reduced False Positives and Negatives:** Our models significantly reduced the rates of false positives and false negatives, enhancing the reliability of phishing detection.
- **Feature Importance:** Critical features such as domain age, URL length, and special character presence played a vital role in accurately classifying URLs.
- **Robustness and Adaptability:** The models proved robust across various phishing techniques, highlighting their potential for real-world applications.

The deployment of our phishing detection system in a real-time environment received positive feedback from users, affirming its practicality and effectiveness in enhancing cybersecurity.

Future Work

While our research has yielded promising results, there are several areas for future work to further enhance the performance and applicability of our phishing detection system:

- **Advanced Phishing Techniques:** Future work will focus on improving the system's ability to detect more sophisticated phishing attacks that closely mimic legitimate sites, potentially incorporating deep learning techniques for better feature extraction and classification.
- **Real-time Adaptability:** Integrating continuous learning mechanisms to ensure the system adapts to new and evolving phishing strategies in real time, maintaining its high detection accuracy.
- **Comprehensive Dataset Expansion:** Expanding the dataset to include a more diverse range of phishing and legitimate URLs from various sources, improving the generalizability and robustness of the models.
- **User Interaction and Feedback:** Enhancing the system's user interface to provide more intuitive alerts and actionable insights, while leveraging user feedback to refine and improve detection algorithms.
- **Cross-platform Integration:** Exploring the integration of the phishing detection system across multiple platforms, including web browsers, email clients, and mobile applications, to provide comprehensive protection for users.
- **Collaborative Efforts:** Collaborating with industry partners and cybersecurity communities to share knowledge, datasets, and best practices, fostering a collective effort to combat phishing attacks.

In conclusion, our research presents a significant advancement in phishing detection through machine learning. The results demonstrate the potential of our approach to enhance cybersecurity measures and protect users from malicious phishing attacks. Ongoing research and development will focus on addressing current limitations and expanding the system's capabilities, ultimately contributing to a safer and more secure digital environment.

REFERENCES

.Abu-Nimeh, S., Nappa, D., Wang, X., & Nair, S. (n.d.). *A Comparison of Machine Learning Techniques for Phishing Detection.*

Jain, A. K., & Gupta, B. B. (2018). PHISH-SAFE: URL features-based phishing detection system using machine learning. *Advances in Intelligent Systems and Computing*, 729, 467–474. DOI: 10.1007/978-981-10-8536-9_44

Jain, A. K., & Gupta, B. B. (2019). A machine learning based approach for phishing detection using hyperlinks information. *Journal of Ambient Intelligence and Humanized Computing*, 10(5), 2015–2028. DOI: 10.1007/s12652-018-0798-z

.Kiruthiga, R., & Akila, D. (2019). Phishing websites detection using machine learning. *International Journal of Recent Technology and Engineering, 8*(2 Special Issue 11), 111–114. DOI: 10.35940/ijrte.B1018.0982S1119

Lee, O. V., Heryanto, A., Razak, M. F. A., Raffei, A. F. M., Phon, D. N. E., Kasim, S., & Sutikno, T. (2020). A malicious URLs detection system using optimization and machine learning classifiers. *Indonesian Journal of Electrical Engineering and Computer Science*, 17(3), 1210–1214. DOI: 10.11591/ijeecs.v17.i3.pp1210-1214

Rashid, J., Mahmood, T., Nisar, M. W., & Nazir, T. (2020). Phishing Detection Using Machine Learning Technique. *Proceedings - 2020 1st International Conference of Smart Systems and Emerging Technologies, SMART-TECH 2020*, 43–46. DOI: 10.1109/SMART-TECH49988.2020.00026

Sahingoz, O. K., Buber, E., Demir, O., & Diri, B. (2019). Machine learning based phishing detection from URLs. *Expert Systems with Applications*, 117, 345–357. DOI: 10.1016/j.eswa.2018.09.029

Shahrivari, V., Darabi, M. M., & Izadi, M. (2020). *Phishing Detection Using Machine Learning Techniques*. http://arxiv.org/abs/2009.11116

Zaini, N. S., Stiawan, D., Razak, M. F. A., Firdaus, A., Din, W. I. S. W., Kasim, S., & Sutikno, T. (2020). Phishing detection system using machine learning classifiers. *Indonesian Journal of Electrical Engineering and Computer Science*, 17(3), 1165–1171. DOI: 10.11591/ijeecs.v17.i3.pp1165-1171

Zheng, X., IEEE ITSS, & Institute of Electrical and Electronics Engineers. (n.d.). *IEEE ISI 2017 :IEEE International Conference on Intelligence and Security Informatics: Security and Big Data :July 22-24, 2017-Beijing, China.*

Chapter 16
Assortment of Social Engineering Attacks in the New Digital Era

Geetha Manoharan
https://orcid.org/0000-0002-8644-8871
SR University, India

Chetan Dudhagara
https://orcid.org/0000-0003-1220-5719
Anand Agricultural University, India

ABSTRACT

Social engineering involves stealing secrets. Assaults seek different information each person. Deception is used to gain passwords, financial data, and viruses. This spyware may steal passwords, financial data, and computer control. Attackers utilize social engineering because victim confidence is easier to influence than program weaknesses. Phishing for a password is easier than cracking it. Fast technical change has increased social engineering assaults, which target psychology rather than technology. Hackers utilize many methods to deceive people into disclosing sensitive information or taking digital security risks. We discuss numerous digital social engineering attacks in this chapter. Discussing phishing, pretexting, baiting, quid pro quo, and whaling. We also explore attackers' psychological manipulation and their massive damage to people and organizations. We emphasize awareness, education, and training to prevent social engineering assaults and protect crucial data in the digital era.

DOI: 10.4018/979-8-3693-6665-3.ch016

INTRODUCTION TO SOCIAL ENGINEERING

Social engineering refers to malicious actions that take place through human connections. It uses psychological manipulation to trick users into disclosing sensitive information or making security mistakes. Social engineering attacks happen in one or more stages. The attacker investigates the target first to gather background information needed to carry out the assault, such as potential avenues of entry and faulty security measures. Subsequently, the attacker attempts to gain the target's confidence by providing triggers for behaviors that breach security standards, such as exposing private data or granting access to critical resources.

Utilizing human weaknesses is the core of social engineering. We are naturally curious, fearful, trustworthy, and want to be of service to others. Psychological manipulation is how attackers trick victims into divulging private information (Singh, D., et al., 2024), allowing unwanted access, or carrying out destructive actions. Observation, thorough study, and the capacity to adopt many personas and circumstances are typically necessary for social engineering to be successful. An individual or group can use social engineering as a tactic to trick and coerce people into revealing private information, carrying out certain tasks, or allowing unwanted access. It frequently uses deceptive and psychologically manipulative methods to take advantage of human psychology and the propensity to trust others. Social engineering plays on people's innate desire to be helpful, inquisitive, or trustworthy, as opposed to traditional hacking techniques, which focus on taking advantage of technological flaws. By using human flaws, social engineering aims to obtain illegal access or obtain private information for malevolent intentions. Users of businesses' protected information systems are the target of more social engineering assaults than ever before, and their ability to withstand these attacks is declining. Machine learning technologies are taken into consideration as a potential solution to this problem, and the requirement of creating tools to safeguard businesses (Manoharan, G., et al., 2024) from social engineering assaults is documented. Here are the findings from the creation of a software program called a resilience scanner, which assesses an organization's workforce to see how resilient they are against social engineering assaults. As demonstrated by Astakhova, L., & Medvedev, I.A. (2021), it has multiple uses, including identifying user vulnerability, involving users more in the process of identifying social engineering attacks and fostering an information security culture within an organization. It also has potential for future development.

Figure 1. Stages of Social Engineering Attacks

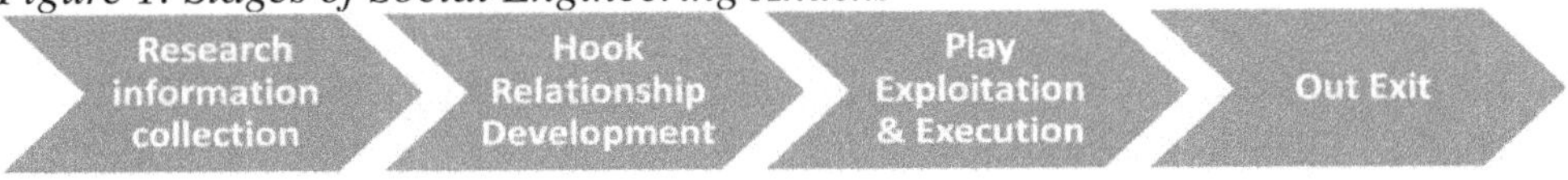

Source: Author compilation

People's communication is becoming easier and more rapid as digital communication technologies advance (Dattatreyulu, C., et al., 2024). However, if social networks and other internet services fail to take the appropriate security safeguards, private and sensitive information may become publicly available. Criminals can easily hack communication networks via social engineering attacks because of their susceptibility. The goal of these assaults is to trick people or organizations into doing tasks that benefit the attackers or give over sensitive information such as passwords, health data, and social security numbers. One of the most serious risks to network security is social engineering, which exploits people's natural urge to trust.

The social engineering assault types, classifications, detection techniques, and preventative measures are all covered in detail in this study. In 2019, Kaabouch, N., and Salahdine, F.

Social engineering is a hacking technique that uses people's psychological vulnerabilities to steal private or sensitive information. T. Nakajima & Y. Kano (2021). This paper investigates the trust factors of social engineering assaults on SNSs using an experiment involving 35 participants and a fake social networking service application. According to the findings, trust is only influenced when a negative response to the post is displayed; other factors, such as the attacker's profile data and the post's content, have no effect.

Multi-university engagement is facilitated through safe collaboration on difficult projects. Various empirical and analytical methodologies need to be employed in the testing and evaluation of safe collaboration tools as educational initiatives geared toward network deployment are developed. In this study, the interaction model of participants in networking educational initiatives is understood to examine the possibilities of forecasting social-engineering assaults on information resources. When selecting an attack plan, it uses an ambiguous attack readiness indicator to display outcomes based on managing roles and activities inside a project. Several tests conducted inside the current networking infrastructure are shown. In terms of educational settings and the creation of safeguards for information resources in networking initiatives, the outcomes are encouraging. In 2021, Parotkin, N.Y., Zolotarev, V.V., Arkhipova, A., and Lvova, A.S.

Literature Support for Social Engineering

Information systems are still vulnerable to potentially disastrous Social Engineering (SE) attacks, according to Al-khateeb, M., Al-Mousa, M.R., Al-Sherideh, A.S., Almajali, D.A., Asassfeha, M., & Khafajeh, H. (2023). As the number of SE events has rapidly expanded and become more aggressive than previously, security information systems are becoming more and more important. Information sharing and exchange have contributed to the evolution of the World Wide Web (WWW). In a quick, efficient, and transparent manner, it makes information sharing possible. Cybercriminals make use of existing lawful users' sensitive information to commit fraud or deception for financial gain. This is known as identity theft or identity misuse. Phishing is the practice of planting harmful URLs behind ones that appear legitimate. The number of malicious websites and the sophistication of their attacks increase with the growth in the number of online pages. In this research, we provide a crawling and classification strategy that supports the automated detection of dangerous links and allows the identification of malicious websites. Even if the page requires partial page refreshes and authentication credentials, the provided solution will allow the crawling session to be completed successfully. Based on three unique applications, the recommended solution outperforms an existing approach with an overall accuracy of 72%. Furthermore, the proposed technology differentiates between risky and lawful links more efficiently by assessing the value and influence of each link on the page. The proposed technique will also include a set of guidelines that can help end users and website administrators learn how to correctly manage these types of SE attacks.

As per the research conducted by Falade, P.V. (2023), the emergence of generative AI models such as FraudGPT, WormGPT, and ChatGPT has presented novel difficulties as well as inventive solutions in the always-changing field of cybersecurity. In addition to providing insights into the changing threat landscape through the use of blog mining techniques, this research explores the many uses of generative AI in social engineering assaults. Hackers now can create individualized and convincing phishing lures, use deepfakes to sway public opinion, and take advantage of cognitive biases in humans. Generative AI models have completely changed the landscape of cyberattacks. ChatGPT, FraudGPT, and WormGPT are three models that have introduced new risks and intensified already-existing problems. We investigate how the armory of hackers is augmented by generative AI, from phishing tactics that imitate reputable firms to deepfake technologies that resemble prominent personalities. Furthermore, they clarified the weaknesses—psychological manipulation, targeted phishing, and the crisis of authenticity—that AI-driven social engineering takes advantage of. We discuss several techniques to tackle these risks, such as collaborative approaches in cybersecurity, AI-powered security solutions, and traditional security measures. They highlight how crucial it is to maintain vigilance, raise awareness, and fortify rules in the fight against social engineering assaults boosted by artificial intelligence. To counteract the growing threat of generative AI, individuals, businesses, and governments must constantly adapt and work together in an environment where AI models are evolving quickly and there is a shortage of training data. The objective of this study is to furnish stakeholders with the necessary information to maneuver through the complex cybersecurity terrain by offering a thorough comprehension of the dynamic interaction between generative AI and social engineering efforts.

According to Yang, Z., Allen, J., Landen, M., Perdisci, R., & Lee, W. (2023), people are the weakest link in cybersecurity and have thus become the primary target of attackers using advanced web-based social engineering tactics. These hackers insert social engineering elements into webpages using low-tier ad networks in an attempt to get visitors to their websites so they may be exploited further. Web-based social engineering attacks, or WSEAs, account for the majority of these exploitations; examples include lottery and incentive schemes. Researchers have developed methods and instruments to identify some WSEAs, however, they are very specialized in terms of certain scam tactics (such as survey and tech support scams). Against a wide range of assault methods, they were not intended to be successful. To effectively identify generic WSEAs, new and more efficient in-browser technologies are desperately needed, given the ever-increasing range and sophistication of WSEAs that every user may encounter. We provide T RIDENT, a cutting-edge defensive system designed to instantly identify and thwart generic WSEAs, to meet this demand. T RIDENT inhibits WSEAs by identifying Social Engineering Ads (SE-ads), which serve as the gateway for widespread online social engineering assaults that are widely disseminated by low-quality ad networks. According to our thorough analysis, T RIDENT is resistant to evasion efforts and has an accuracy of 92.63% for detecting SE-ads, with a false positive rate of 2.57%. Modern ad-blocking techniques were also used to compare T RIDENT's effectiveness. T RIDENT performs 10% more accurately than these instruments, according to the findings. Moreover, the median runtime overhead of T RIDENT is just 2.13%, which is negligible enough for production deployment.

In the real world as much as in online, social engineering assaults are a phenomenon. A. Atyabi, S. Xu, and R.M. Rodriguez (2022). Compared to their internet equivalent, these attacks in the real world have been researched for a lot longer. This drives our research on the similarities and differences between social engineering assaults in the real world and cyberspace. To this aim, we present a methodology to integrate social engineering attacks and defenses in cyberspace and the real world into a single framework. This methodology consists of three main parts: (i) a systematization of defenses against social engineering attacks; (ii) a systematization of attacks themselves; and (iii) a systematic model based on psychological principles for describing these attacks. To effectively fight against social engineering attacks in cyberspace, future research areas will be clarified by the insights gained from our study.

People are being persuaded to provide attackers with critical personal or financial information more frequently as a result of the rise in social engineering scams. More often than phishing emails, telephone schemes are less thoroughly researched. According to our research, a collection of speech actions that are used in social engineering scams can be used to identify the attack. A speech act is any declaration or action made by a person that carries out an activity in addition to communicating information. Scams may be classified based on common speech actions, even when attackers modify their way of speaking and terminology to suit the victim over the phone. A collection of spoken behaviors known as a scam signature is used to distinguish each sort of fraud. We provide a technique to social engineering detection, the Anti-Social Engineering Tool ASsET, that identifies assaults by analyzing the conversation's semantic content. To detect if a scam signature's meaning is present in a discussion, our method leverages word embedding methods from natural language processing. A dataset of telephone scams, authored by volunteers based on authentic scam samples from authoritative websites, has been assembled to assess our methodology. To their knowledge, this dataset is the first of its kind for telephone-based scams. High accuracy was achieved in differentiating between scam and non-scam calls using their detection approach. I.G. Harris, M. Behzadi, and A. Derakhshan (2021).

Reasons for Social Engineering Attacks

This study's main goal is to assess how susceptible an organization's information technology infrastructure is to cyber intrusions. This includes networks that are used for enterprise applications, intranets, transmission media, hardware and software systems, local area networks, wide area networks, and corporate networks (Ananthan, M., et al., 2024). This goal is met by explaining throughout the chapter the significance of social engineering in network intrusions and cyber theft, as well as the causes of the swift growth in cybercrime. The chapter also covers the definition and full explanation of social engineering, its function in cyber identity theft and network intrusion, the causes of the surge in cybercrimes, and the effects these crimes have on businesses. To sum up, the writers provide a few precautionary tips and potential fixes for the risks and weaknesses associated with social engineering. While technology can help lessen the effect of social engineering assaults, human behavior, human emotions, and psychological predispositions remain the main source of vulnerability, according to the chapter's conclusion. In 2021, Schmick, P.J., and Conteh, N.Y.

For information security professionals, risk assessment is a complicated decision-making process. In 2019, Ahmed, S.A., and Khidzir, N.Z. One of the key factors that directly influence individual judgments about risk assessment is the abundance of confusing software domain models and the absence of accompanying ambiguity. Attacks utilizing artificial intelligence technologies for social engineering may occur at all domain levels. However, the risk analysis carried out on the security specifications for artificial intelligence threats made social engineering impossible. Therefore, in the context of information security, the term "social engineering" simply means "the psychological mentality that exploits people to divulge secret information."

A confident approach to gathering data, deception, or gaining entry to the system differs from a conventional "con" in that it frequently involves intricate fraudulent methods. To address the severe impacts of information security, we have thus suggested a theoretical framework in this research that not only shows promise for risk assessment but also can be sensitive and effective in assessing a crucial and unpredictable operational environment. Due to the proliferation of social media apps and mobile technologies, there has been a rise in harmful scams and social engineering (SE) assaults that compromise personal data and result in financial losses. Being aware of the propagation patterns of SE attacks might help you prevent them. AI has shown to be effective at identifying SE assaults; however, it is still unclear whether or not users with varying degrees of SE awareness would find this detection method to be acceptable. The present study involved two investigations: a preliminary study that gathered qualitative data from 20 victims of social engineering attacks to guide the creation of an artificial intelligence (AI) tool for identifying fraudulent messages; and a second study that involved user testing with 48 participants from various professions to ascertain the acceptability of the detection tool. The victims' acts generally revealed six main themes: "experiences: reasons for falling for attacks; attack methods; advice on preventing attacks; detection methods; attack context and victims." Regardless of a user's employment, the user testing research shown that everyone approved the AI-based application. A user's level of SE awareness may be determined by looking at the types of occupation. Since social media platforms are public spaces where information is shared, information security knowledge should not be restricted to corporate levels. Yang (2021) and Banire, B. and Al Thani, D.

The metaverse—a virtual world where users communicate with one another through avatars—has garnered more interest recently as a result of the COVID-19 epidemic and the development of the fifth-generation (5G) mobile network. Nevertheless, like to conventional cyberspace, the metaverse, an online three-dimensional virtual environment, is also susceptible to a range of unforeseen security risks. Furthermore, the metaverse environment has allowed for further growth of several conventional cyberspace threat forms and techniques. That means that depending on the metaverse's features, social engineering assaults can be more useful. We clarify in this work that social engineering assaults in the metaverse are caused by the user's avatar usage demands, psychological needs, and immersion needs. Next, to explain how social engineering assaults function in the metaverse, we provide a conceptual model. The last section presents the outcomes of three metaverse application scenarios using social engineering assaults. By bringing this research to the attention of metaverse environment designers and users, we intend to significantly lower the success rate of social engineering assaults in the metaverse. Deng (2023), Zhai (2023) & Yang (2023) Deng, M. Utilizing human psychology to obtain access to confidential information is known as social engineering in the context of information security. Both strengths and weaknesses may be found in human emotion. Human emotions that have nothing to do with the subject matter are made to seem relevant by social engineering in today's technologically advanced environment. By taking advantage of psychological weaknesses, social engineering uses "traps" to prey on human emotion and its susceptibility. Social engineering is a topic that cannot be ignored in this context because many information security breaches use social engineering tactics. An outline of social engineering assaults and recommended defenses is provided in this research study. About the present trends and associated vulnerabilities, an overview of social engineering assaults is provided. Also provided are the primary causes of the current social engineering attack epidemic. At the conclusion, defense strategies are suggested and attack frameworks are displayed. (2018) Kaushalya, S.A., Liyanage, A., and Randeniya, R.

One major issue is social engineering, which uses both technological and non-technical tricks to obtain information from individuals who are not watching. In the form of email phishing attempts, this article evaluates user awareness of such techniques. In our experiment, participants were instructed to categorize 20 emails—20 real and 20 fraudulent—and provide justification for their choices using an online survey. Findings from this evaluation indicate that 36% of the 179 participants were able to recognize authentic emails, while 45% were able to recognize fraudulent ones. Furthermore, the individuals who accurately recognized fraudulent emails frequently were unable to offer strong justifications for their decisions. Furnell (2006), Papadaki (2006), and Karakasiliotis (2006).

Types of Social Engineering Attacks

When a cybersecurity assault uses psychological manipulation of people's behavior to reveal private information, exchange login credentials, provide access to a personal device, or jeopardize their online security, it's known as a social engineering attack.

Due to their tendency to start small and rely on human mistakes to progress, social engineering attacks are a danger to cybersecurity. Adversaries can often get personal data or the goal itself by evoking empathy, anxiety, and a sense of urgency in the victim. Additionally, this can provide attackers access to enterprise-level assaults if the device is linked to a business (Satpathy, A., et al., 2024) network or has login credentials for corporate accounts. Businesses need to keep ahead of the curve since cybercriminals are always coming up with new, deceptive ways to fool consumers and staff. Ten prevalent forms of social engineering assaults will be examined in this post:

- Phishing
- Whaling
- Baiting
- Diversion Theft
- Business Email Compromise (BEC)
- Smishing
- Quid Pro Quo
- Pretexting
- Honeytrap
- Tailgating/Piggybacking

1. Phishing

Phishing is a kind of cybercrime in which victims—using email, phone, SMS, social media, or other personal communication channels—are duped into clicking on dangerous links, downloading infected files, or revealing personal information such as account numbers or passwords. Usually making ludicrous claims, like a member of the royal family requesting someone's banking information, current phishing scams are far more sophisticated than the well-known ones. Cybercriminals often pass for businesses, service providers, or government agencies to get innocent personal data such as email addresses, phone numbers, the user's date of birth, or family member names.

The frequency of phishing attempts is increasing annually, making it one of the most prevalent forms of cyberattacks. COVID-19–Cyberattacks of all types, including phishing attacks, have grown drastically in 19 years. A phishing effort may be successful because individuals during the lockdown period were more likely to spend time online and feel more emotional. With instances nearly tripling from 2019 to 2020, phishing emerged as the most common type of cybercrime, according to the FBI.

2. Whaling

An example of a phishing assault is a whaling attack, which also uses private correspondence to access a target's device or personal data. It is the degree of customization that separates whaling from phishing. A high-level executive is usually the focus of whaling operations, whereas phishing attempts are impersonal and may be duplicated for millions of individuals. For this kind of assault, a great deal of information about that person is needed, typically through an examination of their public conduct and social media posts. More advanced outreach and a better chance of success come from this in-depth study.

Whaling assaults are more likely to yield large rewards since the targets have access to valuable data or the funds required to further a ransomware campaign, even though they initially need more planning and assistance.

3. Baiting

Con artists fool people into revealing personal information or letting malware be placed on their computers by making false promises, therefore engaging in a type of social engineering attack called "baiting". Enticing adverts or online promos like free music streaming, phone upgrades, game or movie downloads, or other material might be baiting techniques. The attacker hopes that the password the target uses to accept the offer is one they have already used on other websites so they may access the victim's data or sell it to other criminals on the dark web. Physical baiting—most usually transmitted from a flash drive tainted with malware—can also be considered as baiting. The assailant would leave the hacked flash drive somewhere where the victim would most likely find it. The victim would then be asked to insert the flash drive into the computer to ascertain who owned it. Malware installs itself automatically in between.

4. Diversion theft

Cyberattacks with offline origins are known as diversion theft. This assault involves a burglar convincing a courier to deliver a product to the wrong person, pick it up or drop it off at the wrong place, or take it somewhere else. Subsequently, internet schemes have been developed to exploit distraction stealing (Singh, A., et al., 2024). By deceiving the user into transmitting sensitive information to the incorrect person, the malevolent actor takes possession of confidential information. Spoofing is one of the tactics hackers employ to pass for reputable or well-known sources, and it's frequently utilized in this kind of assault. There are several ways to fake an internet or phone, including using phony emails, IP addresses, DNS names, GPS coordinates, websites, and phone numbers.

5. Business email compromise (BEC)

A business email compromise (BEC) is a social engineering method whereby the assailant takes on the persona of a trustworthy executive authorized to handle internal corporate financial problems. Here the fraudster closely monitors the executive's behavior and uses spoofing to create a fake email address. Attaching an email pretending to be someone else, the assailant asks their colleagues to handle financial tasks such as wire transfers, banking information updates, and other responsibilities.

BEC can cause businesses to suffer significant financial losses. These assaults are distinct from previous cyber scams in that they don't rely on bad URLs or software that cybersecurity solutions like firewalls or endpoint detection and response (EDR) systems can identify. BEC assaults, on the other hand, are only carried out through human behavior, which is sometimes more difficult to oversee and control, particularly in large enterprises.

6. Smishing / SMS-phishing

Smishing, also known as SMS-phishing, is a type of social engineering assault that is carried out only through SMS texts. In this assault, con artists try to trick the user into clicking on a link that takes them to a hostile website. The victim is then asked to download dangerous software and material after accessing the website. As more individuals spend time on mobile devices, scammers are using smishing attacks more frequently. Although consumers are now more adept at spotting email phishing, many are much less aware of the dangers of text messaging.

Threat actors often just need to buy a phony phone number and put up the malicious URL to launch a smishing attack.

7. Quid pro quo

A form of social engineering attack called "smishing," often referred to as "SMS-phishing," is limited to using SMS texts. In an attempt to deceive the user into visiting a malicious website, con artists utilize this attack method. After entering the website, the victim is then prompted to download risky software and content. The use of smishing attacks by con artists is increasing as more people spend time on mobile devices. Though many customers are significantly less aware of the risks associated with text messaging, they are becoming increasingly skilled at identifying email phishing attempts. Attackers can initiate a smishing attack by simply purchasing a fake phone number and putting up the malicious URL.

8. Pretexting

Social engineering techniques such as pretexting entail creating believable narratives, or pretexts, that are likely to persuade targets to divulge sensitive information. Pretexters may pose as tax officials, police enforcement officers, or other individuals in positions of power. They may also pose as someone of interest, such as talent agency scouts or sweepstakes organizers. Once the background had been explained, the attacker would interrogate the victim to get important and private information that they might use to access their accounts or develop further attack scenarios.

9. Honeytrap

A honeytrap assault is a kind of social engineering wherein people who are using social media or online dating services to find love are the intended target. By fabricating a character and building a phony internet profile, the criminal establishes a friendship with the victim. Eventually, the criminal uses their friendship as leverage to coerce the victim into paying them money, obtaining personal data, or downloading malicious software.

10. Tailgating/Piggybacking

Called piggybacking or tailgating, this physical breach happens when an assailant begs someone approaching a facility ahead of them to keep the door open or grant access. The assailant might pretend to be a delivery driver or adopt another actual identity to increase their chances. The perpetrator could use their time within the facility for surveillance, theft of lost devices, or access to private information. Another type of tailgating is letting a third party install malware on a worker's laptop or other device without permission.

Literature on the Prevention of Social Engineering Attacks

This research investigates women's cybersecurity knowledge and fortitude at Women Online University in Afghanistan, with a particular emphasis on social engineering vulnerability. The introduction, which emphasizes the danger of social engineering attacks that take advantage of human weaknesses, describes the changing environment of cybersecurity. By filling up a knowledge vacuum on the many aspects that affect women's susceptibility in academia, the study offers insightful information for focused interventions and policy. Employing stratified sampling, 170 women from different faculties participated in the study, which has a strong quantitative approach. Perspectives are obtained from participants using self-administered questionnaires containing closed- and open-ended questions. The study carefully identifies the variables and uses accurate tools, such as surveys, to classify them into independent, dependent, and control variables. The findings show varying degrees of cybersecurity knowledge as well as differences in program efficacy. The necessity of customized program design is highlighted by ANOVA testing, which shows substantial differences. A limited impact from publishing personal information on social media is highlighted by regression studies that examine factors impacting the feeling of vulnerability. Additional research is required since the findings reveal significant variations in risk perception among categories. The study's findings, which emphasize customized treatments and take sociocultural quirks into account, offer sophisticated insights on social engineering weaknesses among women enrolled in online programs. Consequences include future study directions, methods, and policies that will help Women Online University in Afghanistan better fend off social engineering attacks.

Increased human engagement and increased vulnerability to cyberattacks are the results of the internet's and social networks' expansion. With the use of technology as a tool to take advantage of human fallibility, social engineering focuses on interpersonal interactions in the virtual world. Although social engineering assaults have been demonstrated to be capable, there aren't many studies that address how chatbots and automation are developing and how trustworthy they are in supporting these types of attacks. A review of professional (Manoharan, G., et al., 2024) social networks' ability to identify and stop automated social engineering attacks against their users is provided in this research. Through the created technique, we were able to discern the features of the trust relationship that resulted from the interaction between the user, the social network, and the ChatBot, as well as the social network's inability to recognize and prohibit this type of activity. A social engineering bot that is automated was created to achieve this.

Ariza, M., Azambuja, A.J., Nobre, J.C., & Granville, L.Z. (2023) The user's trust connection with the ChatBot is enhanced by the study and discussion of the findings, which demonstrate the security risks inherent in professional networks. A method of breaching information security to get access to networks or systems is called social engineering. When victims are unaware of the techniques, frameworks, and models that can stop them, social engineering attacks happen. The theory, assessment, ideas, frameworks, models, user studies, and techniques to stop social engineering assaults are all explained by the present study. Regrettably, there isn't any particular prior study that does an efficient and methodical analysis of social engineering assault prevention. Health campaigns, user-centric frameworks, human-as-security sensor frameworks, and user vulnerability models are some of the current measures, models, and frameworks used to avoid social engineering attacks. A secure system's policing act as super-recognizers in cybersecurity is likely needed to guide the development of the human as a security sensor framework. This article reviews previous research on the frameworks, models, and preventive techniques for social engineering assaults critically and thoroughly. Following the guidelines provided by Bryman & Bell, we carried out a methodical examination of the literature. We learned from the review how to regulate information sharing on a social network, how to prevent social engineering assaults like health campaigns, and how vulnerable social engineering victims are. To offer recommendations on how to stop social engineering assaults, we have presented this thorough overview of the research. Sulaiman, R., Ibrahim, M.A., Shukur, Z., Mokhtar, U.A., and Syafitri, W. (2022).

Recent years have seen a rise in social engineering assaults that employ phishing emails as the medium and target certain categories of individuals, according to study by He, D., Lv, X., Xu, X., Yu, S., Li, D., Chan, S., & Guizani, M. (2022). Social engineering assaults can compromise corporate systems that are in place now. Furthermore, the effectiveness of the current detection techniques is somewhat low. Consequently, we put out a deep learning-based, double-layer detection system. To begin with, a model for detecting phishing emails is created from an individual security standpoint using Long Short-Term Memory (LSTM) and an extreme gradient boosting tree (XGBoost). Group security is therefore taken into consideration while designing an insider threat detection model that uses a Bidirectional LSTM and an attention mechanism. The social engineering attack and defensive simulation platform is finally built and integrated with the social engineering network attack simulation theory. Utilizing Bi-LSTM in the double-layer framework, they extract user sequence information and long-range dependent email body characteristics. Next, to enhance the classification accuracy and reinforce the network structure even more (Manoharan, G., Durai, S., et al., 2023), XGBoost and the attention method are applied. When comparing our model to other approaches, it can reliably identify insider threats and phishing emails without the need for human feature extraction... Lastly, we validate the two-layer model's efficacy using our suggested social engineering simulation platform. As demonstrated by the experimental findings, our suggested framework can successfully identify insider threats and phishing assaults on business systems by having the features of timely detection and after-the-fact analysis.

Matyokurehwa, K., Rudhumbu, N., Gombiro, C., & Chipfumbu-Kangara, C.T. (2022) set out to create and verify a more robust framework for social engineering defense against such attacks. Based on the advantages and disadvantages of previous social engineering frameworks, as well as Dhillon's balanced control theory, the study developed a theoretical framework. By use of the three-round Delphi procedure, experts confirmed the theoretical framework. The inclusion criteria were satisfied by a sample of twenty-five specialists from three higher education institutions. To fully comprehend the phenomena being studied, the interpretivism philosophy served as the study's compass. The results show that an organization's security strategy, social engineering knowledge, and Internet of Things (IOT) (Thavamani, S., et al., 2023) security all help to lessen social engineering threats. Higher education decision-makers will use the study's results to develop interesting social engineering training initiatives, establish organizational security guidelines, and thwart IOT intrusions to lessen social engineering attacks in higher education. An improved social engineering framework that protects against social engineering assaults is one of the study's contributions to the field of social engineering. In tertiary education, the research contributes to the conceptual framework of social engineering.

Recommended Best Practices to Prevent Social Engineering

There is still a human element of vulnerability despite all technological protections. When properly used, the following solutions can aid in reducing the impact of the social engineering assault methods that are illustrated in the materials above. Make sure your security policy is well-thought-out and takes user and technology-level processes into account.

To protect users against social engineering attempts and to respond to them, the IT support staff will:

- During and after recruiting, users should get instruction and training on cyber security attributes and vulnerabilities.
- Installing technical safeguards to stop users from doing activities that leave them vulnerable to social engineering scams.
- Implementing robust network security measures, such as a whitelist of all accessible domains and a blacklist of dubious websites.
- Protecting data on a variety of levels, in both virtual and real spaces, and for organizations or individuals.
- Perform routine assessments of the organization's cyber security and update data and software. Most of the system's vulnerabilities that hackers could have discovered will be sealed by this phase.

Figure 2. Recommended best practices to avert social engineering attacks

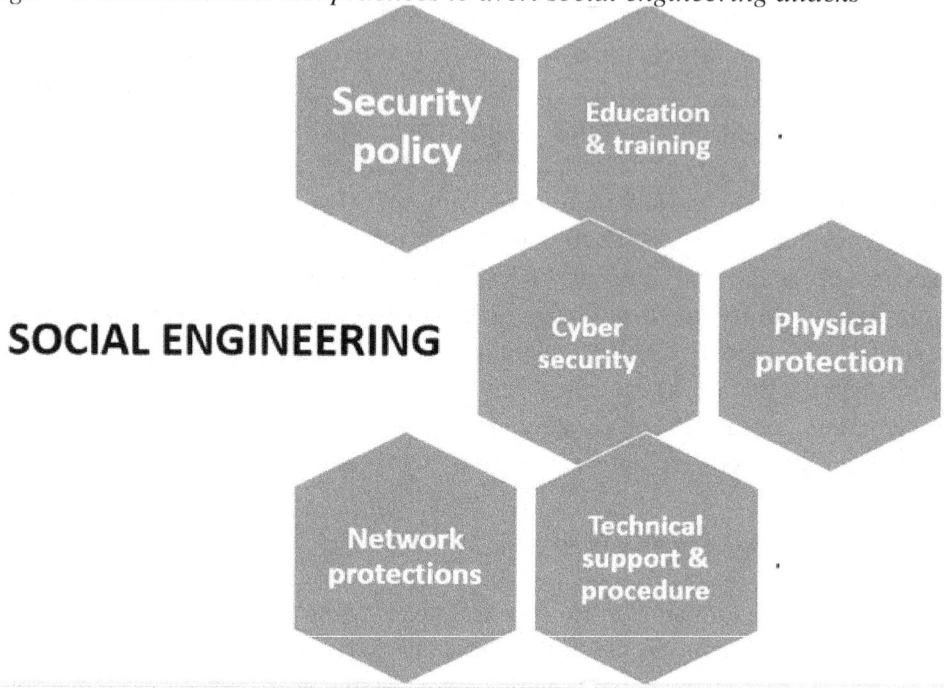

Source: Author compilation

An essential component of the software supply chain is open-source software, or OSS. To compromise dependent software, attackers have been able to become code contributors in recent social engineering assaults against open-source software development teams. From there, they can introduce harmful code or vulnerabilities into the project. To carry out their assaults, the attackers have taken advantage of the social dynamics inside the development team as well as interactions between team members. We provide a security methodology that predicts a software development team's vulnerability to social engineering assaults that allow access to the source code of the open-source software (OSS) project by utilizing team dynamics signs and patterns. According to Giovanini, L.H., Oliveira, D.S., Sánchez, H.A., & Shands, D. (2021), the suggested technique evaluates the artifacts of OSS team interactions rather than OSS code, making it platform-, programming language-, and vulnerability-agnostic.

Most people agree that one of the most important components of successful cyberattacks, particularly in contexts targeted at small and medium-sized enterprises (SMEs), is chat-based social engineering, or CSE. Few research has taken into account the particulars of the language that the attackers employ, despite the need to stop CSE assaults. By putting forth a method for creating and annotating a specific-purpose corpus and demonstrating its use in the CSE domain, this study advances the field of early-stage automated CSE attack identification. Next, a bi-directional long short-term memory (bi-LSTM) neural network is trained with the CSE corpus to assess its performance in named entity recognition (NER). The study's findings highlight how crucial it is to include a wealth of metadata in a dataset to provide essential in-context elements and create a corpus that deepens our knowledge of social engineers' strategies. According to Tsinganos, N., & Mavridis, I. (2021), the results may be used to specific cyber-defense systems used to safeguard SME personnel utilizing Electronic Medium Communication (EMC) software.

Protection from Social Engineering Attacks

A common tactic used in social engineering assaults is basic human mistakes. Thus, make sure you constantly heed the most recent advice on preventing fraud and are informed about new online dangers. Then, adhere to the following advice to protect your family and yourself against social engineering scams:

- Lessen the traces you leave online. Hackers will have a tougher time targeting you if you disclose less information on social media and the internet. Don't share private information online. Things that can be used against you include things like your child's school name or real-time vacation photos.
- Set up your antivirus program. Malware, spyware, and ransomware are more prevalent than ever in today's world. Avoid allowing these dangerous apps to ruin your privacy. Use an antivirus program such as Aura to safeguard your gadgets.
- Examine your bank statements and credit reports regularly. Almost always, con artists target your bank accounts. Look out for clues that point to identity theft, such as unfamiliar accounts or odd transactions on your bank statement. Aura, an identity theft protection service, can keep an eye on your credit and bank accounts and notify you of any suspicious activity.
- When you browse and purchase online, use a VPN. With Aura's VPN, your location is untraceable and your data is jumbled.
- Use two-factor or multi-factor authentication (2FA/MFA) at all times. Every one of your accounts has a second layer of protection in place. Thus, even if a hacker manages to mislead you into giving your password, they will still require a unique code that you are the only one with to access your accounts. Use an authenticator app rather than 2FA over SMS for the highest level of security.
- Keep an eye out for any exposed data on the Dark Web. Your personal information is frequently sold by hackers on the Dark Web.

Protecting our Business From Social Engineering Attacks

Personal information is not the only thing targeted by social engineering attempts. Usually, their goal is to steal confidential information and data from your company or workplace.

- To safeguard your group and business from social engineering scams, consider these last few pointers:
- Establish a culture that values security. Just 3% of victims notify management (Joyce, P. R., et al., 2024) about fraudulent emails. The system has frequently already been seriously shaken by the time they arrive. It is recommended that victims disclose such cybersecurity attacks without worrying about the consequences. Before things worsen, you want to take care of things as quickly as possible.
- Assure continued training on security awareness. Most vulnerable to social engineering assaults, according to more than 60% of IT workers, are recent recruits. Hence, at onboarding, security awareness training is required.
- Test your team regularly. Investigate third-party services that model social engineering assaults. Plan many intrusion tests to determine whether staff members accept the offer. Our goal is not to make team members feel uncomfortable but rather to demonstrate to them how simple it is to fall prey to someone.
- Continually upgrade your gear, software, and website. Malware may be introduced into a webpage by hackers who identify a hole or vulnerability. In an attack known as a "watering hole," this will then quickly infect every user. Ensure that your email spam filters, firewalls, and anti-malware software are up to date.
- Establish data surveillance. Sensitive file tracking ought to be part of your business's data analytics. Verify the access, download, and sharing history of these files. Take note of any strange conduct you observe, such as staff members accessing private data after work.

DISCUSSION AND CONCLUSION

As a social engineering technique, attackers have utilized phishing to get sensitive user data. Whether it occurs offline or online, phishing undermines user security, cybersecurity, and computer security. While phishing assaults on technical devices have been addressed by a number of proposed remedies, user-level action has been lacking. Remaining difficult is user-level involvement. In order to give users better understanding and enable them to quickly identify phishing scams and other similar actions, adequate instructional models and pertinent tools are needed in today technologically evolved environment. The modern social engineering methods have been thoroughly examined in this article, with a focus on phishing attempts. In our opening remarks, we talked about human hacking as a serious problem when individuals are tricked into giving over their personal information. Our conversation covered the many types of social engineering assaults and provided advice on how to prevent them.

This study delves into the complex world of social engineering in the constantly changing field of cybersecurity. It explains the relevance of social engineering, moves through tactics and procedures, comprehends psychological concepts, looks at actual cases, and suggests mitigation solutions. It is clear from considering the main conclusions that social engineering is a deeply ingrained human phenomena that calls for an adaptable and comprehensive solution rather than merely a technological problem. A sophisticated grasp of human behavior, technical innovation, and ethical concerns are necessary for the dynamic task of social engineering. Understanding the complex nature of social engineering is made easier with the help of the insights gathered from this review. It is evident that we need to be alert, flexible, and cooperative in our endeavors to lessen the hazards associated with social engineering as we negotiate the complex relationship between psychology and technology. In order to protect our digital future (Tripathi, M. A., et al., 2023) from the ubiquitous threat of social engineering, it will be crucial to continue the search of knowledge, build resilient solutions, and collaborate across disciplines.

REFERENCES

Al-khateeb, M., Al-Mousa, M.R., Al-Sherideh, A.S., Almajali, D.A., Asassfeha, M., & Khafajeh, H. (2023). Awareness model for minimizing the effects of social engineering attacks in web applications. *International Journal of Data and Network Science*.

Ananthan, M., Shanmugam, V., Udayanan, M., Selvaraj, F., & Manoharan, G. (2024, June). Corporate social responsibility is used as a marketing strategy during Covid-19 pandemic. In AIP Conference Proceedings (Vol. 2971, No. 1). AIP Publishing. DOI: 10.1063/5.0195948

Ariza, M., Azambuja, A. J., Nobre, J. C., & Granville, L. Z. (2023). Automated Social Engineering Attacks using ChatBots on Professional Social Networks. *Anais do XXVIII Workshop de Gerência e Operação de Redes e Serviços (WGRS 2023).*

Astakhova, L., & Medvedev, I. A. (2021). An Information Tool for Increasing the Resistance of Employees of an Organization to Social Engineering Attacks. *Scientific and Technical Information Processing*, 48(1), 15–20. DOI: 10.3103/S0147688221010020

Banire, B., Al Thani, D., & Yang, Y. (2021). Investigating the Experience of Social Engineering Victims: Exploratory and User Testing Study. *Electronics (Basel)*, 10(21), 2709. DOI: 10.3390/electronics10212709

Conteh, N. Y., & Schmick, P. J. (2021). *Cybersecurity Risks, Vulnerabilities, and Countermeasures to Prevent Social Engineering Attacks*. Ethical Hacking Techniques and Countermeasures for Cybercrime Prevention. DOI: 10.4018/978-1-7998-6504-9.ch002

Dattatreyulu, C., Krishna, C. B., & Geetha, M. (2024, June). Assessment of the effect of covid–19 situation on digital marketing. In AIP Conference Proceedings (Vol. 2971, No. 1). AIP Publishing. DOI: 10.1063/5.0195757

Deng, M., Zhai, H., & Yang, K. (2023). Social engineering in metaverse environment. *2023 IEEE 10th International Conference on Cyber Security and Cloud Computing (CSCloud)/2023 IEEE 9th International Conference on Edge Computing and Scalable Cloud (EdgeCom)*, 150-154.

Derakhshan, A., Harris, I. G., & Behzadi, M. (2021). Detecting Telephone-based Social Engineering Attacks using Scam Signatures. *Proceedings of the 2021 ACM Workshop on Security and Privacy Analytics*. DOI: 10.1145/3445970.3451152

Falade, P.V. (2023). Decoding the Threat Landscape: ChatGPT, FraudGPT, and WormGPT in Social Engineering Attacks. *ArXiv, abs/2310.05595.*

Giovanini, L.H., Oliveira, D.S., Sánchez, H.A., & Shands, D. (2021). Leveraging Team Dynamics to Predict Open-source Software Projects' Susceptibility to Social Engineering Attacks. *ArXiv, abs/2106.16067.*

He, D., Lv, X., Xu, X., Yu, S., Li, D., Chan, S., & Guizani, M. (2022). An Effective Double-Layer Detection System Against Social Engineering Attacks. *IEEE Network*, 36(6), 92–98. DOI: 10.1109/MNET.105.2100425

Joyce, P. R., Selvaraj, F. J., Manoharan, G., Priya, C., Vijayalakshmi, R., Dwivedi, P. K., & Veerakumar, K. (2024). To Study The Role Of Marketing In Human Resource Management. *Migration Letters : An International Journal of Migration Studies*, 21(S2), 1191–1196. DOI: 10.59670/ml.v21iS2.7072

Kano, Y., & Nakajima, T. (2021). Trust Factors of Social Engineering Attacks on Social Networking Services. *2021 IEEE 3rd Global Conference on Life Sciences and Technologies (LifeTech)*, 25-28.

Karakasiliotis, A., Furnell, S., & Papadaki, M. (2006). Assessing end-user awareness of social engineering and phishing.

Kaushalya, S. A., Randeniya, R., & Liyanage, A. (2018). An Overview of Social Engineering in the Context of Information Security. *2018 IEEE 5th International Conference on Engineering Technologies and Applied Sciences (ICETAS)*, 1-6.

Khidzir, N.Z., & Ahmed, S.A. (2019). Viewpoint of Probabilistic Risk Assessment in Artificial Enabled Social Engineering Attacks. *Journal of Contemporary Issues and Thought.*

Manoharan, G., Durai, S., Rajesh, G. A., & Ashtikar, S. P. (2024). A Study on the Application of Expert Systems as a Support System for Business Decisions: A Literature Review. Artificial Intelligence and Knowledge Processing, 279-289.

Manoharan, G., Durai, S., Rajesh, G. A., Razak, A., Rao, C. B., & Ashtikar, S. P. (2023). A study on the perceptions of officials on their duties and responsibilities at various levels of the organizational structure in order to accomplish artificial intelligence-based smart city implementation. In *Artificial Intelligence and Machine Learning in Smart City Planning* (pp. 1–10). Elsevier. DOI: 10.1016/B978-0-323-99503-0.00007-7

Manoharan, G., Razak, A., Rajchandar, K., Nithya, G., Durai, S., & Ashtikar, S. P. (2024). Digital Learning for Professional Development in Varied Fields of Service Sectors: Embracing Technological Advancements. In Embracing Technological Advancements for Lifelong Learning (pp. 111-137). IGI Global.

Matyokurehwa, K., Rudhumbu, N., Gombiro, C., & Chipfumbu-Kangara, C. T. (2022). Enhanced social engineering framework mitigating against social engineering attacks in higher education. *Security and Privacy*, 5(5), 5. DOI: 10.1002/spy2.237

Rodriguez, R.M., Atyabi, A., & Xu, S. (2022). Social Engineering Attacks and Defenses in the Physical World vs. Cyberspace: A Contrast Study. *ArXiv, abs/2203.04813*.

Salahdine, F., & Kaabouch, N. (2019). Social Engineering Attacks: A Survey. *Future Internet*, 11(4), 89. DOI: 10.3390/fi11040089

Satpathy, A., Samal, A., Gupta, S., Kumar, S., Sharma, S., Manoharan, G., Karthikeyan, M., & Sharma, S. (2024). To Study the Sustainable Development Practices in Business and Food Industry. *Migration Letters : An International Journal of Migration Studies*, 21(S1), 743–747. DOI: 10.59670/ml.v21iS1.6400

Singh, A., Virmani, D., Kulkarni, N., Tiwari, M., Manoharan, G., & Alanya-Beltran, J. (2024). The Emerging Role and Application of Adopting Revolutionary Internet of Things (IoT) for Future Technology Sustainability. Computer Science Engineering and Emerging Technologies. *Proceedings of ICCS*, 2022, 103.

Singh, D., Makkar, S., Durai, S., Manoharan, G., Purushottamashtikar, S., & Alexrajesh, G. (2024, June). Human resource information system applications in small and medium enterprises: A study (SMEs). In AIP Conference Proceedings (Vol. 2971, No. 1). AIP Publishing.

Syafitri, W., Shukur, Z., Mokhtar, U. A., Sulaiman, R., & Ibrahim, M. A. (2022). Social Engineering Attacks Prevention: A Systematic Literature Review. *IEEE Access, PP*, 1-1.

Thavamani, S., Mahesh, D., Sinthuja, U., & Manoharan, G. (2022, May). Crucial attacks in internet of things via artificial intelligence techniques: The security survey. In AIP Conference Proceedings (Vol. 2418, No. 1). AIP Publishing.

Tripathi, M. A., Tripathi, R., Effendy, F., Manoharan, G., Paul, M. J., & Aarif, M. (2023, January). An In-Depth Analysis of the Role That ML and Big Data Play in Driving Digital Marketing's Paradigm Shift. In *2023 International Conference on Computer Communication and Informatics (ICCCI)* (pp. 1-6). IEEE. DOI: 10.1109/ICCCI56745.2023.10128357

Tsinganos, N., & Mavridis, I. (2021). Building and Evaluating an Annotated Corpus for Automated Recognition of Chat-Based Social Engineering Attacks. *Applied Sciences (Basel, Switzerland)*, 11(22), 10871. DOI: 10.3390/app112210871

Yang, Z., Allen, J., Landen, M., Perdisci, R., & Lee, W. (2023). TRIDENT: Towards Detecting and Mitigating Web-based Social Engineering Attacks. *USENIX Security Symposium*.

Zolotarev, V.V., Arkhipova, A., Parotkin, N.Y., & Lvova, A.S. (2021). Strategies of Social Engineering Attacks on Information Resources of Gamified Online Education Projects.

Compilation of References

Abadi, M.. (2016). Deep learning with differential privacy. In **Proceedings of the ACM SIGSAC Conference on Computer and Communications Security**.

Abass, I. (2018). Social engineering threat and defense: A literature survey. *Journal of Information Security*, 9(4), 257–264. DOI: 10.4236/jis.2018.94018

Abdullah, A., Xu, Y., & Chan, T. (2017). An empirical study on the susceptibility to social engineering in social networking sites: The case of facebook. *European Journal of Information Systems*, 26(6), 661–687. DOI: 10.1057/s41303-017-0057-y

Abe, N., & Soltys, M. (2019). Deploying health campaign strategies to defend against social engineering threats. *Procedia Computer Science, 159*, 824–831. DOI: 10.1016/j.procs.2019.09.213

Abroshan, H.; Devos, J.; Poels, G.; Laermans, E. (2021), Phishing happens beyond technology: The effects of human behaviors and demographics on each step of a phishing process. IEEE Access 2021, 9, 44928–44949.

Abu Hweidi, R. F., & Eleyan, D. (2023). Social engineering attack concepts, frameworks, and awareness: A systematic literature review. *International Journal of Computing and Digital Systems*, 13(1), 691–700. DOI: 10.12785/ijcds/130155

Adnan Afaq, S., Khalida Izhar, S., & Srivastava, S. (2023). The IOT Farming Revolution: Enhancing efficiency and sustainability in agriculture. *International Journal of Engineering Sciences & Emerging Technologies*, 11(2), 160–170.

Afaq, S. A., Husain, M. S., Bello, A. M., & Sadia, H. (2023). A critical analysis of cyber threats and their global impact. * [CRC Press.]. *Journal of Computational Intelligent Security in Wireless*, 20(1), 201.

Afenu, D. S., Asiri, M., & Saxena, N. (2024). Industrial Control Systems Security Validation Based on MITRE Adversarial Tactics, Techniques, and Common Knowledge Framework. *Electronics (Basel)*, 13(5), 917. DOI: 10.3390/electronics13050917

Agarwal, S., Farid, H., El-Gaaly, T., & Lim, S.-N. (2020). Detecting Deep-Fake Videos from Appearance and Behavior. *2020 IEEE International Workshop on Information Forensics and Security (WIFS)*, 1–6. DOI: 10.1109/WIFS49906.2020.9360904

Agarwal, S., Hu, L., Ng, E., Darrell, T., Li, H., & Rohrbach, A. (2023). Watch those words: Video falsification detection using word-conditioned facial motion. In *Proceedings of the IEEE/CVF Winter Conference on Applications of Computer Vision* (pp. 4710-4719).

Ağca, M. A., Faye, S., & Khadraoui, D. (2022). A survey on trusted distributed artificial intelligence. *IEEE Access : Practical Innovations, Open Solutions*, 10, 55308–55337. DOI: 10.1109/ACCESS.2022.3176385

Aijaz, M., & Nazir, M. (2024). Modelling and analysis of social engineering threats using the attack tree and the Markov model. *International Journal of Information Technology : an Official Journal of Bharati Vidyapeeth's Institute of Computer Applications and Management*, 16(2), 1231–1238. DOI: 10.1007/s41870-023-01540-z

Aina-Pelemo, A., Oke, O. A., & Alade, I. T. (2021, November). Deborah., Oke, Olubukola. Abimbola., & Aladec, Iseoluwa Titilayo. (March 2021). Quid pro quo sexual harassment: Comparative study of its occurrences in selected institutions in South-West, Nigeria. *Current Research in Behavioral Sciences*, 2, 100031. Advance online publication. DOI: 10.1016/j.crbeha.2021.100031

Ajder, H., Patrini, G., Cavalli, F., & Cullen, L. (2019). *The State of Deepfakes: Landscape*. Threats, and Impact.

Al Daajeh, S., Selous, H., Alrabaee, S., Barka, E., Breitinger, F., & Choo, K. K. R. (2022). The role of national cybersecurity strategies on the improvement of cybersecurity education. *Computers & Security*, 119, 102754. DOI: 10.1016/j.cose.2022.102754

Albladi, S. M., & Weir, G. R. S. (2018). User characteristics that influence judgment of social engineering attacks in social networks. *Human-Centric Computing and Information Sciences, 8*(1), 5. DOI: 10.1186/s13673-018-0143-8

Albladi, S. M., & Weir, G. R. S. (2020). Predicting individuals' vulnerability to social engineering in social networks. *Cybersecurity, 3*(1). DOI: 10.1093/cybsec/tyaa011

Albladi, S. M., & Weir, G. R. (2018). User characteristics that influence judgment of social engineering attacks in social networks. *Human-centric Computing and Information Sciences*, 8(1), 1–24. DOI: 10.1186/s13673-018-0128-7

Albladi, S. M., & Weir, G. R. S. (2020, December). Predicting individuals' vulnerability to social engineering in social networks. *Cybersecurity*, 3(1), 1–19. DOI: 10.1186/s42400-020-00047-5

Aldawood, H., & Skinner, G. (2018, December). Educating and raising awareness on cyber security social engineering: A literature review. In 2018 IEEE international conference on teaching, assessment, and learning for engineering (TALE) (pp. 62-68). IEEE.

Aldawood, H., & Skinner, G. (2019, May). Challenges of implementing training and awareness programs targeting cyber security social engineering. In 2019 cybersecurity and cyberforensics conference (ccc) (pp. 111-117). IEEE.

Aldawood, H., Alashoor, T., & Skinner, G. (2020). Does Awareness of Social Engineering Make Employees More Secure? *International Journal of Computer Applications*, 177(38), 45–49. DOI: 10.5120/ijca2020919891

Aldawood, H., & Skinner, G. (2019). Challenges of Implementing Training and Awareness Programs Targeting Cyber Security Social Engineering. *2019 Cybersecurity and Cyberforensics Conference (CCC)*, 111-117. DOI: 10.1109/CCC.2019.00004

Aldawood, H., & Skinner, G. (2020). An Advanced Taxonomy for Social Engineering Attacks. *International Journal of Computer Applications*, 177(30), 975–8887. DOI: 10.5120/ijca2020919744

Aldawood, H., & Skinner, G. (2020). Analysis and Findings of Social Engineering Industry Experts Explorative Interviews: Perspectives on Measures, Tools, and Solutions. *IEEE Access: Practical Innovations, Open Solutions*, 8, 67321–67329. DOI: 10.1109/ACCESS.2020.2983280

Aldawood, H., & Skinner, G. 2019, January. An academic review of current industrial and commercial cyber security social engineering solutions. In *Proceedings of the 3rd International Conference on Cryptography, Security and Privacy* (pp. 110-115). DOI: 10.1145/3309074.3309083

Aldwairi, M., & Alwahedi, A. (2018). Detecting Fake News in Social Media Networks. *Procedia Computer Science*, 141, 215–222. DOI: 10.1016/j.procs.2018.10.171

Alexopoulos, C., Saxena, S., & Saxena, S. (2024). Natural Language Processing (NLP)-Powered Legal A (t) Ms (LAMs) in India: Possibilities and Challenges. *Journal of the Knowledge Economy*, 15(2), 8513–8533. DOI: 10.1007/s13132-023-01450-2

Algarni, A., Xu, Y., & Chan, T. (2017). An empirical study on the susceptibility to social engineering in social networking sites: The case of Facebook. *European Journal of Information Systems, 26*(6), 661–687. https://doi.org/DOI: 10.1080/0960085X.2017.1327237

Algarni, A., Xu, Y., Chan, T., & Tian, Y. C. (2013, December). Social engineering in social networking sites: Affect-based model. In *8th International Conference for Internet Technology and Secured Transactisons (ICITST-2013)* (pp. 508-515). IEEE.

Algarni, A., Xu, Y., Chan, T., & Tian, Y.-C. (2013). Social engineering in social networking sites: Affect-based model. *8th International Conference for Internet Technology and Secured Transactions (ICITST-2013)*, 508–515. DOI: 10.1109/ICITST.2013.6750253

Alharthi, D.N., Hammad, M.M., & Regan, A.C. (2020). A Taxonomy of Social Engineering Defense Mechanisms.

Alkhalil, Z., Hewage, C., Nawaf, L., & Khan, I. (2021, March 9). Hewage, Chaminda., Nawaf, Liqaa., & Khan, Imtiaz. (2021). Phishing Attacks: A Recent Comprehensive Study and a New Anatomy. *Frontiers of Computer Science*, 3, 563060. Advance online publication. DOI: 10.3389/fcomp.2021.563060

Al-khateeb, M., Al-Mousa, M.R., Al-Sherideh, A.S., Almajali, D.A., Asassfeha, M., & Khafajeh, H. (2023). Awareness model for minimizing the effects of social engineering attacks in web applications. *International Journal of Data and Network Science*.

Alkhurayyif, Y., & Almarshdy, Y. S. (2024). Adopting Automated Penetration Testing Tools: A Cost-Effective Approach to Enhancing Cybersecurity in Small Organizations. *Journal of Information Security and Cybercrimes Research*, 7(1), 51–66. DOI: 10.26735/RJJT2453

Al-Musib, N. Al-Serhani, Faeiz., Humayun, Mamoona., & Jhanjhi, Noor. (2021). Business email compromise (BEC) attacks. Materials Today Proceedings DOI: DOI: 10.1016/j.matpr.2021.03.647

Almutairi, B. S., & Alghamdi, A. (2022). The Role of Social Engineering in Cybersecurity and Its Impact. *Journal of Information Security*, 13(4), 363–379. DOI: 10.4236/jis.2022.134020

Alotibi, G. (2024). A Cybersecurity Awareness Model for the Protection of Saudi Students from Social Media Attacks. *Engineering, Technology &. Applied Scientific Research*, 14(2), 13787–13795.

Alzahrani, A. A. (2020). Coronavirus Social Engineering Attacks: Issues and Recommendations. *International Journal of Advanced Computer Science and Applications*, 11(5), 154–161. DOI: 10.14569/IJACSA.2020.0110523

Ananthan, M., Shanmugam, V., Udayanan, M., Selvaraj, F., & Manoharan, G. (2024, June). Corporate social responsibility is used as a marketing strategy during Covid-19 pandemic. In AIP Conference Proceedings (Vol. 2971, No. 1). AIP Publishing. DOI: 10.1063/5.0195948

Andrews, L. J. B., Alagappan, A., Sarathkumar, D., Fathima, M., Venkatachary, S. K., Rajeshkanna, R., & Raj, R. A. (2024, February). Investigations on Cyber Security Vulnerability using Distribution Analysis. In *2024 IEEE International Students'Conference on Electrical, Electronics and Computer Science (SCEECS)* (pp. 1-6). IEEE. DOI: 10.1109/SCEECS61402.2024.10482303

Anti-Phishing Working Group. (2020). *Phishing activity trends report.* APWG.

Anwar, S., Milanova, M., Anwer, M., & Banihirwe, A. (2019). Perceptual Judgments to Detect Computer Generated Forged Faces in Social Media. In Schwenker, F., & Scherer, S. (Eds.), *Multimodal Pattern Recognition of Social Signals in Human-Computer-Interaction* (Vol. 11377, pp. 38–48). Springer International Publishing., DOI: 10.1007/978-3-030-20984-1_4

Apostol, A. C., Cristache, N., & Năstase, M. (2022). Societal Resilience, A Key Factor in Combating Hybrid Threats. International Conference KNOWLEDGE-BASED ORGANIZATION, 28(2), 107–115. https://doi.org/DOI: 10.2478/kboo-2022-0057

Ariza, M., Azambuja, A. J., Nobre, J. C., & Granville, L. Z. (2023). Automated Social Engineering Attacks using ChatBots on Professional Social Networks. *Anais do XXVIII Workshop de Gerência e Operação de Redes e Serviços (WGRS 2023).*

Arya, S. (2021). The most effective approaches to combating cyberbullying in educational institutions. *Asian Journal of Research in Social Sciences and Humanities*, 11(10), 468–473. DOI: 10.5958/2249-7315.2021.00134.9

Asadian, H., & Javadi, H. H. S. (2018). Identification of Sybil attacks on social networks using a framework based on user interactions. *Security and Privacy, 1*(2), e19. DOI: 10.1002/spy2.19

Astakhova, L., & Medvedev, I. A. (2021). An Information Tool for Increasing the Resistance of Employees of an Organization to Social Engineering Attacks. *Scientific and Technical Information Processing*, 48(1), 15–20. DOI: 10.3103/S0147688221010020

Atkeson, C. G., Moore, A. W., & Schaal, S. (1997). Locally weighted learning. *. *Artificial Intelligence Review*, 11(1-5), 11–73. DOI: 10.1023/A:1006559212014

Aun, Y., Gan, M. L., Wahab, N. H. B. A., & Guan, G. H. (2023). Social engineering attack classifications on social media using deep learning. *Computers, Materials & Continua*, 74(3), 4917–4931. DOI: 10.32604/cmc.2023.032373

Awasthi, S., Pratap, A., & Srivastava, R. (2017). Framework for Visual Cryptographic based Encryption and Decryption. *International Journal of Computer Applications*, 163(3), 17–20. DOI: 10.5120/ijca2017913485

Baena-Luna, P., & García-Río, E. (2022). BLOCKCHAIN TECHNOLOGY: PRESENT AND FUTURE APPLICATION CHALLENGES. *Rev. Conhecimento Online*, 2, 258–273. DOI: 10.25112/rco.v2.2859

Banire, B., Al Thani, D., & Yang, Y. (2021). Investigating the Experience of Social Engineering Victims: Exploratory and User Testing Study. *Electronics (Basel)*, 10(21), 2709. DOI: 10.3390/electronics10212709

Bhusal, C.S. (2020). Systematic Review on Social Engineering: Hacking by Manipulating Humans. Journal of Information Security.

Biggio, B., Nelson, B., & Laskov, P. (2012). Poisoning behavioral malware clustering. In **Proceedings of the International Conference on Machine Learning** (pp. 327-334). PMLR.

Black, R., Busby, J., Dalbello, G. D., De Coning, C., Maalim, H., McAllister, C., Ndiloseh, M., Smith, D., Cobar, J. F. A., Barn Hoorn, A., Bell, N., Bell-Moran, D., Broek, E., Eberlein, A., Elaw, K., Faller, J., Gander, A., Hegazi, F., Kim, K., . . . Staudenmann, J. A. (2022). *Environment of Peace: Security in a New Era of Risk.* https://doi.org/DOI: 10.55163/LCLS7037

Bouke, M. A., & Abdullah, A. (2024). Smrd: A novel cyber warfare modeling framework for social engineering, malware, ransomware, and distributed denial-of-service based on a system of nonlinear differential equations. *Journal of Applied Artificial Intelligence*, 5(1), 54–68. DOI: 10.48185/jaai.v5i1.972

Bradshaw, S. (2015a). Combating Cyber Threats: CSIRTs and Fostering International Cooperation on Cybersecurity. SSRN *Electronic Journal*. https://doi.org/DOI: 10.2139/ssrn.2700899

Breda, F., Barbosa, H., & Morais, T. (2017). Social Engineering And Cyber Security. *Proceedings of the International Conference on Technology, Education and Development*, Valencia, 4204-4211, http://dx.doi.org/DOI: 10.21125/inted.2017.1008

Britt, M. A., Rouet, J.-F., Blaum, D., & Millis, K. (2019). A Reasoned Approach to Dealing With Fake News. *Policy Insights from the Behavioral and Brain Sciences*, 6(1), 94–101. DOI: 10.1177/2372732218814855

Brown, C., & White, D. (2020). Machine learning approaches for threat detection. *. *IEEE Transactions on Information Forensics and Security*, 14(3), 789–801.

Bryman, A., & Bell, E. (2011). *Business research methods* (3rd ed.). Oxford University Press.

Buczak, A. L., & Guven, E. (2016). A survey of data mining and machine learning methods for cyber security intrusion detection. *. *IEEE Communications Surveys and Tutorials*, 18(2), 1153–1176. DOI: 10.1109/COMST.2015.2494502

Bu, J., Jiang, R. L., & Zheng, B. (2023). Research on Deepfake Technology and Its Application. *ACM International Conference Proceeding Series*. DOI: 10.1145/3603781.3603790

Bullee, J. W., & Junger, M. (2020). How effective are social engineering interventions? A meta-analysis. *Information & Computer Security, 28*(5), 801–830. https://doi.org/DOI: 10.1108/ICS-01-2020-0010

Bullée, Jan-Willem & Junger, Marianne. (2020). How effective are social engineering interventions? A meta-analysis. Information & Computer Security. ahead-of-print. .DOI: 10.1108/ICS-07-2019-0078

Bullée, J.-W., & Junger, M. (2020). Social Engineering. In Holt, T. J., & Bossler, A. M. (Eds.), *The Palgrave Handbook of International Cybercrime and Cyberdeviance* (pp. 849–875). Springer International Publishing., DOI: 10.1007/978-3-319-78440-3_38

Burda, P., Allodi, L., & Zannone, N. (2024). Cognition in social engineering empirical research: A systematic literature review. *ACM Transactions on Computer-Human Interaction*, 31(2), 1–55. DOI: 10.1145/3635149

Burkell, J., & Gosse, C. (2019). Nothing new here: Emphasizing the social and cultural context of deepfakes. *First Monday*. Advance online publication. DOI: 10.5210/fm.v24i12.10287

Business, C. N. N. (2019). *The fight to stay ahead of deepfake videos before the 2020 US election*. https://edition.cnn.com/2019/06/12/tech/deepfake-2020-detection/index.html

Buttan, D. (2020). Hacking the Human Brain: Impact of Cybercriminals Evoking Emotion for Financial Profit (Doctoral dissertation, Utica College).

Cachon, G., & Fisher, M. (2000). Supply chain inventory management and the value of shared information. *. *Management Science*, 46(8), 1032–1048. DOI: 10.1287/mnsc.46.8.1032.12029

Campbell, C. C. (2019). Solutions for counteracting human deception in social engineering attacks. *Information Technology & People*, 32(5), 1130–1152. DOI: 10.1108/ITP-12-2017-0422

Cao, C., Hou, Q., & Zhou, K. (2014). Displaced dynamic expression regression for real-time facial tracking and animation. *ACM Transactions on Graphics*, 33(4), 1–10. DOI: 10.1145/2601097.2601204

Cao, J., Hu, Y., Yu, B., He, R., & Sun, Z. (2019). 3D aided duet GANs for multi-view face image synthesis. *IEEE Transactions on Information Forensics and Security*, 14(8), 2028–2042. DOI: 10.1109/TIFS.2019.2891116

Chen, H., Li, Y., Lin, D., Li, B., & Wu, J. (2023). Watching the BiG Artifacts: Exposing DeepFake Videos via Bi-Granularity Artifacts. *Pattern Recognition*, 135, 109179. DOI: 10.1016/j.patcog.2022.109179

Chen, L.. (2024). Ensemble learning models for authentication. In **Proceedings of the International Conference on Machine Learning**.

Chetioui, K., Bah, Birom., Alami, Abderrahim. Ouali., & Bahnasse, Ayoub. (2021). Overview of Social Engineering Attacks on Social Networks. The Second International Workshop of Innovation and Technologies, doi: . 302.DOI: 10.1016/j.procs.2021.12

Chetioui, K., Bah, B., Alami, A. O., & Bahnasse, A. (2022). Overview of social engineering attacks on social networks. *Procedia Computer Science*, 198, 656–661. DOI: 10.1016/j.procs.2021.12.302

Chio, C., & Freeman, D. (2018). *Machine learning and security: Protecting systems with data and algorithms*. O'Reilly Media.

Chow, M. (2022, June). *What Are The Positive Applications of Deepfakes?*https://www.jumpstartmag.com/what-are-the-positive-applications-of-deepfakes/

Christopher, N. (2020, February). We've Just Seen the First Use of Deepfakes in an Indian Election Campaign. *We've Just Seen the First Use of Deepfakes in an Indian Election Campaign*. https://www.vice.com/en/article/jgedjb/the-first-use-of-deepfakes-in-indian-election-by-bjp

Christopher, M., & Towill, D. (2001). An integrated model for the design of agile supply chains. *. *International Journal of Physical Distribution & Logistics Management*, 31(4), 235–246. DOI: 10.1108/09600030110394914

Ciekanowski, M., Żurawski, S., Pauliuchuk, Y., Ciekanowski, Z., & Marciniak, S. (2024). Strategies for Effective Cybersecurity Management in Organizations. *European Research Studies*, XXVII(1), 365–379. DOI: 10.35808/ersj/3364

Clayton, R., & Moore, T. (2007). Evaluating how website removals affect phishing. In **Proceedings of the Second APWG eCrime Researchers Summit** (pp. 1-12).

Conteh, N. Y., & Schmick, P. J. (2021). *Cybersecurity Risks, Vulnerabilities, and Countermeasures to Prevent Social Engineering Attacks*. Ethical Hacking Techniques and Countermeasures for Cybercrime Prevention. DOI: 10.4018/978-1-7998-6504-9.ch002

Conti, E., Salvi, D., Borrelli, C., Hosler, B., Bestagini, P., Antonacci, F., . . . Tubaro, S. (2022, May). Deepfake speech detection through emotion recognition: a semantic approach. In *ICASSP 2022-2022 IEEE International Conference on Acoustics, Speech and Signal Processing (ICASSP)* (pp. 8962-8966). IEEE.

Cover, R. (2022). Deepfake culture: The emergence of audio-video deception as an object of social anxiety and regulation. *Continuum (Perth)*, 36(4), 609–621. DOI: 10.1080/10304312.2022.2084039

Cozzolino, D., Thies, J., Rössler, A., Riess, C., Nießner, M., & Verdoliva, L. (2018). ForensicTransfer: Weakly-supervised domain adaptation for forgery detection. Retrieved from http://arxiv.org/abs/1812.02510

Custers, B., Sears, A. M., Dechesne, F., Georgieva, I., Tani, T., & Van der Hof, S. (2019). *EU personal data protection in policy and practice* (Vol. 29). TMC Asser Press. DOI: 10.1007/978-94-6265-282-8

Cybersecurity & Infrastructure Security Agency. (2020). *Whaling - Spear phishing attack*. CISA.

Da Xu, L., Lu, Y., & Li, L. (2021). Embedding blockchain technology into IoT for security: A survey. *IEEE Internet of Things Journal*, 8(13), 10452–10473. DOI: 10.1109/JIOT.2021.3060508

Das, A., Baki, S., El Aassal, A., Verma, R., & Dunbar, A. (2020). SoK: A comprehensive reexamination of phishing research from the security perspective. *IEEE Communications Surveys & Tutorials, 22*(1), 671–708. https://doi.org/DOI: 10.1109/COMST.2019.2957522

DasGupta, B., Mobasheri, N., & Yero, I. G. (2019). On analyzing and evaluating privacy measures for social networks under active attack. *Information Sciences, 473*, 87–100. DOI: 10.1016/j.ins.2018.11.038

Das, S., & Gosavi, A. (2019). Reinforcement learning algorithms for decision support in the military. *. *The Journal of Defence Modeling and Simulation*, 16(4), 301–312.

Dattatreyulu, C., Krishna, C. B., & Geetha, M. (2024, June). Assessment of the effect of covid–19 situation on digital marketing. In AIP Conference Proceedings (Vol. 2971, No. 1). AIP Publishing. DOI: 10.1063/5.0195757

de Terwangne, C. (2022). Privacy and data protection in Europe: Council of Europe's Convention 108 and the European Union's GDPR. In *Research Handbook on Privacy and Data Protection Law* (pp. 10–35). Edward Elgar Publishing. DOI: 10.4337/9781786438515.00007

Dean, J., & Ghemawat, S. (2004). MapReduce: Simplified data processing on large clusters. *. *Communications of the ACM*, 51(1), 107–113. DOI: 10.1145/1327452.1327492

Deng, M., Zhai, H., & Yang, K. (2023). Social engineering in metaverse environment. *2023 IEEE 10th International Conference on Cyber Security and Cloud Computing (CSCloud)/2023 IEEE 9th International Conference on Edge Computing and Scalable Cloud (EdgeCom)*, 150-154.

Denning, D. (1987). An intrusion-detection model. *. *IEEE Transactions on Software Engineering*, 13(2), 222–232. DOI: 10.1109/TSE.1987.232894

Derakhshan, A., Harris, I. G., & Behzadi, M. (2021). Detecting Telephone-based Social Engineering Attacks using Scam Signatures. *Proceedings of the 2021 ACM Workshop on Security and Privacy Analytics*. DOI: 10.1145/3445970.3451152

Dhamija, R., Tygar, J. D., & Hearst, M. (2006, April). Why phishing works. In **Proceedings of the SIGCHI Conference on Human Factors in Computing Systems** (pp. 581-590). DOI: 10.1145/1124772.1124861

Dong, X., Bao, J., Chen, D., Zhang, T., Zhang, W., Yu, N., & Guo, B. (2022). Protecting celebrities from deepfake with identity consistency transformer. In *Proceedings of the IEEE/CVF Conference on Computer Vision and Pattern Recognition* (pp. 9468-9478).

Dorri, A., Kanhere, S. S., & Jurdak, R. (2016), "Blockchain in internet of things: challenges and solutions, arXiv preprint arXiv:1608.05187,arxiv.org

Edwards, M., Larson, R., Green, B., Rashid, A., & Baron, A. (2017). Panning for gold: Automatically analysing online social engineering attack surfaces. *Computers & Security*, 69, 18–34. DOI: 10.1016/j.cose.2016.12.013

Ehrenfeld, T. (2014, September). Honey Trap: The buzz about bees is not necessarily good. *The Weekly Standard*, 19(48), •••. http://www.weeklystandard.com/ print/articles/honey-trap_803987.html

Falade, P.V. (2023). Decoding the Threat Landscape: ChatGPT, FraudGPT, and WormGPT in Social Engineering Attacks. ArXiv, abs/2310.05595.

Fan, W., Lwakatare, K., & Rong, R. (2017). Social engineering: I-E based model of human weakness for attack and defense investigations. *Computer Network and Information Security*, 1(1), 1–11. DOI: 10.5815/ijcnis.2017.01.01

Farayola, O. A., Olorunfemi, O. L., & Shoetan, P. O.Oluwatoyin Ajoke Fayay-olaOluwabukunmi Latifat OlorunfemiPhilip Olaseni Shoetan. (2024). Data privacy and security in it: A review of techniques and challenges. *Computer Science & IT Research Journal*, 5(3), 606–615. DOI: 10.51594/csitrj.v5i3.909

Federal Bureau of Investigation. (2021). *The Federal Bureau of Investigation and business email compromise*. BEC.

Federal Trade Commission. *Vishing scams*. FTC. Retrieved from https://www.ftc.gov

Ferrag, M. A., & Shu, L. (2021). The performance evaluation of blockchain-based security and privacy systems for the Internet of Things: A tutorial. *IEEE Internet of Things Journal*, 8(24), 17236–17260. DOI: 10.1109/JIOT.2021.3078072

Finn, A., & Scheding, S. (2010). *Developments and challenges for autonomous unmanned vehicles: A compendium*. Springer Science & Business Media. DOI: 10.1007/978-3-642-10704-7

Fletcher, J. (2018). Deepfakes, Artificial Intelligence, and Some Kind of Dystopia: The New Faces of Online Post-Fact Performance. *Theatre Journal*, 70(4), 455–471. DOI: 10.1353/tj.2018.0097

Frauenstein, E. D., & Flowerday, S. (2020). Susceptibility to phishing on social network sites: A personality information processing model. *Computers & Security, 94*, 101862. DOI: 10.1016/j.cose.2020.101862

Fuertes, W., Arévalo, D., Castro, J. D., Ron, M., Estrada, C. A., Andrade, R., Peña, F. F., & Benavides, E. (2022). Impact of Social Engineering Attacks: A Literature Review. In Rocha, Á., Fajardo-Toro, C. H., & Rodríguez, J. M. R. (Eds.), *Developments and Advances in Defense and Security* (Vol. 255, pp. 25–35). Springer Singapore., DOI: 10.1007/978-981-16-4884-7_3

Furnell, S. (2016). The role of security education, training and awareness (SETA) in enterprise-wide defence. * [IJISP]. *International Journal of Information Security and Privacy*, 10(2), 1–14.

Gaur, A. S., Sharan, H. O., & Kumar, R. (2024). AI in Education: Ethical Challenges and Opportunities. The Ethical Frontier of AI and Data Analysis, 39-54.

Ghafir, I., Prenosil, V., Alhejailan, A., & Hammoudeh, M. (2016, August). Social engineering attack strategies and defence approaches. In 2016 IEEE 4th international conference on future internet of things and cloud (FiCloud) (pp. 145-149). IEEE. DOI: 10.1109/FiCloud.2016.28

Ghaib, A. A. (2024). Future Trends in Cybersecurity: Exploring Emerging Technologies and Strategies. *International Research Journal of Modernization in Engineering Technology and Science.* Advance online publication. DOI: 10.56726/IRJMETS49530

Giovanini, L.H., Oliveira, D.S., Sânchez, H.A., & Shands, D. (2021). Leveraging Team Dynamics to Predict Open-source Software Projects' Susceptibility to Social Engineering Attacks. *ArXiv, abs/2106.16067.*

Godulla, A., Hoffmann, C. P., & Seibert, D. (2021). Dealing with deepfakes – an interdisciplinary examination of the state of research and implications for communication studies. *Studies in Communication and Media*, 10(1), 72–96. DOI: 10.5771/2192-4007-2021-1-72

Gomes, V., Reis, J., & Alturas, B. (2020). Social Engineering and the Dangers of Phishing. 2020 15th Iberian Conference on Information Systems and Technologies (CISTI), 1-7.

Gomes, V., Reis, J., & Alturas, B. (2020). Social engineering and the dangers of phishing. In **Proceedings of the Iberian Conference on Information Systems and Technologies** (pp. 24–27). DOI: 10.23919/CISTI49556.2020.9140445

Goodfellow, I.. (2014). Generative adversarial networks. *Advances in Neural Information Processing Systems.*

Gosain, M. S., Aggarwal, N., & Kumar, R. (2023, April). A study of 5G and edge computing integration with IoT-A Review. In *2023 International Conference on Computational Intelligence and Sustainable Engineering Solutions (CISES)* (pp. 705-710). IEEE. DOI: 10.1109/CISES58720.2023.10183438

Grassegger, T., & Nedbal, D. (2021). The role of employees' information security awareness on the intention to resist social engineering. *Procedia Computer Science*, 181, 59–66. DOI: 10.1016/j.procs.2021.01.103

Grbic, D. V., & Dujlovic, I. (2023). Social engineering with ChatGPT. 2023 22nd International Symposium INFOTEH-JAHORINA (INFOTEH), 1-5.

Gu, Z., Yao, T., Chen, Y., Yi, R., Ding, S., & Ma, L. (2022, July). Region-Aware Temporal Inconsistency Learning for DeepFake Video Detection. In *IJCAI* (pp. 920-926).

Guadagno, R., Muscanell, N., Rice, L., & Roberts, N. (2013). Social influence online: The impact of social validation and likability on compliance. *Psychology of Popular Media Culture*, 2(1), 51–60. DOI: 10.1037/a0030592

Guarnera, L., Giudice, O., & Battiato, S. (2020). Deepfake detection by analyzing convolutional traces. In *Proceedings of the IEEE/CVF conference on computer vision and pattern recognition workshops* (pp. 666-667)

Gupta, N., Sharma, H., Kumar, S., Kumar, A., & Kumar, R. (2022, December). A comparative study of implementing agile methodology and scrum framework for software development. In *2022 11th International Conference on System Modeling & Advancement in Research Trends (SMART)* (pp. 1088-1092). IEEE.

Gupta, S., Singhal, A., & Kapoor, A. (2016). A literature survey on social engineering attacks: Phishing attack. *2016 International Conference on Computing, Communication and Automation (ICCCA)*, 537–540. DOI: 10.1109/CCAA.2016.7813778

Hadnagy, C. (2011). *Social engineering: The art of human hacking*. Wiley. The Verizon Investigations Report on Data Breach (DBIR). Retrieved from enterprise .verizon.com/resources/reports/dbir/

Hadnagy, C. (2018). *Social engineering: The science of human hacking*. Wiley. Marczak, B. (2019). *Social engineering: The human side of hacking*. CRC Press. DOI: 10.1002/9781119433729

Harris, M., & Jackson, E. (2018). Legal Implications of Cybercrime. *International Journal of Legal Studies*, 3(2), 56–71.

Hartanto, F., Budiman, B., Gwei, E., Gunawan, A. A. S., & Edbert, I. S. (2024). An Experiment to Prevent Malicious Actors from Compromising Private Digital Assets Over a Public Network. *Engineering* [EMACS]. *MAthematics and Computer Science Journal*, 6(1), 7–11.

Hatfield, J. M. (2019). Virtuous human hacking: The ethics of social engineering in penetration-testing. *Computers & Security, 83*, 354–366. DOI: 10.1016/j.cose.2018.12.003

Hatfield, J. M. (2018). Social engineering in cybersecurity: The evolution of a concept. *. *Computers & Security*, 73, 102–113. DOI: 10.1016/j.cose.2017.10.008

Hatfield, J. M. (2018). Social engineering in cybersecurity: The evolution of a concept. *Computers & Security*, 73, 102–113.

Heartfield, R., & Loukas, G. (2018). Detecting semantic social engineering attacks with the weakest link: Implementation and empirical evaluation of a human-as-a-security-sensor framework. *Computers & Security, 76*, 101–127. DOI: 10.1016/j.cose.2018.03.001

He, D., Lv, X., Xu, X., Yu, S., Li, D., Chan, S., & Guizani, M. (2022). An Effective Double-Layer Detection System Against Social Engineering Attacks. *IEEE Network*, 36(6), 92–98. DOI: 10.1109/MNET.105.2100425

Hendrycks, D., Burns, C., Chen, A., & Ball, S. (2021). Cuad: An expert-annotated nlp dataset for legal contract review. arXiv preprint arXiv:2103.06268.

Hijji, M., & Alam, G. (2021). A multivocal literature review on growing social engineering based cyber-attacks/threats during the COVID-19 pandemic: Challenges and prospective solutions. *IEEE Access, 9*, 7152–7169. https://doi.org/DOI: 10.1109/ACCESS.2021.3050770

Hijji, M., & Alam, G. (2021). A Multivocal Literature Review on Growing Social Engineering Based Cyber-Attacks/Threats During the COVID-19 Pandemic: Challenges and Prospective Solutions. *IEEE Access : Practical Innovations, Open Solutions*, 9, 7152–7169. DOI: 10.1109/ACCESS.2020.3048839 PMID: 34786300

Hilgenberg, S., & Bosk, C. L. (1988). The Rise and Fall of Social Problems: A Public Arenas Model. *American Journal of Sociology*, 94(1), 53–78. DOI: 10.1086/228951

Hosler, B., Salvi, D., Murray, A., Antonacci, F., Bestagini, P., Tubaro, S., & Stamm, M. C. (2021). Do deepfakes feel emotions? A semantic approach to detecting deepfakes via emotional inconsistencies. In *Proceedings of the IEEE/CVF conference on computer vision and pattern recognition* (pp. 1013-1022).

Huang, Y., Juefei-Xu, F., Guo, Q., Liu, Y., & Pu, G. (2022). FakeLocator: Robust Localization of GAN-Based Face Manipulations. *IEEE Transactions on Information Forensics and Security*, 17, 2657–2672. DOI: 10.1109/TIFS.2022.3141262

Huber, M., Kowalski, S., Nohlberg, M., & Tjoa, S. (2009, August). Towards automating social engineering using social networking sites. In *2009 International Conference on Computational Science and Engineering* (Vol. 3, pp. 117-124). IEEE. DOI: 10.1109/CSE.2009.205

Huseynov, F., & Ozdenizci Kose, B. (2024). Using machine learning algorithms to predict individuals' tendency to be victim of social engineering attacks. *Information Development*, 40(2), 298–318. DOI: 10.1177/02666669221116336

Huy, H., Nguyen, J., & Yamagishi, I. (2018). Capsule-forensics: Using capsule networks to detect forged images and videos.

Ilyas, H., Javed, A., & Malik, K. M. (2023). AVFakeNet: A unified end-to-end Dense Swin Transformer deep learning model for audio–visual deepfakes detection. *Applied Soft Computing*, 136(110124), 110124. DOI: 10.1016/j.asoc.2023.110124

Irani, D., Balduzzi, M., Balzarotti, D., Kirda, E., & Pu, C. (2011). Reverse social engineering attacks in online social networks. In Detection of Intrusions and Malware, and Vulnerability Assessment: 8th International Conference; DIMVA 2011, Amsterdam, The Netherlands, July 7-8, 2011. [Springer Berlin Heidelberg.]. *Proceedings*, 8, 55–74.

Ivanov, M. A., Kliuchnikova, Bogdana. V., Chugunkov, Ilya.V., & Plaksina, Anna M. (March 2021). *Phishing Attacks and Protection Against Them. IEEE Conference of Russian Young Researchers in Electrical and Electronic Engineering (ElConRus)*, doi: 51938.2021.9396693.DOI: 10.1109/ ElConRus

Ivanov, N., Lou, J., Chen, T., Li, J., & Yan, Q. (2021). Targeting the Weakest Link: Social Engineering Attacks in Ethereum Smart Contracts. *Proceedings of the 2021 ACM Asia Conference on Computer and Communications Security*. DOI: 10.1145/3433210.3453085

JAiman. A. (2020, May). *Debating the ethics of deepfakes*. https://www.orfonline.org/expert-speak/debating-the-ethics-of-deepfakes

Jain, A. K., & Gupta, B. B. (2018). PHISH-SAFE: URL features-based phishing detection system using machine learning. *Advances in Intelligent Systems and Computing*, 729, 467–474. DOI: 10.1007/978-981-10-8536-9_44

Jain, A. K., & Gupta, B. B. (2019). A machine learning based approach for phishing detection using hyperlinks information. *Journal of Ambient Intelligence and Humanized Computing*, 10(5), 2015–2028. DOI: 10.1007/s12652-018-0798-z

Jain, A. K., Sahoo, S. R., & Kaubiyal, J. (2021). Online social networks security and privacy: Comprehensive review and analysis. *Complex & Intelligent Systems*, 7(5), 2157–2177. DOI: 10.1007/s40747-021-00409-7

Jain, A., & Gupta, B. B. (2018). Kumar, & Gupta, B.B. (December 2017). Rule-Based Framework for Detection of Smishing messages in Mobile Environment. Science Direct: Procedia. *Procedia Computer Science*, 125, 617–623. Advance online publication. DOI: 10.1016/j.procs.2017.12.079

Jaiswal, A., & Kumar, R. (2023). Breast cancer diagnosis using Stochastic Self-Organizing Map and Enlarge C4.5. *Multimedia Tools and Applications*, 82(12), 18059–18076. DOI: 10.1007/s11042-022-14265-1

Jajodia, S., Shakarian, P., Subrahmanian, V., Swarup, V. S., & Wang, C. (2011). *Cyber warfare: Building the scientific foundation*. Springer.

Jamil, A., Hassan, M. S., Salleh, N. M., & Yaakob, R. (2020). Non-financial risk disclosure: From narratives to an index based on Delphi technique. *Asian Journal of Government, 14*, 1–19. DOI: 10.17576/AJAG-2020-14-10

Jardine, A. K., Lin, D., & Banjevic, D. (2006). A review on machinery diagnostics and prognostics implementing condition-based maintenance. *. *Mechanical Systems and Signal Processing*, 20(7), 1483–1510. DOI: 10.1016/j.ymssp.2005.09.012

Jia, L., Chen, X., Liu, L., Wang, X., Xiao, K., & Xu, G. (2023). Blockchain data secure sharing protocol based on threshold Paillier algorithm. *High-Confidence Computing*, 3(4), 100132.

Jobin, A., ... (2019). The Global AI Ethics Consortium (GAIEC) data protection framework for artificial intelligence. *arXiv preprint arXiv:1907.07788*.

Johnson, E., & Smith, K. (2024). Continuous authentication with AI. *. *Security Management*, 17(1), 78–91.

Joyce, P. R., Selvaraj, F. J., Manoharan, G., Priya, C., Vijayalakshmi, R., Dwivedi, P. K., & Veerakumar, K. (2024). To Study The Role Of Marketing In Human Resource Management. *Migration Letters : An International Journal of Migration Studies*, 21(S2), 1191–1196. DOI: 10.59670/ml.v21iS2.7072

Junger, M., Montoya, L., & Overink, F.-J. (2017). Priming and warnings are not effective to prevent social engineering attacks. *Computers in Human Behavior, 66*, 75–87. https://doi.org/DOI: 10.1016/j.chb.2016.09.045

KAgyepong, E., Cherdantseva, Y., Reinecke, P. and Burnap, P. (2019). Challenges and performance metrics for security operations center analysts: A systematic review. *Journal of Cyber Security Technology*, 0(0), 1–28.

Kamruzzaman, A., Thakur, K., Ismat, S., Ali, M. L., Huang, K., & Thakur, H. N. *(2023)*. Social Engineering Incidents and Preventions. *IEEE 13th Annual Computing and Communication Workshop and Conference (CCWC)*, Las Vegas, NV, USA, 2023, pp. 0494-0498, DOI: 10.1109/CCWC57344.2023.10099202

Kano, Y., & Nakajima, T. (2021). Trust Factors of Social Engineering Attacks on Social Networking Services. 2021 IEEE 3rd Global Conference on Life Sciences and Technologies (LifeTech), 25-28.

Kapoor, K., Bigdeli, A. Z., Dwivedi, Y. K., & Raman, R. (2021). How is COVID-19 altering the manufacturing landscape? A literature review of imminent challenges and management interventions. *Annals of Operation Research. Annals of Operations Research*, 335(3), 1567–1599. DOI: 10.1007/s10479-021-04397-2 PMID: 34803204

Karakasiliotis, A., Furnell, S., & Papadaki, M. (2006). Assessing end-user awareness of social engineering and phishing.

Kashmar, N., Adda, M., Atieh, M., & Ibrahim, H. (2021). Access Control in Cybersecurity and Social Media. Cybersécurité Médias Sociaux, 69-105.

Kaushalya, S. A. D. T. P., Randeniya, R. M. R. S. B., & Liyanage, A. D. S. (2018, November). An overview of social engineering in the context of information security. In 2018 IEEE 5th International Conference on Engineering Technologies and Applied Sciences (ICETAS) (pp. 1-6). IEEE. DOI: 10.1109/ICETAS.2018.8629126

Kaushalya, S. A., Randeniya, R., & Liyanage, A. (2018). An Overview of Social Engineering in the Context of Information Security. 2018 IEEE 5th International Conference on Engineering Technologies and Applied Sciences (ICETAS), 1-6.

Khidzir, N. Z., Ahmed, S. A., & Guan, T. T. (2019). Management policies for the prevention technique of social engineering (SoE) attacks in the organization. *IJCSNS International Journal of Computer Science and Network Security, 19*(10), 78–82. DOI: 10.22937/IJCSNS.2019.19.10.11

Khidzir, N.Z., & Ahmed, S.A. (2019). Viewpoint of Probabilistic Risk Assessment in Artificial Enabled Social Engineering Attacks. *Journal of Contemporary Issues and Thought.*

Khlobystova, A. O., Abramov, M. V., & Tulupyev, A. L. (2019). *An Approach to Estimating of Criticality of Social Engineering Attacks Traces.* Recent Research in Control Engineering and Decision Making. DOI: 10.1007/978-3-030-12072-6_36

Kim, H.. (2021). Malware detection using deep learning. *. *Journal of Information Security Research*, 5(2), 101–115. DOI: 10.33778/kcsa.2021.21.1.101

Kobis, P. (2021). Human Factor Aspects in Information Security Management in the Traditional It and Cloud Computing Models. *Operations Research and Decisions*, 31(1). Advance online publication. DOI: 10.37190/ord210104

Kothamasu, G. A., Angara Venkata, S. K., Pemmasani, Y., & Mathi, S. (2023, April). An Investigation on Vulnerability Analysis of Phishing Attacks and Countermeasures. *International Journal of Safety and Security Engineering*, 13(2), 333–340. DOI: 10.18280/ijsse.130215

Krasadakis, P., Sakkopoulos, E., & Verykios, V. S. (2024). A survey on challenges and advances in natural language processing with a focus on legal informatics and low-resource languages. *Electronics (Basel)*, 13(3), 648. DOI: 10.3390/electronics13030648

Krombholz, K., Hobel, H., Donko-Huber, M., & Weippl, E. (2014). Advanced social engineering attacks. *Journal of Information Security and Applications.*, 22, 113–122. Advance online publication. DOI: 10.1016/j.jisa.2014.09.005

Kumar Ashutosh, Pant Kumar Vinay (2016), "DNA Optimized Playfair Cipher to Enhance the Security of Cloud Data", Int. J. Eng. Res. Manag. Technol, Vol.3, Issue.4, Pages.7-14.

Kumar, A., Saini, R., & Kumar, R. (2023, December). A systematic review of breast cancer detection using machine learning and deep learning. In 2023 10th IEEE Uttar Pradesh Section International Conference on Electrical, Electronics and Computer Engineering (UPCON) (Vol. 10, pp. 1128-1133). IEEE. DOI: 10.1109/UPCON59197.2023.10434530

Kumar, N., & Dabas, P., & Komal. (2019). Detection and prevention of profile cloning in online social networks. In *Proceedings of the 5th International Conference on Signal Processing and Computing Control (ISPCC)* (pp. 287–291). DOI: 10.1109/ISPCC48220.2019.8988394

Kumar, P., Kumar, M., & Kumar, R. (2024). The Proposed Framework of View-Dependent Data Integration Architecture. In The Ethical Frontier of AI and Data Analysis (pp. 343-361). IGI Global. DOI: 10.4018/979-8-3693-2964-1.ch021

Kumar, P., Kumar, R., Singh, K. B., & Kumar, M. (2023). Identification of the problem and research methodology. In Effective AI, Blockchain, and E-Governance Applications for Knowledge Discovery and Management (pp. 289-308). IGI Global. DOI: 10.4018/978-1-6684-9151-5.ch017

Kumar, A., Saini, R., & Kumar, R. (2024). A Comparative Analysis of Machine Learning Algorithms for Breast Cancer Detection and Identification of Key Predictive Features. *TS. Traitement du Signal*, 41(1). Advance online publication. DOI: 10.18280/ts.410110

Kumar, R., Hamid, A., Bakar, A., Inayah Binti Ya'akub, N., Sharma Gaur, M., & Kumar, S. (Eds.). (2024). *Futuristic E-governance Security with Deep Learning Applications*. IGI Global. DOI: 10.4018/978-1-6684-9596-4

Kwok, A. O. J., & Koh, S. G. M. (2021). Deepfake: A social construction of technology perspective. *Current Issues in Tourism*, 24(13), 1798–1802. DOI: 10.1080/13683500.2020.1738357

Lahcen, R. A. M., Caulkins, B., Mohapatra, R., & Kumar, M. (2020). Review and insight on the behavioral aspects of cybersecurity. *Cybersecurity, 3*(1), 10. DOI: 10.1093/cybsec/tyaa003

Laskov, P., Biggio, B., & Nelson, B. (2012). Poisoning malware clustering behaviour. In **Proceedings of the International Conference on Machine Learning** (pp. 327-334). PML.

Latif, S. A., Wen, F. B. X., Iwendi, C., Li-li, F. W., Mohsin, S. M., Han, Z., & Band, S. S. (2022). AI-empowered, blockchain and SDN integrated security architecture for IoT network of cyber physical systems. *Computer Communications*, 181, 274–283. DOI: 10.1016/j.comcom.2021.09.029

Lee, J., & Bagheri, B. (2015). Cyber-physical systems in future maintenance. *. *IFAC-PapersOnLine*, 48(21), 185–190.

Lee, J., & Kim, S. (2022). User behavior analytics for social engineering defence. *. *Computers & Security*, 18(3), 211–224.

Lee, O. V., Heryanto, A., Razak, M. F. A., Raffei, A. F. M., Phon, D. N. E., Kasim, S., & Sutikno, T. (2020). A malicious URLs detection system using optimization and machine learning classifiers. *Indonesian Journal of Electrical Engineering and Computer Science*, 17(3), 1210–1214. DOI: 10.11591/ijeecs.v17.i3.pp1210-1214

Li, T., Wang, K., & Horkoff, J. (2019). Towards Effective Assessment for Social Engineering Attacks. 2019 IEEE 27th International Requirements Engineering Conference (RE), 392-397.

Liang, P., Liu, G., Xiong, Z., Fan, H., Zhu, H., & Zhang, X. (2023). A facial geometry based detection model for face manipulation using CNN-LSTM architecture. *Information Sciences*, 633, 370–383. DOI: 10.1016/j.ins.2023.03.079

Li, G., Zhao, X., & Cao, Y. (2023). Forensic Symmetry for DeepFakes. *IEEE Transactions on Information Forensics and Security*, 18, 1095–1110. DOI: 10.1109/TIFS.2023.3235579

Lin, H. (2019). The existential threat from cyber-enabled information warfare. *Bulletin of the Atomic Scientists*, 75(4), 187–196. DOI: 10.1080/00963402.2019.1629574

Liu, B., Liu, B., Ding, M., Zhu, T., & Yu, X. (2023). TI2Net: temporal identity inconsistency network for deepfake detection. In *Proceedings of the IEEE/CVF Winter Conference on Applications of Computer Vision* (pp. 4691-4700).

Lorenzo, D. A. M. I. "Analysis and conceptualization of deepfake technology as cyber threat." (2022). magazine, P. (2018, July). *When AI Blurs—The Line Between Reality And Fiction*. https://www.magzter.com/stories/Science/PC-Magazine/When-AIBlurs-The-Line-Between-Reality-And-Fiction

Lundberg, S. M., & Lee, S. I. (2017). A unified approach to interpreting model predictions. *Advances in Neural Information Processing Systems*.

Lu, T., Bao, Y., & Li, L. (2023). Deepfake Video Detection Based on Improved CapsNet and Temporal–Spatial Features. *Computers, Materials & Continua*, 75(1), 715–740. DOI: 10.32604/cmc.2023.034963

Mahammad, A. B., & Kumar, R. (2022, April). Design a linear classification model with support vector machine algorithm on autoimmune disease data. In 2022 3rd International Conference on Intelligent Engineering and Management (ICIEM) (pp. 164-169). IEEE. DOI: 10.1109/ICIEM54221.2022.9853182

Mahammad, A. B., & Kumar, R. (2022). Progression of Digital Healthcare with Deep Learning and Blockchain Methods for Smart Cities. In *Advances in Deep Learning Applications for Smart Cities* (pp. 248–266). IGI Global. DOI: 10.4018/978-1-7998-9710-1.ch012

Mahammad, A. B., & Kumar, R. (2023, April). Scalable and security framework to secure and maintain healthcare data using blockchain technology. In *2023 International Conference on Computational Intelligence and Sustainable Engineering Solutions (CISES)* (pp. 417-423). IEEE. DOI: 10.1109/CISES58720.2023.10183494

Mahmud, B. U., & Sharmin, A. (2020). Deep Insights of Deepfake Technology: A Review. *DUJASE*, 5(1 & 2), 13–23.

Mahmud, B. U., & Sharmin, A. (2021). *Deep Insights of Deepfake Technology: A Review*. DOI: 10.48550/ARXIV.2105.00192

Malin, C. (2017). *H., Gudaitis, Terry., Holt, Thomas. J. & Kilger, Max.* Phishing, Waterhole and Scareware. Book Chapter - Deception in the Digital Age., DOI: 10.1016/B978-0-12-411630-6.00005-0

Manoharan, G., Durai, S., Rajesh, G. A., & Ashtikar, S. P. (2024). A Study on the Application of Expert Systems as a Support System for Business Decisions: A Literature Review. Artificial Intelligence and Knowledge Processing, 279-289.

Manoharan, G., Razak, A., Rajchandar, K., Nithya, G., Durai, S., & Ashtikar, S. P. (2024). Digital Learning for Professional Development in Varied Fields of Service Sectors: Embracing Technological Advancements. In Embracing Technological Advancements for Lifelong Learning (pp. 111-137). IGI Global.

Manoharan, G., Durai, S., Rajesh, G. A., Razak, A., Rao, C. B., & Ashtikar, S. P. (2023). A study on the perceptions of officials on their duties and responsibilities at various levels of the organizational structure in order to accomplish artificial intelligence-based smart city implementation. In *Artificial Intelligence and Machine Learning in Smart City Planning* (pp. 1–10). Elsevier. DOI: 10.1016/B978-0-323-99503-0.00007-7

Marrero, K. (2012). Miller, J. Voas, and G. Hurlburt. Byod: Security and privacy considerations. *IT Professional*, 14(5), 53–55. DOI: 10.1109/MITP.2012.93

Masood, M., Nawaz, M., Malik, K. M., Javed, A., Irtaza, A., & Malik, H. (2023). Deepfakes generation and detection: State-of-the-art, open challenges, countermeasures, and way forward. *Applied Intelligence*, 53(4), 3974–4026. DOI: 10.1007/s10489-022-03766-z

Mattera, M., & Chowdhury, M. M. (2021). Social Engineering: The Looming Threat. 2021 IEEE International Conference on Electro Information Technology (EIT), 056-061. DOI: 10.1109/EIT51626.2021.9491884

Matyokurehwa, K., Rudhumbu, N., Gombiro, C., & Chipfumbu-Kangara, C. T. (2022). Enhanced social engineering framework mitigating against social engineering attacks in higher education. *Security and Privacy*, 5(5), 5. DOI: 10.1002/spy2.237

Mayeke, N. R., Arigbabu, A. T., Olaniyi, O. O., Okunleye, O. J., & Adigwe, C. S. (2024). Evolving Access Control Paradigms: A Comprehensive Multi-Dimensional Analysis of Security Risks and System Assurance in Cyber Engineering. *Available atSSRN*. DOI: 10.2139/ssrn.4752902

Medhane, D. V., Sangaiah, A. K., Hossain, M. S., Muhammad, G., & Wang, J. (2020). Blockchain-enabled distributed security framework for next-generation IoT: An edge cloud and software-defined network-integrated approach. *IEEE Internet of Things Journal*, 7(7), 6143–6149. DOI: 10.1109/JIOT.2020.2977196

MIHINDUKULASURIYA. R. (n.d.). *Why the Manoj Tiwari deepfakes should have India deeply worried*. Retrieved June 21, 2024, from https://theprint.in/tech/why-the-manoj-tiwari-deepfakes-should-have-india-deeply-worried/372389/

Miller, P., Kozu, J., & Davis, A. (2001), "Social influence, empathy, and prosocial behavior in cross-cultural perspective," in Proc. Pract. Social In_uence Multiple Cultures, 2001, pp. 63_77.

Ming, T. S., Shi, N. L., & Taha, A. M. (2020). Awareness of the risks and dangers of social networking: Exploration on four types of Malaysian secondary schools. *Jurnal Komunikasi, Malaysian Journal of Communication, 36*(1), 147–165. DOI: 10.17576/JKMJC-2020-3601-09

Mishra, Sandhya., & Devpriya, Soni. (2019). SMS Phishing and Mitigation Approaches. Conference: Twelfth International Conference on Contemporary Computing (IC3), DOI:.DOI: 10.1109/IC3.2019.8844920

Mitnick, K., Telecom system security. *Security Engineering: A Guide to Building Dependable Distributed Systems, 17.*

Mitropoulos, D., & Douligeris, C. (2012). USB AutoRun worms propagation: Modeling and analysis. In **Proceedings of the International Conference on Critical Infrastructure Protection** (pp. 71-85). Springer, Berlin, Heidelberg.

Mohtashim Mian, S., & Kumar, R. (2023). Deep Learning for Performance Enhancement Robust Underwater Acoustic Communication Network. In Maurya, S., Peddoju, S. K., Ahmad, B., & Chihi, I. (Eds.), *Cyber Technologies and Emerging Sciences. Lecture Notes in Networks and Systems* (Vol. 467). Springer., DOI: 10.1007/978-981-19-2538-2_24

Mokhtar, R., & Rohaizat, A. (2024). Cybercrimes and cyber security trends in the new normal. In *The New Normal and Its Impact on Society: Perspectives from ASEAN and the European Union* (pp. 41–60). Springer Nature Singapore. DOI: 10.1007/978-981-97-0527-6_4

Montañez, R., Atyabi, A., & Xu, S. (2022). Social engineering attacks and defenses in the physical world vs. cyberspace: a contrast study. In *Cybersecurity and Cognitive Science* (pp. 3–41). Academic Press. DOI: 10.1016/B978-0-323-90570-1.00012-7

Mouton, F., Malan, M. M., Leenen, L., & Venter, H. S. (2014). Social engineering attack framework. *2014 Information Security for South Africa*, 1–9. DOI: 10.1109/ISSA.2014.6950510

Mouton, F., Leenen, L., & Venter, H. S. (2016). Social engineering attack examples, templates and scenarios. *Computers & Security*, 59, 186–209. DOI: 10.1016/j.cose.2016.03.004

Možnik, D., Delija, D., Tulčić, D., & Galinec, D. (2023). Cybersecurity and Cyber Defense Insights: The Complementary Conceptual model of Cyber resilience. *ENTRENOVA - ENTerprise REsearch InNOVAtion, 9*(1), 1–12. https://doi.org/DOI: 10.54820/entrenova-2023-0001

Mughal, A. A. (2018). The Art of Cybersecurity: Defense in Depth Strategy for Robust Protection. *International Journal of Intelligent Automation and Computing*, 1(1), 1–20.

Mustafa, H. (2019). Digital Social Engineering Threatens Cybersecurity. *International Journal of Innovative Technology and Exploring Engineering*, 9(1), 4016–4025. DOI: 10.35940/ijitee.A5289.119119

Nabie C, Paul S. (2016), Cybersecurity: risks, vulnerabilities and countermeasures to prevent social engineering attacks. Int J Adv Comput Res. 2016; 6:31–8. . 2016.623006.DOI: <ALIGNMENT.qj></ALIGNMENT>10.19101/ IJACR

Nagarjuna, B., Aarif, M., Shamina, H., Sawant, P. D., Bhadane, J. R., & Manoharan, G. (2022). An empirical analysis of efficacy of digital marketing techniques on tourism entrepreneurs. *European Journal of Molecular and Clinical Medicine*, 9(8).

Naitali, A., Ridouani, M., Salahdine, F., & Kaabouch, N. (2023). Deepfake Attacks: Generation, Detection, Datasets, Challenges, and Research Directions. In Computers (Vol. 12, Issue 10). DOI: 10.3390/computers12100216

Neupane, A., Satvat, K., Saxena, N., Stavrinos, D., & Bishop, H. J. (2018, December). Do social disorders facilitate social engineering? A case study of autism and phishing attacks. In *Proceedings of the 34th Annual Computer Security Applications Conference* (pp. 467-477). DOI: 10.1145/3274694.3274730

Nevarez, N. (2023). Integrating Cyber Resilience Strategies for OT Data Acquisition Devices. *The International Journal of Social Sciences (Islamabad)*, 7(30), 488–500. DOI: 10.52096/usbd.7.30.33

Nirkin, Y., Wolf, L., Keller, Y., & Hassner, T. (2022). DeepFake Detection Based on Discrepancies Between Faces and Their Context. *IEEE Transactions on Pattern Analysis and Machine Intelligence*, 44(10), 6111–6121. DOI: 10.1109/TPAMI.2021.3093446 PMID: 34185639

O'Brien, S. A. (2018, August). Deepfakes are coming. Is Big Tech ready? *Deepfakes Are Coming. Is Big Tech Ready?*https://money.cnn.com/2018/08/08/technology/deepfakes-countermeasures-facebook-twitter-youtube/index.html

O'Sullivan, D. (2019, October 18). We asked a hacker to try and steal a CNN tech reporter's data. Here's what happened. *CNN*. https://www.cnn.com/2019/10/18/tech/reporter-hack/index.html

Okoli, U. I., Obi, O. C., Adewusi, A. O., & Abrahams, T. O. (2024). Machine learning in cybersecurity: A review of threat detection and defense mechanisms.

Orujo, Z. (2023). CYBER SECURITY: CONTEMPORARY CYBER THREATS AND NATIONAL STRATEGIES. *Distance Education in Ukraine: Innovative, Normative-Legal. Pedagogical Aspects*, 2, 100–116. DOI: 10.18372/2786-5495.1.17309

Owusu-Oware, E., & Effah, J. (2024). Biometric system for protecting information and improving service delivery: The case of a developing country's social security and pension organisation. *Information Development*, 40(1), 61–74. DOI: 10.1177/02666669221085709

Pant Kumar Vinay., Prakash Jyoti, Asthana Amit (2015), Three step data security model for cloud computing based on RSA and steganography, International Conference on Green Computing and Internet of Things (ICGCIoT), IEEE,490-494.

Papatsaroucha, D., Nikoloudakis, Y., Kefaloukos, I., Pallis, E., & Markakis, E. K. (2021). A survey on human and personality vulnerability assessment in cybersecurity: Challenges, approaches, and open issues. arXiv preprint arXiv:2106.09986.

Papernot, N.. (2016). Distillation as a defence to adversarial perturbations against deep neural networks. In **IEEE Symposium on Security and Privacy**.

Parri, J., Patara, F., Sampietro, S., & Vicario, E. (2020). A framework for Model-Driven Engineering of resilient software-controlled systems. *Computing*, 103(4), 589–612. DOI: 10.1007/s00607-020-00841-6

Parthy, P. P., & Rajendran, G. (2019). Identification and prevention of social engineering attacks on an enterprise. *2019 International Carnahan Conference on Security Technology (ICCST)*, 1-5. DOI: 10.1109/CCST.2019.8888441

Patel, R., & Gupta, S. (2021). Deep learning techniques for cybersecurity. *. *International Journal of Network Security*, 10(1), 67–79.

Paterson, T., & Hanley, L. (2020). Political warfare in the digital age: Cyber subversion, information operations and 'deep fakes.'. *Australian Journal of International Affairs*, 74(4), 439–454. DOI: 10.1080/10357718.2020.1734772

Patil, M. Harl. (1997). People Hacking: "The Psychology of Social Engineering". [Online]. Available: http://www.text_les.com/russian/cyberlib.narod.ru/lib/cin/se10.html

Pawelec, M. (2022). Deepfakes and Democracy (Theory): How Synthetic Audio-Visual Media for Disinformation and Hate Speech Threaten Core Democratic Functions. *Digital Society : Ethics, Socio-Legal and Governance of Digital Technology*, 1(2), 19. DOI: 10.1007/s44206-022-00010-6 PMID: 36097613

Pei, S., Wang, Y., Xiao, B., Pei, S., Xu, Y., Gao, Y., & Zheng, J. (2022, September). A bidirectional-LSTM method based on temporal features for deep fake face detection in videos. In *2nd International Conference on Information Technology and Intelligent Control (CITIC 2022)* (Vol. 12346, pp. 311-318). SPIE.

Pharris, L., & Perez-Mira, B. (2023). Preventing social engineering: A phenomenological inquiry. *Information and Computer Security*, 31(1), 1–31. DOI: 10.1108/ICS-09-2021-0137

Pitchan, M. A., Omar, S. Z., & Ghazali, A. Ḣ. A. (2019). Amalan keselamatan siber pengguna internet terhadap buli siber, pornografi, E-mel phishing dan pembelian dalam talian. *Jurnal Komunikasi, Malaysian Journal of Communication, 35*(3), 212–227. https://doi.org/DOI: 10.17576/jkom-2019-3503-14

Praveen, A., Boini, R., Ravi, K., & Geetha, M. (2024, June). A contemplation on the seven significant characteristics of an engineering instructor in TLP. In AIP Conference Proceedings (Vol. 2971, No. 1). AIP Publishing. DOI: 10.1063/5.0195780

PurpleSec. (2021). 2021 cyber security statistics: The ultimate list of stats, data & trends. https://purplesec.us/resources/cyber-security-statistics/

Rachman, D. A., Muhyidin, Y., & Sunandar, M. A. (2023). Analysis Quality of Service of Internet Network Fiber to the Home Service Pt. Xyz Using Wireshark. *Jurnal Informatika dan Teknik Elektro Terapan, 11*(3s1).

Rafique, R., Gantassi, R., Amin, R., Frnda, J., Mustapha, A., & Alshehri, A. H. (2023). Deep fake detection and classification using error-level analysis and deep learning. *Scientific Reports*, 13(1), 7422. Advance online publication. DOI: 10.1038/s41598-023-34629-3 PMID: 37156887

Raghavan, S.. (2007). PhishGuru: A system for enterprise-wide phishing education. In **Proceedings of the 16th USENIX Security Symposium**.

Rahman, M. R. A. (2020). Online scammers and their mules in Malaysia. *Jurnal Undang-Undang dan Masyarakat, 26*(2020), 65–72. DOI: 10.17576/juum-2020-26-08

Rashid, J., Mahmood, T., Nisar, M. W., & Nazir, T. (2020). Phishing Detection Using Machine Learning Technique. *Proceedings - 2020 1st International Conference of Smart Systems and Emerging Technologies, SMART-TECH 2020*, 43–46. DOI: 10.1109/SMART-TECH49988.2020.00026

Rehman, S. Ur., Sowerby, K evin. W., & Coghill, Colin. (March 2021). Analysis of impersonation attacks on systems using RF fingerprinting and low-end receivers. *Journal of Computer and System Sciences*. Advance online publication. DOI: 10.1016/ j.jcss.2013.06.01

Reuters. (2019, November 29). *China seeks to root out fake news and deepfakes with new online content rules*. https://www.reuters.com/article/idUSKBN1Y30VT/

Ribeiro, M. T.. (2016). Why should I trust you? Explaining the predictions of any classifier. In **Proceedings of the ACM SIGKDD International Conference on Knowledge Discovery and Data Mining**. DOI: 10.1145/2939672.2939778

Rodriguez, R.M., Atyabi, A., & Xu, S. (2022). Social Engineering Attacks and Defenses in the Physical World vs. Cyberspace: A Contrast Study. *ArXiv, abs/2203.04813*.

Rosmansyah, Y., Hendarto, I. L. S., & Pratama, D. (2020, October 05). Hendarto, Ignatius Leo Sri., & Pratama, Demby. (April 2021). Impersonation Attack-Defense Tree. [iJET]. *International Journal of Emerging Technologies in Learning*, 15(19), 239. Advance online publication. DOI: 10.3991/ijet.v15i19.12699

Ru, Y., Zhou, W., Liu, Y., Sun, J., & Li, Q. (2021, August). Bita-net: Bi-temporal attention network for facial video forgery detection. In *2021 IEEE International Joint Conference on Biometrics (IJCB)* (pp. 1-8). IEEE.

Saberi S., Kouhizadeh M., Sarkis J., Shen L.(2019) “Blockchain technology and its relationships to sustainable supply chain management”, International journal of production research, Taylor & Francis, pp. 2117-2135

Sabharwal, D., Sood, R. S., & Sood, S. (2024). *Media and AI: Navigating the Future of Communication*. Post Script.

Sabir, E., Cheng, J., & Jaiswal, A. AbdAlmageed, W., Masi, I., & Natarajan, P. (2019). Recurrent convolutional strategies for face manipulation detection in videos. Retrieved from http://arxiv.org/abs/1905.00582

Sachs, M. A.. (2015). Human-centered security: Putting users first in security design and evaluation. *. *IEEE Security and Privacy*, 13(2), 24–33.

Sahingoz, O. K., Buber, E., Demir, O., & Diri, B. (2019). Machine learning based phishing detection from URLs. *Expert Systems with Applications*, 117, 345–357. DOI: 10.1016/j.eswa.2018.09.029

Salahdine, F., & Kaabouch, N. (2019). Social engineering attacks: A survey. *Future Internet, 11*(4). https://doi.org/DOI: 10.3390/fi11040065

Salahdine, Fatima. & Kaabouch, Naima. (February 2019). Social Engineering Attacks: A Survey. Future engineering, DOI: .DOI: 10.3390/fi11040089

Salama, R., Al-Turjman, F., Bhatla, S., & Yadav, S. P. (2023, April). Social engineering attack types and prevention techniques-A survey. In *2023 International Conference on Computational Intelligence, Communication Technology and Networking (CICTN)* (pp. 817-820). IEEE. DOI: 10.1109/CICTN57981.2023.10140957

Sánchez, D., Domingo-Ferrer, J., & Martínez, S. (2018). Co-utile disclosure of private data in social networks. *Information Sciences, 441*, 50–65. DOI: 10.1016/j.ins.2018.03.009

Sandhu, B. S., Kaur, J., & Brar, H. S. (2023). Cybersecurity in the Age of Interconnectedness: Challenges, Strategies, and Opportunities. (2023). *International Research Journal of Modernization in Engineering Technology and Science*. Advance online publication. DOI: 10.56726/IRJMETS46003

Sarma, B., Liles, R., & Poojary, P. (2018). Detecting phishing websites using machine learning. *arXiv preprint arXiv:1801.04406*.

Satpathy, A., Samal, A., Gupta, S., Kumar, S., Sharma, S., Manoharan, G., Karthikeyan, M., & Sharma, S. (2024). To Study the Sustainable Development Practices in Business and Food Industry. *Migration Letters : An International Journal of Migration Studies*, 21(S1), 743–747. DOI: 10.59670/ml.v21iS1.6400

Scarfone, K. A., Souppaya, M. P., Cody, A., & Orebaugh, A. D. (2008). Technical guide to information security testing and assessment. (NIST SP 800-115; 0 ed., p. NIST SP 800-115). National Institute of Standards and Technology. DOI: 10.6028/NIST.SP.800-115

Scarfone, K., Souppaya, M., Cody, A., & Orebaugh, A. (2008). *Technical guide to information security testing and assessment recommendations of the National Institute of Standards and Technology (SP 800-115) *. NIST Special Publication, 800, 1–80. Retrieved from https://csrc.nist.gov/publications/detail/sp/800-115/final

Schaab, P., Beckers, K., & Pape, S. (2017). Social engineering defence mechanisms and counteracting training strategies. *Information & Computer Security, 25*(2), 206–222. DOI: 10.1108/ICS-03-2017-0012

Sendjaja, T., Irwandi, , Prastiawan, E., Suryani, Y., & Fatmawati, E. (2024). Cybersecurity In The Digital Age: Developing Robust Strategies To Protect Against Evolving Global Digital Threats And Cyber Attacks. *The International Journal of Science in Society*, 6(1), 1008–1019. DOI: 10.54783/ijsoc.v6i1.1098

Setia, P., & Sandosh S. (2023). Enhancing Cybersecurity Defense of IoT Ecosystem Using Blockchain. *Suranaree Journal of Science and Technology, 30*(4), 010238(1-14). https://doi.org/DOI: 10.55766/sujst-2023-04-e01071

Settles, B. (2009). *Active learning literature survey*. University of Wisconsin-Madison.

Shaari, A. H., Kamaluddin, M. R., Fauzi, W. F. P., & Mohd, M. (2019). Online-dating romance scam in Malaysia: An analysis of online conversations between scammers and victims. *GEMA Online Journal of Language Studies, 19*(1), 97–115. DOI: 10.17576/gema-2019-1901-06

Shahrivari, V., Darabi, M. M., & Izadi, M. (2020). *Phishing Detection Using Machine Learning Techniques*. http://arxiv.org/abs/2009.11116

Shammar, E. A., Zahary, A. T., & Al-Shargabi, A. A. (2021). A Survey of IoT and Blockchain Integration: Security Perspective. *IEEE Access : Practical Innovations, Open Solutions*, 9, 156114–156150. DOI: 10.1109/ACCESS.2021.3129697

Sharma, A.. (2023). Deception technologies for cyber defence. *. *International Journal of Cybersecurity*, 9(3), 167–180.

Sharma, V., Sharma, K. K., Vashishth, T. K., Panwar, R., Kumar, B., & Chaudhary, S. (2023, November). Brain-Computer Interface: Bridging the Gap between Human Brain and Computing Systems. In *2023 International Conference on Research Methodologies in Knowledge Management, Artificial Intelligence and Telecommunication Engineering (RMKMATE)* (pp. 1-5). IEEE. DOI: 10.1109/RMKMATE59243.2023.10369702

Shukla, R. K., Prakash, V., & Pandey, S. (2020, December). A perspective on Internet of Things: Challenges & applications. In *2020 9th International Conference System Modeling and Advancement in Research Trends (SMART)* (pp. 184-189). IEEE.

Siciliano, B., & Khatib, O. (2016). *Springer handbook of robotics*. Springer. DOI: 10.1007/978-3-319-32552-1

Siddiqi, M., Pak, W., & Siddiqi, M. (2022). A Study on the Psychology of Social Engineering-Based Cyberattacks and Existing Countermeasures. *Applied Sciences (Basel, Switzerland)*, 12(12), 6042. Advance online publication. DOI: 10.3390/app12126042

Si, H., Sun, C., Li, Y., Qiao, H., & Shi, L. (2019). IoT information sharing security mechanism based on blockchain technology. *Future Generation Computer Systems*, 101, 1028–1040. DOI: 10.1016/j.future.2019.07.036

Singh, C. B., Gupta, A., & Kumar, R. (2022, April). Diabetes Care Survey Using Supervised and Unsupervised Machine Learning. In 2022 3rd International Conference on Intelligent Engineering and Management (ICIEM) (pp. 207-210). IEEE. DOI: 10.1109/ICIEM54221.2022.9853085

Singh, D., Makkar, S., Durai, S., Manoharan, G., Purushottamashtikar, S., & Alexrajesh, G. (2024, June). Human resource information system applications in small and medium enterprises: A study (SMEs). In AIP Conference Proceedings (Vol. 2971, No. 1). AIP Publishing.

Singh, A., Virmani, D., Kulkarni, N., Tiwari, M., Manoharan, G., & Alanya-Beltran, J. (2024). The Emerging Role and Application of Adopting Revolutionary Internet of Things (IoT) for Future Technology Sustainability. Computer Science Engineering and Emerging Technologies. *Proceedings of ICCS*, 2022, 103.

Smith, J., & Jones, A. (2020). Effective strategies for social engineering defence. *. *Journal of Cybersecurity*, 8(2), 123–135.

Sobur, A., Hossain, A., Nazrul Islam, K., & Kabir, M. H. (2023). A Contradiction study of pysical vs cyberspace social engineering attacks and defense.

Sobur, A., Hossain, A., Nazrul Islam, K., & Kabir, M. H. (2023). A Contradistinction Study of Physical Vs. Cyberspace Social Engineering Attacks and Defense. Cyberspace Social Engineering Attacks and Defense (June 14, 2023).

Solsman, J. E. (2019, July 12). Deepfakes freak YouTubers out. Vidcon offers a way to prepare. *Deepfakes Freak YouTubers out. Vidcon Offers a Way to Prepare*. https://www.cnet.com/tech/computing/deepfakes-freak-youtubers-out-vidcon-offers-a-way-to-prepare/

Sommer, R., & Paxson, V. (2010). Outside the closed world: On using machine learning for network intrusion detection. In **Proceedings of the 2010 IEEE Symposium on Security and Privacy**. DOI: 10.1109/SP.2010.25

Southers, L. (2019, March). How Reuters is training reporters to spot 'deepfakes.' *How Reuters Is Training Reporters to Spot 'Deepfakes.'* https://shorturl.at/epjML

Southwick, S. M., Bonanno, G. A., Masten, A. S., Panter-Brick, C., & Yehuda, R. (2014). Resilience definitions, theory, and challenges: interdisciplinary perspectives. https://doi.org/DOI: 10.3402/ejpt.v5.25338

Srivastava, S., & Ahmed, T. (2023, March). An Approach to Monitor Urban Growth through Deep Learning based Change Detection Technique using Sentinel-2 Satellite Images. In *2023 10th International Conference on Computing for Sustainable Global Development (INDIACom)* (pp. 832-838). IEEE.

Srivastava, S., Soni, M. K., & Pratap, A. (2023). A Critical Study of Challenges and Risk in Healthcare sector based on Cloud Computing," *2023 14th International Conference on Computing Communication and Networking Technologies (ICCCNT)*, Delhi, India, 2023, pp. 1-5, DOI: 10.1109/ICCCNT56998.2023.10307861

Srivastava, S., & Ahmed, T. (2022). Correlation Between Built-Up and Land Surface Temperature Using Sentinel-2 and Landsat-8 Images through Semi-Supervised Deep Learning Model for Efficient Land Surface Monitoring. *Mathematical Statistician and Engineering Applications*, 71(4), 3000–3023.

Srivastava, S., & Ahmed, T. (2024). DLCD: Deep learning-based change detection approach to monitor deforestation. *Signal, Image and Video Processing*, 18(S1, Suppl 1), 167–181. DOI: 10.1007/s11760-024-03140-1

Srivastava, S., Ahmed, T., & Saxena, A. (2023). An approach to secure IOT application of smart city using blockchain technology. *International Journal of Engineering Sciences & Emerging Technologies*, 11(2), 71–78.

Srivastava, S., Ahmed, T., & Saxena, A. (2023). An approach to secure IOT applications of smart city using blockchain technology. *International Journal of Engineering Sciences & Emerging Technologies*, 11(2), 71–78. DOI: 10.5281/zenodo.10434277

Stojanovic, N., & Dhabliya, R. (2023c). Empowering Edge Security An Advanced Encryption Strategies for Enhanced Cyber Resilience in Edge Computing. *Research Journal of Computer Systems and Engineering*, 4(1), 74–83. DOI: 10.52710/rjcse.65

Sun, Y., Zhang, Z., Echizen, I., Nguyen, H. H., Qiu, C., & Sun, L. (2023). Face forgery detection based on facial region displacement trajectory series. In *Proceedings of the IEEE/CVF Winter Conference on Applications of Computer Vision* (pp. 633-642).

Syafitri, W., Shukur, Z., Mokhtar, U. A., Sulaiman, R., & Ibrahim, M. A. (2022). Social Engineering Attacks Prevention: A Systematic Literature Review. IEEE Access, PP, 1-1.

Syafitri, W., Shukur, Z., Asma'Mokhtar, U., Sulaiman, R., & Ibrahim, M. A. (2022). Social engineering attacks prevention: A systematic literature review. *IEEE Access : Practical Innovations, Open Solutions*, 10, 39325–39343. DOI: 10.1109/ACCESS.2022.3162594

Syed, R. (2019). Enterprise reputation threats on social media: A case of data breach framing. *Journal of Strategic Information Systems, 28*(3), 257–274. DOI: 10.1016/j.jsis.2019.01.003

Syed, R. (2019). Enterprise reputation threats on social media: A case of data breach framing. *The Journal of Strategic Information Systems*, 28(3), 257–274. DOI: 10.1016/j.jsis.2018.12.001

Symantec Corporation. (2020). *2020 Internet security threat report*. Symantec.

Szegedy, C., ... (2014). Intriguing properties of neural networks. *arXiv preprint arXiv:1312.6199*.

Taherdoost, H. (2022). A critical review of blockchain acceptance models—Blockchain technology adoption frameworks and applications. *Computers*, 11(2), 24. DOI: 10.3390/computers11020024

Taib, R., Yu, K., Berkovsky, S., Wiggins, M. W., & Bayl-Smith, P. (2019). Social Engineering and Organisational Dependencies in Phishing Attacks. IFIP TC13 International Conference on Human-Computer Interaction. DOI: 10.1007/978-3-030-29381-9_35

Tanium. (2020, October 19). Your people are being hacked: How to defend against social engineering during WFH. *CIO*. https://www.cio.com/article/190874/your-people-are-being-hacked-how-to-defend-against-social-engineering-during-wfh.html

Taylor, P. J., Dargahi, T., Dehghantanha, A., Parizi, R. M., & Choo, K.-K. R. (2020). A systematic literature review of blockchain cyber security. *Digital Communications and Networks*, 6(2), 147–156. DOI: 10.1016/j.dcan.2019.01.005

Tenove, C. (2020). Protecting Democracy from Disinformation: Normative Threats and Policy Responses. *The International Journal of Press/Politics*, 25(3), 517–537. DOI: 10.1177/1940161220918740

Ternovski, J., Kalla, J., & Aronow, P. M. (2021). *Deepfake Warnings for Political Videos Increase Disbelief but Do Not Improve Discernment: Evidence from Two Experiments*. DOI: 10.31219/osf.io/dta97

Thavamani, S., Mahesh, D., Sinthuja, U., & Manoharan, G. (2022, May). Crucial attacks in internet of things via artificial intelligence techniques: The security survey. In AIP Conference Proceedings (Vol. 2418, No. 1). AIP Publishing.

Thomopoulos, G. A., Lyras, Dimitrios. P., &Fidas, Christos. A. (March 2023). A Systematic review and research challenges on phishing cyberattaks from an electro-encephalography and gaze-based perspective. *Personal and Ubiquitous Computing*. Advance online publication. DOI: 10.1007/s00779-024-01794-9

Tian, G., Zhang, C., Fathollahi-Fard, A. M., Li, Z., Zhang, C., & Jiang, Z. (2023). An Enhanced Social Engineering Optimizer for Solving an Energy-Efficient Disassembly Line Balancing Problem Based on Bucket Brigades and Cloud Theory. *IEEE Transactions on Industrial Informatics*, 19(5), 7148–7159. DOI: 10.1109/TII.2022.3193866

Trabelsi, Z., Parambil, M. M. A., Qayyum, T., & Alomar, B. (2024, May). Teaching DNS Spoofing Attack Using a Hands-on Cybersecurity Approach Based on Virtual Kali Linux Platform. In *2024 IEEE Global Engineering Education Conference (EDUCON)* (pp. 1-8). IEEE. DOI: 10.1109/EDUCON60312.2024.10578851

Tripathi, M. A., Tripathi, R., Effendy, F., Manoharan, G., Paul, M. J., & Aarif, M. (2023, January). An In-Depth Analysis of the Role That ML and Big Data Play in Driving Digital Marketing's Paradigm Shift. In *2023 International Conference on Computer Communication and Informatics (ICCCI)* (pp. 1-6). IEEE. DOI: 10.1109/ICCCI56745.2023.10128357

Tsinganos, N., & Mavridis, I. (2021). Building and Evaluating an Annotated Corpus for Automated Recognition of Chat-Based Social Engineering Attacks. *Applied Sciences (Basel, Switzerland)*, 11(22), 10871. DOI: 10.3390/app112210871

Tuli, R. (2023). Analyzing Network performance parameters using wireshark. *arXiv preprint arXiv:2302.03267.*

Vági, R. (2023). How Could Semantic Processing and Other NLP Tools Improve Online Legal Databases? *TalTech Journal of European Studies*, 13(2), 138–151. DOI: 10.2478/bjes-2023-0018

van Schaik, P., Jansen, J., Onibokun, J., Camp, J., & Kusev, P. (2018). Security and privacy in online social networking: Risk perceptions and precautionary behaviour. *Computers in Human Behavior, 78*, 283–297. DOI: 10.1016/j.chb.2017.09.010

Vashishth, T. K., Sharma, V., Pandey, A., & Tomer, T. (2024). Innovative Advancements in Big Data Analytics: Navigating Future Trends with Hadoop Integration. In Recent Trends and Future Direction for Data Analytics (pp. 234-258). IGI Global.

Vashishth, T. K., Sharma, V., Sharma, K. K., Kumar, B., Chaudhary, S., & Panwar, R. (2024). Transforming Classroom Dynamics: The Social Impact of AI in Teaching and Learning. In AI-Enhanced Teaching Methods (pp. 322-346). IGI Global.

Vashishth, T. K., Sharma, V., Sharma, K. K., Kumar, B., Kumar, A., & Panwar, R. (2024). Artificial Intelligence (AI)–Powered Chatbots: Providing Instant Support and Personalized Recommendations to Guests 24/7. In Technology and Luxury Hospitality (pp. 211-236). Routledge.

Vashishth, T. K., Sharma, V., Sharma, K. K., Kumar, B., Chaudhary, S., & Panwar, R. (2024). Security and Privacy Considerations in Cloud-Based Data Processing Solutions for Sensitive Data. In *Developments towards Next Generation Intelligent Systems for Sustainable Development* (pp. 35–61). IGI Global. DOI: 10.4018/979-8-3693-5643-2.ch002

Vasserman, E. Y., & Hopper, N. (2011). Vampire attacks: Draining life from wireless ad hoc sensor networks. *IEEE Transactions on Mobile Computing*, 12(2), 318–332. DOI: 10.1109/TMC.2011.274

Velayudhan, S. P., & Somasundaram, M. S. B. S. (2019). Compromised account detection in online social networks: A survey. *Concurrency and Computation: Practice and Experience, 31*(20), 1–15. DOI: 10.1002/cpe.5623

Venkatesha, S., Reddy, K. R., & Chandavarkar, B. R. (2021). Social Engineering Attacks During the COVID-19 Pandemic. [Erratum in: SN Comput Sci. 2021;2] [3] [:134. PMID: 33585823; PMCID: PMC7866964]. *SN Computer Science*, 2(2), 78. DOI: 10.1007/s42979-020-00443-1 PMID: 33585823

Verizon, N. A. J., & Scobell, A. (2020). *2020 Data Breach Investigations Report*. Retrieved from https://enterprise.verizon.com/resources/reports/2020-data-breach-investigations-report.pdf

Vidas, T.. (2012). A survey of user-centered design techniques towards usable security and privacy. In **Proceedings of the 28th Annual Conference on Computer Security Applications**.

Waddell, M. (2023). Human factors in cybersecurity: Designing an effective cybersecurity education program for healthcare staff. *Healthcare Management Forum*, 37(1), 13–16. DOI: 10.1177/08404704231196137 PMID: 37684060

Wang, J., Wu, Z., Ouyang, W., Han, X., Chen, J., Jiang, Y.-G., & Li, S.-N. (2022, June 27). M2TR: Multi-modal Multi-scale Transformers for Deepfake Detection. Proceedings of the 2022 International Conference on Multimedia Retrieval. Presented at the ICMR '22: International Conference on Multimedia Retrieval, Newark NJ USA. DOI: 10.1145/3512527.3531415

Wang, Z., Sun, L., & Zhu, H. (2020). Defining social engineering in cybersecurity. *IEEE Access, 8*, 85094–85115. https://doi.org/DOI: 10.1109/ACCESS.2020.2993060

Wang, Z., Zhu, H., & Sun, L. (2021). Social engineering in cybersecurity: Effect mechanisms, human vulnerabilities and attack methods. *IEEE Access, 9*, 11895–11910. https://doi.org/DOI: 10.1109/ACCESS.2021.3050294

Wang, Z.; Zhu, H.; Sun, L. (2021), Social engineering in cybersecurity: Effect mechanisms, human vulnerabilities and attack methods. IEEE Access 2021, 9, 11895–11910.

Wang, Zuoguang., Zhu, Hongsong., Liu, Peipei., & Sun. Limin. (2021). Social engineering in cyber security: a domain ontology and knowledge graph application examples. Springer Open, doi: https://doi.org/.DOI: 10.1186/s42400-021-00094-6

Wang, C.. (2019). HAQ: Hardware-aware automated quantization with mixed precision. In **Proceedings of the IEEE Conference on Computer Vision and Pattern Recognition**. DOI: 10.1109/CVPR.2019.00881

Wang, X., & Li, Z. (2022). Clustering techniques for anomaly detection. *. *ACM Computing Surveys*, 49(1), 1–38.

Wang, Z., Sun, L., & Zhu, H. (2020). Defining Social Engineering in Cybersecurity. *IEEE Access : Practical Innovations, Open Solutions*, 8, 85094–85115. DOI: 10.1109/ACCESS.2020.2992807

Wang, Z., Zhu, H., & Sun, L. (2021). Social engineering in cybersecurity: Effect mechanisms, human vulnerabilities and attack methods. *IEEE Access : Practical Innovations, Open Solutions*, 9, 11895–11910. DOI: 10.1109/ACCESS.2021.3051633

Wan, J., Li, J., Imran, M., Li, D., & Fazal-e-Amin, . (2019). A blockchain-based solution for enhancing security and privacy in smart factory. *IEEE Transactions on Industrial Informatics*, 15(6), 3652–3660. DOI: 10.1109/TII.2019.2894573

Waseem, S., Abu-Bakar, S. R., Omar, Z., Ahmed, B. A., & Baloch, S. (2022, June). A multi-color spatio-temporal approach for detecting deepfake. In *2022 12th International Conference on Pattern Recognition Systems (ICPRS)* (pp. 1-5). IEEE.

Washo, A. (2021). An interdisciplinary view of social engineering: A call to action for research. *Computers in Human Behavior Reports*, 4, 100126. DOI: 10.1016/j.chbr.2021.100126

What are digital doubles? Everything you need to know. (n.d.). Retrieved June 19, 2024, from https://di4d.com/what-are-digital-doubles-everything-you-need-to-know/

Xu, Y.. (2023). Adaptive deception strategies using reinforcement learning. *. *Journal of Machine Learning Research*, 19(2), 345–358.

Xu, Y., Yin, H., & Zhu, X. (2016). Understanding behavioral biometrics: Towards a science of measuring human behavior. *. *ACM Computing Surveys*, 49(1), 1–38.

Yadav, V., Soni, M. K., & Pratap, A. (2024). Secured Identity and Access Management for Cloud Computing Using Zero Trust Architecture. In Chaturvedi, A., Hasan, S. U., Roy, B. K., & Tsaban, B. (Eds.), *Cryptology and Network Security with Machine Learning. ICCNSML 2023. Lecture Notes in Networks and Systems* (Vol. 918). Springer., DOI: 10.1007/978-981-97-0641-9_47

Yang, J., Xiao, S., Li, A., Lu, W., Gao, X., & Li, Y. (2022). MSTA-net: Forgery detection by generating manipulation trace based on multi-scale self-texture attention. IEEE Transactions on Circuits and Systems for Video Technology: A Publication of the Circuits and Systems Society, 32(7), 4854–4866. DOI: 10.1109/TCSVT.2021.3133859

Yang, R., Zheng, K., Wang, X., Wu, B., & Wu, C. (2023). Social Engineering Attack-Defense Strategies Based on Reinforcement Learning. *Computer Systems Science and Engineering*, 47(2), 2153–2170. DOI: 10.32604/csse.2023.038917

Yang, X., Wang, Z., Wang, Q., Wei, K., Zhang, K., & Shi, J. (2024). Large language models for automated q&a involving legal documents: A survey on algorithms, frameworks and applications. *International Journal of Web Information Systems*, 20(4), 413–435. DOI: 10.1108/IJWIS-12-2023-0256

Yang, Z., Allen, J., Landen, M., Perdisci, R., & Lee, W. (2023). TRIDENT: Towards Detecting and Mitigating Web-based Social Engineering Attacks. *USENIX Security Symposium*.

Yan, X., Yan, K., Rehman, M. U., & Ullah, S. (2022). Yan, Ke., Rehman, Meezan. Ur., & Ullah, Sami. (October 2022). Impersonation Attack Detection in Mobile Edge Computing by Levering SARSA Technique in Physical Layer Security. Applied Science, doi. *Applied Sciences (Basel, Switzerland)*, 12(20), 10225. DOI: 10.3390/app122010225

Yasin, A., Fatima, R., Liu, L., Yasin, A., & Wang, J. (2019). Contemplating social engineering studies and attack scenarios: A review study. *Security and Privacy, 2*(4), 1–14. DOI: 10.1002/spy2.124

Ye, Z., Guo, Y., Ju, A., Wei, F., Zhang, R., & Ma, J. (2020). A Risk Analysis Framework for Social Engineering Attack Based on User Profiling. *Journal of Organizational and End User Computing*, 32(3), 37–49. DOI: 10.4018/JOEUC.2020070104

Yilmaz, A., & Gunes, A. (2024). A Model to Protect Disaster Recovery Centers from Cyber Threats with Multi-Layered Network Security Architecture.

Yusof, Y. M., & Singh, D. (2021). Civil servants awareness guideline towards computer security policy: A case study at the manpower department, ministry of human resources. *Asia-Pacific Journal of Information Technology and Multimedia, 10*(8), 86–99. DOI: 10.17576/apjitm-2021-1001-08

Yusuf, A., Khairil, K., & Rohmawan, E. P. (2024). An Analysis of Service quality on VSAT using Wireshark. *Jurnal Media Infotama*, 20(1), 73–78.

Zaini, N. S., Stiawan, D., Razak, M. F. A., Firdaus, A., Din, W. I. S. W., Kasim, S., & Sutikno, T. (2020). Phishing detection system using machine learning classifiers. *Indonesian Journal of Electrical Engineering and Computer Science*, 17(3), 1165–1171. DOI: 10.11591/ijeecs.v17.i3.pp1165-1171

Zambrano, P., Torres, J., & Flores, P. (2019). How does grooming fit into social engineering? In *Advances in Intelligent Systems and Computing* (Vol. 924, pp. 629–639). Springer., DOI: 10.1007/978-3-030-14471-8_63

Zambrano, P., Torres, J., Tello-Oquendo, L., Yánez, Á., & Velásquez, L. (2023). On the modeling of cyber-attacks associated with social engineering: A parental control prototype. *Journal of Information Security and Applications*, 75, 103501. DOI: 10.1016/j.jisa.2023.103501

Zaoui, M., Yousra, B., Yassine, S., Yassine, M., & Karim, O. (2024). A Comprehensive Taxonomy of Social Engineering Attacks and Defense Mechanisms: Towards Effective Mitigation Strategies. *IEEE Access : Practical Innovations, Open Solutions*, 12, 1–1. DOI: 10.1109/ACCESS.2024.3403197

Zeng, Y. (2022). AI Empowers Security Threats and Strategies for Cyber Attacks. *Procedia Computer Science*, 208, 170–175. DOI: 10.1016/j.procs.2022.10.025

Zhang, C., Jiang, H., Cheng, X., Zhao, F., Cai, Z., & Tian, Z. (2021). Utility analysis on privacy-preservation algorithms for online social networks: An empirical study. *Personal and Ubiquitous Computing, 25*(6), 1063–1079. https://doi.org/DOI: 10.1007/s00779-021-01509-3

Zhang, R., Sun, W., Liu, J., Li, J., Lei, G., & Guo, H. (2020). Construction of two statistical anomaly features for small-sample apt attack traffic classification. *arXiv preprint arXiv:2010.13978.*

Zhang, Z., & Gupta, B. B. (2018). Social media security and trustworthiness: Overview and new direction. *Future Generation Computer Systems, 86*, 914–925. DOI: 10.1016/j.future.2018.04.055

Zheng, X., IEEE ITSS, & Institute of Electrical and Electronics Engineers. (n.d.). *IEEE ISI 2017 :IEEE International Conference on Intelligence and Security Informatics: Security and Big Data :July 22-24, 2017-Beijing, China.*

Zheng, Y., Bao, J., Chen, D., Zeng, M., & Wen, F. (2021). Exploring temporal coherence for more general video face forgery detection. In *Proceedings of the IEEE/CVF international conference on computer vision* (pp. 15044-15054).

Zhong, H., Xiao, C., Tu, C., Zhang, T., Liu, Z., & Sun, M. (2020). How does NLP benefit legal system: A summary of legal artificial intelligence. arXiv preprint arXiv:2004.12158. DOI: 10.18653/v1/2020.acl-main.466

Zhou, Y., Jiang, X., & Heidemann, J. (2007). Detecting mass web spying: Pitfalls, challenges, and solutions. In **Proceedings of the First Usenix Workshop on Large-scale Exploits and Emergent Threats** (pp. 1-8).

Zolotarev, V.V., Arkhipova, A., Parotkin, N.Y., & Lvova, A.S. (2021). Strategies of Social Engineering Attacks on Information Resources of Gamified Online Education Projects.

About the Contributors

Rajeev Kumar is a proficient academician and academic administrator with more than 14 years of experience in developing the strategy towards the excellence in professional education. Prof. Kumar is currently serving as Professor of Computer Science and Engineering Department, Moradabad Institute of Technology, Moradabad, Uttar Pradesh, India. Prof. Kumar, earned the intellect in distinction as Ph.D. (Computer Science), D.Sc. (Post-Doctoral Degree) in Computer Science, Postdoctoral Fellowship (Malaysia). He has done certification in Data Science and Machine Learning using python and R Programming from IIM Raipur and certification from IBM, Google, etc, Senior member of IEEE and core team member of IEEE young professional committee and he is having membership of Computer Society of India, and AIEEE. He has participated many training programs in leadership, and also delivers the expert talks on how to develop or enrich the curriculum, development of PO, PSO, PEOs, and how to design the vision and mission and the implementation. His academic areas of interest and specialization include Artificial Intelligence, Cloud Computing, e-governance and Networking. Prof. Kumar actively associated in NAAC SSR preparations at universities interface. He has visited international countries- London (United Kingdom), Mauritius, Dubai for academic promotional activities. under his supervision awarded 9 scholars their Ph.D. and 4 Scholar is Ongoing their research work in the field of computer science. He is awarded 3 times Best project supervisor award; Prof. Kumar guides the institutions towards the academic excellence; promotes a culture of research, innovation and leads new curricula and program development efforts. He is expert in designing & deployment academic curriculum, and Program inception. he organizes the seminar, workshops for the students and faculty to promote the research. Prof. Kumar also nurtures the ecosystem for incubation for the students as well as mentors. Under the leadership of Prof. Kumar many ideas are under incubation and few are incubated and develop the prototypes.

Saurabh Srivastava is working as a Assistant Professor in Department of Computer Science Engineering (Data Science), Moradabad Institute of Technology, Moradabad, India. He received P.hD. from Integral University Lucknow in 2023, and Master of Computer Application (MCA) from Dr. A.P.J. Abdul Kalam Technical University Lucknow in 2015. He is associated with research after MCA, and he has approx. 9 years of experience in research including Computer Vision & Image Processing, Satellite Image Interpretation and Analysis, Land Cover Mapping, Time Series Analysis, Requirement Engineering, Multi-Agent System, etc

Ahmed A. Elngar is an Associate Professor and Head of the Computer Science Department at the Faculty of Computers and Artificial Intelligence, Beni-Suef University, Egypt. Dr. Elngar is also, an Associate Professor of Computer Science at the College of Computer Information Technology, American University in the Emirates, United Arab Emirates. Also, Dr. AE is Adjunct Professor at School of Technology, Woxsen University, India. Dr. AE is the Founder and Head of the Scientific Innovation Research Group (SIRG). Dr. AE is a Director of the Technological and Informatics Studies Center (TISC), Faculty of Computers and Artificial Intelligence, Beni-Suef University. Dr. AE has more than 150 scientific research papers published in prestigious international journals and over 35 books covering such diverse topics as data mining, intelligent systems, social networks, and smart environment. Dr. AE is a collaborative researcher He is a member of the Egyptian Mathematical Society (EMS) and International Rough Set Society (IRSS). His other research areas include the Internet of Things (IoT), Network Security, Intrusion Detection, Machine Learning, Data Mining, and Artificial Intelligence. Big Data, Authentication, Cryptology, Healthcare Systems, Automation Systems. He is an Editor and Reviewer of many international journals around the world. Dr. AE won several awards including the Young Researcher in Computer Science Engineering", from Global Outreach Education Summit and Awards 2019, on 31 January 2019 (Thursday) in Delhi, India.

Farooq Ahmad is currently working as Assistant Professor and Training Coordinator (IUCAT) in the Department of Computer Application, Integral University, Lucknow, INDIA. Dr. Farooq holds a bachelor's degree in Science from DDU University, a Master's degree from Harcourt Butler Technological Institute, Kanpur and achieved his PhD degree in Computer Application from Integral University, Lucknow. He has diverse background of 24+ Years of total experience in IT software development industry and education with over 7 years of project management, 4 years of Database Architect, 4 years of Programmer Analyst and 9 years of Academic/Research, Teaching, Technical Training and coordination of the Technical Trainings. He has published quality research papers in Journals, National and International Conferences of repute. He is contributing his knowledge and experience as speaker and member of technical committee in various international Journals/Conferences of repute. His areas of interest are Web Technologies, RDBMS, SQL, PLSQL, C, C++, Python, Java, R Programming, DSA, MERN & MEAN Stack, Artificial Intelligence, Machine Learning, Data Warehousing and Mining.

Vinod Kumar Bagar completed his graduation from CCS University Meerut (U.P), Law graduate from CCS University Meerut (U.P), MBA from AKTU, Lucknow and Ph.D. in Commerce from CCS University Meerut (U.P). He is net qualified in management in 2012 . Presently he is working as Assistant Professor in Dewan Institute of Management Studies in Management Department. He is having 12 year of teaching experience. His area of specialization is finance and marketing.

Sachin Chaudhary completed his Graduation from MJPRU, Bareilly, and Post Graduation from IFTM, Moradabad, U.P. Currently Pursuing his Ph.D. in Computer Science and Engineering from Govt. Recognized University. Presently, he is working as an Assistant Professor in the Department of Computer Science and Applications, IIMT University, Meerut, U.P, India. He has been awarded as Excellence in teaching award 2019. He is the reviewer member of some reputed journals. He has published several book chapters and research papers of national and international reputed journals.

Nishant Chaturvedi, an Assistant Professor in Management, has more than 6 years of teaching and research experience. His areas of teaching include Management and Personality Development. He has been certified as an Accredited Management Teacher (AMT) in Human Resources by AIMA, New Delhi.

Gauri Giri is very hardworking and innovative researcher of Amity Institute of Information Technology, Amity University Uttar Pradesh Lucknow campus. She is involved in various research activities under the supervision of her guide Dr. Ajay Pratap.

Himani Grewal has obtained her Ph.D in Corporate Social Responsibility. She has ten years of experience in academics and research. She has published more than 12 research papers in Scopus, ABDC and different international peer reviewed journals. She has presented her research papers in different international conference organized by a variety of reputed institutions like IIM Kashipur, IIM Indore and so on. Hear area of interest in CSR, ethics and general management.

Sachin Kaushik completed his Graduation from Chaudhary Charan Singh University Meerut and Post Graduation from U.P. Technical University Lucknow U.P. Presently, he is working as a Associate Professor in the Department of Computer Science and Applications, HRIT University, Ghaziabad, U.P. He has been a huge teaching experience of 15 years.

Rachit Kumar Gupta is an Assistant Professor at Anand Engineering College in Agra, Uttar Pradesh, India. With a robust academic background, he earned his PhD in Finance from Uttarakhand Technical University. Dr. Gupta has many years of teaching experience, previously working with GL Bajaj Group of Institutions. He has a keen interest in finance and accounting, with significant contributions to the field.

Geetha Manoharan is currently working in Telangana as an assistant professor at SR University. She is the university-level PhD program coordinator and has also been given the additional responsibility of In Charge Director of Publications and Patents under the Research Division at SR University.

Manvi Mishra, Associate Prof. Department of Computer Science & Engineering at Shri Ram Murti Smarak College of Engineering Technology and Research Bareilly, (UP) India. I am having 17 Years of Academic Experience. I received Bachelor's degree in Information Tecnology from Dr. A.P.J. Abdul Kalam Technical University Lucknow, India in 2006 and further Master degree with honors in Software Engineering from the same university in 2011. I have achieved Doctorate in Computer Science Engineering field from the same prestigious Dr A.P.J. Abdul Kalam Technical University Lucknow India. My Area of Interest includes Bio Medical Imaging, Cryptography and Network Security, Data Compression, Software Engineering. My research work has been published in various national and international journals and Conferences. I participated and organized various FDPs, Conferences, Webinars, Seminars, and Workshops at national and international levels. I am a life member of Institution of Engineers IEI India, Computer Society of India CSI, and IEEE etc. I have received "Bharat Vikas Award" on the occasion of citizen's day on 19 Nov 2017 by Institute of Self Reliance, Bhubaneswar Odisha, for loyalty, diligence and outstanding performance in the field of Cryptography and network security. I also have been endorsed with "Young Woman Educator and Researcher" Award on 8th March '2021 for significant contribution to Teaching and Research activities in the field of Computer Science and Engineering by National Foundation for Entrepreneurship Development (NFED) Coimbatore Tamil Nadu, India Recently I endorsed with Woman Power India Awards 2024 powered by WE Raise Raj Square Charity Foundation MSME Chamber of Commerce and Industry of India on 8 march 2024 for recognition of exceptional contribution and remarkable work in the realm of social and corporate impact through service and management.

Ajay Pratap is working as an Assistant Professor and Member Secretary-Research Cell in AIIT, Amity University Uttar Pradesh. Dr Ajay is emerging data scientist and cyber-security expert and recipient of University Gold-Medal for Master of Computer Application program by Chairman- University Grand Commission. Dr Pratap has published more than 25 national and international research papers and has been granted with national and international patents. Dr Pratap has chaired various national and international conferences and delivered guest lectures and also been honored at STF-Head Quarter for training STF cops about investigating cyber crimes. He has also completed and received Certificate of Excellence for research projects based on Internet of Things and QUIC and TCP in 5G Core Network assigned by Samsung PRISM. Currently six students of master program and four students of Ph.D. program are doing their research work under the guidance of Dr Pratap. He has been assigned the responsibility of Chairman - HSL Welfare Society, Lucknow which has served 2000+ people in different ways.

Gauri Rastogi is very innovative researcher of AIIT, Amity University Uttar Pradesh. She is involved in various research activities under her guide Dr Ajay Pratap.

Shirina Samreen is an Assistant Professor in the Department of Computer Science, College of Computer and Information Sciences, Majmaah University, Saudi Arabia. She has done her Ph.D in CSE from JNTUH in 2016. She is actively involved in research activities and is continuing with her post-doctoral research. She has 30 research papers to her credit in various IEEE International conferences / Journals. She received Best paper awards twice for her research papers at IEEE ICCIC, a renowned international conference. She acted as a reviewer for IEEE Wireless Communication Magazine, Journal of Engineering and Applied Sciences (JEAS), Majmaah University and various IEEE International Conferences held in India and abroad. She has over 13 years of experience in technical teaching and research at various Engineering Colleges.

Kewal Krishan Sharma is a professor in computer sc. in IIMT University, Meerut, U.P, India. He did his Ph.D. in computer network with this he has MCA, MBA and Law degree also. He did variously certification courses also. He has an overall experience of around 33 year in academic, business and industry. He wrote a number of research papers and books.

Vikas Sharma completed his Graduation and Post Graduation from Chaudhary Charan Singh University, Meerut, U.P. Currently Pursuing his Ph.D. in Computer Science and Engineering from Govt. Recognized University. Presently, he is working as an Assistant Professor in the Department of Computer Science and Applications, IIMT University, Meerut, U.P. He has been awarded as Excellence in teaching award 2019. He is the reviewer member of some reputed journals. He has published several book chapters and research papers of national and international reputed journals.

Rohit Kumar Singh is currently employed as an Assistant Professor in the Computer Science Department at Moradabad Institute of Technology, Moradabad, U.P. With over a decade of experience, he has authored several research papers that have been presented at both international and national conferences and published in reputable journals. His areas of expertise include Software Engineering, Cryptography, Database, and Logical Analytics. Throughout his tenure, Rohit Kumar Singh has demonstrated exceptional teaching abilities, positively impacting the lives of numerous students with his contagious enthusiasm for learning. His classrooms serve as dynamic platforms for intellectual exchange, where students are encouraged to question, explore, and innovate. Through his guidance, countless students have discovered their passion for computer science, setting the stage for prosperous careers in the field of technology.

Priyanka Tyagi is an Assistant Professor at Anand School of Engineering, Sharda University Agar where she has been a faculty member since October 2022. With over 10 years of teaching experience, she has established herself as a dedicated educator and mentor in the field of Computer Science and Engineering. Tyagi holds a B.Tech. and M.Tech. in Computer Science & Engineering and is currently pursuing her Ph.D. at Sharda School of Engineering and Technology, Noida. Her research interests span across Artificial Intelligence, Machine Learning, Internet of Things (IoT), Cyber Security, and Digital Image Processing. She has guided numerous final-year computer science students in their projects, fostering innovation and practical application of theoretical knowledge. Priyanka Tyagi is an ambitious and goal-oriented professional, recognized for her excellent communication skills and her ability to effectively facilitate teamwork. She seeks opportunities to leverage her expertise as a Technical Trainer, designing and delivering engaging technical training programs.

Gopalji Varshneya is an esteemed Assistant Professor in the Department of Computer Science and Engineering at Anand School of Engineering and Technology, Sharda University Agra . With over 14 years of combined experience in academia and the software industry, he has significantly contributed to the field of computer science. Varshneya holds a B.Tech. and an M.Tech., and is currently pursuing a Ph.D. in Computer Science and Engineering. Throughout his career, Varshneya has achieved numerous accolades. He secured the 410th All India Rank in GATE and was selected as an Assistant Scientific Officer at the National Informatics Centre (NIC). His research interests include deep learning, 3D object watermarking, machine learning, information retrieval, and wireless sensor networks. He has published 18 research papers in reputable journals and conferences, with 3 indexed in SCI and 5 indexed in Scopus. Varshneya's academic contributions include assisting in 4 Ph.D. projects, 5 M.Tech. projects, over 54 B.Tech. projects, and 48 web-based mini projects. He has also served as the principal consultant for 25 web portals and numerous application projects. His accolades include an award at the National Project Presentation Competition for a project developed for the DRDO. With 5 professional certifications, Varshneya is recognized for his expertise and contributions to technological innovation and education.

Tarun Kumar Vashishth is an active academician and researcher in the field of computer science with 22 years of experience. Currently he is working as an Associate Professor in IIMT University Meerut U.P India. His qualification is MCA, M.Tech. Ph.D. He served several academic positions such as HoD, Dy. Director, Academic Coordinator, Member Secretary of Department Research Committee, Assistant Center superintendent and Head Examiner in university examinations. He is involved in academic development and scholarly activities. He is member of International Association of Engineers, The Society of Digital Information and Wireless Communications, Global Professors Welfare Association, International Association of Academic plus Corporate (IAAC), Computer Science Teachers Association and Internet Society. His research interest includes Cloud Computing, Artificial Intelligence, Machine Learning and Operations Research; published more than 35 research articles with 2 book and 40 book chapters in edited books. He is contributing as member of editorial and reviewers boards in conferences and various computer journals published by CRC Press, Taylor and Francis, Springer, IGI global and other universities.

Index

I

K

M

N

O

P

www.ingramcontent.com/pod-product-compliance
Lightning Source LLC
LaVergne TN
LVHW080345011026
849161LV00009B/2196
* 9 7 9 8 3 6 9 3 6 6 6 5 3 *